LOVE'S COLD RETURNING

LOVE'S COLD RETURNING

*John Clare's 1841 Odyssey
from Essex to Northamptonshire*

❧

Ellis Hall and Bridget Somekh

Maps by Jon Harris
Illustrated by Pam Smy

𝕋hirteen 𝔼ighty 𝕆ne

Thirteen Eighty One Press
Cambridge, United Kingdom

info@thirteeneightyone.com
www.thirteeneightyone.com

Text © 2019 Ellis Hall and Bridget Somekh
Photography © 2019 Ellis Hall
Original verse © 2019 Bridget Somekh

First published 2019

The moral rights of the authors have been asserted.

All rights reserved. No part of this publication may be reproduced, stored in a retrieval system, or transmitted in any form, or by any means, without the prior permission of the copyright holders.

ISBN 978-0-9926073-1-9

I've wandered many a weary mile
Love in my heart was burning
To find a home in Mary's smile
But cold is love's returning

John Clare
Northborough, July 23rd 1841

Acknowledgements

Thanks are due to the following, without whose inspiration, advice and support this book could not have been written:

Reviewers: Anne-Louise Coldicott, Judy Findlay, Lindsay Fursland, Melissa Good, Eleanor Grene, Bryony Hall, Lilian Hall, Jon Harris, Brandon High, David Jones and Lesley Saunders.

Specialist advisers: Nicky Blandford, psychotherapist; Vic Gattrell, author of *The Hanging Tree* and *City of Laughter*; Chris Wilson of the Thurlow Press.

Clare scholars: James Canton, Paul Chirico, Peter Cox, John Goodridge, Mina Gorji, Bob Heyes, Sarah Houghton-Walker, Simon Kövesi, Valerie Pedlar, Roger Rowe, Roger Sales, Stephen Sullivan and Emma Trehane.

Poets: Roger Garfitt, John Gallas, Michael Longley, David Morley, Lesley Saunders and Penelope Shuttle; The Cambridge Stanza of the Poetry Society; CB1 Poetry Cambridge.

Historical advisers: Roy Baines, The Stilton Tunnels; Dennis Bird and Mike Noronha, Barnet Museum; Jim Brown, Gamlingay and District History Society; Jon-Paul Carr, Northamptonshire Public Library; Andy Chapman, Lemsford Historical Society; John Clark, Enfield Local Studies Library and Archive; Sue Jarrett, Eatons Community Association; Brendan King, Baldock Museum; Kerry Rolison, The Suntrap Education Centre; Anna Towlson, London School of Economics Library; Sir Hereward and Lady Julia Wake; Brian Warren, Potters Bar Library; Tom Wheeley, Hinchingbrooke School; Cambridge University Library; Stevenage Museum.

Carry Akroyd, President of the John Clare Society; Lucy Sheerman and David Dykes of the John Clare Trust; The University of Cambridge Centre for John Clare Studies.

Lesley Newitt and her colleagues at the Bluebell, Helpston.

Verses from the Clarendon edition of Clare's poetry appear by kind permission of Roger Rowe on behalf of the estate of Prof Eric Robinson.

Edward Villiers Rippingille's 'The Stage Coach Breakfast' is reproduced by kind permission of The National Trust, Charles Dickinson Langley's 'Landscape with Two Gentlemen' by kind permission of the Cromwell Museum, Huntingdon, and George Cruikshank's 'The Radical Ladder' by kind permission of the National Portrait Gallery.

The photograph of brick workers on page 101 is reproduced by kind permission of Pat Tookey.

Every effort has been made to trace the copyright holders and obtain permission to reproduce the images in this book. Please contact us with any enquiries or any information relating to them or to the rights holders.

Contents

An Invitation	vii
A Clare Chronology	x

THE POET

Paradise Lost	3
The Hero Home at Last	5

THE JOURNEY

Essex

Musings I	12
The Voice of Freedom	14
Musings II	28
The Transience of the Record	30
Musings III	44
Plunging through Timescapes	46

Middlesex

Musings IV	56
Hemmed in and Channelled	58
Musings V	82
Loops and Landgrabs	85
Musings VI	99
Bars, Bricks and Baptists	100

Hertfordshire

Musings VII	110
Money Speaking Power	111
Musings VIII	129
Lions and Lambs	130
Musings IX	141
Faded Fashion in a Rural Backwater	142
Musings X	156
The Ruins of Utopia	158
Musings XI	172
A Puzzle with a Missing Piece	174
Musings XII	188
Notes Scribbled under a Dry Hedge	191
Musings XIII	198
Boom Town	200

Bedfordshire (with a brief excursion into Cambridgeshire)

Musings XIV	212
Nowhere in Particular	214
Musings XV	223
A Fearfully Open Sky	224
Musings XVI	237
The Beacon Moon	238
Musings XVII	245
Ever-present Whispers	246
Musings XVIII	259
A Shot Fox	260
Musings XIX	264
A Very Odd House	265
Musings XX	271
King of the Heap	272

- Huntingdonshire
  - *Musings XXI* — 282
  - The Stupid Road — 284
  - *Musings XXII* — 293
  - Out Cold on the Causeway — 294
  - *Musings XXIII* — 302
  - An Eagle for a Slave — 304
  - *Musings XXIV* — 311
  - A Fistful of Pennies — 312
- Northamptonshire
  - *Musings XXV* — 316
  - Where is Angel Mary Now? — 318

THE MAN
- Authors' Note — 329
- *Father of the Queen of England* — 330
- Lunatic, Lover and Poet — 331
- *Emma and Johnny* — 334
- "Beautious Emma" — 335
- *Poet with an Oaken Bludgeon* — 340
- A Man of No Party — 341
- *Lament* — 346
- "Inclosure like a Buonaparte" — 347
- *The Education of a Man of Taste* — 352
- Clare's Science of Sensibility — 353
- *Laying Out Plans for an Iron Railway* — 356
- Guilt for Steam — 357
- *Sent by Train* — 358
- Clare and the Railways — 359
- *Writing a Song, the Evening He Returned* — 360
- Romantic Sensibilities — 361
- *MS 8, John Clare Collection, Northampton Library* — 362
- John Clare, Writer and Man — 363

THE RETURN
- *Love's Cold Returning* — 369

Notes and Indexes
- Abbreviations — 375
- Notes to Prose — 377
- Notes to Verse — 393
- Index of Persons — 399
- Index of Places — 402
- About the Authors — 408

An Invitation

Come and join us. Creating this book has been our obsession, and now we are looking for readers to explore it. We have both loved John Clare's poetry ever since it was set for A level in 1974 (yes, it really was), so we were intrigued to hear about Iain Sinclair's *Edge of the Orison: in the traces of John Clare's 'Journey out of Essex'*. But, having admired the combination of astute observation and personal experience in his *London Orbital*, we were disappointed to find that Sinclair had diverged from his original impulse to track Clare's walk and taken a more circuitous approach. True, the nineteenth-century roads were no longer there to follow, but might there be another way?

We decided to make our own attempt, taking Clare's *Journey out of Essex* as our guiding text. Never published during his lifetime, this account of his trek from Matthew Allen's asylum at High Beach in Epping Forest to his home at Northborough in Northamptonshire is less than three and a half thousand words long. In line with its brevity, we initially set out to produce a slim volume of photographs and poems that would attempt to reflect his experience during his great escape.

Our intention was to uncover what we could of the roads he trod, but since many had vanished beneath urban development and the dual carriageways of the A1, walking his route was out of the question. Instead, we resolved to make focused visits by car to the sections that remained.

We always arrived early in the morning before cars cluttered the streets. In rain and sun, Ellis took hundreds of photos and I filled notebooks with ideas for poems. Empathy was our aim: what had Clare been thinking and feeling when he passed these houses, crossed this bridge, negotiated the first railway line he had ever seen? How much was he carrying, and did he have a knapsack? What were these houses like when newly built? How had the view from this location changed since he was here?

Questions like these focussed our attention on the materiality of the road and the social conditions of the time, and gradually it became clear there was more to do if we were to capture the essence of his adventure. Also, since our investigations often turned into minor adventures of their own, they seemed worth recording as part of a broader narrative. Ellis therefore began to produce some prose to accompany the photos and poems: a description of Clare, newly arrived home, writing down the first line of the *Journey*, and an account of our trip to High Beach, where we were shown the register recording his arrival at Allen's asylum.

By this time I was composing what I came to call 'poetic musings'. I wanted to honour Clare in my own style, with a continuing form that would allow me to experiment within its constraints. I chose a five-line stanza with some internal rhyme and assonance and a broadly pentameter rhythm, and borrowed occasional quotes from his work as a means of keeping his presence alive to me. These pieces have no title: they catch glimpses of Clare on the road, touching on books he loved and happenings in his life—his violin-playing, his friendship with the gypsies, his trips to London.

The prose was growing in length, and we soon realised it needed to cover the whole journey. It was a useful change of focus for me, then, to share the writing of it with Ellis.

As the book began to take on the features of a scholarly research project, the purpose of our visits changed. We scrupulously followed Clare's account of where he walked as far as he tells us, sometimes finding that close reading of the text paid off in sudden realisations of his meaning. But there is a large section of his journey on the first day, between Enfield and Stevenage, which he covers in what would have been a single sentence had he bothered with punctuation:

> I walked down the lane gently and was soon in Enfield Town and bye and bye on the great York Road where it was all plain sailing and steering ahead meeting no enemy and fearing none I reached Stevenage

I took over from Ellis to write the account of that part of the journey. It involved detailed study of maps from the 1830s and 40s, tracking down the Enclosure Act relating to Enfield Chase, learning how roads were improved during the age of the stagecoach and how inns were closed and roads re-routed when the railways sent coaching into decline. I also tried to imagine what might have claimed Clare's attention along the way, although the rest of his account suggests that his only real interest was in the people he met. Perhaps it was not until the second day that he realised the scale of his adventure and began to think about turning it into a story.

Ellis, too, was engaged in research, visiting local studies libraries to amass detail on the places Clare had passed through, and to fill in gaps in the narrative. The second night of the journey posed a particular challenge for him, as Clare became lost after leaving Potton and had no idea where he was until he stumbled on a tollgate at what must have been Tempsford. In order to narrow down the various paths Clare might have taken to get there, Ellis sought out not only the tithe and Enclosure maps of the area, but also the meteorological and ephemeris records for the night in question.

As the prose accumulated, we realised there was a need for maps. When Jon Harris agreed to become our cartographer, our meetings and field trips became even more interesting—and time-consuming—as he had no hesitation in challenging our assumptions with insights of his own. Most importantly, his profound knowledge of nineteenth-century architecture brought a fresh confidence to our deliberations, and our intense discussions with him became central to the detective process. These discussions have been reproduced as passages of dialogue so that readers can weigh up the opposing arguments, and come to their own conclusions about which of us comes closest to the truth.

The poetry also began to take off in unexpected directions, with two ballad-style poems, 'Paradise Lost' and 'Love's Cold Returning', which weave a myth around Clare the poet. They include quotations and allusions to his poetry and prose, and are ascribed as 'after John Clare'. But if these are 'after' him, what about the musings, for which the starting point was always a kind of meditation on his imagined presence? Drawing on Geoff Reid's collection *For and After*, I decided that the musings are 'for' Clare. The next question was how to acknowledge him. My first approach was to place double quotation marks around the quotes from his work (just as he had done when inserting lines from Ovid's Fifth Elegy into 'The Lovers Meeting'), but rather than creating the echoes in homage that I had intended, this only gave them an unduly obtrusive prominence. Instead, I have provided references to them at the end of this book.

Inescapably our work also involved close engagement with the growing body of Clare scholarship. Research of this kind often leads to new discoveries, and however small the gains in knowledge turn out to be, the process is invariably exhilarating, particularly when it is a collaborative venture. In 'A Shot Fox', we describe the hiatus in our thinking caused by the discovery that the pub long thought to be where Clare intended to spend his second night did not exist in 1841. In 'Beloved Emma' we relate how we unearthed, in the Clarendon edition of his poetry, the poem Eliza Emmerson called 'The Invitation to Emma', previously thought to have been lost. Establishing a link between this poem and another in the same volume has enabled us to shed new light on why Clare interpolates a tender love song to the mysterious Eliza Phillips in the middle of the most scurrilous passage of his 'Don Juan', which he wrote just before escaping from the asylum at High Beach.

Alongside the excitement of this detective work, there was also a cross-fertilisation of ideas between Ellis and myself. For example, my poem 'Poet with an Oaken Bludgeon' laid bare the inconsistencies in Clare's political writings, which prompted Ellis to research the literature and produce, in 'A Man of No Party', a reassessment of the seemingly contradictory views within them. Likewise, 'The Education of a Man of Taste' led him to consider the role that education played in Clare's notion of the poetic sensibility.

Finally, in 'John Clare, Writer and Man', I was able to draw together the insights gained from months of reading the *Journey out of Essex*. In particular, scrutinising this text preparatory to writing the Huntingdonshire and Northamptonshire sections of the book led to epiphanies about its focus and structure, and Clare's intention—at least at the time he wrote it—to prepare it for publication.

This book is divided into three major sections: 'The Poet', 'The Journey' and 'The Man'. The second, dealing with Clare's walk, consists of 25 sets of poetic musings and prose pieces organised within the counties he passed through, with the musings acting as introductions to the prose. Ellis's photographs, Harris's maps, Pam's drawings and various other photos and illustrations have been placed where they best support the text. The book begins and ends with biographical poems that draw closely on Clare's own writing.

We have not reproduced the *Journey out of Essex* in its entirety, but quote from it fully and frequently. The complete text can be found in Robinson and Summerfield's *John Clare by Himself* (Carcanet, 2002), and also in the *Selected Poems and Prose of John Clare* (Oxford University Press, 1973), which was our A-level set text and is still, in our view, the best available introduction to his work.

BS

A Clare Chronology

1788		Birth of Byron.
1789		Storming of the Bastille.
1793	Born Helpston, Northamptonshire, July 13th, with twin sister who dies within days.	
1795		Birth of Keats.
1796		Death of Burns.
1798	Attends Mrs Bullimore's dame school. Birth of sister, Sophy, only sibling to reach adulthood.	Coleridge and Wordsworth's *Lyrical Ballads*.
1800	Attends school in the vestry of Glinton church, a two-mile walk away, where he meets Mary Joyce.	Bloomfield's *The Farmer's Boy*.
1804	Is shown a fragment of Thomson's *The Seasons* and buys his own copy for a shilling. Begins writing poetry.	Napoleon declared Emperor.
1805	Leaves school and embarks on 'self-tuition', supported by friends such as John Turnill (mathematics) and Tom Porter (botany).	Battle of Trafalgar.
1807		First London street lit by coal gas.
1808	Works for a year as general help at the Bluebell public house, next door to his cottage.	Byron leaves England.
1809		Enclosure Act for Helpston passed. Work begins enclosing the commons.
1810		Crabbe's *The Borough*.
1811	Sees the dead body of a carter fallen from a hay wagon. (Later cites this as the root cause of his recurrent chronic depression.) Sworn into Northamptonshire militia; three weeks' basic training at Oundle.	Bloomfield's *Banks of Wye*.
1812	Spends time with gypsy families; 'Boswell's Crew, Smiths and Grays'. Learns to play the fiddle 'by the ear' from them.	Byron's *Childe Harold (I & II)*. Assassination of Prime Minister Spencer Perceval.
1814	Takes casual labouring work, including Enclosure-related fencing and ditching. Temporarily abandons writing poetry.	Cary's translation of Dante's *Divina Commedia*.
1815		Battle of Waterloo.

A CLARE CHRONOLOGY

1816	Employed as 'extra labourer' at Burghley Park Nursery and Plantations. Learns 'irregular habits' from fellow workers.	Byron's *Childe Harold (I & II)*. The 'Year without a Summer'.
1817		Keats' *Poems*. Enclosure of Helpston complete.
1818	Works as a lime-burner at Pickworth in Rutland. Starts a manuscript collection of *Songs, Airs and Dances for the Violin* (over 250 in all). Sees Martha 'Patty' Turner walking in the fields and falls in love 'at first sight'.	Keats' *Endymion*. Lamb's *Works*. Mary Shelley's *Frankenstein*. Prizefighter Jack Randall at the peak of his fame.
1819		Byron's *Don Juan, Cantos 1 & 2* published anonymously. Peterloo Massacre. Herbert Marsh ordained Bishop of Peterborough.
1820	January: *Poems Descriptive of Rural Life and Scenery*. March: First visit to London. Meets his publisher John Taylor, the writers of the *London Magazine*, and painter Peter de Wint. Meets Eliza Emmerson and acquires the sponsorship of Admiral Lord Radstock. Has his portrait painted by William Hilton. Marries Patty at Great Casterton church. Is given a Cremona violin as a wedding present by his publishers Taylor and Hessey. June: Birth of first child, Anna Maria. Epidemic of fen-fever in Helpston. Death of Sophy's newborn son, also named John. June-July: Trust fund set up by Taylor, Hessey, Radstock and Earl Fitzwilliam to provide annual income.	Keats' *Lamia*. The Queen Caroline controversy. General fear of Revolution. The Cato Street Conspiracy. Loyalty of troops in doubt following mutiny of 3rd Regiment of Guards. *Poems Descriptive* a great success, runs to four editions. Madame Vestris sings Haydn Corri's setting of 'The Meeting' at the Theatre Royal, Drury Lane.
1821	*The Village Minstrel and other Poems*. Fourth edition of *Poems Descriptive*. Birth of second child, who does not survive. Begins friendship with Herbert Marsh and German-born wife Marianne.	Death of Keats, 23rd February. Disappointing sales of *The Village Minstrel*.
1822	January: Stays at Milton Hall. Forms close friendships with the steward Edmund Tyrell Artis, an amateur archaeologist and antiquarian, and with head gardener and noted botanist Joseph Henderson. May-June: Second visit to London. Attends Taylor's dinner for *London Magazine* writers, including essayists Hazlitt and Lamb, and translator Henry Cary. Befriends painter Edward Villiers Rippingille. June: Birth of third child, Eliza Louise, named after godmother Mrs Emmerson.	Death of Shelley, 8th July.

1823	Receives from Lamb a signed presentation copy of the *Elia* essays.	Lamb's *Elia*, essays which have appeared under that signature in the *London Magazine*. Death of Gilchrist, 30th June. Death of Bloomfield, 19th August.
1824	January: Birth of fourth child, Frederick. March: Joins the 'Primitive Methodists' or 'Ranters'. (The association does not last.) April: Exhibits signs of clinical depression. May-August: Third visit to London. Is examined by Keats' physician Dr Darling. Visits bare-knuckle bouts, brothels, drinking dens and theatres with Rippingille. Attends a *London Magazine* dinner where Coleridge is guest of honour. Receives from Cary a copy of his translation of Dante. Witnesses Byron's funeral cortège. Is advised to abandon poetry for prose. September: Begins two books of prose: an autobiography, and a natural history of Helpston modelled on Gilbert White's *Selborne*, to be called 'Biographies of Birds and Flowers'. December: Stays four nights with Artis and Henderson at Milton Hall. Is shown a copy of Linnaeus' *Botany*.	James Hogg's *Confessions of a Justified Sinner*. Death of Byron, 19th April. The demand for poetry in decline.
1825	Begins contributing to literary annuals such as Thomas Pringle's *Friendship's Offering* and S. C. Hall's *The Amulet*. January-March: Suffers extreme mental and physical distress. Draws up a will in the belief he is dying. Drinks heavily. April: Is accused of being a poacher while 'birding and botanizing'. Compiles a record of over 100 birds he has observed. May: Finishes the autobiography and sends it to Cary for comment. It is subsequently lost. June: Meets surveyors in Royce Wood, 'laying out plans for an "iron rail way"' from London to Manchester'. August: Is visited at Helpston by Eliza and Thomas Emmerson. September: Arranges for 1,000 copies of his satire 'The Parish' to be printed locally. (The plan is never realised.) October: Begins affair with a local woman of his former acquaintance (thought to be Betsey Sell).	Stock market crashes: six London banks and 60 country banks fail. Bank of England narrowly avoids collapse. Death of Admiral Lord Radstock, 20th August. Taylor and Hessey dissolve their partnership. Opening of the Stockton and Darlington Railway.

1825	November: His essay 'On Popularity in Authorship' appears in the *European Magazine*.	
1826	January: Is temporarily estranged from his family.	First photographic image taken by Joseph Nicéphore Niépce at Le Gras, France.
	March-April: Stays with Henderson at Milton Hall, and Frank Simpson in Stamford.	
	June: Birth of fifth child, John ('Jack'). Ends his affair and returns home. Money worries compounded by a demand for £40 from Edward Drury.	Artis leaves Milton Hall following the death in childbirth of a milkmaid.
	July-September: Works in the fields.	
	October: Helps Artis excavate Roman remains near Helpston. His account of Artis' dig appears in the *New Monthly Magazine*.	
1827	April: *The Shepherd's Calendar*.	De Quincey's *On Murder Considered as one of the Fine Arts*.
	June-August: Is occupied with botanical research. Accompanies Henderson on orchid-hunting expeditions. Attends a dinner in his honour at Peterborough Bishop's Palace.	*The Shepherd's Calendar* receives mixed reviews; sells poorly.
	August-September: Works in the fields.	Death of William Blake, 12th August.
	October: Is found by Herbert Marsh locked out of his cottage.	
	November-December: Suffers from ague, lethargy, headaches and nightmares.	
1828	January-February: Fevers, headaches and feelings of dread worsen. Believes he may have contracted a sexually transmitted disease. Contemplates suicide.	Duke of Wellington appointed Prime Minister.
	February-March: Fourth visit to London. Lodges with Eliza Emmerson. Consults Dr Darling. Takes sulphur baths. Finds himself marginalised in a changed London literary scene. Forms a close friendship with Harry Behnes, who takes his bust. Arranges with Taylor to sell some of his books himself.	Night Poaching Act: setting of mantraps to catch poachers made illegal; poaching made punishable by transportation. Raising the 'Hue and Cry' abolished.
	April: Birth of sixth child, William Parker.	
	August-September: Works at harvesting. Drinks heavily.	
	September-October: Is invited to spend two weeks in Boston, Lincolnshire. Is fêted by the town's literary circle. Sees the sea for the first and only time. Collects a 'sea serpent' and seaweed for Henderson.	
	October-November: He and his family suffer 'a very bad Fen fever'. Unable to leave his cottage for six weeks.	

1829	March-May: Takes labouring job at Burghley for 12 shillings a week.	The Rainhill Trials won by George Stephenson's 'Rocket'.
	August-September: Works at harvesting.	Metropolitan Police Service created by Sir Robert Peel.
	November: Discovers that sharp practice in Taylor and Hessey's accounting has left him owing them money. Asks Taylor for clarification. Taylor responds with promise to amend the figures.	
1830	July: Creates disturbance at a performance of 'The Merchant of Venice' in Peterborough. Has hallucinations of devils. Birth of seventh child, Sophie.	Tennyson's *Poems, Chiefly Lyrical*. Cobbett's *Rural Rides*. Accession of William IV. 'Captain Swing' riots in southern and eastern counties.
1831	Is unwell the entire year with stomach pains, headaches and a burning sensation in groin and 'fundament'. Believes he is under the influence of 'evil spirits'.	Taylor unable to find a publisher for 'The Midsummer Cushion'. General fear of revolution. Riots in Bristol and Merthyr suppressed by troops. Miners destroy enclosure fencing in the Forest of Dean.
	March: Is given a blank book of 600 pages. Starts copying into it poems for 'The Midsummer Cushion', a projected volume of his best uncollected and unpublished work.	
1832	January: Desperate to clear his debts, asks Taylor to cash in his trust fund, but this proves impossible.	Death of Sir Walter Scott, 21st September. Second Cholera Pandemic reaches Britain.
	April: Leaves Helpston with his family for a larger cottage with smallholding and orchard at Northborough, three miles distant. Writes 'The Flitting'.	Great Reform Act enfranchises owners of property worth at least £10. Last gibbeting of a criminal.
	May-June: Suffers prolonged bout of illness, and is unable to work.	
	July: Resumes work on the new volume, to be financed by subscription.	
	September-November: Prospectus for 'The Midsummer Cushion, or Cottage Poems', circulated in London. Jeremiah How of printers Whittaker & Co agrees to produce the collection. 'The Nightingale's Nest' appears in *Friendship's Offering* and *The Bee*.	
	December: Over 100 subscribers secured for 'The Midsummer Cushion' (the subscription model is later dropped). Feels isolated from old friends. Falls prey to familiar symptoms of depression, lethargy and fever. Hallucinations return.	
1833	January: Conviction returns that he is bewitched by evil spirits. Is ordered by his doctor to abstain from reading and writing. Birth of eighth child Charles.	Slavery Abolition Act makes the practice illegal throughout most of the British Empire.

1833	August: Finishes the manuscript of 'The Midsummer Cushion'. Sends it to Eliza Emmerson for editing. She suggests an alternative title of 'The Rural Muse'. September-December: Return of depression and debility.	Factory Act sets a minimum age and limits the working hours for children.
1834	January: Family falls ill. Convinced he is the victim of witchcraft. Is in debt to the tune of £35. March: Receives £40 from Whittaker's for copyright to first edition of 'The Rural Muse'. July: Relapse of illness. A trip to consult Dr Darling in London is called off due to the temporary absence of Eliza Emmerson from the capital. December: Decline in health continues. Becomes reclusive.	Death of Coleridge, 25th July. Death of Lamb, 27th December. The Tolpuddle Martyrs, six Dorset farm labourers, are transported for forming a trade union. Poor Law Amendment Act forces able-bodied unemployed into the workhouse.
1835	January: Is too weak 'to move around the house'. Receives £50 from the Royal Literary Fund. Birth of ninth child, who does not survive. July: *The Rural Muse* published. December: Mother, Ann Clare, dies aged 78.	Death of Hogg, 21st September. Favourable reviews of *The Rural Muse*. Encouraging sales.
1836	Undergoes erratic mood swings. Shows signs of violence. Is sometimes uncontrollable. Writes about 300 poems in a frenzy of creative output, but is burnt out by the autumn. November: Makes plans for a new volume entitled 'The Fields, a poem; Tales of the Farm; Autumn, and Sonnets'. Is visited by Taylor who notices him acting strangely, and exhibiting the delusion that Mary Joyce is his first wife and Martha his second.	Dickens' *The Pickwick Papers*. Last hangings in England for robbery and arson.
1837	January-June: Episodes of violent agitation continue. July: Is committed to Matthew Allen's private asylum at High Beach in Epping Forest, with fees paid by Taylor and Lord Milton. Is treated with 'great kindness' and settles to a routine of writing and walking in the forest undisturbed for almost three and a half years. Symptoms of mental distress abate during this time, but delusions continue.	Accession of Queen Victoria. Matthew Allen's *On the Classification of the Insane*. W. A. F. Browne's *What Asylums Were, Are and Ought to Be*. The pillory abolished. Patent filed for the electric telegraph. Euston Station opened.

1838		Mary Joyce dies in a fire at her home in Glinton, 14th July.
		Chartist movement founded.
		Charles Darwin formulates theory of evolution by natural selection.
		Opening of the London and Birmingham Railway.
1839	December: Is certified as still insane.	Death of Herbert Marsh, 1st May.
1840	Undertakes gardening and field work in and around the asylum.	Rowland Hill introduces pre-paid postage with the 'Penny Black'.
	Is described by Allen as physically 'in his best state' with a mind that is 'not worse'.	London and Eastern Railway opens a single-track line from Stratford, East London, to Broxbourne in Hertfordshire.
1841	January-June: Changes in treatment regime lead to a deterioration in his mental condition. Convinced he has two wives. Assumes the personae of Byron and Regency prizefighter Jack Randall. Begins two long poems, 'Child Harold' and 'Don Juan' in imitation of Byron.	
	July: Escapes High Beach and walks home over three and a half days without money or provisions. Finds 'first wife' Mary Joyce absent, and refuses to believe she is dead. Writes an account of his adventure for her, which later becomes known as *Journey out of Essex*.	
	December: Is admitted to Northampton General Asylum, from which he is never released.	
1849		Death of de Wint, 30th January.
1854		Death of Eliza Emmerson, 11th March.
1864	Dies 20th May of a stroke, aged 70. Body sent by train to Helpston for burial. A delay informing his family causes it to be kept overnight in the Exeter Arms before being interred the following day.	

The Poet

Paradise Lost

After John Clare

In the heat and sweat of July,
on her marriage bed under the thatch
Ann laboured and gave birth to twins:
a boy skinny enough to fit a pint pot
and a lively bonny wench, expected to live.

All hail! A sooty crow flew high,
two thrushes opened snails on a stone,
a blackbird warbled joy
in the golden russet apple tree,
and starnels darkened down the sky.

Then came the Fiend of the Fen
breathing fire and flame,
angered by the delight of birds:
'One must die as ransom for the other,'
and he reached out to snatch the boy.

But King Boswell's crew stepped in:
'Wrest your filthy claw away from him,
for it is set down in gypsy lore
he carries the muse of song, is marked
with the music of rhyme.

'He has his run-a-gate grandfather's
blood, the gift of fiddler's fingers
to charm the throng. Take the girl instead.'
And the fiend agreed and wrenched her
from her mother, letting be the boy.

King Boswell wove a willow basket for his crib.
The babe lay still and gazed at the sky,
his eyes blue as forget-me-nots;
a fallow deer came to the garden,
skittish on legs like carriage springs.

Under Helpstone's tower they baptised him, John,
in holy water, and he looked into the brook
and saw heaven in the stars by night
and shadow-shaping clouds by day
and knew that he was centre of the world.

He heard landrails drawing young lads away
from their eggs loose in the long grass,
deep-blotched and nearly round, and he saw
the hedgehog's nest of grass and sedge
and little trotty wagtails and frogs' eggs.

Growing to boyhood he first saw Mary,
the stillest and most good-natured child;
he loved her secretly but one day, in play,
lobbed a walnut in her eye and made her cry
and was afraid to comfort her and show his love.

In the high hopes of youth he set out
for the orison, to find the brink of the world
and see Earth's secrets below, but the great pit
he imagined was not there, and the lanes and fields
shifted so that home was never again the same.

Growing to manhood, he lay long days with Patty
in the shadow of a willow, wash of the stream;
she was with child and wound him in her hair
and he was tied to her with promises,
pressures of gossip, sin closing in.

His brain burned with rhymes, pouring out words
on scraps of paper and round the crown of his hat,
wandering lost in fields and byways.
He relished sounds and rhythms imitating birds
– wagtails trotting and tottering sideways.

Time concertinaed into hectic scribbling
and dreams of images and rhymes all night;
and other times of darkening gloom
and failed purpose, all hope gone, too weak
to swing a flail or scare birds from the corn.

And seeing his fractured life, King Boswell
reads the tarot cards and tea leaves
and finds the Muse of Poetry struggling
for his fortune with the God of Helpstone's tower.
Neither will let go, so John Clare splits in two.

BS

The Hero Home at Last

Northborough, Northamptonshire
The evening of July 23rd 1841

In our mind's eye there is a room.

It has a low ceiling, a flagstone floor and lime-washed walls. Level evening sun streams in through a casement window, striking the wall opposite and lighting the pictures that hang there—lithographs of the local aristocracy, rustic scenes, and the watercolour of a handsome, strong-featured man in his mid-twenties. Much else remains in shadow, though a plain oak bookcase crammed with scuffed and battered volumes can be made out in the coppery gloom, and beside the bookcase, a scratched and scored kitchen table.

In the room, there is a man.

He is sitting at the table, body thrown back in an attitude of reverie, head cocked to one side and legs thrust out before him. One of his feet is booted; the other is bandaged with clean rags. Though the room is warm and close—it is summer, the end of haymaking—he is wearing the clothes he arrived in: a pair of mud-stained breeches and a pea-green fustian jacket white with dust from the road. One broken shoe and an old hat with a battered crown lie discarded on the floor nearby, as forgotten as the half-finished meal of bread, cheese and beer set before him. His attention is wholly focused on the notebook that lies open in his hands. Slowly he reaches for a pen and on a fresh page writes the day's date. It is the 23rd of July 1841.

The man has not seen this room in four years. He left it utterly broken, with a body weak from hard labour, poor nutrition and strong drink, and a mind fractured by bitter disappointment and the depredations of rural poverty. His mood, which at no notice swung from hopeless apathy to violent raving, made him unsafe to his family, and for that he was sent into exile. Today, barely two hours since his return, his transformation from the human wreck he once was into something preternaturally strong—elemental even—has become abundantly clear.

In stature he is below medium height, and his frame is compact and muscled—the sinewy body of a bantam-weight boxer. His face no longer flickers and jumps with inner conflict. Now, with the lines of middle age upon them like creases in fine linen, his features are smooth and calm. Only his pale blue eyes betray the confusion he is feeling: confusion at having come home to a place he does not recognise, though it is in every way familiar to him; confusion at having ended his long pilgrimage but not completed it. Although he has reached his destination, it is somehow not the one he was making for.

He straightens himself in his chair and dips the pen in ink. Writing quickly and confidently, he adds a single line beside the date. He writes as easily as he breathes —indeed he is a compulsive writer, a word addict. Rhyming is a drug for him, some would say a vice. Half his lifetime ago, when the watercolour on the wall was painted, this compulsion had garnered him celebrity and brought him influential and powerful friends. And though today they are gone—lost or perished—and he himself has passed out of public memory, the impulse to commit thought to paper is as insistent as ever, an irresistible pressure in the brain.

He has decided to record every detail of his journey here. Perhaps he believes that by doing so he will unravel the mystery of how he comes to be in a house that looks like his own, but feels like a stranger's. Perhaps this act will be the key to solving the puzzle of his misplaced life. He murmurs aloud this first brief entry, reading the final words "And how can I forget?" not as a question but as the desolate cry of yearning and bewilderment it actually is; a cry barely held in check by the lowness of his voice with its flat, unaffected midland vowels.

It suddenly comes to him that the question is not of forgetting, but of recalling the woman whose absence in this place has knocked away the pivot of his universe. Every day he has blessed her on lying down to sleep in barns and ditches, and on rising again in the dew-sodden dawn. For it is she who has drawn him here from almost a hundred miles away, a beacon to his soul's spyglass and a lodestone to the iron in his loins. But it seemed that the more he walked towards her the more distant she became. The bliss of their union, so clearly captured in her steadily fading call, has dwindled from absolute fact to a sketchy hypothesis. Though he is not fond of classical allusion, a dark, lumbering image of Sirens and seafarers breaks surface on the choppy waters of his imagination.

The light from the window is dimming fast, its bright copper fading to burnished bronze. Shadow engulfs the bookcase and falls across the table. Someone—a woman certainly, though not the one he craves—enters the room and wordlessly places a lighted candle by his side. He takes no notice, even when she touches his arm with a wife's tender familiarity, so she retreats, face resolutely blank, to where her children have crowded in the doorway. They crane past each other to view the novelty of a grown man sitting in their parlour. The smallest gazes on him wide-eyed and curious, but his older siblings watch guardedly, as though observing a wild beast that has blundered its way into the house: though there is excitement at the improbability of the event, their expressions seem to say, there is also danger.

Whispers and nudges and looks of wary appraisal: the man is oblivious to them all. Even were he not, he would judge his audience to be strangers to him rather than who they truly are—his own progeny. The chasm between the burning anticipation of the road and the ashen reality here at its end is too wide; it has rendered him incapable. For the present he has no family. There has been no joyous reunion with his two wives and their collective brood (whose names and faces presently elude him), and most grievous of all, his first wife—his favourite, his childhood sweetheart, his muse, his Siren—is nowhere to be found. The freshly written words stare up at him from the white desolation of the page:

> July 23rd 1841 Returned home out of Essex & found no Mary – her & her family are as nothing to me now, though she herself was once the dearest of all – & how can I forget?

He has begun the account of his journey at its wretched end, but he must return to the start to have any chance of comprehending how he became pitched into this strange world, where half his family, and all that he loves, has quite vanished into air.

In our minds' eye there is a room. And in the room there is a man.

The man, perpetual poet and sometime lunatic John Clare, picks up his pen once more, and in the candle's buttery light resumes writing.

EH

The Journey

Essex

Day 1, 20th July 1841:
High Beach to the River Lea

Musings I

He speaks:

'What is it Allen's always telling me –
about self-identity? To know myself
and own myself for that will make me free,
standing among the trees, firm and strong and sure,
growing to God's heaven, wanting no more.

'Jack Randall is the one I know I am
with courage to stand up to any man,
stamping my feet in the sand of the ring,
hearing the crowd roar as I come through
with my fist, afraid neither to die nor kill.

'Byron I'll be. I saw his funeral pass
down Oxford Street, crowds of common folk
standing to honour him: satirical rhymer,
flogger of Tories, favourite with the ladies
lucky feller, fond of getting into scrapes.'

Fevered, tied to his bed, not right in his head,
the storm battered him: through open shutters
clouds backlit by jagged streaks of light,
rolls of monstrous sound, God's heaven
despoiled, great trees torn from the ground.

❧

A hornbeam brought down by wild winter winds
has fallen across another from the great storm
of 1822; the trunk on its side,
half its roots torn from the earth, half clinging to life
with leaves growing on the ground all summer.

Bones of branches, stripped to the white wood
like a whale carcass; oak tree bark, crusty,
rugged home for bugs; and a stretched tree,
the speed of its growth written in rips
of green up its creamy trunk.

❧

The Voice of Freedom

Ellis begins the story...

Clare's *Journey Out of Essex* is a remarkable document—at once the diary of a man who endures extreme physical and mental anguish to return to his family; the record of an 85-mile walk undertaken on almost no food or water; the story of how obsessive love can inspire heroic fortitude, and the tale of a quest that is doomed to end in disappointment and despair.

Though he was a poet of the Romantic age, Clare's background as the son of an agricultural labourer fostered a sensibility at variance with that of his contemporaries. His relationship with the natural world was rooted in the day-to-day experience of the rural working poor, and his descriptions of it were grounded in the kind of detailed, first-hand observation practised by the natural scientists of his day. His was a unique voice—that of a lone traveller who had to pick his own path through the intellectual and spiritual landscapes being charted by the Romantic movement. Yet even if he was not a 'Romantic' as the term has been commonly understood, Clare possessed qualities indispensable to the Romantic hero: he was a passionate lover of women; a man of intelligence, introspection and feeling; a creative power-house, and an artist who suffered for his art.

The *Journey* cannot be improved upon in its depiction of a certain kind of Romantic protagonist: the solitary outcast who tramps the high road like a vagabond, wanders through woods and heathland, and passes houses at dusk whose windows glow with family cheer while he seeks out shelter in barns and ditches, struggling on through wind and rain, his soul aching for a lost love. It paints so archetypal a picture that it could have been inspired by Schubert's *Winterreise*, and might have inspired Stevenson's *Songs of Travel* in its turn. Yet if Clare is to be believed—and there is no reason not to—it did happen; the *Journey* is a work of fact, not fiction.

At least, insofar as any piece of reportage can be.

The facts of the case present no difficulties. One July morning in 1841, Clare walks out of the asylum at High Beach, where he has lived for four years, and instead of taking his habitual ramble among the hills of Epping Forest, simply keeps on going. As he later explains in a letter to Matthew Allen, the asylum's director, he has "heard the voice of freedom and started". He is heading for home.

On the first day he marches 25 miles to Stevenage, where he spends the night in a farm outbuilding. On the second day, despite becoming lost and breaking the sole of a shoe, he covers another 25 miles, resting up in countryside south of Eynesbury. By the end of the third day he is 20 miles further on, in the vicinity of Sawtry, and on the fourth he reaches the village of Werrington—four miles short of his home—where he is met by his wife with a horse and cart.

So far so straightforward. But in noting the details of what he reports—and does not report—the attentive reader might begin to suspect that this is not quite as clear cut as it might first appear. That would hardly be a surprise, The Clare of the *Journey* is a complex man in a highly emotional state whose grip on reality has been weakened by pain, exhaustion, lack of sleep and the onset of delusional episodes. Added to which, he is writing about his experiences—for the most part without the aid of notes—in retrospect, allowing a potentially faulty memory to compound an impaired grasp of events as they unfolded. The *Journey* is, inevitably, the product of a doubly unreliable narrator.

He writes the first half immediately on arriving home, in what must have been a befuddled, exhausted state. The next morning—after his first proper night's sleep in days—he resumes his task by first copying the previous night's text into a fresh notebook. It is worth remarking that in doing so he makes virtually no changes beyond amending a couple of inconsequential phrases. We do not know if he finishes his account in another single burst of activity or over a number of sittings, but three days later he composes a dedication to Mary Joyce. "I have written an account of my journey—or rather escape—from Essex for your amusement", he writes, "and hope it may divert your leisure hours."

Clare's first biographer Frederick Martin states that "in the Spring of 1841— having been nearly four years at Fairmead House—he made several attempts to escape, but was frustrated each time, being brought back by people who met him wandering at a distance".[1] Martin offers no corroborating evidence for these attempts, but had they taken place, Matthew Allen, with an eye to his professional reputation and the success of his business, would certainly have covered them up. It is worth noting that Martin wrote his *Life of John Clare* in 1865, within the lifetimes of many who might have witnessed or heard of them, and very likely interviewed Clare's acquaintances and their descendants.[2] In any event, it is undeniable that during those early months of 1841 there was an abrupt decline in Clare's mental state—graphically documented in his notes, poems and letters—and that the idea of fleeing what for him had become a living hell was never far from his mind.

Fortunately for Clare, Allen's establishment did not fit the mould of the traditional asylum. As June Wilson, another of his biographers, points out, it offered "a system of treatment which was entirely new", based on the principle that kindness and compassion worked better than cold baths and straitjackets:

> [Allen's] theory was to allow the patients the maximum amount of freedom, to encourage them to occupy themselves with healthy work and amusement. [...] He believed that if the patient was treated with honesty and frankness, he would give his trust in return, [affording] the doctor power to work on his mind and help his condition.[3]

Under this benign regime, Clare spends his first three years at High Beach in relative good health and tranquillity. The fainting fits, hallucinations and bouts of rage that brought him here fall away almost at once. As early as November 1837—just four months after his committal—he writes to his wife Patty that he has "met with great kindness", and is getting better. The communication consists of no more than a couple of lines: "I can't write a long letter", he apologises, before adding optimistically, "but shall do better."[4] The following April she receives news that he is continuing to make progress, but at the end of 1839—almost two and a half years into his confinement—Allen certifies him as still insane. The improvement in his mental condition appears to have plateaued, and in July 1840 he is described as being "in his best state" physically, with a mind that is "not worse".[5]

Around this time there are reports in the press that Clare has died, and Allen, stung by the potential slur on his own reputation, publishes a fierce rebuttal. This contains a more detailed account of Clare's condition, in which Allen remarks that despite a cheerful disposition and a capacity to write beautiful and coherent verse, Clare "is full of very strange delusions" and "has never been able to obtain in conversation, nor even in writing prose, the appearance of sanity for two minutes or two lines together".[6]

The delusions are manifold. Clare not only believes himself to be a bigamist but also a prizefighter. Moreover, a growing obsession with Lord Byron apparently leads him to identify so closely with the poet that he imagines they are one and the same.[7] As if to prove it, in the early spring of 1841 he embarks on his own versions of 'Childe Harold's Pilgrimage' and 'Don Juan', both of which—as they unfold over the ensuing months—come to reveal the depths of his despair and desperation.

Canto 6 of his 'Child Harold', penned in either April or early May, begins "My Mind Is Dark & Fathomless & Wears / The Hues Of Hopeless Agony & Hell".[8] At about this time he starts to capitalise every word he writes, an eccentricity that hints at a derangement transcending either melancholy or depression. Yet to those who meet him he seems perfectly amiable, with the "cheerful disposition" that Allen describes still very much to the fore. Visiting in early May, literary gent-about-town Cyrus Redding finds him working in a field near the asylum. "He was communicative", writes Redding, "and answered every question put to him in a manner perfectly unembarrassed." Clare, with "a continued smile playing upon his lips", comments on the quality of the soil he is hoeing, talks about the difference between the landscapes of Epping Forest and his fenland home and, apart from dropping sudden non-sequiturs about prize-fighting into the conversation, appears perfectly rational. "To our seeming," Redding concludes, "his affection was slight; and it is not at all improbable that a relief from mental anxiety might completely restore him."[9]

The other subject Clare mentions—namely "his loneliness away from his wife" and a desire to have "the society of women"—reveals a powerful driver of his growing distress. In May, he drafts a letter to Mary Joyce, the childhood sweetheart to whom he is now convinced he is married. Its tone swings wildly from tenderness to violent reproach and back again. "No one knows how sick I am of confinement possessing two wives that ought to be my own & cannot see either one or the other," he complains, adding that even convicted felons are allowed conjugal visits though he is not. Enforced celibacy is fuelling a violent rage within him, and it erupts suddenly onto the page:

> what is the use of shutting me up from women in a petty paltry place as this merely because I am a married man & I dare say though I have two wives if I got away I should soon have a third & I think I should serve you both right in the bargain by doing so

Just as suddenly, the rage vanishes. "My dear Mary", he writes, "take all good wishes from me as your heart can feel for your own husband & kiss all your dear family for their abscent father & Pattys childern also."[10] He is fondly picturing his two wives and their broods gathered around a single hearth, an image that will persist in his mind's eye until he reaches home. Canto 18 of 'Child Harold', probably composed within a couple of weeks of the letter, begins:

> Where are my 'friends' & childern where are they
> The children of two mothers born in joy
> One roof has held them — 'all' have been at play
> Beneath the pleasures of a mothers eye [11]

And in Canto 22, picturing himself "in cowslip fields" at the head of a household under Edenic skies, he describes:

> My cot this awthorn hedge this spreading tree
> — Mary and Martha once my daily guests
> & still as mine both wedded loved and blest [12]

The verses composed at this time are shot through with meditations on these women. Among them are two 'Ballads', written for inclusion in 'Child Harold'; one a pastoral idyll describing his courtship of Martha Turner—his 'Patty'—and the other an account of his wooing, and eventual winning, of Mary Joyce. The first we know to be the product of memory, but the second is almost certainly pure invention. To what extent he believed it to be otherwise is anyone's guess, but the point here is that both poems deal with conquest and possession. The subject uppermost in his mind is sex, and the getting of it.

In the absence of his wives he is looking closer to home for intimacy, or at least fantasizing about doing so. On Easter Monday—a day in early April—he attends the meeting of the local hunt and is much taken with two strangers he encounters there. "I Saw A Tall Stout Woman Dressed In A Darkish Flowerd Cotton Gown As A Milkmaid Or Farm Servant", he writes, "And Stood Agen Her For Some Minutes Near A Small Clump Of Furze." He makes no attempt to speak to her but later wishes he had, and finds that he cannot rid her from his thoughts. The other he spies stepping down from a gig "With A Large Scotch Shawl On And A Pretty Face."[13] The yearning for female companionship in these lines is palpable, and as it increases with the passing weeks his diffidence wanes. Over the course of May and June he lends out copies of Byron's works to various women in the locality. Perhaps he thinks that the lord's reputation as a seducer will make them more pliable, or perhaps he hopes the books will create some common ground—even intimacy. The stratagem, if such it is, fails, and the recipients—Mrs. Pratt the labourer's wife, Miss Fish of the Owl public house, and Mrs. King, late of the parish and now of Enfield Highway—do not respond, or at least not in any way worth recording. In any event, they are ranked in his affections well behind the mysterious Eliza Phillips, the woman who is then dominating his thoughts. In a letter to her drafted sometime in May, he writes:

> I do not much like to write love letters but this which I am now writing to you is a true one—you know that we have met before & the first opportunity that offers we will meet again—I am now writing a New Canto of Don Juan which I have taken the liberty to dedicate to you in remembrance of Days gone bye...[14]

The canto, simply entitled 'Song', entreats Eliza to stray among the woods with him. "Come & spend a day with me / underneath the forest tree" he begs, adding that "Though flowers bloom now on every hill / Eliza is the fairest still."[15] The fact that he includes it in 'Don Juan' rather than 'Child Harold' is odd. Its naïve sentiment sits awkwardly alongside the former's bawdy verses and seems more properly to belong to the latter, whose paeans to Mary and Martha it most closely resembles.

Unlike Clare's other women, Eliza Phillips has left no detectable trace. She is absent from both the parish register and Allen's admissions book. As for other Elizas, there are three at the asylum in 1841—a Palmer, a Rackshaw and a Roberts—

and at the end of June, just when 'Don Juan' is taking shape, a patient named Mary Phillips takes up residence. This raises the intriguing possibility that rather than being an actual person, his Eliza is an amalgam of some or all of these women, fused by his imagination into one erotic ideal.

On the other hand, the reference to "Days gone bye" suggests passions past, not present. The most important Eliza in his life—barring his daughter Eliza Louise—was his close friend and confidante Mrs Eliza Emmerson. Perhaps the newly-arrived Mary Phillips resembles her, and has triggered memories of an affair. For while there is no evidence that one took place, from time to time she and Clare behaved as though they were bound together by more than simple friendship.[16] The most telling example relates to a portrait which she sent to Clare along with instructions to keep it hidden.[17] He had asked for her picture in a letter, framing his request with allusions to Nelson and Lady Hamilton. (Coincidentally or otherwise, Eliza habitually signed her missives to him 'Emma'.) The portrait—kept discreetly in a red Morocco case—was later hung in the cottage at Helpston, and possibly at Northborough too. It may have prompted the reference in a poem composed at the end of his long walk—"Here on the wall with smileing brow / Her picture used to cheer me"—though the poem's subject was not Eliza Emmerson but his beloved Mary Joyce.[18]

Although he shows no apparent guilt at the idea of having committed adultery, his conviction that he is married to both Mary Joyce and Martha Turner seems to be plunging him deeper into a state of mental distress. On the one hand they are legitimate objects of desire because as wives they offer sexual relations sanctioned by God, but on the other his marriage to each is bigamous, and therefore sinful. It is a circle he cannot square. "My life hath been one chain of contradictions", he writes in a fit of self-loathing, recalling youthful visits to London brothels with the artist Edward Villiers Rippingille.[19] He groups such places with those other Victorian institutions of misery and shame, the prison and the madhouse. His recollections are no longer the narrative of laddish adventure they once were; a deep sense of religious guilt hangs over the contemplation of his carnality. "Never doubt", he continues,

> But that my life hath had some strong convictions
> That such was wrong — religion makes restrictions
> I would have followed — but life turned a bubble
> & clumb the jiant stile of maledictions
> They took me from my wife & to save trouble
> I wed again and made the error double [20]

But even as he turns this disgust in upon himself, he also directs it outward. The first stanza of 'Don Juan' sets the tone:

> "Poets are born" — & so are whores — the trade is
> grown universal — in these canting days
> Women of fashion must of course be ladies
> & whoring is the business — that still pays [21]

In the lines that follow he presents a verbally rendered Gillray cartoon of outwardly respectable wives engaging in illicit sex at every possible opportunity. But if—in line with Byron's own mockery of high society—these females are meant to represent the rapacity of the landowning classes, the point is somewhat overtaken by his graphic depiction of their proclivities. What may have begun as metaphor is now a theme in itself: namely the faithlessness and depravity of women. In his fevered imaginings they are all whores—even "little Vicky" the monarch, who in a fit of prurient *lèse-majesté*, he pictures cavorting with her cabinet while the Prince Consort is away in Germany. "I wsh [sic] prince Alberts queen was undefiled" he remarks, pointing the finger squarely at Whig Prime Minister Lord Melbourne, "— & every man could get his *wife* with child."

When he breaks the narrative and addresses the reader directly, as in verse 5, he gives vent to his overriding preoccupation:

> Shopmen are fond of good sigars and brandy
> & I of blunt — & if you change the letter
> To C or K it would be quite as handy
> & throw the next away — but I'm your debtor
> For modesty — yet wishing nought between us
> I'd hawl close to a she as vulcan did to venus

And though he is imitating Byron's raciness here, he is nonetheless sincere in what he says. When he revisits the subject some verses later, the tone is wistful and full of yearning:

> How I would like to purchase some sweet woman
> Or else creep in with my two wives to night
> —Surely that wedding day is on the comeing
> Absence like physic poisons all delight
> Mary & Martha both an evil omen
> Though both my own — they still belong to no man

As he writes this, in June or early July, he is very likely considering how to hasten that day along. Perhaps all he needs to make it happen is a spur, or an opportunity.

His previous three years at High Beach have been tranquil and restful. He has spent them exploring the wooded countryside around the asylum, either on his own or accompanied by friends—local artist Juan Buckingham Wandesforde, fellow inmate Thomas Campbell (son of the Scots poet of the same name) and Stockdale, one of the more congenial attendants. These years have also been productive. He has been writing verse. Not much survives, but what does is cogent and beautiful, full of descriptions of the forest in every season. It gives no hint of derangement. Neither does it convey any discontent beyond homesickness and a wish to be back with Patty and the children. One has the sense that Allen is correct: the mental state that led him here was brought on by the worry of supporting a large family and the neglect he suffered following his all-too-brief moment of literary fame.

Removal from home and the suspension of domestic responsibilities has calmed if not cured him. On 17th March 1841, responding to a letter from one of his sons

Matthew Allen's asylum at High Beach, where Clare was admitted in July 1837. He spent four years there—three and a half at Fairmead House followed by six months at Lippitts Hill Lodge.

—most likely the 17-year-old Frederick—he writes, "You Will All Be As Well Pleased To Hear That I Have Been So Long In Good Health & Spirits As To Have Forgotten That I Was Any Otherways", adding that he does not know why he is still being kept at the asylum, "For I Have Been No Otherways Than Well A Couple Of Year's At The Least & Was Never Very Ill Only Harrassed By Perpetual Bother."[22] The letter, though coherent and for the most part even-tempered, bears the first unambiguous sign that all is not well. The postscript contains an odd, elliptical reference:

> P.S. Give My Love To The Dear Boy Who Wrote To Me & To Her Who Is Never Forgotten

Fairmead House, the Allen family home, where Clare spent his first three years at High Beach. Copperplate circa 1830.

Fairmead Cottage circa 1865. Originally consisting of a single range, it was expanded by Matthew Allen in 1837 to house his most seriously afflicted patients.

There can be little doubt that "her who is never forgotten" is Mary Joyce, though it is hard to decipher in what capacity he believes her to be a member of the family, if he does at all. Throughout the letter he addresses Patty as his sole wife and helpmate: "It Was My Lot To Seem As Living Without Friends Untill I Met You," he writes, "& Though We Are Now Parted My Affection Is Unaltered." But Mary is hovering in the wings of his imagined household, and over the weeks prior to his escape she will increasingly take centre stage, pushing Patty so far into the background as to reduce her status to that of a housekeeper. At this point, in mid-March, the worst he can say about High Beach is that he is impatient to be away. By May it will have become a living nightmare.

The asylum was divided among several neighbouring properties. Fairmead House, on Church Road, was reserved for the least-afflicted and best-behaved patients. Allen lived there with his family, and it was run more like a country retreat than a sanatorium. At one point he offered Thomas Carlyle lodging there (the offer was politely declined) on the basis that its setting would be conducive to contemplative thought. It housed both men and women, and promotional literature made much of the fact that, provided they conducted themselves well, residents were permitted to mingle socially, were not restrained in any way, and could come and go as they pleased.

The more seriously disturbed were kept in separate buildings close by; the men at Lippitts Hill Lodge and the women at Springfield. These two establishments, standing close together on the Lippitts Hill Road, were run along more orthodox lines. Inmates were closely watched and restricted to the asylum grounds unless accompanied by attendants. With the exception of the disruptive or the fearful, who were kept in individual cells, they slept in dormitories and during the day were encouraged to work and play together. Excessively noisy or uncontrollable patients were locked in a building a hundred yards or so from Fairmead House, in conditions that Allen would not have wished widely advertised. All the properties but Springfield were linked by a double hawthorn hedge that not only hid promenading patients from inquisitive outsiders, but also acted as a deterrent to escape.

The admissions ledger does not record which house Clare was taken to when he arrived at High Beach in July 1837, and he does not say. But in a letter to Patty sent the following November he describes an entirely benign environment. "The place here is beautiful & I meet with great kindness," he assures her, observing that "the country is the finest I have seen."[23] He is encouraged to take daily walks in the forest as part of his recuperation, and from references in his verse to local landmarks it is clear that he roams the countryside around High Beach without hindrance. The degree of freedom afforded him, as well as the sense he gives of being in a benevolent and restful setting, makes it certain that he has been installed at Fairmead House. This may in part explain the sudden crisis that overtakes him in early 1841. The reply to Frederick's letter, dated 17th March, is headed "Leppitts Hill"—which means he is writing from Lippitts Hill Lodge. Allen moved patients between houses as their condition worsened or improved, so there would be nothing unusual in his being placed here if circumstances warranted. However, anyone accustomed to the relative ease of Fairmead House would find adjusting to the Lodge's regime a challenge, and in Clare's case the change in status from 'guest' to 'inmate', along with the imposition of restrictions, the constant surveillance, and above all the loss of female companionship, would have been bound to aggravate his mental condition.

The origins of that condition are somewhat mysterious. Its suddenness points to some external cause—an event, perhaps, that resulted in his expulsion from Fairmead. In the light of his sexual frustrations, it is not hard to imagine what sort of event this might have been. When he writes, "what is the use of shutting me up from women in a petty paltry place as this merely because I am a married man", he may not be making a general point at all. Rather, he may be dwelling on something more specific—something he did that Allen could not tolerate, and for which he now finds himself exiled to an all-male environment.

Such an eviction may well be at the root of his distress. Far from necessitating a move to Lippitts Hill, his mental decline may well be the result of having to live there. And when viewed in the context of how the asylum was organised, his status does indeed appear incongruous. Though supposedly too unstable for Fairmead House and fit only for the Lodge, he is free to wander the forest—something that has the decided look of exile from one establishment rather than confinement to the other.

At all events there is a definite note of grievance when he writes "I Would Sooner Be Packed In A Slave Ship For Affrica Than Belong To The Destiny Of Mock Friends & Real Enemies."[24] On the evidence of his past behaviour, we cannot doubt he would have taken his removal from Allen's home as an act of personal betrayal.

And if Allen is not among the 'mock friends' in March, when these words are written, by June he is well and truly in Clare's sights. There are two stanzas of 'Don Juan', composed at about this time, that deal with High Beach. The first begins by introducing us to "Doctor Bottle imp" who "deals in urine". Allen, investigating possible links between kidney dysfunction and mental illness, regularly examined his patients' nightly output for clarity and colour, and the action is vividly conjured up by Clare's grotesque appellation. But 'bottle imp' was also contemporary slang for a heavy drinker, insinuating something that those in regular contact with the asylum's director would already have known.

The dual meaning renders Allen not just a figure of fun but also one of opprobrium, and shaming him is very much Clare's intention. The verse continues:

> A keeper of state prisons for the queen
> As great a man as is the Doge of Turin
> & save in London is but seldom seen
> Yclep'd old All-n — mad brained ladies curing
> Some p-x-d like Flora & but seldom clean
> The new road oer the forest is the right one
> To see red hell & further on the white one

These hells are not figurative but real, and the directions to get to them clear: the road "oer the forest" is Lippitts Hill Road; the red hell is the brick-built Lodge, and the white hell Springfield, whose walls are faced with pale stucco. Far from being retreats, these are places where people are held against their will and, as the following stanza reveals, subjected to sexual assault:

Lippitts Hill Lodge, circa 1950. Clare was moved here from Fairmead House at the start of 1841, and it was from here that he escaped.

>Earth hells or b-gg-r shops or what you please
>Where men close prisoners are & women ravished
>I've often seen such dirty sights as these
>I've often seen good money spent & lavished
>To keep bad houses up for doctors fees

Lippitts Hill Lodge in 2016, restored and partially remodelled.

The accusation could not be plainer; Allen is running High Beach as a prison and a house of ill repute. It has become an amalgam of those three socially sanctioned dens of vice identified earlier in the poem; the jail, the madhouse and the brothel.

How much of this is only happening in Clare's head is hard to judge, but there is a clue in the line that describes Doctor Bottle Imp as being "seldom seen". At about this time Allen is in London, raising capital for a new project, and without his personal oversight the moral order of High Beach appears to be unravelling. While the lunatics may not be taking over the asylum exactly, the attendants are definitely taking liberties. Evidence for this can be found in an angry poem that deals with the theft of inmates' possessions, in which Clare writes:

> They'll cheat you of your money friend
> By takeing too much care o't
> & if your wives their cun-ys send
> They're sure to have a share o't [25]

—suggesting that the attendants are helping themselves to more than just property. If this is so, his characterisation of the asylum as a hell is more than justified, as is his urgent need to escape.

On returning home he wrote Allen a courteous letter explaining the reasons for his abrupt departure:

> I can be miserably happy in any situation & any place & could have staid in yours on the forest if any of my friends had noticed me—but the greatest annoyance in such places as yours are those servants styled

keepers who often assumed as much authority over me as if I had been their prisoner & not likeing to quarrel I put up with it till I was weary of the place altogether so I heard the voice of freedom & started [26]

The air of menace at Lippitts Hill may also have caused him to adopt the guise of a professional boxer. Clare's father, in his youth, had been a noted local wrestler at a time when the boundaries between wrestling and boxing were blurred, and as an aficionado of the 'Fancy'—the murky, illegal world of bare-knuckle fighting—Clare himself attended bouts at the Fives Court in London. Boxing had long been a passion, and it chimed perfectly with his Byronic persona.

On the first of May he composes "Jack Randalls Challenge To All the World", which dares anyone to meet with him for a purse of £500 or £1000 "Aside A Fair Stand Up Fight half Minute Time Win Or Loose". Randall—a Regency boxer dead for over a decade—is a hero of Clare's, so it is no surprise that he takes on his identity in the edgy atmosphere of the Lodge. Two months later, writing to Eliza Phillips, he is still playing the role for all he is worth:

> Having been cooped up in this Hell of a Madhouse till I seem to be disowned by my friends & even forgot by my enemies for there is none to accept my challenges which I have from time to time given to the public I am almost mad in waiting for a better place & better company & all to no purpose. It is well known that I am a prize fighter by profession & a man that never feared any body in my life either in the ring or out of it [27]

The adoption of this belligerent role might suggest that he is slipping deeper into psychosis, but it could equally be evidence of his mental resilience in the face of insupportably grim conditions—that he is becoming the dangerous Jack Randall to ward off the abuse meted out to other inmates. By this time, he is waging a war on two fronts—with the fractured world of the asylum and with his own conflicted feelings. It is exhausting. He gives voice to this fatigue in verses to 'Child Harold' entitled 'Written in a Thunder storm July 15th 1841', where not even the overwhelming *son et lumière* of an electrical storm is able to excite his imagination or provoke his fear. He is deadened to all stimulus:

> My soul is apathy — a ruin vast
> Time cannot clear the ruined mass away
> My life is hell — the hopeless die is cast
> & manhoods prime is premature decay [28]

But even as he writes these lines he is nursing hopes of better times to come because, seeking solace in the woods the previous Sunday, he chanced upon the means of making a successful escape.

Musings II

Proud-veined, corrugated leaves float free,
drifting and lifting on currents of air
and we stretch to catch and make a wish
that we may find him here, rhyming his life away
in the spreading yellow of the hornbeam fall.

❦

This rectangular dip is the chapel's footprint
cut across by saplings and strong young trees,
new growth. This is where John Clare
was brought to pray, where his habit of rhyming
made him stand apart like a prophet in the fire.

The little chapel, built of brick, stood at the foot
of the rise to Fern Hill, where Clare saw the
breakneck hills that headlong go, half the world below.
Here is his brook without a bridge, meandering
through leaf mould soft to our feet under the oaks.

❦

The double, densely-layered blackthorn hedge,
where patients were paraded out of sight
and out of mind, axed and gone; heavy bars
that shot into the slots of the Noisy Patients'
bedroom doors, heaved aside.

This is where the knocking can be heard at night
through the memories and myths of generations,
the poor mad people throwing their weight
against the hefty oak. How many times
was John Clare locked up here? how often let run free?

❦

Leopard's Hill Lodge where Allen kept screamers
and incontinents, the seriously deranged:
a fortress still – high walls topped with stone prongs,
barbed wire, electric fence, CCTV.
It was from here that Clare escaped.

Today, refused entry even to the yard,
we feel his dread; troublers banged up at the back,
he was still with his key, but watched going out
and coming in, wild with adrenaline
he's off through the forest to Ponders Green.

❦

Springfield where keepers locked them for protection –
women in dirty pinafores, giddy
with delight at sight of him, bound to their beds;
the tyranny of goodness
stifling their minds, binding their mouths,

women not safe with knives, slashing
their own flesh, playing with dirt from the pot,
restrained for fear they would tear off their clothes
and open their legs to local lads,
breeding babies, extra work for keepers.

For whose good were they locked up here, stunned
to cower from the light? Poor mad creatures
abandoned – cash down to stow them away
on day after day like today – restrained
in case they ran amok, extra work for keepers.

❦

The Transience of the Record

Bridget and I are driving through the heart of Epping Forest, so a road sign bearing the silhouette of a cow comes as a bit of a surprise. Deer, yes, obviously; but cows? It seems so unlikely that we wonder if there's been an error: some mix-up at the signage depot, perhaps, or a misdirected work crew. Through the car's windows the scenery unfolds at speed. Under a leaden sky the forest's hornbeams are shedding leaves that twist and spin in the still, damp air of late October. The lane in front of us dips and dives, curving past large, well-maintained gates. We glimpse an expanse of roof, a flash of Mock-Tudor timbering, a brace of black-windowed Range Rovers —*Welcome to Essex, Ladies and Gents*—and then the bend is behind us and we begin to climb again. We are almost at our destination, High Beach, three hundred feet above the Essex flood plain.

We have come here to meet Kerry Rolison, who has kindly agreed to show us around. Kerry runs the Suntrap Forest Educational Centre, a field-trip destination for inner city schoolchildren that stands on the former site of Fairmead House. Over the years she has accumulated a fund of knowledge about Clare's stay at High Beach from the scholars and devotees who turn up on her doorstep, and she also knows where to find the various locations he wrote about. Much to our delight, she was completely unfazed by our request for a visit. We seemed to come under the heading of 'business as usual'.

Driving into the car park, we see the Centre for the first time: a large late-Victorian building with the oversized windows, deep balconies and wide verandas of the TB sanatorium it once was. Before the invention of antibiotics, consumptive children from London's impoverished East End came here for the only treatments then on offer; bed-rest, fresh air and a good diet. During the Second World War it was annexed to Plaistow Maternity Hospital, so that expectant mothers could have their babies away from the docks that were being targeted by Luftwaffe bombers. After the war, and throughout the 1950s, the building served as accommodation for homeless families. It became a residential field studies centre in 1967, when the London Borough of Walthamstow purchased it from two elderly spinsters for the princely sum of £500.

Kerry leads us through corridors thronged with children and up a staircase to the first floor. Here, the rooms are still recognisable as hospital wards, though now they are furnished with the trappings of a modern schoolroom; white-topped tables, stackable chairs, data projectors and smart screens.

The room we are taken to has been set out with a small collection of exhibits— sketches of Fairmead House, maps of the immediate area, photos of the room when it was a maternity ward and, most wonderful of all, the asylum's Admissions Ledger, open at Clare's entry. His details are written in flowing copperplate: a 44-year old labourer and poet from Northborough, admitted on 15th July 1837 on his wife's instructions. His departure is not recorded. Other individuals on the same page are logged as 'dead', 'cured', 'improved' or 'withdrawn by family', but his status has been left blank. Unwilling to admit that a patient had escaped but equally wary of putting a lie down on paper, Matthew Allen did neither, and in the process consigned Clare to a bureaucratic limbo.

Bridget takes notes while I photograph the exhibits in the daylight streaming through the room's wide, high windows. Glancing down at the car park, I see children being shepherded along by their teachers in a brightly coloured crocodile. Happy and animated, they chatter like birds, clutching worksheets and pencils, impatient to be exploring among the trees. When we descend again, the building is quiet and deserted—an echoing labyrinth.

One of Kerry's friends has dropped by to accompany us on our tour. She knows Austin Darby, the owner of Fairmead Cottage, who is in the process of selling up and moving away. The four of us walk the short distance along Church Road amid the pirouetting leaves, hoping we'll be allowed inside, but on arriving we find the gate padlocked. Peering through a gap in the hedge, we see that the property has already been vacated. Its bare windows stare back at us blankly.

Far from being a cottage, Fairmead Cottage is in fact a handsome, double-roofed two-storey house; in size and appearance more like a classic English rectory. Allen spent a good deal of money enlarging and extending its seventeenth century core while Clare was his 'guest'. Not only was business booming for Allen—Clare was, after all, his forty-fifth patient—but he had also managed to extract a total of £7,000 from the family of Alfred Lord Tennyson for another project: one that would ultimately land both men in dire financial straits.[29]

The asylum Admissions Register, showing Clare's committal as patient 45.

It used to be thought that Clare was installed at the cottage on his arrival here, the assumption being that Allen had reserved it for the least-afflicted because its seclusion would protect them from the asylum's more alarming occupants. Plausible, if circumstantial, evidence for Clare's residency was provided by a poem, 'The Water Lilies', which describes a nearby pond, and by references in other poems to St Paul's Chapel just across the road. But in 2003, Clare's biographer Jonathan Bate found Allen's plans for the asylum, which specified that Fairmead Cottage was to be equipped with cells for restraining what he termed "noisy patients".[30] Far from being a sanctuary for the timid, then, the building was a prison for the violent.

Austin Darby, the owner, told the author Nicholas Haggar a macabre story about the place. Because Victorians viewed the souls of the insane as unfit for Heaven, inmates who died at Fairmead Cottage were buried in its garden instead of the consecrated space of a graveyard. Darby had dug up their bones while turning the earth of the grounds. He'd also, he said, grown up hearing their voices, as had the rest of his family. When I mention this to Kerry's friend, she confirms that the Cottage has long had a reputation for being haunted.

Ghostly manifestations aside, there is no doubt that it was a place of extraordinary suffering. Quite apart from the misery of their own afflictions, inmates had to endure rough handling and close confinement, locked up in individual cells whose outward-opening doors were secured by heavy iron bars. Even the décor reflected its oppressive atmosphere, with interior walls painted a dark brown to hide the soot stains made by oil lamps.[31]

Even before he arrived at the asylum, Clare was familiar with the kind of behaviour exhibited by the occupants of Fairmead Cottage. Mental illness was the companion of rural poverty, and for the afflicted there were few refuges other than the family. Even then, the stigma of insanity could cause them to be driven away.

In Clare's work we find figures like 'Crazy Nell', who wanders the countryside in a state of inconsolable mental agony. While she comes from a newspaper report, he describes other madwomen as though from actual experience.[31] His blank-verse poem 'The Crazy Maid', written in 1819 or 1820, has the power and immediacy of first-hand observation:

> Poor wretch she howls her fancied terrors now
> But short existance each gives leave to each
> As like the hasty tide they ebb & flow
> As like to Aprils skye her passions change
> Sun shine & rain clear sky & cloud
> All mingling in an hour
>
> So song & sorrow mingles tears & smiles
> Laughing & howling at she knows not what
> Nor feels not—a minute goes grief dies
> She fancies shes in heaven prays & sings
> To trees & bushes calling them her angels
> Then again a moment shifts the scene

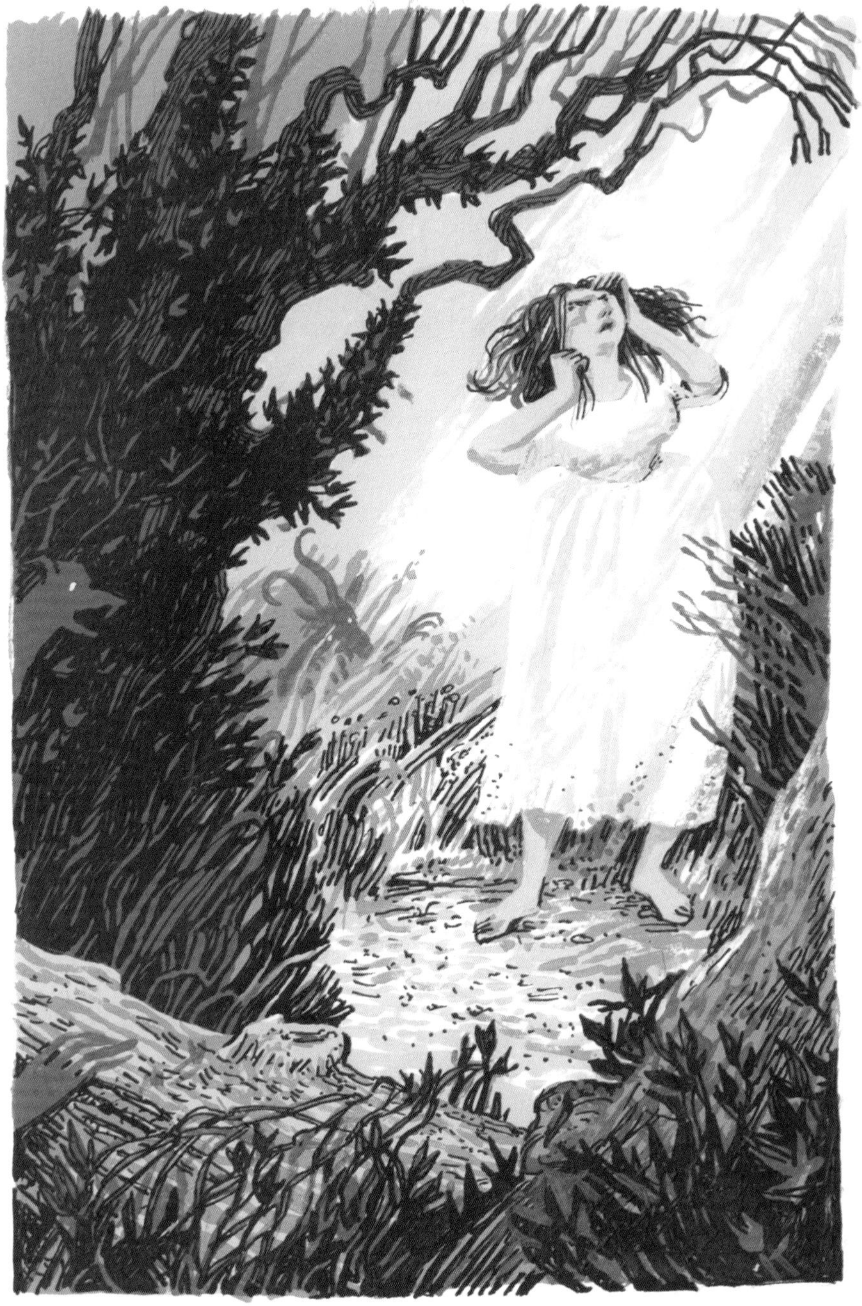

> Black horror fill[s] her brain she howls her rage
> & frighted flies from every thing that stirs
> Cows shine her devils then with tails & horns
> & hogs & sheep her imps of dreaded hell
> Again composd wild gushing joys again
> Burst from her laughing soul poor hagged wretch [32]

I get out my notes and read these lines aloud as we imagine the screams of inmates, the shouts of attendants, the slam of doors and clang of iron bars. Then we turn to cross Church Road, and head into the forest.

Following Kerry, we walk down a narrow track until the enfolding trees muffle our voices and the air falls quiet. Clare's lily pond still exists here, fed by a brook that rises behind Fairmead Cottage and flows beneath the road to Hill Wood, near the site of the chapel. As in Clare's day, it is a tortuous slot in the ground, winding through closely-set oaks and beeches and snaking its way out of sight. We cross it by a narrow footbridge, and soon we are climbing as the land swells gently upward, lifting the forest canopy. This slope, which he christened "Fern Hill", was bare when he was here, but on reaching the top we find it crowned by a large pollarded hornbeam. The broad, open vistas he used to enjoy are now blocked by golden treetops, and woodland falls away on every side.

Looking down on this tranquil landscape, it's hard to imagine that it was once a battleground for commoners' rights, but there is a history here that Clare was familiar with and felt strongly about: "I could not bear to see the tearing plough / Root up and steal the forest from the poor", he writes in one of his High Beach poems, recapitulating the distress he felt when the woods and copses of his childhood were felled for agriculture.[34] During his stay here, scenes from those days were being replayed in the countryside around him.

Between the twelfth and seventeenth centuries Epping had been a Royal Forest, kept by kings and queens for hunting deer and wild boar. The Crown owned the land and the game, while commoners were free to collect wood and graze their cattle—

Clare's 'Brook without a Bridge'.

an arrangement that stayed unchanged for four centuries to the mutual benefit of all. Following the Civil War, however, the restored monarchy turned its back on field pursuits and the Forest began to fall into neglect. Commoners still held their rights to lop firewood and put animals out to graze, but the place was now increasingly the haunt of brigands and outlaws. Poaching, too, was endemic, so much so that the Crown no longer bothered to enforce Forest Law.

By the 1720s the situation had reached its nadir. In Essex, as elsewhere, criminality was soaring. The economic crash that followed the collapse of the South Sea Bubble was being felt at all levels of society, and otherwise law-abiding citizens were poaching simply to survive. Draconian legislation passed by Parliament to deal with a nationwide epidemic of property theft only inflamed what was fast becoming a class war, and in 1735 Epping Forest—already a place of dread for travellers—saw its most famous son, Dick Turpin, take to the roads.

Against this background of neglect and disorder, local manorial lords seized their chance to enclose Forest land on their own initiative. By 1793, the year of Clare's birth, fully one third of its 9,000 acres was in their hands with the blessing of the Forest Warden, the Duke of Wellington's dissolute and incompetent nephew, William Wellesley Pole. For its part the Crown, unwilling to spend money on the upkeep of an asset it no longer required, was happy to turn a blind eye as Pole lost large tracts of it. By 1809, the year that Clare's home village of Helpston began to be carved up with Parliament's approval, this wholly unsanctioned Enclosure had deprived Epping's commoners of half their land. The Forest was still being appropriated when Clare arrived twenty-eight years later. We know that locals were collecting wood at the time because one of his asylum poems, 'A Walk on High Beach, Loughton', mentions a 'sticker', but friction with the Enclosers was ongoing, and continued long after his departure. It culminated in 1866 with litigation between a Loughton man, Thomas Willingdale, and the lord of the manor, the Rev. John Whitaker Maitland, a voracious Encloser who had taken over 1,000 acres of the Forest for himself, after which there were barely 3,500 left. Maitland sued Willingdale and his friends, accusing them of damaging his property. They countered by insisting they had been exercising their rights to lop.

Various interested parties, including the Corporation of London, were so alarmed at the speed with which the Forest was disappearing that they weighed in on the side of the defendants. Though Willingdale died before the matter was resolved, Maitland and his fellow Enclosers were forced to stop. In 1871 the Corporation took the Forest over from the Crown by Act of Parliament, bought up the manors, and began to manage it as an open space for all. Though a victory for conservation, it was a defeat for the commoners. William Morris, who as a young boy roamed the Forest while Clare was at Allen's, recalls that

> except for a piece about Queen Elizabeth's Lodge, and for the part about High Beech, the Forest was almost wholly made up of pollard hornbeams mixed with holly thickets. But when the Corporation of London took it over [...] the topping and lopping, which was part of the old commoners' rights, came to an end and the trees were let to grow.[35]

The commoners were given compensation of a sort in the form of a public building, Lopping Hall in Loughton, which opened in 1884, but many must have reckoned this was far too little and far too late. It almost goes without saying that the Enclosers received their compensation in hard cash, and a good deal more promptly.

As we retrace our steps down the hill, Kerry tells us about two traditional methods of managing woodland: pollarding, which involves cutting wood from the tops of the trees, and coppicing—cropping them at ground level. Because these practices encouraged new growth, they ensured a constant supply of wood for fuel and construction, and in some species could even prolong a tree's life. Another vital activity is keeping the ground free of undergrowth. Here it was done by putting cattle out to graze, but the practice fell into a slow decline, and finally ended in 1996 with the BSE crisis. Over the years since, unwanted plants such as holly have proliferated, severely impacting the Forest's biodiversity. The subject of grazing prompts Bridget to mention the rather surreal road sign we saw warning of cows, and Kerry assures us we weren't hallucinating—in recent years, herds of Longhorn and Red Poll have been reintroduced to help tackle the rampant undergrowth. These magnificent beasts have no fear of traffic. Drivers who value their no-claims bonuses, on the other hand, might well be advised to show them respect.

We re-cross the footbridge and turn south, following the brook until we meet a path that takes us back towards the road. Within earshot of the occasional passing car, we emerge at a clearing. This, Kerry tells us, is Church Plain, the spot where St Paul's Chapel used to stand. There is the barest footprint of a building impressed in the earth, a straight-sided hollow heaped with leaf litter, but that is all. The rest is left to our imagination, and to Clare:

A hornbeam toppled by gales in Hill Wood—Clare's 'Fern Hill'.

The summit of Hill Wood, once bare but now clothed in mature trees.

> So beautifull the chapel peeps between
> The hornbeams—with its simple bell—alone

he writes in 'Child Harold', and again:

> Here is the chapel yard enclosed with pales
> & oak trees top its little bell

Oaks still stand at the clearing's margin among the hornbeams and beeches. Of the picket fence there is no trace.

When, in 1836, this spot was chosen as the site of High Beach's first church, it had been known for generations as Blencow's Green. Just before Clare's arrival, builders had cleared away the grass and wild flowers, laid foundations, and raised an iron roof over walls of red brick. The result, completed at a cost of £900, was described in the 1848 edition of the Essex Directory Gazetteer as "a small mean structure".[36] It is perhaps a measure of how much Clare revered the spiritual, how close he felt it was to Nature, that he viewed it not as an ugly intrusion but a living part of the forest. Every Sunday he came here with his fellow inmates to sing hymns and hear sermons from men whose goodness and piety were deemed—at least by themselves—to be beyond reproach. Allen himself often preached here. But St Paul's did not survive long. Built on miry ground, it fell into such a state of disrepair that in 1862 it had to be abandoned. It was finally demolished in 1885, following years of vandalism by East-End 'excursionists'.

On the path to Old Church Plain.

By the early twentieth century there was little to testify it had ever existed, apart from the graves in its overgrown churchyard.[37] Today there is no evidence even of those. It is something, we remark to each other, that Clare would have appreciated —a vindication of his intense awareness of the transience of things: a very personal riff on the themes of Gray's 'Elegy' and Young's 'Night Thoughts'.

We rejoin Church Road opposite the grounds of Fairmead Cottage. Behind us we can hear the chatter of schoolchildren and the raised voice of a teacher reminding them to look at—*but not touch*—any berries or fungi they come across. This prompts Kerry to relate how in recent years the forest's biodiversity has acquired a new threat: professional foragers, who come up from London to pick wild produce for trendy restaurants. No fungus, berry or herb is safe from these gastronomic asset strippers. It's an unsustainable situation, she says, but one with no immediate remedy.

Back at the car we take leave of our guides and head to the Owl for a late lunch. Clare would have walked across the fields to get there, but we have to go the long way round, driving to the end of Church Road and taking the right-hand bend at the foot of Lippitts Hill. The good news is that both Lippitts Hill Lodge and Springfield are on our route.

Just before the bend there is a gate flanked by stone turrets in the French style, complete with arrow slits and conical roofs. They rather remind me of the toy castle that my children, when small, used to garrison with barmily smiling Duplo people. To the side of each a smooth sandstone block has been set into a high wall, bearing the elegantly incised legend 'Lippitts Hill Lodge'.

We continue round to where the Lodge's west wing abuts the road. The tradesmen's entrance is here, and by sheer good luck the door is standing open. A courier is handing a parcel to a severely dressed woman who is evidently some kind of manager or personal assistant. She signs for it and he drives off, but before she can retreat Bridget runs up and accosts her. A conversation ensues. I can't hear what is being said, but I do see the woman shake her head and shut the door. "She won't even let us look around the yard," Bridget reports, disappointed. This doesn't surprise me. I have been scanning the building and musing on how the high perimeter wall and security cameras at every corner give it the air of a military compound. People were locked away from the world here but now it's the world that's locked out. It makes me wonder whether, these days, those in need of restraint are inside or outside. I'm mulling this over when Bridget spots a plaque high above the door informing us, not quite accurately, that "John Clare the Famous Poet Lived Here in Lippits (sic) Hill Lodge 1837-1841". As we stroll away, we wonder if it prompts passers-by to ring the bell, and if so, whether the owners rue the day they allowed it to be fixed to their home.

It is only a few steps to Springfield, which in Clare's day was the asylum's all-female institution. Its proximity suggests that the women there would have been able to hear—and occasionally see—the men in the Lodge, and vice-versa. The high-voltage sexual charge that permeates the description of "Allen's hells" in 'Don Juan' may well have resulted from this tantalizing state of affairs—pheromones wafting between the houses, driving the inmates into frenzies of lust.

The gates of Lippitts Hill Lodge on Church Road.

It was sex that caused Allen to acquire Springfield in the first place. He had started out with a mixed population at the Lodge, but in 1832 a potential scandal forced him to reconsider this arrangement. One of his patients, a Mrs Dutton, had been transferred there from Fairmead House because her condition had deteriorated and she needed closer supervision. Her husband objected, citing a supposed contractual obligation on Allen's part to keep her at Fairmead, and refused to pay her fees until she was returned there. When the case went to trial, he insinuated that she had been molested at the Lodge, possibly by Allen himself—something she may well have claimed under the influence of her illness.[38] In 1834, mindful of Dutton's accusations and keen to avoid any chance of future scandal, Allen bought Springfield and moved the entire female complement of the Lodge there. When Clare arrived at High Beach three years later, it was home to 15 women.[39]

Today Clare's 'white hell' is a handsome private residence with a weather-boarded front, elegant sash windows and a gabled roof. It stands in a large garden bordered by a picket fence and, unlike Lippitts Hill Lodge, is completely open to the road. With no-one around to ask for a closer look, we lean on the five-bar gate at the entrance and content ourselves with viewing it from the public highway.

Our destination, the Owl, lies less than a hundred yards away at the top of the hill. It's a large modern pub-restaurant well and truly geared to the family market. Out front is a children's playground, complete with swings and slides, and in the garden there's a scattering of wooden tables with red and yellow parasols tightly furled against the autumn weather. There is no-one about, and as we push at the door we wonder whether the place is even open.

The landlady confirms that business has wound down for the year. The pub makes most of its money from summer visitors; trade drops off in September, and though things get livelier during the run up to Christmas it is usually Easter before there's a reliable upswing. When Iain Sinclair came here in 2004 he commented on the proximity of the Metropolitan Police Firearms Centre, a large complex of buildings hidden behind trees on the other side of the road, and reported seeing a sign warning of "Sudden Loud Noise from This Camp".[40] Today there are no gunshots to shatter the autumnal hush. We are left to wander the garden in peace, savouring the fine southerly view of Epping's wooded hills. Looking back the way we came, we see

Springfield, on Lippitts Hill, Matthew Allen's all-female institution.

Lippitts Hill Lodge, just a few yards down the hill, where Clare was billeted.

the double roof of Fairmead Cottage peeping out from among the burnished trees. We imagine Clare toiling up the hill of an evening to spend his gardening money on a couple of pints, chatting up Mrs King the landlady, or after she has decamped to Enfield Highway, young Miss Fish, the publican's nubile daughter, pressing into their hands his books of Byron like paper aphrodisiacs.

The original Owl was demolished in 1977. It dated from the early eighteenth century and, like Springfield, was built in the traditional Essex fashion with white-painted weatherboard walls. At a time when the area was little visited, Clare knew it as a public house frequented by locals. That was before the arrival at Loughton of the Eastern Counties Railway in 1856, and the crowds of East End pleasure seekers who descended on the forest at weekends and bank holidays, leaving—if their vandalism of St Paul's Chapel is anything to go by—no small amount of destruction in their wake. Clare's forest was still a tranquil, semi-wild and untouched place, one that he came to love as much as his own native woods and fields. He wrote about it at this very spot, looking across, as we are doing now, at "the breakneck hills, that headlong go, / And leave me high, and half the world below."[41]

But not even the beauty of the landscape could lift the tide of depression that was threatening to engulf him as the spring of 1841 turned to summer. During the second week of July, while roaming the forest close to High Beach and feeling, as he put it, "melancholly", he encountered a band of gypsies. This would have been a common occurrence. Romanies frequently stayed in the area, and it had been the setting for his sonnet 'The Gipsy Camp', which paints a stark, unsentimental picture of the Traveller's life in the depths of winter. Many who regularly came were members

The Owl public house in 1903, virtually unchanged from when Clare was a patron.

of the Smith clan, a large and sprawling family with whom he'd had dealings going back to his childhood.

Whether he knew the individuals he met that day is unclear, but the encounter was a turning point in his life. Perhaps it triggered an impulse in him to flee, or perhaps—if, as his biographer Frederick Martin claims, he had already tried to escape—he saw them as allies in securing the freedom that had so far eluded him. Either way, he expressed a wish to be gone, and one of them, as he writes,

> offered to assist in my escape from the mad house by hideing me in his camp to which I almost agreed but told him I had no money to start with but if he would do so I would promise him fifty pounds and he agreed to do so before Saturday

The claim of being able to lay hands on £50—an implausibly large sum for the time—must have sounded to the gypsies like madness talking. They clearly regretted making the deal. He saw them again the following Friday but they temporised, and when he went to their camp two days later he found it deserted:

> On Sunday I went and they were all gone — an old wide awake hat and an old straw bonnet of the plumb pudding sort was left behind — and I put the hat in my pocket thinking it might be usefull for another opportunity and as good luck would have it, turned out to be so

He does not record his reaction to their disappearance, but he might well have expected something of the sort. In his autobiography he had written of gypsies that "Their friendships are warm and their passions of short duration but they are not to be relied on".[42] Perhaps, in the end, he'd considered the strategy a long shot and was philosophical about its outcome.

One thing this turn of events did not do was dissuade him from trying to escape. One of the band had given him directions that would take him at least as far as Enfield. We do not know if they guided him further because he only mentions them once, when he misses a turn between Ponders End and Enfield on account of "being careless in mapping down the rout as the Gypsey told me". In any event he did not need to be shown a way out of the woods; during his four years at Allen's he had wandered far and wide, both alone and accompanied by keepers, and knew the lie of the land for miles. This much is clear from his writings—verses such as 'A Walk on High Beach Loughton' in which he looks down on "pleasant Edmonton", "Wild Enfield Chase" and "Giant London", and the canto of 'Don Juan' in which he confides his love of "the moor and marsh and Ponders end"—all places beyond the Forest's western edge. What he really needed was a way of leaving Lippitts Hill Lodge unseen and evading immediate capture, and for that the gypsy's advice proved invaluable.

The following day, a Monday, he did nothing—or at any rate nothing out of the ordinary. He set out the morning after, taking the first steps on the longest walk of his life.

Musings III

He speaks:

'Gone – nought but two hats lying on the ground –
they've grabbed my freedom and gone –
left me in Allen's madhouse, caged and living –
such bursting in my chest, raging and hollering
till I fall and darkness closes in.

'What did the gypsy say? down the forest track,
but then which path? Dare I lose my way?
but what's worse than here? lost to hope,
truth shut up in prison, forgotten,
losing myself, no escape unless I dare.'

He speaks:

'I'm marching – making good speed at a steady pace
like the troops at Waterloo – a Northants
militiaman with many miles to go,
my courage in tow, tracking the ruts
from the gypsies' cart like a birding dog.

'This route's not often used, criss-crossed
with briars where the forest thins;
white bramble flowers, torn and trampled
by the cart. And here's a great oak
tumbled by last week's gale, branches in lush leaf.

'They'll be after me, soon as I'm missed, for sure,
just like the times before. But I got a good start
and they don't know this secret route. Wisdom
I'll call him, like my friend from Langley Bush,
for I'll not let on his real name.

'Wisdom said to keep going up, till the trees
come to the brink and all London is in sight:
the snaking Thames to Greenwich, the city and smoke;
then down to my right, by the forest's edge,
through the marsh to the bridge o'er the Lea.'

Plunging through Timescapes

Bridget and I do not return to High Beach until the following summer. The trees that nine months ago were golden and threadbare are now heavy with foliage, and the stewed-tea perfume of dead leaves has yielded to a heady chlorophyll sweetness. It is six in the morning on 20th July, one hundred and seventy-four years to the day since Clare started for home, and by happy coincidence the weather is as it was then —close and warm, with intervals of sunshine and the threat of showers. We are standing outside the tradesman's entrance of Lippitts Hill Lodge under the vigilant eye of a CCTV camera, about to retrace the first few of miles of his walk. I check my equipment with some shots of the blue plaque, and one of the camera for luck, and then we are off down the hill. As we go, we picture Clare, the gypsy's hat rammed on his head and a knapsack swinging at his shoulder, stealthily hastening to reach the turn in the road.

"Reconnitered the rout the Gipsey pointed out and found it a legible one to make a movement," he wrote, neglecting to mention where the route was actually leading him. Reconstructing it is relatively straightforward, however, as there were only two places where he could have crossed the marshes, and very few ways to get to them. The first ran north past the Owl to the end of Lippitts Hill road, and then via a succession of paths and tracks to the village of Enfield Highway. From there, Enfield Town could be reached from Nag's Head Lane, a short distance south along Ponders End High Road.

Initially, this was the route we thought he had taken. But our minds were changed when we came across two letters at Enfield Library written in the 1980s by Graham Dalling—then head of Local History—in response to queries on this very subject. In both, Dalling points out that Clare missed Nag's Head Lane *before* arriving in Enfield Highway, which means he must have gone north along Ponders End High Road after taking the more southerly path across the marshes. James Canton, in his collection of essays *Out of Essex*, describes how his conversations with Dalling helped him trace the route.[43] When we came across Canton's book a little later in our researches, it became invaluable in helping us navigate our way between High Beach and Enfield Highway.

The gypsy's route had several advantages, the first of which becomes obvious when we cross the road at the corner by the Lodge and make a right turn, as Clare did, onto a path leading west towards Ludgate Plain. Hidden by trees, we are almost immediately out of the Lodge's line of sight. Anyone looking from the windows would have had mere seconds in which to spot him. The path itself, which follows the forest's north-western boundary, has undergone profound changes since his time. The muddy trail he hurried down in 1841 is now a broad, well-maintained cinder track which even at ten past six in the morning is busy with people. Middle-aged joggers with shiny faces and sweat-stained armpits lurch past us at a trot, asthmatically acknowledging us with a grunt or a distracted nod. Out of nowhere a

'Tyrolean hiker' on the track to Sewardstonebury.

peloton of sleekly helmeted twenty-somethings swoops around us from behind with a popping of tyres on loose stones and the whir and *snicker-snack* of dérailleur gears, all Gallic insouciance and fluorescent Lycra. As they power out of sight, it occurs to me that despite appearances this is not the countryside at all—just a wooded interstice in the fabric of suburbia where the city's more masochistic workers start their days of thankless toil by ritually exhausting themselves. "It's called exercise," Bridget reminds me when I share this epiphany with her.

My hiking boots are already uncomfortably hot, so I stop to remove my sweater in the irrational hope that this might help. At that moment a lone figure appears in the distance. We try not to stare as it resolves into a sprightly old man. He is dressed, like a waiter from a *Bierkeller*, in Tyrolean hat, short-sleeved shirt and leather braces. No *Lederhosen*, sadly, but he's wearing shorts, long brown socks and tan leather shoes—close enough to pass muster. Holding a stick like a wizard's staff, he is white-haired and spry, and as he passes us, he *twinkles*—there's really no other word for it. We mutter a "Morning" and keep our eyes fixed resolutely forward. When he turns a bend in the track, Bridget gives me a 'did you see *that*?' look. "That *was* bizarre, even by our standards", I concede, "but in the very likely case no-one will believe us, I have the evidence right here", and I pat one of the cameras slung around my neck.

At Ludgate Plain the track forks in two. The left-hand branch plunges deep into the forest making for Woodman's Glade, but we take the other, which brings us to the hamlet of Sewardstonebury and the grounds of the West Essex Golf Club. We emerge at the bottom of Hornbeam Lane—practically all that is left of the old settlement—where we are confronted by a huge half-timbered Tudorbethan villa. Next door to it is an equally grand pile in the New England Colonial Style, and next door to *that* is a mock-medieval mansion, and then another—this time with a triple garage attached—and so on, all the way down the road. The whole of the lane, we realise, is made up of properties with seven-digit price tags. Behind it all, manicured fairways stretch away in that shade of emerald green you only find on Metroland posters. "The sun has got his hat on, hip hip hip hooray!" I sing, and not just because it seems appropriate given our surroundings. A break in the cloud is pouring golden light like honey over the successful and the prosperous, as is only their due.

In 1841 this was an incomparably meaner place—a handful of foresters' cottages by Sewardstone Green. The golf course had yet to be built, and Hornbeam Lane was an unnamed woodland trail that ended at a junction with four other ways. Three of those were footpaths and the fourth was a cart track bisecting the Forest from north to south. The junction is still here, though the paths are now buried in undergrowth and the track is a busy A road linking Sewardstone and Chingford.

We cross it and take the footpath that Clare followed, which charges straight up the northern spur of Pole Hill, making absolutely no concessions to an out-of-shape walker like me. As we trudge up the unfeasibly steep slope, Bridget comments that Clare could not have wished for a better escape route. I agree. Passing through thick vegetation, this path was made by cottagers and other poor locals who would have taken as little interest in an escaped lunatic as they did in the gypsies who habitually used it to enter and leave the forest.

Hornbeam Lane, Sewardstonebury, where substantial Metroland villas have replaced foresters' cottages.

Such is the density of the trees and bushes around us that, despite climbing for what seems like a geological age, there is still no view. This, I believe, is why we take a wrong turn. We have been skirting the northern boundary of the Hawk Wood, an elongated tongue of the Forest that climbs Yardley Hill. On reaching its westernmost edge, we arrive at a well-trodden track running at right angles to us, on the other side of which our own path disappears into dense undergrowth, looking for all the world like a dead end. Without bothering to consult the map on my phone I decide our only sensible course of action is make a right turn. Though we're unaware of it at the time, the track we are joining is in fact a section of the London Outer Orbital Path—a 240-kilometre M25 for ramblers also known by the acronymically-minded as the 'Loop', which draws a circle around the capital touching cardinal points at Enfield, Upminster, Croydon and Uxbridge. As soon as we join it we find the going easier, and not just because we are almost at the top of the hill. The footing has become much firmer, due—as we later learn—to the local authority's obligation to keep it in a walkable state.

We are passing a tall, straight hedge on our right—a field boundary, we guess—when out of a gap leaps a golden Labrador. He is gripping a tennis ball in his jaws and wagging his tail so hard it looks in danger of flying off. Behind him emerges a good-looking, well-heeled couple in their late thirties. I immediately have them pegged as residents of Hornbeam Lane. The man looks as though he's starring in an after-shave commercial and the woman seems to be modelling conditioner for shiny bouncy hair. Both are tanned, and have a health and vigour about them that is positively unnatural, but they greet us affably enough while yelling at the Lab not to jump—*"No Rollo!"*— just as two muddy paws thump against my chest. Rollo immediately sits, drops the ball, and studies it quizzically as though he's never seen it before, tail a-wag in the grass like a strimmer.

"I say, nice cameras," drawls Mr Hornbeam-Lane—his opening gambit in the tricky game of Talking to Complete Strangers, "You a photographer then by any chance?" His manner suggests an expensive schooling followed by a career in something insanely lucrative but intellectually undemanding: marine insurance, maybe, or ship brokerage. There is of course only one sensible answer I can give, and when I do the woman's face lights up as if I have surprised—even delighted—her. Bridget tells them we are on our way to the Lea but does not mention why, as we've found that explaining our project to strangers only leads to bemusement on their part and embarrassment on ours. "No, no!" Mr Hornbeam-Lane replies, shaking his head, "You won't get any good shots by the Lea. It's all very ugly. Reservoirs and whatnot. For a really spectacular shot you need to go up *there*." And he points through the gap in the hedge where the field climbs to a flattish summit. "We come here every morning," gushes his wife, instantly giving herself away as a native of the Golden State. "It's totally *awesome*. Rollo loves it, don't you fella?" Of course he loves it, I want to say, gritting my teeth; he's a Labrador, he loves everything.

We trade platitudes about the weather and the scenery, then pat Rollo goodbye before they stride off down the hill. When they're about fifty yards away Mr Hornbeam-Lane turns and yells, "That way!" jabbing his finger at the field. We nod vigorously and wait until they are out of sight. Then we go on our way.

The Beach Boys' 'California Girls' is still playing in my head when we come to another junction, this time with a path running east-west. We need to get off the hill, and here is an opportunity to do so. A quick look at my phone confirms what I already knew but was too embarrassed to admit—we've come way too far north. It's a bad start to our attempt at following Clare. We can either return to our original route—the one he took—and fight our way through a tangle of brambles, or follow the invitingly clear and unobstructed path before us. We discuss it for a while and finally agree to take the correct one, in reverse, on our return leg. This is how we end up picking our way gingerly down a steep, slippery trail that dumps us without ceremony into the brick and concrete of suburban North London. As we slither and slide, the trees and bushes thin out, then vanish altogether. Back gardens appear on our right and left, and then, in a final surreal twist, we realise—as we exit a narrow alley between two houses and our feet touch pavement—that a couple more steps will take us through the open doors of a waiting double-decker bus.

We have emerged at the Yardley Lane Estate bus stop on the Sewardstone Road, where a number 215 Routemaster is ingesting a long line of commuters. It is half past seven in the morning, and all over London semi-conscious men and women are boarding buses like this one to take their daily ride to work. The sudden switch from sunny hillside to cheerless street is disorienting; for a moment or two we feel out of place and out of time, like a pair of anthropologists observing the baffling, joyless rite of some primitive tribe. But even the psychically dislocated need to eat. A signboard on the pavement is advertising the Valley Golf Course Café, so without further ado we head on over for a much-needed breakfast.

Inside, there's a group of telecomms engineers wolfing down plates of full English and holding about fifteen conversations at once. They are middle-aged and balding, and their banter fills the café with boisterous bonhomie. One of them waves me over. He is built like a brick outhouse, with a magnificent beer belly and a thatched beard. I'd lay odds on him being a Morris dancer. "'Ere," he says grinning, "Come over tonight and take some pictures of the wife, will ya?"

"Sure," I reply, "and I'll do some prints for your mates, if you like."

The table erupts with good-natured, ribald laughter. A whippet-thin bloke with John Lennon specs taps my arm and asks a question about lenses for shooting wildlife. "Do you go birding then?" I ask. "Dogging, more like," quips the Morris dancer, to more guffaws and table slapping. I'd like to stay and trade banter with them but my stomach is rumbling audibly, so I say goodbye and drift over to the counter where Bridget has been ordering for us.

We take our coffees to an empty table and I dig out my phone to search for 'Valley Golf Course Chingford'. I discover it's a "nine-hole pitch-and-putt par three", which conjures up absolutely nothing in my head beyond the thought that it must be a tongue twister. I look through the windows for enlightenment but to no avail. The view is obstructed by a high fence. All I can see is a pair of BT vans standing side by side in the gravel car park.

As we eat, we review the morning so far. It strikes us that there are traces of Clare's landscape at Ludgate Plain and the Hawk Wood but none at all hereabouts; Yardley Hill is encrusted with housing, and the marshes at its feet lie drowned beneath the Chingford Reservoirs, whose massive grass-covered embankments confine millions of metric tonnes of water pumped directly out of the Lea. Vital though they are to millions of people, these artificial lakes have wrecked the local landscape on a truly geological scale.

Clare's route therefore took him through a locality that is now extinct—one that had its own geography and landmarks.

After descending the hill from the Hawk Wood, he made his way down Marsh Lane, over the Lea at Dell Ford, and onto the grassy expanse of South Marsh. About halfway across he negotiated a bridge over the Mar Dyke, then followed a track that took him to the southern towpath of the Lea Navigation. Like the river, the Navigation still exists, but nine tenths of the land in between—hundreds of hectares of grass and sedge—vanished for good in 1913, when King George's Reservoir was filled.

The Lea Valley bore more than a passing resemblance to the countryside around Northborough, and Clare would have found its wildlife familiar; lapwing, heron, reed bunting and bittern were all common, as were adders, grass snakes and lizards. From medieval times the marshes had been carefully managed to ensure a plentiful supply of fodder; locals observed a seasonal cycle of leaving the grass to grow until summer, harvesting it at Lammas Tide (the weeks leading up to August 1st), and then grazing cattle on the regrowth until the following spring. In late July Clare would have experienced the valley as a place of tall, dry grass peopled with scythe-wielding mowers.

South Marsh was something of an exception as it was on the route to Smithfield Market and thus grazed the whole year round. While making his way across it he must surely have encountered drovers with their beasts slogging the last few weary miles to market. They may have reminded him of his days as a boy watching highland cattle pass through Helpston on their trek down the Great North Road, as he relates in *The Shepherd's Calendar*:

> Along the roads in passing crowds
> Followd by dust like smoking clouds
> Scotch droves of beast a little breed
> In sweltered weary mood proceed
> A patient race from scottish hills
> To fatten by our pasture rills
> Lean wi the wants of mountain soil

The bridge over the Lea at Dell Ford circa 1860.

> But short and stout for travels toil
> Wi cockd up horns and curling crown
> And dewlap bosom hanging down

Equally strange were the herders, at whose "uncouth dress" and outlandish appearance "the shepherds dog will rise [...] Draw back and waffle in affright",

> To witness men so oddly clad
> In petticoats of banded plad
> Wi blankets oer their shoulders slung
> To camp at night the fields among [44]

 Though he had never seen the Lea before this moment, it was already familiar to him. From a young age, Izaak Walton's *The Compleat Angler* had been one of his most cherished books. He wrote in his journal, "One may almost hear the water of the river Lea ripple along and the grass and flags grow and rustle in the pages that speak of it", having just taken refuge in those very pages from a dull, rainy morning cooped up at home. Walton fished on the Lea and set his great work on its banks, so that the river and the Navigation must have felt to Clare like a piece of home unmoored from his poetic imagination and laid beneath his feet. I picture him striding along, absorbed in its familiarity and only half-aware of oncoming cattle, his hat rammed low to hide his face, his eyes fixed firmly on the track, and with nothing in his head beyond the fear of capture and the voluptuous promise of his two wives.

 After saying goodbye to the café's staff and customers, we resume our walk. To our right a straggly hedge hides the golf course and the built-up riverside, so that the illusion of being in the countryside is almost perfect, compromised only by a long street of 1950s semis perched high on the hill opposite. The view from up there must be spectacular, especially for those into reservoirs and sewage treatment plants. I wonder out loud whether it's something estate agents make much of—*Properties ideal for DIY enthusiasts, aficionados of Edwardian civil engineering and connoisseurs of post-industrial blight*. This being prime London commuter belt, very probably.

 I'm sharing this thought with Bridget when we come across an uncomfortable reminder of Clare's world, though I don't suppose he would have recognised it as such: a huddle of trailers, circled like pioneer wagons under attack, in the car park of a derelict industrial site. Children whoop and scream as they chase each other round them, dodging obstacles and ducking under lines of washing. One little girl stands apart, watching us narrowly. Her hands grip the torn chain-link fence that was meant to keep her family out—to make them travel on, to stop anywhere but here on this apron of rotted concrete. I'd like to think we have stumbled on a direct connection to Clare; that these are Smiths or Boswells following the old network of Romani ways, but it's pointless to consider asking them. Like the cloistered rich, they are wary of those they do not know. In its own way this camp is as impregnable to the likes of us as Lippitts Hill Lodge with its security cameras and unscaleable walls.

The site they have broken into stands on a remnant of South Marsh—once common land on which their forebears camped without fear of eviction. As far as we can judge, the line of Clare's track runs just to the right of the trailers, close to the boundary with the golf course. We'd like to stand where it meets the Lea—near to the place where, crossing a wooden bridge along the river's old course, Clare left Essex behind him forever—but the camp is in the way. Bridget suggests we double back along the river, and as it happens there's a place just adjacent where we might be able to do this. I've seen aerial photos from the 1960s which lead me to expect a post-industrial brownfield site littered with concrete, but a sign at the gate welcomes us to 'Sewardstone Paddocks'. To my great delight I see the land has been restored to its natural semi-wild state—an expanse of rough grasses studded with meadow-sweet and ox-eye daisy, and punctuated by bushes and mature trees.

On the other side of the Lea the great green earthwork of King George's Reservoir rears up, flecked with dirty-white sheep. Heads down, jaws working, they stand so disconcertingly upright on the steeply rising slope that we strongly suspect them of having telescopic legs. Above where they graze, at the embankment's rim, there's a chain-link fence for keeping out undesirables—skinny-dipping teens off their heads on glue, maybe, or terrorists hell-bent on poisoning North London—and through it we can see the tops of distant pylons marching along the reservoir's farther shore. Bridget grips my arm and points to a dot in the sky high above us: a kestrel, hovering on beating wings while it watches for movements in the grass—testament to the resilience of the local wildlife, which for over a century has prevailed against the cataclysmic arrival of the reservoirs.

There's a head-high fence of galvanized steel lining the river front, and two more running either side of the Paddocks up to the road. We are in a sealed unit isolated from its neighbours: a cul-de-sac from which no further progress can be made. There were no such obstacles for Clare. This was all open country—well-drained and firm underfoot from the summer's warmth. Ahead of him lay the bustling commercial hub of the Lea Navigation, where narrow boats and barges thronged as they waited to pass through Ponders End lock, or lay moored at wharves where local produce—sacks of flour, crates of vegetables, bolts of fabric and bundles of basketwork—lay piled, ready to be lowered into holds. There would have been freshly unloaded cargo, too—grain for the flour mill, liquor for the public houses, engine coal and dyes and bolts of raw silk for the factory across the Navigation. On the quayside, dockers hauled goods to and from wagons while teams of horses waited patiently in their harnesses. Contemporary records suggest a crowded, noisy and chaotic scene, so Clare very likely hurried as he turned left onto the towpath and walked the short distance to Ponders End Lock, where he crossed the Navigation.

Bridget and I abandon our quest as neither of us had the foresight to bring along an oxy-acetylene torch; not only do the fence's steel pickets make it impossible for us to pass through, but they won't even let me jam a camera lens between them to take a photo. Defeated, we decide to press on to the lock, though unlike Clare we cannot take a direct route. Instead we will have to skirt St George's reservoir, which involves a two-mile hike along busy A-roads.

Middlesex

Day 1, July 20th 1841:
The Lea Navigation to Potters Bar

Musings IV

The river, reflecting the morning blue
and fret of cobweb clouds, is banked by sedge
and osier beds. He dare not stop, so scarcely sees
the bobbing heads and tumbler tails
of topsy-turvy ducks, probing bills of snipe;

marshland cut by long straight drains, reeds and teasel heads
like soldiers with skeleton helmets;
arrow flights of geese caught by the sun
over their feeding grounds, and swans' beaks
tucked in feather coats with one protruding foot.

THE JOURNEY – MIDDLESEX – MUSINGS IV

It's very hard to find the River Lea
at Ponders End: lines of late Victorian semis
and pre-war terraces conspire
to hide all trace. Even Pickett's Lock Lane
misinforms us with a dead-end sign.

Divided from the river by two giant
reservoirs, the old canal sheers under
a dual carriageway. Two anglers
show us four hands'-breadth perch in a keepnet:
'nah, we frow 'em back, woon't eat nuffink from 'ere.'

Clare tramped over this bridge by the lock, barges
lined up along the bank, horses with nosebags
jangling and munching, men stopped for a smoke,
women busy over pots. Today's lime tree
of giant girth was a younker then, watching him pass.

We walk the towpath, used by cyclists now:
two geese fly upstream honking urgently,
a cormorant rises plashy from the flags,
stretching its wings and long black head,
a heron sleuths the flooding overspill.

Eerie country calm for us, under the marching line
of pylons feeding London's energy;
downstream the Olympic Park and Canary Wharf;
above, the Epping Forest heights. There's Clare
breaking through hornbeams down the gypsy path.

Brash industrial noise for him. These locks
were modernised in 1771; barges bearing
the heaviest loads, beyond the horse power
of wagons and carts: coals from Nottingham,
timber from Sherwood, drawing afloat to London.

Today, narrow boats in leisure colours
are tied up by the old boat builder's yard:
white roses in flower, garden chairs and table.
He's there again at the lock keeper's cottage
priming the pump to fill his wooden bottle.

Hemmed in and Channelled

It is just a short walk—the length of a couple of bus stops—to the Crossways, a major junction with the A110. Gridlocked by morning commuter traffic, this intersection could be on the margins of any British city, and is only noteworthy for being where the Chingford reservoirs meet. To our right, the Lea Valley Road passes between their high embankments as if through a dead-straight valley, and it's down this exhaust-polluted gauntlet that we'll have to run if we're to reach Ponders End.

As Bridget and I make the turn, the reservoirs loom in front of us—King George's on our right, and to our left its younger companion, the equally massive William Girling. We pause a moment where the road crosses the Lea to take in the view. On the bank opposite, the dinghies of the King George Sailing Club lie beached in an untidy row, masts jostling and clashing at odd angles. The club sails them up on the reservoir, but today, abandoned and forlorn, they look like they're awaiting their fate in a breaker's yard. Directly above, the domed buildings of a pumping station stand atop the embankment like a pair of astronomical observatories. Two fat intake pipes snake up to them from the river, and as I study the massive blue-painted tubes I imagine I can hear them slurping greedily just below the rumble of the traffic.

The Lea Valley Road was not here in 1841, but was built some thirty years later by public subscription. Today it is a vehicle-clogged two-lane artery in urgent need of widening. Limes and sycamores, some dating from the road's inauguration, line either side, along with head-high barriers of galvanized steel that fence it off from its surroundings. The stuff is everywhere, so prevalent in this area's mosaic of tarnished meadows and derelict lots that a Martian botanist would be bound to mistake it for a native species. Here it not only dissuades the public from trespassing on Thames Water land, but more importantly prevents livestock from becoming roadkill. For behind its thorny pickets there are sheep everywhere: parked placidly on the thin strips of meadow that line the road, or roaming the grassy embankments where they crop away with endearingly daft single-mindedness. It's as though a slice of Clare's marsh has fallen through a hole in time and draped itself over this artificial valley, creating a landscape that might have been hallucinated by Samuel Palmer on acid. We slog on past the weirdly bucolic embankments and the alternately crawling and stationary traffic until both run out, and we arrive at the junction with Wharf Road —the turning that will lead us down to the Lea Navigation.

I came here on the first Sunday in May, taking advantage of fair weather and good light to do an early-morning photo shoot. The sun was just clearing the horizon as I crested Daws Hill in the car. Below me, still in shadow, were the reservoirs, like indigo blankets on a field at twilight. Beyond them I could see a dark muddle of sheds and warehouses by the Navigation, while the tower blocks of the Alma Estate, struck face-on by the rays of the sun, blazed pink against an azure sky. When I reached the Lea Valley Road it was empty of traffic, and as I turned into Wharf Road I had the strange impression I was the only one awake in the whole wide world.

I tell Bridget about this as we make our way down to the Navigation through the Meridian Business Park. Its entrance may be tricked out with flagpoles bearing smart company logos, but the place itself is decayed and down at heel—post-industrial even: the term 'Edgelands' could have been coined especially for it. Everywhere we look Nature has established beachheads: ivy smothers chain-link fences, buddleia has burst through tarmac parking lots, and rosebay willow herb is choking the drains where iridescent puddles linger after last night's rain. The only sign of resistance to this vegetable invasion is an exquisitely maintained park, no bigger than a children's playground, complete with artfully placed trees and stylish steel benches. Its presence here is a surreal puzzle; perhaps it only exists because of some long-forgotten contract with the local authority that no-one thought to cancel. Only a few years ago, when this was still a centre of manufacturing, there were people to use it. A fading sign draws our attention to a pair of gates that have not opened since a large bush seeded itself and grew to head height behind them. They used to lead to an electronics factory that employed hundreds before it was shut and demolished in 2009.

The site—now a wasteland of rubble—faces the Navigation, and it is there that we'll hook up with Clare again, for along the towpath is the place where he stepped off South Marsh. We leave Wharf Road and descend a ramp to where houseboats and cabin cruisers are moored in a long line. The dock is quiet; the waterway empty. Though Ponders End Lock still functions there's an air of neglect about it. Paint is flaking off the gates and graffiti balloons in silver gibberish across the long-defunct keeper's cabin.

Narrowboats crowd by the bridge on Wharf Road close to Ponders End Lock.

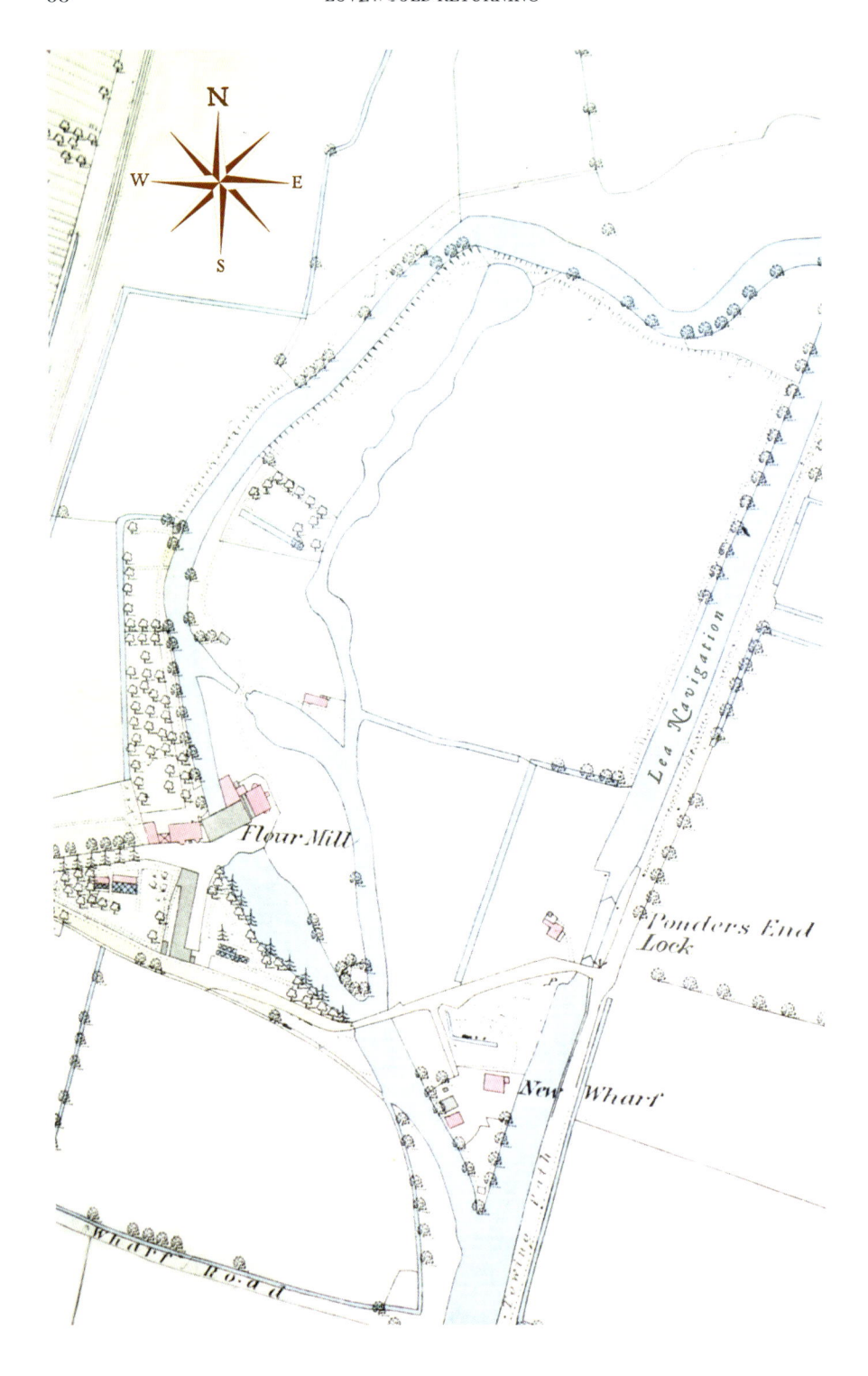

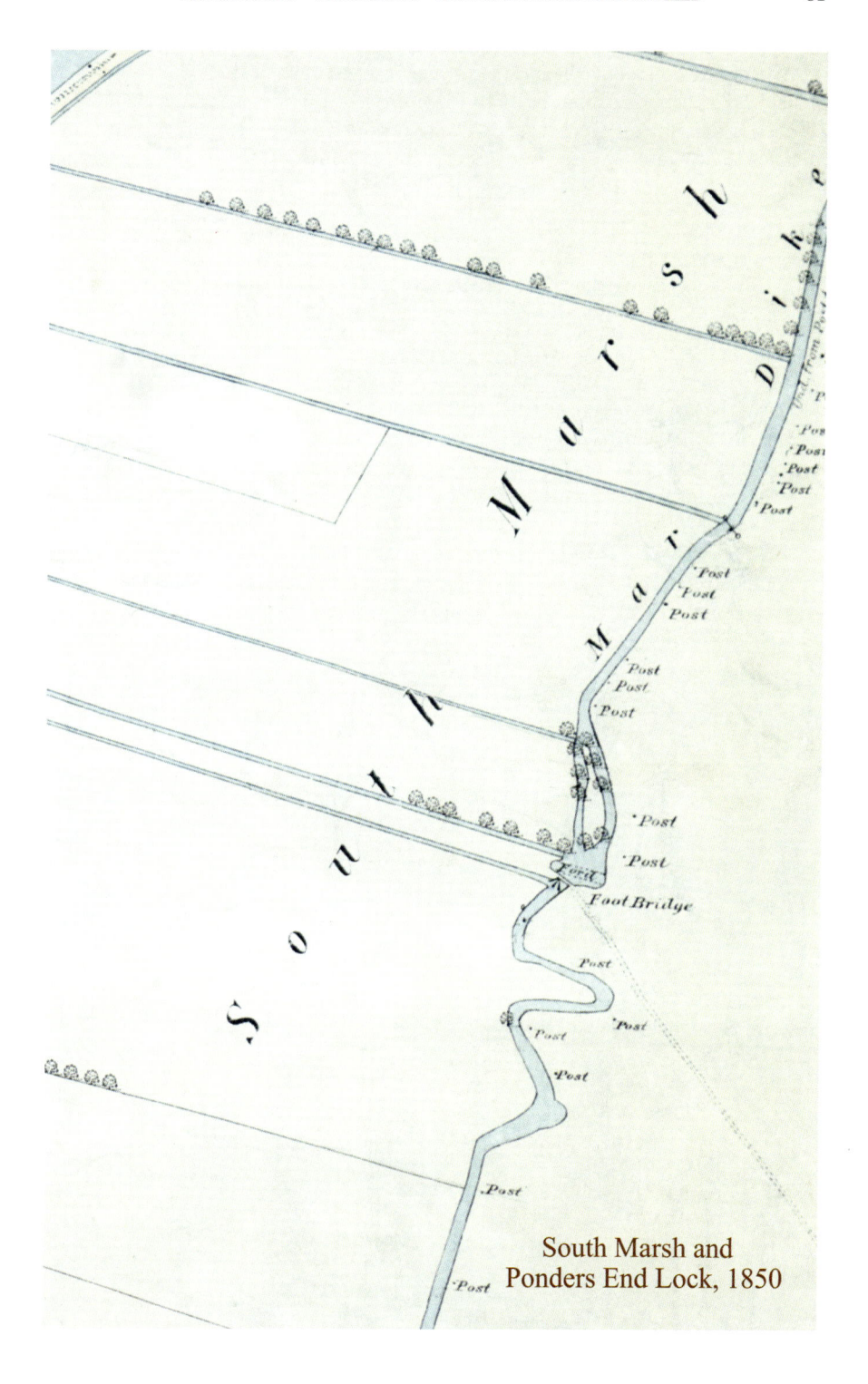

South Marsh and
Ponders End Lock, 1850

When Clare crossed it, the lock was twenty metres or so upstream and known as Enfield Mill Lock for its proximity to the mill race. This nearness was a source of conflict as the mill and the Navigation were in constant competition for water, and at times of low rainfall there was not enough to go around. In 1878 a Navigation Engineers' Survey noted that:

> the Miller frequently draws down the water of the Enfield Mill Stream to the great inconvenience and obstruction of the Navigation and that Notice has many times been given him to desist but without effect [...] In getting to Enfield Lock a case in point was observed by the Committee [in which] the water was 9 inches below head and a barge could not get into the Lock in consequence.[1]

Such was the severity of the problem that the same committee recommended passing an Act of Parliament to make the miller stop. The matter was not resolved until 1913, when the arrival of King George's Reservoir provided the mill with a more reliable source of water for driving its wheels. Ironically, it switched to using electric power not long after.

Having crossed the lock, Clare took a lane that passed through the mill grounds to South Street. Today the lane is gone, its route blocked by a row of industrial sheds and a steel fence guarding the mill's perimeter—obstacles that we'll have to

The place where Clare left South Marsh, with the embankment of King George's Reservoir and the hills of Epping Forest to the east.

The old water works pumping station on the Lea Navigation. Now a restaurant, it once housed a steam engine and sported a tall chimney stack.

circumnavigate. Before we do, however, we make a point of visiting the spot where he came off the marsh. A bridge carrying the Lea Valley Road now straddles the Navigation where the old lock used to stand. We slowly walk beneath it and out the other side, following the towpath until the GPS readout on my phone informs us that we have arrived.[2]

I look intently in the direction of Clare's approach, almost willing him to come into view. On the horizon a brush stroke of green marks the escarpment down which he walked to reach the marshes. I lower my gaze and half expect to see an unbroken expanse of grass and sedge with a wooden bridge spanning the Lea in the middle distance. Instead, a hundred yards from where we are standing, King George's Reservoir rises to block the prospect. On the thin remnant of marsh in between there are horses grazing beneath the same pylons we glimpsed from Sewardstone Paddocks. I'm suddenly reminded of a foal I photographed at this spot in the spring. He may have been moved or simply grown out of all recognition, but at this distance I don't see him and I can't get any closer because there's a wire mesh fence and a padlocked gate in the way.

It seems that ever since coming off Yardley Hill we have been negotiating a chequerboard of fenced-off plots that make progress over the landscape impossible except by the public roads. I suddenly grasp, in a very visceral way, Clare's rage against the Enclosures. A sense of constantly being hemmed in and channelled—of being simultaneously *imprisoned* and *exiled*—is finally driving me to trespass: something I'm generally loath to do. But before I can climb the gate, a pair of lady joggers approaches us along the towpath.

Beneath the bridge carrying Ponders End Road, at the site of the old lock.

Ponders End Lock at its present site, with the bridge to the north.

When we've exchanged pleasantries, one of them points to a building on the far bank. "Is it a school?" she asks. Well, no. It used to be a pumping station, and had the good fortune—or misfortune, depending on your taste in architecture—to be built at the very end of the nineteenth century, when the fashion was to disguise the merely functional as something more picturesque. This is why it looks like a cross between a medieval barn and a Tudor manor house, with quaintly gabled half-timbered wings facing the canal and a broad central range of pitched tile roof and red brick walls. In its original incarnation, this magnificent folly also boasted a chimney stack and a ramp for hauling coal into its cavernous interior—features generally missing from manors and barns but vital to the operation of steam engines. They were lost in 1995 when the building was converted into a pub called 'The Navigation Inn'. Today, rechristened simply 'The Navigation', it is owned and beautifully maintained by a nationwide restaurant chain. Like the sheds and warehouses, it was built after Clare's time. What he saw around the wharves was a place still largely rural, made up of pastures, orchards and market gardens. There were only two centres of industry then—the flour mill, which had existed in some form for at least eight centuries, and the crape factory, a much newer arrival.

Crape was a sombre fabric made from crimped silk that rocketed in popularity during the early nineteenth century, when an emerging middle class took to wearing it as mourning attire. A high mortality rate, a fashion for sentimentalising death, and a population with increasingly deep pockets presented Victorian entrepreneurs with opportunities for (as it were) making a killing. Two such men were Norfolk-based brothers George and Joseph Grout, who in 1809 turned from manufacturing saddles and harnesses to producing their very own crimped black silk, which they branded 'Norwich Crape'. They teamed up with like-minded individuals to form a company with the suitably Dickensian name of 'Grout, Baylis, Ringer, Martin & Co', though for the sake of brevity this was usually shortened to 'Grout & Baylis'. Such was their success that two decades later they owned several manufactories across Britain and one in India. Their first modest workshop, meanwhile, had grown to cover much of the Norwich parish of St. Benedict. Describing it in 1829, the antiquarian and topographer John Chambers wrote:

> One of the buildings is five stories high, and each floor contains an area of about 220 square yards. The other buildings are of a much greater extent; one of them contains machinery which is worked by a steam engine of twenty-horse power, erected by Messrs. Boulton and Watt, of the Soho foundry, near Birmingham [...] The principal business performed here is the winding and throwing of silk: the silk thus prepared is delivered out to the weavers, who manufacture it into crape, or more properly gauze, the craping being an after operation, and performed near London.[3]

By 1841 the company boasted a workforce of more than 3,000, mostly women and children, of which the Ponders End factory employed about two hundred. The factory was purpose-built for the "after operation" of craping—that is, of crimping and dyeing the silk. Its location, a hundred miles from Norwich, was chosen for good reasons. The craping process was a closely guarded secret, and carrying it out at arm's length lessened the risk of industrial espionage. Ponders End was the perfect place—sufficiently distant, yet easy to supply with raw materials via the Navigation. But the overriding consideration that persuaded the company to build its factory here was the local geology.

Workers at Grout & Baylis, Ponders End, circa 1870. Background detail gives some hint of the size and height of the factory buildings.

Ponders End stands at the eastern edge of a formation known as the London Basin, whose heavy clays cover strata of porous rock into which vast quantities of rainwater have flowed over the millennia. Crimping and dyeing required exceptionally clean water, and fossil rainwater was considered ideal for the purpose. The factory was built on top of a borehole that provided a continuous supply through hydraulic pressure alone. By tapping into what was effectively a self-emptying, self-replenishing subterranean lake, Grout & Baylis had a free manufacturing resource that was under their complete control, unlike the coal that powered the machinery or the gas that provided light for the workers.

Of those workers we know very little. Thumbnail sketches of a few survive, thanks to John Fuller Russell, the Curate-in-Charge of St James' Church in Enfield Highway. During 1841 he took it upon himself to assess the 'spiritual health' of the Grout & Baylis workers by visiting them in their homes. Overall, what he found was not encouraging. Of one woman, Betsy Nicholls, he wrote, "character doubtful"—probably because she'd had an illegitimate child—and he described another, Anne Carrington, as "a slovenly, ignorant woman" whose three daughters had been "badly conducted before marriage". Nicholls had worked at the factory since childhood and was paid eight shillings a week to make up packets of crape. Carrington was employed to "turn a reel to dry crape" for nine. Neither was entitled to sickness allowance. Russell did not find the workers universally reprehensible, however. He saw promise in a dyer called David Conyard who earned twenty shillings a week and whose wife did piecework for seven. "Good servant. Civil man", was his conclusion, "Perseverance here might do some good".[4]

When Conyard and his fellow dyers had finished with it, the water so ingeniously sourced from the ground was simply poured away into the tributaries of Brimsdown Ditch, earning the factory its nickname of 'The Black Dyke Works'. The industrial pollution of Clare's day was mild by comparison with what was to come, however. By the end of the 1860s Ponders End was also home to a jute mill, a linoleum factory and a gas works. The mill was taken over by the Ediswan light bulb company in 1886, and in 1894 the crape factory was closed and acquired by a firm that made flexible steel tubing. This intensification of heavy industry produced a landscape more reminiscent of the industrial North than the Home Counties, and photos of the Navigation from the early twentieth century show smoke-belching factories bordering a polluted and lifeless waterway.

Now that the area has slumped into post-industrial senescence, the Navigation is once again supporting healthy populations of fish. On our way back to the lock we pass a row of anglers hunched like garden gnomes in a silence broken only by the whizzing and whirring of reels. When I was last here I engaged one in conversation only to have my ear bent about the perfidy of cormorants. "You ain't one of them *twitchers* are you?" he asked, eyeing my cameras with suspicion. When I assured him I wasn't, he explained there was a spat in progress between the angling fraternity and—well—just about everyone else you could think of: ornithologists; conservationists; the CPRE; the RSPB; the RSPCA; DEFRA; the newspapers, and so on.

Angler heading down Wharf Road to the Navigation.

Wharf Road and South Street,
Ponders End, 1850

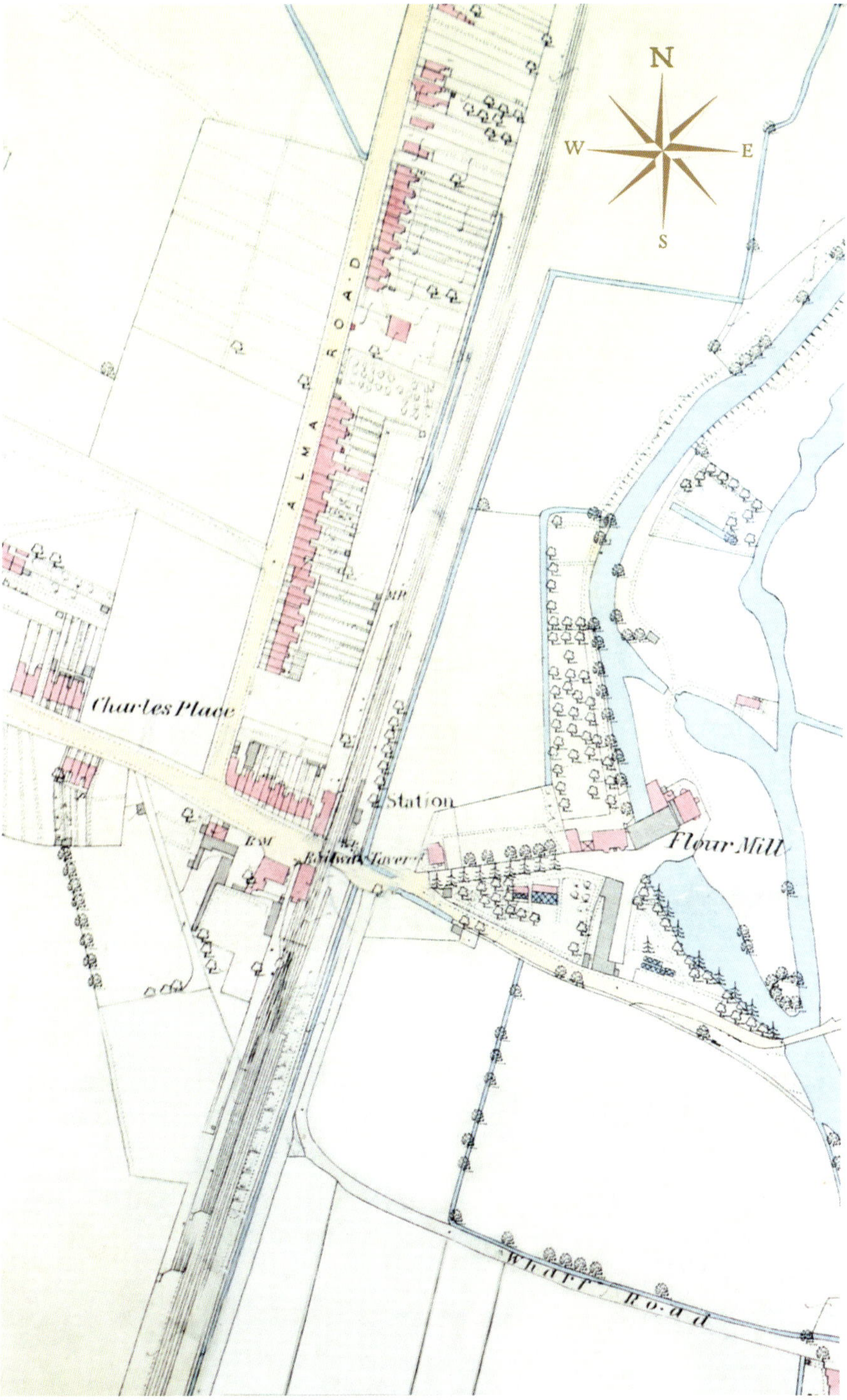
N
W
E
S
ALMA ROAD
Charles Place
Station
Flour Mill
Wharf Road

This was because the anglers, in defence of their sport, were proposing a widespread cull of "them fish-pinching sods" (his words) while their opponents were—or so he claimed—threatening legal, and very possibly actual, violence to stop a cull from going ahead.[5] Having endured his rant, which went on for some minutes, I should have been wary of the man's siege mentality. Instead I made the mistake of asking him about otters. "Otters?" came the lugubrious reply, "If I ever see one of them buggers I'll wring its bloody neck." I had to suppress a smile. It was a sentiment Clare would have recognized from reading Walton:

> Piscator: ...my purpose is to bestow a day or two in hunting the Otter...of helping to destroy those villainous vermin, for I hate them perfectly because they love fish so well, or rather, because they destroy so much.
>
> Viator: Why sir I pray, of what Fraternitie are you, that you are so angry with the poor Otter?
>
> Piscator: I am a brother of *the Angle*[6]

I'd only broached the subject because of a signboard down by the lock. Without ever quite stating that otters exist on the Navigation, it suggests—in the sort of slippery language you expect from used-car salesmen and equity brokers—that we should look out for them because they are a sure sign of a healthy waterway. Maybe,

The gatekeeper's lodge at Wright's flour mill, viewed from the bridge over Meridian Way, Brimsdown Ditch and the Liverpool Street Line.

THE JOURNEY – MIDDLESEX – HEMMED IN AND CHANNELLED   71

Ponders End station in 2016, looking north.

The station in the early 1900s, with the buildings Clare would have seen on the left, and on the right a waiting room erected in the 1870s for London-bound passengers.

as I remark to Bridget when we view it together, it was put up more in hope than expectation, or perhaps there was money on offer for making the Navigation otter-friendly and installing an 'educational resource' was part of the deal. Like the bijou park at the top of Wharf Road, it is a minor mystery.

Leaving the Navigation behind, we resume our progress down Wharf Road, walking in parallel with Clare as he made his way through the mill grounds. These now lie on the other side of a high brick wall, which bears multiple signs warning of 'Razor Wire'—another native species for our Martian botanist to catalogue. The wall runs to the end of the road, where it makes a hairpin turn into what is left of Clare's lane. There's a gate-keeper's lodge here dating from 1820, with latticed ogive windows and a hipped roof of Welsh slate—nothing special in the architectural scheme of things perhaps, but a positive jewel in this post-industrial landscape. Clare, one suspects, would not have given it a second glance as he left the grounds and stepped out onto South Street.

South Street has moved, however. It now starts on the other side of Meridian Way, an urban clearway dating from the 1970s, and can only be reached by a high concrete footbridge straddling not just the road, but also Brimsdown Ditch and the Liverpool Street railway line. From the top we look down on Ponders End Station; not the building Clare saw, alas—that one was pulled down in 1967—but a mean, flat-roofed public convenience of a structure that was once a manned ticket office. Today it houses nothing more than drifts of fast-food packaging and a couple of armour-plated ticket machines.

The Falcon Inn, South Street, photographed in 1890. It was replaced in 1907 by an Edwardian public house.

The view south-west from Daws Hill at sunrise, showing King George's reservoir with the old pumping station half hidden behind its western embankment, the silos of Wright's flour mill, and the towers of the Alma Housing Estate.

    The bridge stands where Clare crossed the single track of the Northern and Eastern Railway, whose arrival at Ponders End just ten months earlier had caused no small amount of excitement. We don't know if he held any strong opinions about it—he certainly makes no mention of it in the *Journey*—but we do know that railways, and their potential for environmental destruction, had come to his notice very early on in their history: sixteen years earlier, in fact. This is his journal entry for June 4th, 1825:

> Saw three fellows at the end of Royce wood who I found were laying out the plan for an 'Iron rail way' from Manchester to London — it is to cross over Round Oak Spring by Royce Wood Corner for Woodcroft Castle   I little thought that fresh intrusions would interrupt and spoil my solitudes after the Inclosure   they will despoil a boggy place that is famous for Orchises at Royce Wood end [7]

That year had seen the opening of the world's first steam railway, built to transport coal the 25 miles or so from collieries at Shildon to the towns of Stockton and Darlington, so it is remarkable that plans for linking towns over 200 miles apart were also under way. Remarkable too, that Clare was a witness to preparations for bringing them to fruition. But as things turned out, he need not have worried; funding for the line collapsed, and the orchids in Royce Wood were left undisturbed.

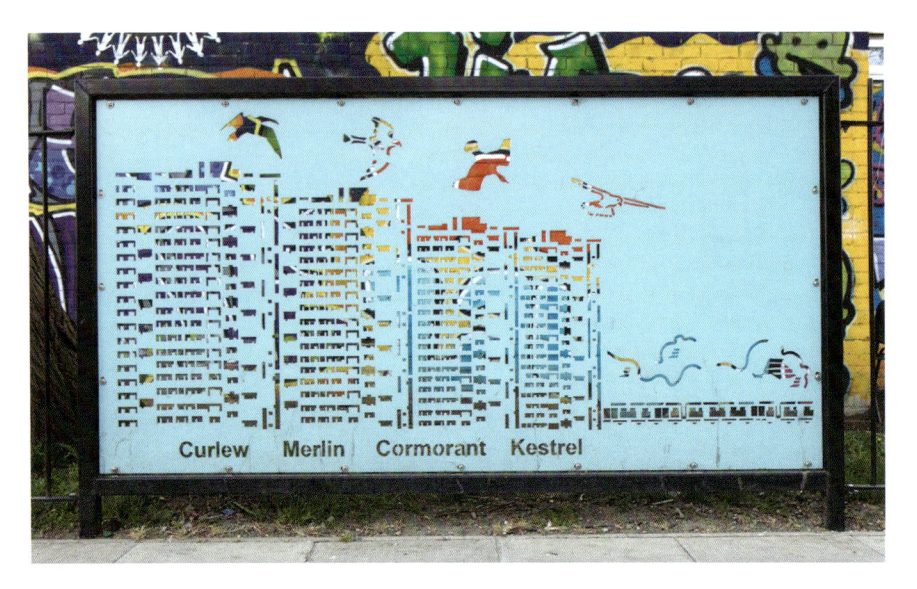

Public art on South Street showing the Alma Estate's four towers and their avian namesakes. The piece is made from a sheet of locally manufactured punched steel that lets through the colours of the wall behind it.

Crossing into South Street, Clare passed the newly built station, where it is just possible that a train was standing: six a day ran between Stratford, in London's East End, and the Hertfordshire village of Broxbourne. A second track was already under construction, and the line itself was being extended to Bishops Stortford, from where it would eventually reach Cambridge.

Beyond the station there was a baker's, a butcher's, a grocer's, a shoemaker's, and a seventeenth-century inn called the Falcon. Today the street is served by a blocky 1970s shopping parade. As we pass it, we note a couple of convenience stores, a café, a newsagent's, a chip shop, and a laundrette, all looking prosperous and well-kept. In fact the whole street feels good—pleasantly open, with trees and grass at intervals on either side. It's clear that a lot of money has been spent on regenerating the area: most prominently on a new school whose timber and glass façade is fronted by a broad plaza, complete with trees and marble seating. It occupies the site of the old gas works, the last relics of which—three latticed gas holders—were demolished in 2010.

Opposite the school, the gargantuan tower blocks of the Alma Road Estate loom over South Street. When these 23-storey monoliths were built in 1968 they stood next to the gas works—an enterprise so vast that the Liverpool Street line ran through it, hemmed in on both sides by sooty buildings and crossed high overhead by coal chutes. Now that all trace of heavy industry has vanished from the street, it is almost possible to see them as part of its brighter, gentler twenty-first-century self. Almost, but not quite. From the top of Daws Hill, lit by the rising sun, they looked majestic. Up close, they simply look their age.

THE JOURNEY – MIDDLESEX – HEMMED IN AND CHANNELLED   75

Perhaps all too predictably, they were named to reference the long-vanished marsh, and specifically its birds. A nearby piece of public art lists them in sequence: "Curlew House, Merlin House, Cormorant House, Kestrel House". All sorts of ironies might be wrung from this piece of Housing Committee hamfistedness, but by far the most telling is the fact that the towers have become vertical marshes in their own right. Severe damp and flooding caused by leaky plumbing have plagued them so intractably over the decades that in 2012 the council finally decided to pull them down.[8] Four years on they are still standing tall while the massive bureaucratic machine gathers speed to level them and put in their place a housing complex to match the school's slick, clean lines, and complete South Street's propulsion into the present century.

We plough on past them, searching for something—anything—that Clare might have seen with his own eyes, but everywhere we look there are post-war semis and 1960s apartment blocks vying for dominance with late Victorian terraces. The oldest structure we can identify is St Matthew's Church, built in 1877. There is nothing at all to suggest where Grout & Baylis stood.

Clare walked past the factory's gates before reaching the end of the street, where he turned right. Now heading north along Ponders End High Road, he should have been looking out for Nag's Head Lane on his left, as this would have taken him directly to Enfield Town. Instead, he missed the turning and soon found himself in the village of Enfield Highway.

View east along South Street towards the railway station in 2016, with the towers still in place. Demolition of these iconic 1960s landmarks began the same year.

If Frederick Martin is right and he had already tried to escape, it's highly likely he already knew the lie of the land hereabouts. The High Road formed part of the Old North Road from London to York, which was also known by its Anglo-Saxon name of Ermine Street. This series of old Roman roads passed through Hertford and Ware to Royston, and from there, via Huntingdon, to Alconbury Hill, Stilton and Norman Cross. Clare's own route would veer westward through Enfield Town and Potters Bar before rejoining Ermine Street at Alconbury Hill, some 50 miles away, so why he did not simply stay on Ermine Street and save himself the detour is something of a puzzle. Most likely he believed—or was advised by the gypsies—that taking the less obvious road would reduce his chances of being captured by Allen's men. Or perhaps he'd used Ermine Street on a previous escape attempt and been caught on it.

Ponders End High Road is now the High Street, and designated the A1010. Here we come across a parade of shops that was very likely around in Clare's day. The only clue to its antiquity—rather bizarrely—is a long balustrade, complete with ornamental stone ball, perched on top of a flat Regency roof. He would have been baffled by a couple of the establishments here—an internet café and a laptop repairer —but the rest he might have understood as modern incarnations of things he was familiar with: a hardware store, a hair salon (called "Heir Kutz", no less), and an eating house. Apart from this small find, we are at a loss to identify anything contemporary to his world, the street being pretty much wall-to-wall late Victoriana and twentieth-century infill.

It goes without saying that the road has become a slow-motion traffic jam. The turn into Nag's Head Lane is now a crossroads, created by the construction, in the 1880s, of a residential street. Sensibly enough for a continuation of the lane, this was christened 'Nags Head Road', but at about the same time—and for reasons best known to the local authority—the lane itself was renamed 'Southbury Road'. Heading over the crossroads in a deliberate reconstruction of Clare's navigational error, we glance left and see, as expected, a vehicle-choked urban artery.

As a major route northwards out of London, Ermine Street in 1841 was thronged with all kinds of traffic: mail and stage coaches; horse-drawn wagons; carts pulled by mules, nags and donkeys; gentlemen on horseback like Cowper's John Gilpin; men and women on foot—some pushing hand carts—and drovers with their sheep, cattle, geese and pigs. Clare, hurrying among them, inadvertently passed the turn. He did not realise his mistake, but by a stroke of luck soon met an acquaintance who was able to put him right. "I missed the lane to Enfield town and was going down Enfield highway till I passed 'The Labour in Vain' Public house," he writes, "where a person I knew coming out of the door told me the way." He says nothing more about the encounter, so the identity of his friend remains a mystery. Neither are we any the wiser about the public house. Graham Dalling, at the Enfield Local Studies Centre, wrote the following in response to a request for information about it:

> We have no knowledge of a pub at Enfield Highway called the 'Labour in Vain'. Robson's Directory (1839) lists no less than twelve pubs in Enfield Highway. Nine of these are mentioned by name, but the remaining three are listed under the name of the proprietor. Perhaps the 'Labour in Vain' was one of these three un-named pubs.[9]

In a note penned on the road, Clare records he was "offered a bit of bread and cheese at Enfield", but again does not elaborate.[10] Given he did not yet resemble a travel-stained vagrant, we might reasonably surmise his benefactor was a friend or acquaintance rather than a charitable stranger, and if we allow that by 'Enfield' he meant Enfield Highway, the 'Labour in Vain' might well be the place where he was fed. What's more, the statement that he was "offered" the meal makes it sound as though he was being treated as a guest. So—other things being equal—might his benefactor have been the publican? We know he was acquainted with a pub landlady living in Enfield Highway, because on returning home he wrote to Matthew Allen asking for the books he'd lent to various women in High Beach to be forwarded to him.[11] Among the recipients he lists "Mrs King late of the Owl Public house Leppits Hill & now of Endfield Highway". So if—as seems likely—Mrs King was plying her trade in her new home, she must count as a strong contender for being both the person who fed him and the acquaintance who put him on the right road.[12] And if she was, his use of an untraceable name for the pub could have been deliberate, to protect her from the charge of aiding and abetting a fugitive.[13]

'The Labour in Vain' might therefore be a pseudonym for one of the establishments listed in Robson's Directory.[14] Of the twelve, five are still identifiable: the Plough; the Kings Arms (now called the Sporting Green); the Rose and Crown; the Red Lion and the Bell. One has been rebuilt, and all but two have gone out of business. The Bell—one of those still trading—is technically in Enfield Wash, and too distant to be a credible candidate.

Shortly after the junction with Southbury Road, the A1010 ceases to be Ponders End High Street, a place in its own right, and becomes the Hertford Road, a route to somewhere else. The transition would have been self-evident in 1841 because Ponders End had boundaries that were signalled by the onset of countryside. Inter-war development has done away with such cues, however, and only a lack of shops indicates that we're in between settlements. Arrival at our destination is flagged by a sign welcoming us to 'Enfield Highway Shopping Centre', though there isn't a shop in sight. We have just passed the 'College of Haringey, Enfield and North-East London' (no help there for the geographically bamboozled), and on our right the lawns and flower beds of Durant's Park are opening up to reveal a rare local survivor from the early nineteenth century: St James' Church.

When Clare tramped by it in 1841, St James' was the object of no small controversy. John Fuller Russell, the Curate-in-Charge who was taking such a prurient interest in the Grout & Baylis workers, was also a fervent disciple of the Oxford Movement, and his Anglo-Catholic leanings were causing *frissons* of unease amongst the Diocesan authorities. At the same time, the fabric of his church was also turning out to be suspect—less than ten years old, it was already unsafe. As a money-saving measure the beams supporting the roof had been laid directly on top of damp brick walls, with the result that their ends were rotting away and putting the entire roof in imminent danger of collapse. I'd like to think that the pleasing symmetry of the situation—dodgy architecture mirroring dodgy doctrine—would have raised a wry chuckle with Clare.

St James' structural shoddiness was by no means unique; like most churches of the time it was built in the style known as 'Commissioners' Gothic', which was defined not so much by its aesthetics as its cheapness. During the previous century, most new churches had been neoclassical, requiring costly porticoes that served no practical purpose, and even worse—from the Victorian perspective at least—were redolent of pagan temples. The move to a medieval style not only chimed with the Gothic Revival, but also appealed to the parsimony of the Church Commissioners. St James' was typical of the trend—severe, plain and spare. When Clare saw it he no doubt registered another new, if rather unlovely, place of worship—hundreds had been erected around the country following the Church Building Act of 1818. Today, rising gaunt from a sea of crumbling headstones, its resonances are more Hammer-Horror than Anglo-Catholic.

There used to be a pub across the road called 'The Plough'. James Canton came across it shortly after it closed in 2009. Seeing it boarded up, he must have thought it earmarked for demolition, but it is still standing and currently occupied by a suite of solicitors' offices. Having somehow retained its original façade of brown tile, wooden fascia and lead flashing, it's recognisably the sort of place that would have been patronised by the likes of Grout & Baylis workers Betsy Nicholls and Anne Carrington, and shunned by their 'good' and 'civil' colleague David Conyard.

There's another pub further on, at the corner of Green Street. Clare would have known it as the Kings Arms but today it is 'The Sporting Green'. Whether this is because it's named for the street, or because it's an Irish pub that screens live football, or even because it used to be painted green until 2015 (when for some reason it turned red) is hard to say. Even more perplexing is the sign outside it, which shows a tractor ploughing up a winter field. It takes us a few moments to realise that we've seen it before, in an old photograph of the Plough. Now, with the old establishment gone, it serves as a memorial to better days in Enfield Highway.

There has been a tavern here since at least 1716, when it catered to stockmen driving their cattle and sheep onto South Marsh for grazing. Did Clare encounter his acquaintance here? James Canton, at least, thinks it a possibility. He imagines a shepherd, after a morning's watch on the marsh, going up Green Street to the Kings Arms to quench his thirst, and later on leaving, "just as he was stepping out of the door, [bumping] into that strange poet from the madhouse over in the forest, smoking his pipe and humming to himself".[15]

If the Kings Arms was not the place, Clare would have marched on for another hundred yards before encountering, in short order, the Rose and Crown and the Black Horse. The former is now a Turkish supermarket and only recognisable by its half-timbered Mock-Tudor gable—a staple of Late-Victorian pub design that testifies to a major rebuilding. The latter was rebuilt during the early 1960s as a modern pub-hotel and is now closed and awaiting demolition to make way for a housing development.

Enfield Highway's most northerly public house, the Red Lion, is about ten minutes' walk away: an imposing three storey pile purpose-built in the 1830s as a coaching inn. To our eyes at least it's way too grand to be the one he stopped at, and besides, as Canton remarks, it's also too far along the road. At this point on our 1836 map

THE JOURNEY – MIDDLESEX – HEMMED IN AND CHANNELLED 79

St James' Church circa 1900—a forbidding example of 'Commissioners' Gothic'. Clare passed it on his right as he arrived in Enfield Highway.

View south from the summit of Yardley Hill over Chingford and the City of London.

the road enters a brief stretch of countryside before arriving at Enfield Wash, so somewhere on our walk we must have passed Clare's so-called 'Labour in Vain'—or at any rate the spot it used to occupy. We're no wiser now about its location or name than we were when we set out, but then we didn't expect to be: others have made the search before us and would surely have found traces if any still existed. For our part, we're just happy to have made the pilgrimage.

A number 491 Routemaster takes us back as far as the Crossways, and soon we are plodding back up the Sewardstone Road. At the Paddocks we turn right onto Yardley Hill, tracing Clare's route in reverse. A post-war housing estate now blankets the hillside, making it tricky to find the line of the old track among curving, intersecting streets. The route we've chosen, up Deerleap Grove, is the one James Canton descended in his reconstruction of Clare's walk. At Antlers Hill a flight of steps takes us up between two houses and past an old electricity substation, and then suddenly we're in a scrubby field littered with lager cans, disposable barbecues and other, less savoury, mementoes of good times had by all.

The path we're climbing is the one we should have come down earlier in the day, following Clare and Canton, and it's not nearly as difficult to negotiate as I was expecting. We soon arrive at the junction where I led us onto the Loop, and looking back I realise that the dead-end I thought I'd seen was just a dense tangle of bushes. I'm about to apologise to Bridget for my blunder when a dog starts barking in the undergrowth close by. The noise is familiar, as is the animal himself when he rushes into view, tongue lolling and tail whisking. Voices close behind confirm that we've run into the Hornbeam-Laners once more.

"Hey!" says Mrs as they appear, beaming at the sight of us, "How ya doin'?" Her husband tries to rein in the dog, making grabs for its collar while it races round him in excited circles. He lunges and misses repeatedly before giving up. Straightening, he asks us how we liked the view.

"Actually," I lie, feigning British embarrassment, "We didn't get to see it. We sort of, well, lost our way, I'm afraid."

Mrs opens her mouth in exaggerated surprise like a Disney princess. "Oh! My!, she exclaims, "We gotta put that right *this very minute*! Follow me!", and she leads us, without waiting for a reply, onto the meadow at the top of the hill. At first I don't understand why we're here. The view *is* good, if nothing spectacular, with the ridges of Epping Forest stacked behind each other all away to the horizon. Then I realise everyone is looking the other way, and when I do the same I catch my breath.

This must be the prospect Clare wrote about on Buckhurst Hill: the vast ocean of stone and brick that is London. Beneath us, the land drops away in waves, bearing on its back the suburb of Chingford with its tiled roofs and brick chimneys. Between streets draped like caterpillars over the gentle summits there are copses and stretches of heathland—a faint echo of the landscape Clare must have seen—while beyond them the diorama of the city half-encircles us in a shallow arc, shaded by distance to a misty blue and capped by a canopy of cerulean air. Instead of huddling to the ground beneath a pall of smoke, as it did for Clare, London now soars; to our left stands the glittering complex of Canary Wharf, monumental and intimidating, like the citadel of some master race. In front of us the turrets of the City crowd together, with 30 St Mary Axe rising blue and bulbous in front of the Shard and Tower 42. To our right, past countless grey and brown monoliths, the silver pencil of St George Wharf Tower stands poised like a rocket about to leap into orbit. The view is vast and dizzying; no photograph can do it justice, but I take a sequence of shots anyway. Mrs Hornbeam-Lane approaches me. "Well," she asks, grinning, "Whaddaya think?"

I grin back. "It's awesome," I reply, without the slightest trace of irony.

Musings V

Enfield market is running an Italian theme –
decked out in bunting, red and white and green.
Mario, in brown overalls, is laying out
a giant hog on shiny steel, under the spit
where it cooked in a fug of flame and steam.

A pity Clare's not here to share a tasty off-cut,
or see the fruit and veg stall: a spread of apples,
tomatoes, squash and sweetcorn, leeks rich in mud:
products of Lea Valley – fertile still,
its husbandry squeezed around the reservoirs.

Water carriers came from the New River Loop
in his day, barrels on yokes hooked round their necks,
boots sodden from slops. Inside the tarpaulin wall
of a sweet stall we find a late Victorian pump:
progress came slow and then was long forgot.

Today the renovated Loop is green with weed
and reflected light from sycamores and willows;
water was essential treasure then, flowing
in boarded banks along the contour lines to London.
Now, the Loop's a water feature in a leisure park.

Clare pauses here to take his bearings
by the church and Vestry Offices:
two bastions of Parish rectitude
whose machinations he knows well.
He hurries past the fingerpost and up the hill.

The Ridgeway runs straight to the north along the chalk.
A straggle of hovels at the edge of the heath
was known then – and still today – as Botany Bay.
Clare is aware of the threat of desolation.
Rich men's accusations are all it takes

to lock the poor away on pain of death.
His first fiddle came from a gypsy
sentenced to hang for stealing a horse,
then transported instead. He has smelled
the crossroads stench of the gibbeted dead.

We park our car on the crest of the hill
and stand astride the view: a valley
runs up to woodland, on the other side
cows framed in a green field, enclosed land;
the grey haze of London far away beyond.

After the hamlet, a cottage painted white
marks the entrance to former West Lodge drive.
Here's Clare flexing strong legs and breathing sweet air;
above, a puddock sails high on stilly wings
and starnels rush the sky with dark lassoes.

He's walking fast, with single-minded purpose
but the fresh smell of grass and wild flowers
floods each inward breath and bends his memories
to Emmonsale's Heath.   That's where we go next
to visit the strip of land that still remains:

a mix of grassland, scrub and trees,
oaks, ash and hazels where Clare took Mary nutting;
and there in a grassy firebreak riding,
a heavy-antlered fallow buck stares at us
with careless poise, then quits with a single leap.

Workmen with a truck are clearing weed
from ponds to let frogs spawn and grass snakes
sun themselves and lay their eggs; rampant nettles
are scythed away and thickets of thorns burned,
the smoke of gypsy ghosts rising through the trees.

And where the scrubland meets a line of ash,
we hear the russet brown bird singing,
and can see, because he shows us in his poetry,
its trembling wings and feathers pricked on end.
Yes, the nightingale's thrilling fills the air!

A section of the New River Loop running beside Southbury Road—Clare's Nag's Head Lane—Enfield, which delivered fresh drinking water to the town.

Loops and Landgrabs

Bridget continues the narrative...

It was still mid-morning when Clare turned into Nag's Head Lane and started towards Enfield Town. He was back in open country, feeling cheered, perhaps, by the song of skylarks and blackbirds, the flocks of field fares and starlings swooping over the trees, and the crows scavenging for carrion on the unmade road.

Nag's Head Lane—today's Southbury Road—still carries traffic to the middle of Enfield. As was the case in Clare's day, it is joined on the outskirts of the town by the New River—a 20-mile-long aqueduct built during the seventeenth century to deliver clean water to the growing population of North London. It now forms the central feature of a park, but Clare would have seen it as a place of work, crowded with water sellers filling their barrels and loading them onto mules and donkeys, and sometimes even their own backs, to hawk around the town.

Made all the more remarkable for having taken place thirty years before the Civil War, the construction of the New River was an impressive feat of engineering: complex in its planning and sophisticated in its execution. To prevent leakage, its channel was lined throughout with wooden planks soaked in pitch and caulked with oakum—a technique borrowed from the boat builders of the time—while securing its course involved complex negotiations with landowners, many of whom were reluctant to sell. The uneven topography around Enfield, where ancient streams created a meeting point of valleys, meant that it had to take a meandering course as it followed the 100-ft contour line, resulting in a section that became known as the New River Loop.

When completed, the New River ran from the Hertfordshire village of Ware to Stoke Newington at the edge of the capital. It is a testament to the skill of the builders that when Clare encountered it, almost a hundred and fifty years later, it was still fulfilling its original purpose. Indeed, so efficient had it become that it was causing significant problems elsewhere—taking as much as a third of the water from the Lea and its tributaries, and occasionally leaving the Navigation high and dry.

Clare arrived in Enfield Town at the crossroads where Silver Street met the London Road running past the bowed front of the Nag's Head Inn. From there he continued into Church Street, the thoroughfare that would take him up Windmill Hill and out into countryside once more.

On the way he passed the Market Place and its Neo-Gothic cross of Bath stone. Erected in 1824 as an early exercise in urban regeneration, this monument had been praised by no less a personage than Sir David Wilkie, President of the Royal Academy, who had declared it to be "equal in quality to some of my own work", and in the words of local historian David Pam, "what higher commendation could anyone give or receive?"[16] Behind the Cross stood the Market Place and the parish church of St Andrew, and close by, Enfield's former manor house, which had long been a private

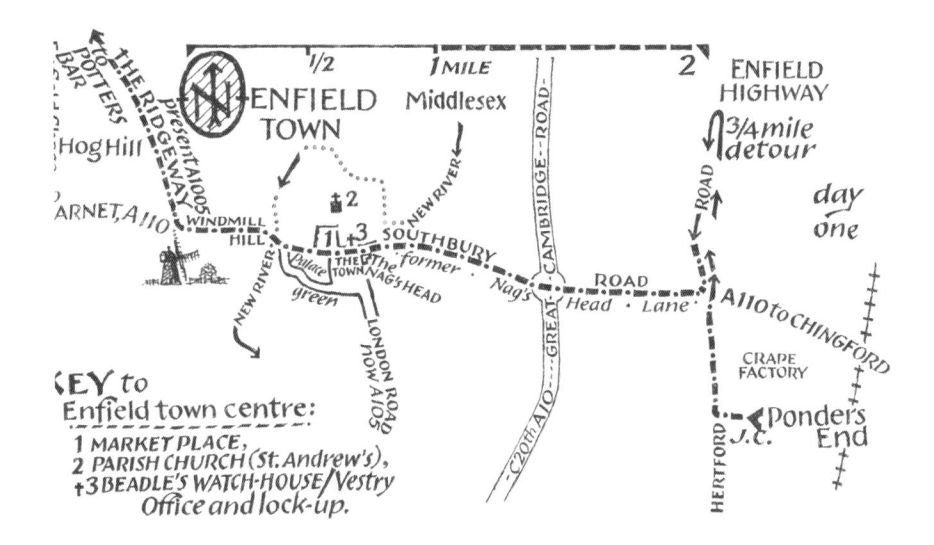

[Map of Enfield area with labels including: POTTERS BAR, THE RIDGEWAY, Hog Hill, ARNET A110, WINDMILL HILL, ENFIELD TOWN, Middlesex, NEW RIVER, SOUTHBURY, Palace, The Former TOWN NAG'S HEAD, green, LONDON ROAD now A105, CAMBRIDGE ROAD, GREAT A10 HERTFORD ROAD, Nag's Head Lane, CRAPE FACTORY, J.C., ENFIELD HIGHWAY, ¾ mile detour, day one, A110 to CHINGFORD, Ponders End, ½ / 1 MILE / 2]

KEY to Enfield town centre:
1 MARKET PLACE,
2 PARISH CHURCH (St. Andrew's),
✝3 BEADLE'S WATCH-HOUSE/Vestry Office and lock-up.

school. Numerous pubs lined the Market Place, including the town's oldest, the King's Head, along with houses and wooden cottages, some of which also stood in the market itself.

The market was set up by Royal Charter in 1613 after years of antagonism between the vicar and townspeople over the issue of Sunday trading. Matters came to a head one Sunday morning in 1582, when Leonard Thickpenny, a curate, stormed out of the church and in a demonstration of muscular Christianity assaulted a butcher, overturning his stall in front of a crowd of customers. The incident prompted a petition to the Queen's Chief Minister Lord Burleigh, signed by nearly all the parish householders, begging him to intervene on their behalf.

Burleigh eventually brokered a deal that allowed the market to flourish unhindered by further acts of thuggery. It did so well, in fact, that in 1632 the Parish Vestry, which rented out stalls to the vendors, increased the size of the square by demolishing an adjoining inn. Fifteen years later the market comprised 14 tiled stalls, seven boarded stalls, and 90 tiled trestles. It had also acquired a pump, and a surrounding rail and gate to protect the stallholders' property (and more to the point, one suspects, the Vestry's).[17]

By the mid-1820s St Andrew's had fallen into disrepair through a combination of vandalism and neglect. It underwent restoration at the same time as the Cross was erected, with the porch and muniment room being replaced with a gallery for renting to the gentry, and the south aisle undergoing a complete rebuild. It was hoped that, along with the introduction of the Cross, these renovations would help revive trade, but a difficulty in obtaining funds for the project reflected a lack of local interest in it, and the market failed to thrive.

Twenty years later, in 1841, Enfield was a backwater cut off from London by poor public transport. The only direct means of reaching the capital was Glover's Omnibus, which made a round trip to the Flower Pot in Bishopsgate three times a day, taking an hour and a half to complete each leg. Passengers paid half a crown to ride on an open deck exposed to the elements, while those who forked out an additional shilling could enjoy the dubious privilege of sheltering in a kind of canvas coupe at the front. At such exorbitant prices, many chose to walk to neighbouring Edmonton for the horse-drawn bus, which only cost a shilling each way. The poor walked the entire route, or hitched a lift on a passing cart for a few pennies.

Enfield was also suffering from the economic ascendency of neighbouring Ponders End, which not only bordered the Lea Navigation but was also connected to London via gas-lit streets patrolled by the newly-formed Metropolitan Police Force. Meanwhile, the opening of a railway station at Ponders End in 1840 dealt Enfield's prospects a further blow. Yet being in the doldrums had its advantages, and Enfield's quiet ambience amid the drowsy orchards of the Lea Valley made it an ideal place for educating the young. Since the seventeenth century the old manor house had been occupied by the Palace School, which broke away from the town's grammar school over a dispute about how many private pupils it could admit. Other establishments flourished there, too, including Cowden Clarke's school, where as a boarder the young John Keats first developed his passion for poetry. The railway eventually caught up with the town when the Eastern Counties Railway established a branch line

View north from The Town into Enfield Market Place circa 1895, showing left to right the King's Head public house, St Andrew's church, the Market Cross and the Greyhound Inn. Clare would have entered the frame from the right.

The King's Head, in the Market Place. This splendid Victorian drinking palace replaced the Regency pub Clare walked past, but still retains its original sign.

The Vestry watch house, built in 1824 with cells for detaining wrongdoers and vagrants, is now the office of the Enfield Charitable Trust.

there in 1849, and the school became the station house.[18] Today there is a blue plaque in Keats' memory on display to the left of the modern station's entrance hall. Clare was most likely unaware of Keats' connection to Enfield. It's doubtful, too, whether he knew that his old friend Charles Lamb had lived there in Clarendon Cottage, Gentleman's Row, before moving to Edmonton, where he died in 1834.

On a sunny October morning Ellis and I make our first visit to the town, where we find the market doing brisk trade. Many of the vendors are Italian. Their stalls, decorated red, white and green, display an expansive sweep of cooked meats and street food under the banner of 'Retro Gusto Meats'. While Ellis takes photographs, I wander around the square, viewing landmarks from Clare's day: St Andrew's in its spacious churchyard, and the former Greyhound Inn. There is also a pub called the King's Head, but it's not the building Clare would have seen. That was swept away in a rebuilding of 1899 and replaced by this ornate example of late-Victorian splendour, with its brass door fittings and etched window glass.

Around the corner is a small Georgian building called 'The Old Vestry Offices'. Now housing the Enfield Charitable Trust, it was erected during the makeover of the Market Place as a watch house for the newly appointed parish beadle. Since the renovations to St Andrew's were costing a huge sum of money, the Vestry was determined to stamp out the vandalism that had made them necessary in the first place, and to this end provided the watch house with cells for the summary imprisonment of offenders. Under the Vagrancy Act of 1824 beggars and tramps could also be kept in parish lockups, so the sight of this building in its commanding position beside the Greyhound Inn must have had a chilling effect on Clare. The difficulty he was to face over the next three days in finding a place to sleep was almost certainly due to his fear of being apprehended and put behind bars.

From Enfield Town Clare says he was "bye and bye on the Great North Road where it was all plain sailing". If this means he covered the distance to the road in short order, it still doesn't tell us exactly where he joined it. We can be sure that he continued along Church Street and up Windmill Hill, but there the road divided, and he had to choose which way to go. One branch continued west and joined the Great North Road at Chipping Barnet, while the other, known as the Ridgeway, took a more northerly route across the high ground of Enfield Chase to Potters Bar.

View north across The Town to the watch house standing beside the Greyhound Inn, with the Market Place just visible on the left of the picture. Clare would have walked into view from the right. Photo circa 1870.

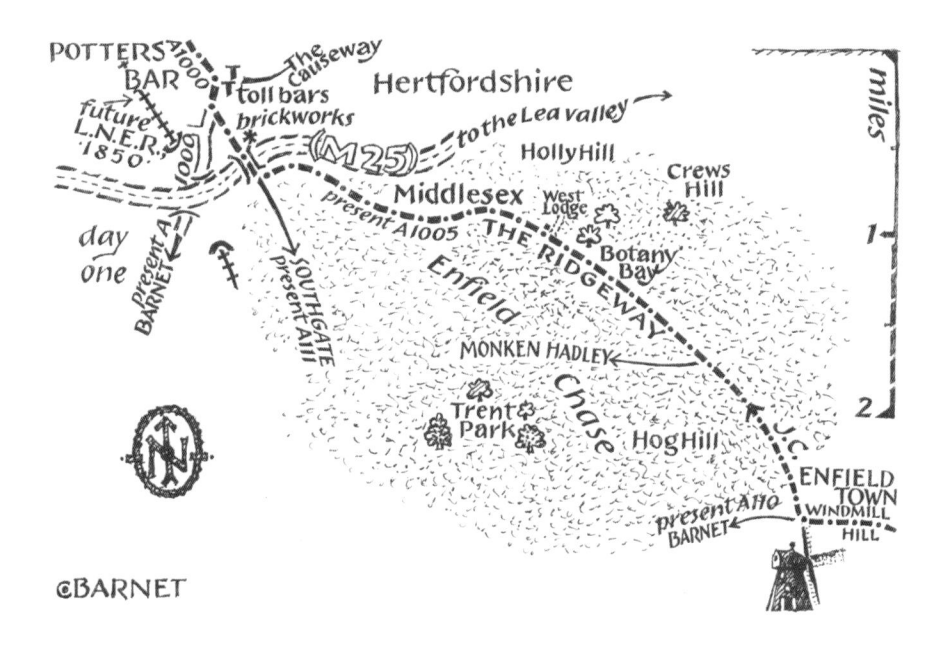

Clare's onward path will have depended on the information he had to hand. There may have been cues such as milestones and fingerposts. The former were obligatory for turnpikes but rare on other roads, and though fingerposts indicated turnpike destinations it is unclear how common they were on ordinary highways. There may be a clue, however, in his description of how, for recreation, he would ramble, 'And green lane traverse heedless where it goes / Nought guessing till some sudden turn espies / Rude battered fingerpost that stooping shows / Where the snug mystery lies'.[19]

Was there a fingerpost at Windmill Hill showing a route up the Ridgeway? And if not, was there sufficient movement on it to persuade him it was a viable route to take? On the enclosure of Enfield Chase in 1777 the first one and a quarter miles of the Ridgeway were put in the care of the Parish of Enfield. Parishes were notoriously poor at keeping roads in good order, so it was probably not well maintained. Also, given that its steep rise to the Chase made it a challenge for horse-drawn vehicles, it likely carried less heavy traffic than the turnpiked Barnet road with its easy gradients and macadamised roadbed. From the position of the sun Clare would have known that it headed north, but if it lacked a fingerpost he might have feared it was a local path, or worse still a dead end.

Another consideration is the extent to which his coach journeys to and from London coloured his choice of route. On his way up Windmill Hill he passed a milestone giving the distance to Barnet, and if he saw it he may well have recalled stopping there aboard the Regent twenty years earlier. Did such a memory prompt him to take the longer but more certain way?

Botany Bay, Enfield Chase, circa 1870, looking along the Ridgeway in Clare's direction of travel. The brick house, foreground right, is still standing but the other buildings in the picture have all been replaced by twentieth-century housing.

These are the questions in our minds when, on a cold February morning, Ellis and I visit Barnet Museum. Dennis Bird, one of the volunteers running it, specialises in the history of turnpikes and coach travel. He and the museum's director, Mike Noronha, listen as we set out our thinking on Clare's possible routes from Enfield to the Great North Road. Much to our surprise, they react with frank incredulity to our suggestion that he might have gone via Chipping Barnet. They assure us that in his time, as now, the Ridgeway was the most obvious route north, and are certain he would have seen plenty of traffic using it. After much discussion over maps of the area, we take our leave, persuaded that, on the balance of probabilities, this must have been the road he took.

Climbing to the high ground on the lip of the London Basin, the Ridgeway is one of the ancient trails of England. During Anglo-Saxon times, men with shields and long-handled axes marched down tracks like it to join the *fyrd* against Viking incursions, while high above, as 'The Battle of Maldon' tells us, ravens and eagles circled, attracted by the clank of metal they associated with feasting on the slain.[20] More recently, generations of schoolchildren have been taught that this is where the chalk and sandstone escarpments of Hertfordshire and Essex meet the clay lowlands and safe harbour of the Thames Estuary.

During his four years at Allen's, Clare was able to gaze down on London: "a shrub among the hills" that had been, from his high vantage point, "lower than the bushes".[21] On the Ridgeway it was again in full view, and perhaps it brought back memories of Taylor, Hessey and the *London Magazine* circle, who had transformed the compass of his writing and had served, in Roger Sales' words, as "his university".[22] If so, it must have been a reminder of all he had lost, with his letter-writing lapsed and friends like Octavius Gilchrist dead.

At the top of Windmill Hill, he entered the wild country of Enfield Chase. Few people lived here in 1841. The only settlement was the isolated hamlet of Botany Bay, established following the Enclosure Act of 1777. He would have understood the name's connotations. He said of the day he left home to join the Northampton Militia that "our mothers parted with us as if we was going to Botaney Bay and people got at their doors to bid us farewell and greet us with a sort of Job's comfort that they doubted we should see Helpstone no more".[23]

During his youth, transportation to the convict colony in New South Wales had been common—he had inherited his first violin from a gypsy sent there for horse stealing. Yet this dreadful punishment was the lesser sanction. Between 1826 and 1830, over six and a half thousand men and women were condemned to hang in England and Wales, of whom 307 were actually executed, 93 pardoned and the remainder transported.[24] In *The Shepherd's Calendar*, a mother tells her children how

> In her younger days, beside the wood,
> The gibbet in its terror stood:
> Though now decay'd, 'tis not forgot,
> But dreaded as a haunted spot— [25]

Clare writes this as a memory from his own mother's childhood, yet public execution was still a popular spectacle in 1820s London, and gibbeted bodies were displayed for months on Hounslow Heath. *The Shepherd's Calendar* was published in 1827, the same year a public outcry overturned a court ruling that the body of a murderer should be hung in chains on the road to Brigg in Lancashire.[26]

The Chase had a long history. In the twelfth century a part of the forest that stretched twelve miles north of the City of London was declared the king's hunting ground, and by Chaucer's day it was known as 'Enfield Chase' in recognition of this royal function. Locals from Edmonton and Enfield claimed common law rights to lop wood and graze animals on it, and the future Queen Elizabeth hunted there after her brother, Edward VI, gifted her the estate of West Lodge Park. The people of Enfield recognised their privileges from Edward by naming their grandest inn 'The King's Head' and displaying his portrait on its sign board.

The first incursion into the people's rights happened in the time of the Commonwealth, when the Chase was carved up and handed over to Roundhead veterans following the disbandment of Cromwell's army. Resentment built up among the locals, who could no longer collect wood or graze their animals. David Pam gives a vivid description of what happened next: "At midsummer 1659, as the crops were ripening in the new fields, the people made a mass incursion onto Enfield Chase and, having destroyed the new hedges and fences, drove their cattle on to the growing crops." The new landowners brought in troops and threatened to burn houses in Enfield Town. On July 10th reinforcements were met by a crowd of men and women who "fought with inveterate fury, pitching long poles into the ground, with colours flying from the top, making great shouts and calling for the restoration of Charles II".[27] A sergeant and ten soldiers were taken prisoner. Three Enfield residents—two men and a woman—were killed. The following year the monarchy was restored and common law rights on the Chase reinstated.

Friction blazed up again during the early eighteenth century. At that time the Chase was being leased from the Duchy of Lancaster by Major General John Pepper, who was greatly hated by the people. Pepper vigorously enforced the laws against poaching, and his zeal often spilled over into vindictiveness. The historian E. P. Thompson notes that he petitioned Parliament with a Private Member's Bill to increase the penalty for stealing deer to a £50 fine, and supported the Law Officers in extending the punishment for wounding a deer from a moderate fine to seven years' transportation.[28]

Commoners had no rights to hunt deer, and poachers dispensing venison were local heroes. In 1721 William 'Vulcan' Gates, a blacksmith from Edmonton, was caught with venison on the Chase and sentenced to twelve months in Newgate prison followed by an hour in the pillory at Enfield Market. News that his release had been countermanded by Pepper led to a serious riot of the crowd gathered to welcome him home. After being pilloried, he was returned to Newgate under armed escort to face further charges and later released. His liberty was short-lived, however, as three years later he went on to a hero's hanging under the notorious Black Act for shooting and carrying off a fallow buck.

Pepper was also determined to stamp out lopping. Each year a large quantity of wood was needed for a bonfire to be lit in Enfield Marketplace on November 5th, which had been sanctioned a holiday by the new Protestant monarchs William and Mary. However, in 1721 three wood collectors were arrested on his orders without warning and sentenced to three months with hard labour in the Clerkenwell lockup to be followed by a public whipping. Such was the public outcry at the savagery of the punishment that Charles Viscount Townshend released the men on behalf of the Crown, thus humiliating the General in a rare victory for the commoners.

At the time of its enclosure the Chase covered an area of 7,900 acres.[29] Slightly over half was allocated to local parishes, and of the remainder some was given to existing manors and lodges and some to Trinity College Cambridge in return for yielding rights to tithes on church lands. The remaining portion, 3,218 acres in all, was allotted to the King. Work began at once to fence and plough the land adjacent to the parishes and to build paved roads where grassy tracks like the Ridgeway already ran. Some Crown land reverted to its former use as a deer park, while the rest was advertised for leasehold sale on the understanding that its trees would be protected and preserved. In the event, many leases were bought by speculators in wood who immediately set about felling them for a quick profit. The extent and speed of the clearance not only degraded the soil but also depressed the price of

Enfield Chase, now mature farmland—the view south-west from Botany Bay.

timber, which led to a collapse in the market. Yet change to the landscape did not happen overnight. The arduous work of turning forest and heath into farmland was necessarily a gradual process, and it was not until 1796 that the systematic application of chalk and lime began a transition to sustainable agriculture.

We drive up to Botany Bay on a sunny October morning and park the car at the Robin Hood pub, on a shoulder of land with stunning views across the valley; it comes as no surprise when Ellis's phone reports that we are 269 feet above sea level. Hazel shells crunch beneath our feet as we stroll along the road, bringing to mind Clare's accounts of the joys of nutting. Among the twentieth-century houses and bungalows on either side of us are cottages dating from a time when this was still a wild and lonely place, named for its remoteness and discomfort, with drifted snow and icy roads in winter, and the need to haul most of life's necessities up from the town. Was there a blacksmith here, we wonder, or a butcher? Or an undertaker?

We come to a large Victorian house set back from the road in its own grounds. It appears deserted, so I venture a little way in, attracted by the bushes and shrubs in their rich autumn hues. Here, hidden from prying eyes behind a garden wall, I find other things to remind me of how late in the season it is—a badly tended plot of blackening maize, an apple orchard carpeted with rotting windfalls, and a pile of yellow and orange gourds drying out for Halloween. There's an outbuilding, too, faced with rough planking; something Clare would have called a 'hovel'. Whatever it once was—a garage probably—it is now derelict, evoking a time when Botany Bay consisted of wooden shacks for poorly paid labourers: pioneers sent by landowners to stake out their claims and begin the long, gruelling process of subduing the chase into farmland.

We are just past the mid-point of the Ridgeway. There's not much else here; a traffic camera, a bus stop, a shack-like chapel and a low building that looks like a toll keeper's cottage but is in fact the former gatehouse of West Lodge Park. Though most of the trees had been felled when Clare was here, agriculture had yet to take hold and great tracts of heath lay all around him. He could revel in the clear air, away from the noise and dust of coaches and wagons down in the valley. These last three miles before he joined the Great North Road must have been among the most serene of his entire walk.

A roebuck leaps into undergrowth at Castor Hanglands Nature Reserve.

The effects of the Enclosures were permanent and all-pervasive, but we cannot see our loss because we never knew what came before. Clare, by contrast, saw it everywhere. The destruction of heath and woodland in his youth had not been a slow, imperceptible evolution from wilderness to farmland, but a sudden depredation over a period of maybe five years. The huge blackthorn at Langley Bush, with the sheltering cave in its hollow stump, was rooted out; the old elm tree by his house was felled, and the sweet winding brooks were channelled and straightened. As one of the casual labourers employed to effect this havoc, he would have known that the shack dwellers of Botany Bay were likewise being paid a pittance to destroy their children's birthright.

To recapture something of his experience, Ellis and I visit the Castor Hanglands Nature Reserve, two miles from Helpston. Perhaps this last remnant of Emmonsales Heath, where Clare roamed as a child, can bring us closer to his sense of loss. Here he spent long days collecting pooty shells to string over the hearth as winter decoration, and dared to enter a ruined house reputedly haunted by the murdered dead.

We arrive early, while the daylight is still new, parking up near a locked gate on the Langley Bush Road. There's a ploughed field standing between us and the reserve. We cross it slowly, noting how stems of broken stubble still cling to the earth, while high above us a fighter jet screams through the silence of a deep blue sky. The woods, when we get to them, are in the fullest flush of autumn. Leaves have fallen in drifts, and crimson berries hang in the hedges. As we stop a moment to catch our breath, a roebuck crashes out of the undergrowth just yards away. He pauses to inspect us, raises his antlered head, then plunges straight back in.

The poet David Morley tells of coming here straight after reading to the English Faculty in Cambridge. He set up his ash-wood easel on the heath and read again from *The Gypsy and the Poet*, his homage to Clare. His imagined memory presses into the lane with me, declaiming to the birds and flowers whose 'biographies' Clare intended to write, but never did.

At the gate there's a map showing the reserve's various terrains—woodland, grassland, heath and scrub. Twenty or so metres in we arrive at a clearing where grasses come up to our shoulders. Here, the rosebay willowherb is dying back, its stalks holding wisps of dead flower heads, while all around us the dew sparkles on hawkweed flowers, and pink seed pods with frothy silver feelers drift in the air. There are teasels, too, with haloes of green fuzz and long curving spikes that catch the light, standing in the grass like luminous warriors of a fabled land. An orange-and-black butterfly flits past—here and gone in a flash—and at my feet there's a freshly dug molehill. It reminds me of Clare sitting on ant heaps and calling them molehills, which makes me wonder where all the ants have gone.[30]

There should be some nuts left on the trees, but we look for them in vain. A party of rangers from English Nature are here clearing the undergrowth from ponds to improve conditions for amphibians and grass snakes. When I ask one of them, he searches a bank of hazels and presents me with a twig that holds just two. He explains that nowadays the nuts are hard to come by as grey squirrels eat them while they are still green. The ripe ones the village girls picked in Clare's youth are no longer found here.

Dry teasel heads in heathland, Castor Hanglands Nature Reserve.

We follow the trail towards the scrub: in Clare's time the habitat of nightingales. Their song, now a rarity, was a common feature of summer woodlands night and day. This morning, low in the undergrowth, a bird is singing loudly, pouring out a cascade of liquid syllables. We decide it must be a black cap or song thrush as the season for nightingales is long past, but as the phrases flow on I recall Clare in his poem 'The Nightingale's Nest', crouching still and silent over many hours until he is rewarded by the bird's song, which guides him to her home, secret in the grass beneath a thorn bush.[31]

Musings VI

Plain sailing on the Great York Road.
Making a good pace on the grass beyond the ruts,
he's passed by a mule and wagon, its driver
white with dust, and a haywain carrying casuals
in smocks and bonnets with a stack of rakes.

He stands back when the beat and clatter of hooves
reaches a pitch with the coming coach:
the driver riding high, whipping four in hand,
a trail of barking dogs close on the wheels
and hazards of flying chips of stone.

Potters Bar – a ribbon of wooden shacks for the poor
by the toll house that gives the place its name
and three or four great houses with their own estates;
this is the perfect place to find Clare's "Crooked Old Man"
of natural honour whom everyone likes to blame.

Caught in a stream of coaches, wagons and carts,
Crooked Old Man's voice like a kite on a string
has satirical force, dangerous as steam;
he catches all the flak and always cocks a snook –
scurrilous stories swarming around him like bees.

Crooked Old Man plays magic tricks for the poor,
smells out villains, is never beaten down;
John Clare shouts about workers starving as they toil,
and his shadow struts by his side in pride,
champion of the poor. Money is not power.

Bars, Bricks and Baptists

The sun was high when Clare crossed the remnant of Enfield Chase between Botany Bay and Potters Bar. As he passed through North Lodge, there would have been long grass bordering the clearings between the trees, with wild flowers tangled in among the year's new growth. He may even have seen a bevy or two of does with their high-antlered bucks and half-grown juveniles.

As he entered Potters Bar by Southgate Road, he passed a brickworks. Like others all over England, this was turning out hand-made bricks to meet local demand. He had grown up close to Stamford, where the homes of the wealthy were built of Barnack rag, but here at the edge of Enfield Chase there was no stone to quarry. Grand houses were made of brick, produced nearby because transporting it any great distance was prohibitively expensive.

The 1840s heralded a great boom in brickmaking. This was the first age of the railways, with its voracious need for stations, viaducts, engine sheds and workers' cottages. In *Bleak House,* published in 1853, Dickens describes an extensive works at St Albans where labourers toiled to make bricks by hand. This involved digging out the clay, mixing it with sand and water, and pugging it to remove stones and air, all of which produced a mixture that could be moulded, dried and fired in kilns. At every stage the clay's dead weight had to be shifted in barrows or carried in moulding trays, and lifted and stacked and unstacked and packed, while the heat of the kilns was raised and maintained by roaring flames. Working conditions were at best dangerous and at worst lethal. Firing produced a poisonous gas that, in Dickens' words, glowed "with a pale blue glare" and could overcome the unwary, as Jo the crossing sweeper is warned on settling down by a kiln for warmth. Living conditions were no better: filthy, damp, disease-ridden, and unsanitary even by the standards of the day. The book's heroine, Esther Summerson, contracts smallpox after visiting brick workers in their homes and helping a sick child.[32]

The Potters Bar brickworks was smaller than Dickens' fictional one, but it still employed whole families. The work was seasonal. The clay was dug out in winter so it could be broken up by frost, and the moulding, drying and firing was done during the summer.[33] If Clare turned to look, he would have seen children packing dried bricks into kilns; the industrial equivalent of his rural childhood labour driving cows, scaring birds, and threshing corn.

Situated on a pebble ridge above the London Basin, Potters Bar was scarcely a place at all, more a continuation of the Ridgeway. According to the Census of 1841, it had 179 houses and a population of 846—so tiny that the only Parish amenity was a pound for stray animals.

Its history had been shaped by its proximity to London. During the sixteenth century, a number of country houses were built on its well-drained upland, while two hundred years later it became a fashionable place for wealthy Londoners to lay out Palladian villas in exquisitely landscaped parks. The first part of the settlement's name came from its local industry. Clay was fired here for thousands of years. A

A rare photograph of Victorian brick workers taken near Hadleigh, Essex in 1901.

thirteenth-century parish document records a 'Pottere' living in 'a croft and grove', and in the 1950s the remains of a Roman tile factory, complete with kiln, were unearthed close to the present town. The second part of the name referred to a gate that led onto Enfield Chase when it was a royal hunting ground. In Clare's day it was also apt because of the presence of a major tollgate at the northern end of the town.

Originally, the road from Potters Bar to Hatfield was a series of local byways with inconvenient right-angled bends. A tollgate was first set up beyond the High Street at the top of the hill, at a place called Little Heath. To accommodate the complexity of the local roads and ensure that travellers could not evade paying their tolls, an additional gate was set to the east of the town on Coopers Lane.[34] In 1802 the Galley Corner Turnpike Trust constructed a more direct route to Hatfield, and as a result the main gate was moved to the corner of the new road and the High Street, and the additional one placed beside it to guard the southern end of the old road.

In the 1830s the Great North Road between Barnet and Hatfield was exceptionally crowded, and though Potters Bar was never a major staging post for coaches, it had a number of inns serving drovers and waggoners. By the time Clare walked the route, traffic was in steep decline due to competition from the London and Birmingham Railway. Trains were faster and cheaper than coaches and—for some, at least—more comfortable. While third-class passengers stood in open wagons and second-classers sat on wooden benches, those in first class rode in compartments offering a level of privacy and protection from the elements only otherwise afforded to stagecoach 'insiders', for a fraction of the cost. By 1841 the resulting switch to rail meant that road traffic through Potters Bar was much reduced, and increasingly local.

Ellis and I visit the town on a wet, freezing-cold day in March. This has been the warmest spring in living memory, but the gods of meteorology have made today a notable exception in our honour. We start our exploration at the Baptist Church on Barnet Road where, in the window of its modern entrance, there's a cheery multi-coloured banner welcoming us inside. Today, though, salvation is not on offer. The door is locked, and we are left looking into the dry, warm space of God's elect while icy rain trickles down our necks, fogs the lenses of Ellis's cameras, and turns the pages of my notebook to soggy papier-mâché. We are here not because Clare passed this way—he didn't—but because a contemporary witness reported that, on busy days, the queue of wagons and carts waiting to pass through the tollgate at the end of the High Street stretched back to this point: a distance, we estimate, of just under a mile.[35]

The Baptists' arrival in Potters Bar was just one tiny event in the widespread religious revival that was taking place during Clare's childhood. A naturally contemplative soul, he could not help being affected by the tide of religious fervour that was sweeping the country. In his youth he flirted with the idea of joining the Nonconformists, and for a time during the 1820s, when fears about his own mortality led him to consider the state of his soul, he attended meetings of the local Primitive Methodists. Neither encounter with organized religion lasted, however. Instead, as he tells us in 'Child Harold', he found God in the natural world:

> & he who studies natures volume through
> & reads it with a pure unselfish mind
> Will find God's power all round in every view
> As one bright vision of the almighty mind

Clare walked through this town less than twenty years before the publication of Darwin's *On the Origin of Species*; in fact, at the time it was being written. In his passion for botanising and birding, he played a small but significant part in the Victorian zeal for documenting God's works in Nature.

He approached his subject not only with a poet's eye but also a naturalist's, his observations leading him to expound a law involving the number five: "With the odd number five strange natures laws / Plays many freaks nor once mistakes the cause", he wrote in 'The Eternity of Nature', citing five spots on a cowslip, five pale leaves on each bindweed stem, the clutches of five eggs laid by many species of bird, and the abundance of plants whose flowers have five petals.[36] In this he was following in the footsteps of Linnaeus, with whose work he was familiar through his friendship with Joseph Henderson.[37]

It's time to move on to the crossroads where Barnet Road becomes the High Street. We are looking for the former unnamed beer shop on the corner of Southgate

Road that was run in Clare's day by the brewer James Wanstall. It was later upgraded to an inn called 'The Lion', but here it is, transformed again, this time into an American-themed restaurant called 'Potty's Diner'—a startling vision in black and white. Once a fine establishment that catered to drovers coming off the Ridgeway, it still retains an elegant lintelled door and four Georgian windows, each of which has double shutters carved with tiny hearts. The whitewashed bricks of its walls were almost certainly made at the old works just a hundred yards up the road.

We cross over into the High Street, formerly the western boundary of Enfield Chase. Somewhere along here parishioners crossed the bar into forested land to exercise their common-law rights—keeping a goose or a pig, running an old cow for milk, lopping wood, collecting kindling.[38] The buildings we are seeking from Clare's time are on the right-hand side of the street, built illegally on the Chase during the previous century: a map dating from 1769 shows such encroachments running the street's entire length.[39] In fact, so commonplace was the illegal appropriation of Chase land that at the time of its enclosure a demand was made (and successfully resisted) for parishes to buy the stolen plots from the Crown retrospectively.

In 1901 Charles Harper described Potters Bar as "not a place of delirious delights".[40] Today its High Street still answers to that description, being mostly twentieth century stock in the form of inter-war shopping parades and office buildings from the sixties, seventies and eighties. At this end of the street only one building pre-dates 1841: a pub called 'The Cask and Stillage' which according to my notes was formerly the White Horse. I go in to check while Ellis hangs back, aware that his

The old Lion Inn, at the junction of Barnet Road and the High Street. Having approached along Southgate Road (background left), Clare passed it on his left before immediately turning right into the High Street.

The Cask and Stillage, in Clare's day 'The White Horse', at the south end of Potters Bar High Street—one of the few local buildings to pre-date the mid-nineteenth century.

cameras can arouse suspicion—and sometimes even hostility—in the alcoholically relaxed. The atmosphere inside is subdued, even for a wet Thursday afternoon. I glimpse locals passing the time listlessly, dazed into apathy while economic austerity eats at the fabric of their lives. The Eastern European barman refers me to an elderly gent in the snug, who confirms my understanding of the facts and goes on to tell me that we can find another historic pub, the Green Man, further down the street. "It's in a shocking state," he adds, shaking his head, "You'll see when you get there." Back outside, I take a few moments with Ellis to examine the exterior, which features a pair of beautiful Georgian timber-pillared doorways set between bowed bay windows. On the pillars of the far door there are two hooks, each with a iron loop. For what, we wonder? Tethering dogs? Or keeping a horse's reins above the mud while the rider nips inside for a quick pint? I wonder out loud whether anyone alive today could give a definitive answer. Such inconsequential mysteries seem to make the past more solid and real in their refusal to be solved: a defiant avowal that it still lives on, no matter how ignored or unnoticed.

As we continue on, the street opens out to reveal the imposing gates and driveway of Oakmere House, whose grounds were once part of the Oakmere Estate; a property so large that according to H. J. Butcher it was "practically half the village".[41] Today it is a public amenity with trees, lawns and lakes arranged in the form of a Victorian country park. The house, a large Regency-style villa peeping between the trees, replaced one that was destroyed by fire in 1864, and is now a restaurant owned by the same chain that acquired the pumping station at Ponders End. From here we can see to the end of the High Street and the former site of the Potters Bar toll

A fitting from Clare's era—most likely a tethering hook—on a door pillar of the Cask and Stillage: a reminder that the past is still with us in the small, often overlooked, details of the built environment.

house, which stood between two gates at a fork in the road. The gate on the left gave access to the Hatfield Road, while the one on the right led to a road called 'The Causeway', and from there to the maze of narrow lanes which the Hatfield Road was built to replace. I have seen old photographs of the tollgate so many times that I'm keen to find if anything of it remains, but a few yards short of my goal I stop, arrested by the sight of a beautiful seventeenth century building left derelict on a patch of wasteland.

This used to be the Green Man, and just as the gentleman in the Cask and Stillage warned me, it's a sorry sight. Originally built as a grand house, it was converted to an inn in 1730 and traded without interruption for almost three hundred years—until 2014 in fact, when the brewery that owned it decided there was more money to be made in land speculation than selling beer. With finely proportioned Georgian windows and a long tiled roof, it is a place that has been lived in, extended and remodelled over centuries. We are appalled: allowing a building of such distinction to rot away in a town with so little architectural heritage seems nothing short of criminal neglect.

In its heyday the Green Man was perfectly positioned to offer refreshment to drovers and waggoners queuing up at the toll bar in deference to priority vehicles such as mail coaches, which as agents of the Crown went free, and long-distance stage coaches whose companies paid their tolls in advance. The guards on these vehicles carried horns with distinctive calls to give a three-minute warning for the gates to be opened so they could thunder through unimpeded.

Because the toll bar stood at the meeting-point of three roads, operating it was a complex undertaking. A keeper supervised operations from an office between the gates while a small team of staff did the actual work of assessing charges, collecting moneys, operating the barriers and keeping a lookout for new arrivals. Though custom was declining by 1841, manning the gates was still a round-the-clock operation.

The Green Man, a drovers' stopping place during the heyday of the Great North Road and a roadside inn for over 400 years, abandoned and awaiting redevelopment.

Charles Harper made this sketch of the Potters Bar toll house prior to 1897, when it was demolished following damage sustained in an automobile crash.

The view today from roughly the spot where Harper sketched the scene above.

It is worth the long walk, the cold hands and the soggy notebook just to see where the toll house stood. The trees in the fork of the road look very much as they do in Victorian photos, tall and ill-kempt, signalling the end of town. Looking down the Hatfield Road to where the last few houses run out, it's clear that a nineteenth-century traveller would have no trouble recognising the scene—cars, tarmacked road and street furniture notwithstanding. As was the case in those days, open

The toll house, with the new Hatfield Road on the left of the picture and the old road—known as the Causeway—on the right. Photograph circa 1860.

countryside still takes over almost immediately after the parting of the ways, with the triangular space in between filled by lush pastureland belonging to Morven Park, a country estate now owned by the National Trust.

On turning back we spot a refuge from the rain in the form of the Sugarloaf Café, and dive inside, our glasses steaming up in the beautiful warmth. It's an up-market tea shop, packed with refugees from the weather. We learn from the waitress that the Green Man is to be converted into a care home, but because it's Grade II listed the exterior will be preserved.[42] We explain our interest in the town's history, and mention that during the coaching era traffic used to reach back from here to the Baptist Church. "It still does," she laughs, "You should see it in the mornings!"

I gaze through the windows and see in my mind's eye a short, stocky figure swinging down the street beside queuing vehicles and droves of animals. Horses were always a pleasure to Clare, a luxury beyond his family's reach. They reminded him of the time he worked at the Bluebell next door to his parents' tenement. He loved the independence the job brought him, and the daily routines of grooming, feeding and watering the landlord's nag.[43]

As he approached the gates among the crowd of bystanders, he would have needed to watch where he placed each foot. I imagine crossing sweepers, like Dickens' Jo, wielding brushwood brooms to keep a clean path for smart boots and long skirts. I imagine, too, horses tossing their heads to shake up the fodder in their nose bags, blinkers shielding them from distractions like this man who is walking purposefully past, the whole of his attention fixed ahead as he pauses to check which gate he should take. Then, having made his choice, he slips free of the crowd and through, out onto the leafy highway.

Hertfordshire

Day 1, 20th July 1841: Bell Bar to Stevenage
Day 2, 21st July 1841: Graveley to Baldock

Musings VII

There's a fine wrought iron gate and post box
with Victoria's mark where the road crossed
into Hatfield Park, and by the Lodge a pond;
did Clare look to see if there were fish,
hating water to be clogged with weed and barren?

He thought Walton's discourse of fish ponds and fishing
a marvel full of sound advice; for sure
he never used bear's hair to tie a fly,
but always looked for sandy places for fish to spawn,
and brushwood to protect young fry from ducks.

But no! The road lay a hundred yards from this gate.
So, I stop and look in his place – is there gravelly ground
for carp, and shallows to sport themselves? Is there mud
for tench and eels? and are there willows planted about,
and a sluice to take away the flood?

❦

The road intruded into Hatfield park
to the left of wrought iron gates, brickwork pillars
and screens of fretted stone. The huge house watches
John Clare pass here around noon of the first day,
making good pace, his legs still fresh.

At the head of the hill, by the palace wall
where a king once hid the daughters of his former wives,
the coach turns under the arch of the Inn
and passengers climb down for lunch. Clare tramps
on down Fore Street past St Etheldreda's church.

❦

Money Speaking Power

Half a mile down the Hatfield Road, Clare rejoined the old highway at Little Heath.[1] From there he made his way to Swanley Bar and skirted the eastern edge of Brockman Park at the 16th milestone near Shepherds Way junction.

To his left, grass and mature trees swept down to the manor house, a fine piece of landscaping that had resulted from a deal struck in 1711 between the manor's owner, Charles Cocks, and the Churchwarden and Overseers of the Poor. For the sum of £70, Cocks persuaded the parish officers to enclose four acres of North Mymms Common between the road and the manor on his behalf. The fact that they had taken the bribe without demur would not have surprised Clare in the slightest. Nor would he have raised an eyebrow at the dealings of the then current owner, Robert William Gaussen, who was in the process of evicting tenants in pursuit of increased profits.[2]

Gaussen owned inns at Bell Bar, employed a large community of labourers, family servants and craftsmen, and had nine tenant farmers paying him rent. The Gaussen family moved to Brockman Manor from London in 1786, having made their fortune through trade and a succession of advantageous marriages. After the death of his father, Robert continued the work of enlarging the estate. An astute businessman and a canny investor in land, he provided his family with a fine country house and his sons and daughters with generous endowments. As a member of the landed gentry, and hence a trustee of the Galley Corner Turnpike Trust, he supported Lord Salisbury in moving the Great North Road away from Brockman Manor and Hatfield House, even though this led to the loss of Bell Bar's trade. When in 1850 he was unsuccessful in stopping the passage of the Great Northern Railway through three of his tenant farms, he quickly found ways of profiting from it, sending beasts and hay to the London markets in railway wagons, and using the same wagons to bring back night soil for manuring his fields. He was, in sum, a natural entrepreneur.

It would have been after noontime when the first houses of Bell Bar came into view, and perhaps Clare was beginning to feel safe from pursuit. Despite its small size, the hamlet had three large inns. When coaching was undergoing its first wave of expansion in the 1750s there had been four: the Swan, with eight beds and stabling for 20 horses; the Bell, with two beds and stabling for 10, and the Bull and the White Hart, which between them had another 12 beds and stabling for 20. These establishments would expand to keep pace as coach travel boomed, so that by the 1830s, when dozens of services a day were plying the routes between London, York and Edinburgh, Bell Bar had become a major staging post.

Servicing the coaches was labour-intensive. Inns had to be a combination of hotel, public house, stable, forge and repair shop, and required ostlers, farriers, blacksmiths, wheelwrights, boot boys, provisioners and servants. In 1805 the Swan was described as:

John Chessell Buckler's 1840 engraving of the Great North Road at Bell Bar. The three-storeyed house at the end of the row is Upper Farm, and the building two doors down is Carpenter's Cottage. Clare arrived here walking out of the far distance on a visibly awful road.

The same view in 2019. The timber-faced building has been replaced with twentieth century housing, as has the row of labourers' dwellings between Upper Farm and Carpenter's Cottage. The cottage itself has lost its outsize chimney but is otherwise perfectly recognisable. The road surface has undergone considerable improvement.

Upper Farm, the first house Clare encountered as he entered Bell Bar.

> most eligibly situated by the side of the Great North Road, opposite to the 17th Mile-stone, a regular station for the changing of Stage-Coach Horses, and otherwise a well-frequented House of good business; containing a good sized Parlour, Tap-room, Bar, and small parlour adjoining, all in front, a back Kitchen, Pantry and two Cellars and five neat bed-Rooms and a Lumber Room, plus the outbuildings.[3]

In 1841, as at Barnet and Potters Bar, Bell Bar's trade was being lost to the London and Birmingham Railway. Once he'd ousted the family that lived there, Robert Gaussen would go on to demolish the White Hart on the grounds that "the railroad had done so much injury to the North Road". Even greater damage would occur nine years later, when the road was moved east to coincide with the opening of the Great Northern Railway and its station at Hatfield.

Today most of Bell Bar is set back to the west of the 1850 road along the original coaching route. Verges and cottage gardens have doubtless spread to fill in the space created by its closure, but parts were narrow and cramped even when it was in use. Dorothy Colville, writing in 1971, records that at the turn of the twentieth century grandparents in the village could remember standing in their doorways as children, "watching great coaches lumber by, sometimes so close that it had been possible to touch the sides of the vehicles".[4]

The western end of the old road is now cut off by the high fence of Brookman Park Golf Course, while the remaining stretch, known as Bell Lane, is mostly lined with twentieth century housing. Nonetheless, Ellis and I manage to find four buildings marked on a tithe map of 1844. The first is Upper Farm, at the lane's western end, a three-storey Georgian red-brick villa built for a well-to-do farmer. It has survived

Lower Farm—Bell Bar's first Swan Inn. By the time Clare passed through the hamlet in 1841, the Swan had moved next door to a premises since demolished.

in its original form without obvious alteration, unlike the seventeenth-century Carpenter's Cottage three doors down, which has been restored to death with *faux*-latticed windows and a brash modern chimney stack, and which—like the Old Bakery at the corner of Bulls Lane—bears a name with pretensions to heirloom status. The building that most carries the weight of this hamlet's past, however, is the beautiful half-timbered Lower Farm, which dates from 1540. In 1726 it housed the Swan Inn, an establishment whose history mirrors perfectly the advances in travel and transport that took place between the late eighteenth century and our own time. The Swan began life as a wayside tavern, but moved in 1768 to a premises just a few yards down the road the better to accommodate the burgeoning coaching trade. This was the inn described in 1805 as "a regular station for the changing of Stage-Coach Horses, and otherwise a well-frequented House of good business". It was also the one Clare trudged past on the humid, overcast afternoon of July 20th 1841. Like so much else of his world, however, it has vanished—abandoned when the new road opened in 1850 and the business was forced to move again, this time to a purpose-built house at the junction of the old and new roads, where it was rechristened 'The White Swan'.

In the summer of 1877, author and journalist James Greenwood found himself taking refreshment there. He was undercover, posing as a vagrant, having joined the annual migration of itinerant labourers northward through Hertfordshire as they worked the ripening hay fields. He published his experiences in a book called

On Tramp, which details the privations he suffered and the characters he met while on the road. Though three decades separate him from Clare, his vivid description of a vagrant subculture gives us a window into the world Clare must have engaged with as he made his way homeward. Greenwood's ragged disguise earned him the opprobrium of 'decent' folk. On one occasion a gentleman leaning on his gate accused him of being a ruffian and, when Greenwood protested his innocence, challenged him to prove his worth by weeding an overgrown garden for twopence. On the whole such prejudice against vagrants was unjustified; many of those Greenwood met were honest tradesmen who had temporarily abandoned their occupations in the hope of earning more money as field hands. One was a French-polisher who had taken to the road only recently, and having got through all he had in his bundle had "sold the hankycher it was tied up in"; others included a potter, a hatter, a blacksmith and a stableman.

At the White Swan, however, he witnessed the kind of incident that gave them a bad name. He observed a woman, "brown as a berry" and with with one bandaged eye "scorched out by a stroke of the sun", attempting to sell a jacket to the landlady for two shillings and claiming the cash would relieve her husband, an out-of-work tailor with a paralysed leg. Greenwood finished his pint and left, and soon met the man in question lounging against the 18th milestone—"a stout and hearty grizzly bearded ruffian smoking a filthy pipe"—who cheerfully explained that his wife had

The former Great North Road through Bell Bar, after it was bypassed by Lord Salisbury's re-routing of 1850. This photograph dates from around 1877, when James Greenwood took part in the annual haymaking migration through Hertfordshire.

The third and final incarnation of the Swan at Bell Bar—the White Swan, later renamed the Swan Hotel. Dating from 1850, it was situated at the corner of the old Great North Road leading away to the left of the picture and the new road leading off to the right. Clare walked along the old road left-to-right. Photograph taken in 1900.

performed this pantomime at other pubs: the jacket was far too worn to be worth buying, but her hard-luck story generally yielded the sum she was asking for it. The ruse had provided them with "beer and bacca and wittles" for days, he said, and with luck would continue to do so for the rest of the summer. As for his wife's scorched eye, he added, he had "blacked it".[5]

Reprehensible behaviour of a less calculated sort was noted a century earlier by John Byng, who spent a night in Bell Bar at haymaking time and recorded the event in his journal:

> The roads were hot and bad, my pace was slow, and the mare jolts me to powder.[...] Had I been young and on an active trotter, I had got to Wellwyn: but those days are past, and, as relative to folly, all the better. So I put up at the White-Hart, Bellbar, whose landlord I have long known, and tho' it is an alehouse, yet there was a pretty display upon my supper board of cold ham, cold fillet of veal and sage cheese; with the daughters of the White Hart attendant. [...] There was much noise and drunkenness of the haymakers in the alehouse kitchen. Then one wishes for an elegant tavern, but it is summertime and may be endured.[6]

Though the White Hart, where Byng stayed, was shut in 1842 because of falling revenue, the White Swan continued to trade—latterly as 'The Swan Hotel'—until the 1960s, when it was finally and fatally bypassed by the A1. It then became a private residence known as Swan Lodge: a handsome double-fronted house of great character facing both Bell Lane and the 1850 road. Its considerable size proved its downfall, however. When we visited Bell Bar in the spring of 2016 it had just been sold for demolition, despite heroic efforts by the North Mymms District Green Belt Society to save it. Since then, developers have thrown up in its place a dull but no doubt fabulously profitable block of eight commuter apartments.[7]

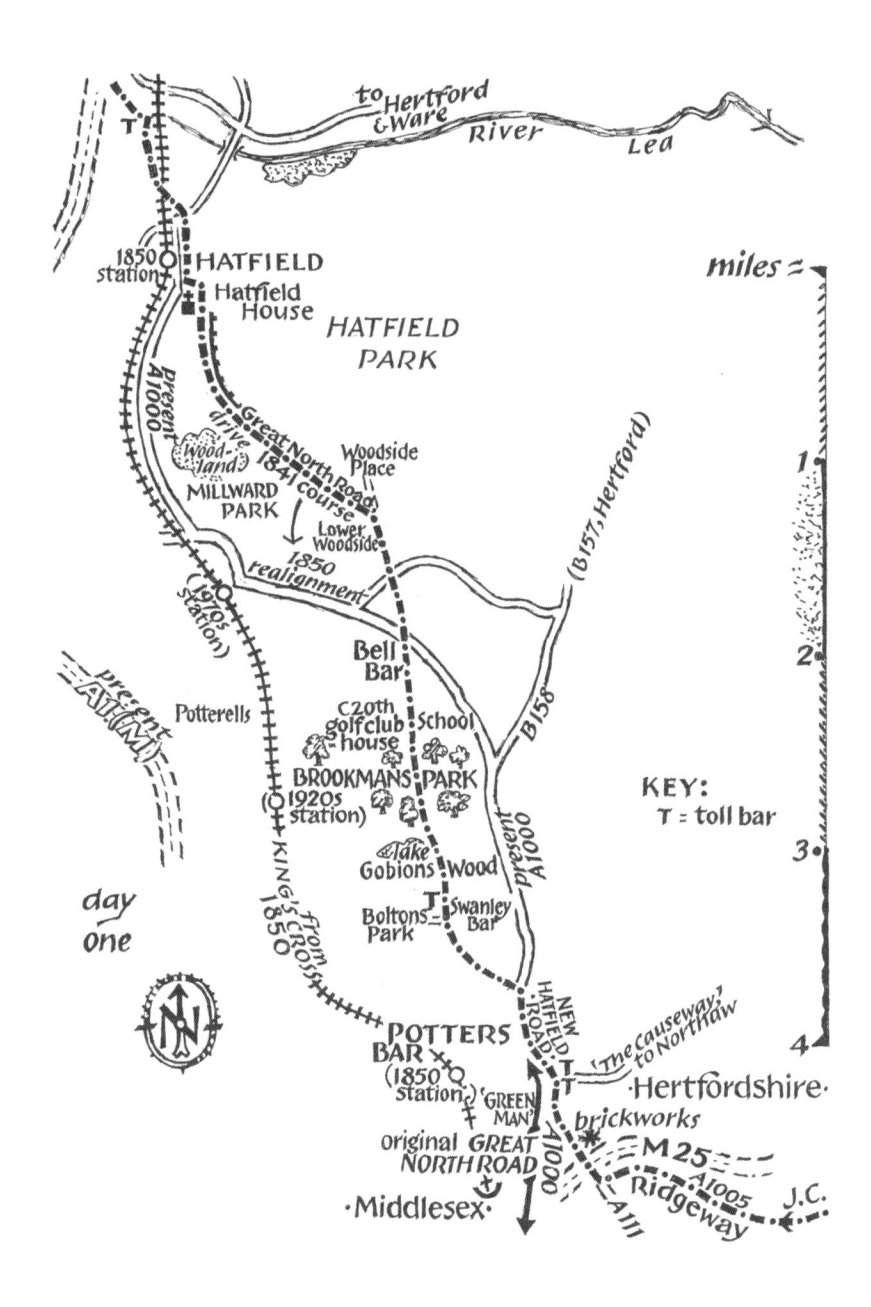

A Victorian letterbox at Woodside. These did not become commonplace until the 1850s, although Rowland Hill's nationwide system of pre-paid postage was already in operation when Clare came through Hatfield Park.

The lodges at Woodside guarding the grand avenue across Hatfield Park. The left-hand lodge was there when Clare passed this way, but the right-hand one had yet to be built.

In Clare's day the road between Swanley Bar and Hatfield was bordered by grassland and mature trees. The northern limit of Gaussen's manor, Brockman Park, extended as far as Bell Bar, while the southern edge of the Hatfield estate almost touched the hamlet at Woodside—so close, in fact, that residents enjoyed the privilege of walking to Hatfield through Hatfield Park. That privilege was rescinded in 1850 with the opening of Salisbury's new road, whose sole purpose was to keep out the riff-raff who plied the Great North Road. As Charles Harper remarked acidly, "And now, forever and a day, those who use the road between Potters Bar and Hatfield village must go an extra half mile. This is indeed a free and happy country."[8]

Somewhere near the Swan, drovers directed their livestock away from the turnpike and onto green lanes to the west in the direction of Lemsford, but the crush of horse-drawn traffic on the Great North Road remained, and this particular stretch was notorious for being difficult to negotiate. Following it out of Bell Bar, Clare passed between high tangled banks bordering farmers' fields before crossing into woodland of sycamore, holly, ash and elm. In less than half a mile he came to the Greyhound Inn at Hatfield Park's Woodside gate, which—hemmed about by dense forest—had been a dreaded haunt of Dick Turpin.

Woodside still lives up to its name, standing as it does at the edge of closely set trees. To reach it, we drive north through a landscape reminiscent of Epping Forest until we come to a junction with the aptly named Wildhill Road. There we turn left and a couple of hundred yards further on arrive at our destination: a pair of lodges that flank the start of an avenue across the park. The one on the left—a single storeyed octagon of stone and red brick—was built during the seventeenth century, while its companion, also octagonal but with two storeys and a square addition,

The old road at the top of Hatfield Park as it approached the Palace Gate, with the parish church of St Etheldreda foreground left and the south front of Hatfield House in the background. Hand-tinted engraving by John Hassell, 1818.

dates from the mid-1840s and so did not exist when Clare was here. We climb out of the car and view the scene. To one side there is a large pond, which I inspect with interest, having just read Chapter XX, 'Of Fish Ponds', in Walton's *Compleat Angler*. Did it hold fish in Clare's day? Only if, as Walton advises, it had been maintained with "bavins in some places not far from the side, and in the most sandy places, for fish both to spawn upon, and to defend them and the young fry from [predators]".[9] I poke around in weeds beneath the willow trees, wondering why small-scale fish farming has died out. Clare said that the sight of a pond with no fish always made him feel sad, so although I'm seeking him out I'm glad he's not here today.

My eye is caught by a Victorian post box let into a wall to the left of the gate: by its appearance one of the first to be installed after their introduction in 1852. In 1840 the first postage stamps, Rowland Hill's 'Penny Blacks', began to be issued for sale at inns and turnpike gates, handy for the mail coaches. Was Clare, isolated at Allen's, aware of this new system of pre-paid postage? If so, it would have pleased him given the difficulties he'd experienced in paying for letters when, in 1820, he became famous overnight. Unsolicited communications arrived from complete strangers and would-be poets, as he complained in his journal entry for Sunday, February 27th 1825: "Received a letter in rhyme from a John Pooley a very dull Fooley who ran me 10^d further into debt as I had not money to pay the postage—I have often been bothered by these poet pretenders."[10]

The encroaching woodland was the reason travellers dreaded this stretch of the Great North Road. Now and then there might be footpads lurking in the undergrowth, but a more constant threat was the waterlogged road—a churned-up quagmire in which carriages and waggons became stuck and could only be released with great effort. in 1831 the Welwyn Turnpike Trust explored the idea of moving the road away from the overhanging trees that were preventing it from drying out after bouts of rain, but nothing came of the plan and the problem persisted until 1850, when the Great North Road was diverted around the Park.

The old road entered the park a hundred yards to the west of the lodges, and climbed towards the top end of Hatfield Town. Clare would have made good speed along the gentle upward slope, a walk of 15 minutes or so through parkland stretching away to the crest of the hill. Passing the house and outbuildings of Lawn Farm he would have seen, to his right, the great south front of Hatfield House. As the road grew steeper he must have overtaken wagons toiling their way up to the Old Palace Gate. Alongside the largest, drivers would have been walking, forbidden to ride for fear they might fall asleep and lose control of their horses. At the top, opposite the Palace's great archway, the road turned sharply left into Fore Street, and the start of Hatfield Town. Coaches and waggons paused here to fit skid pans so they could safely descend the street's alarmingly steep slope. Shovel-shaped and made of steel, these devices were placed beneath the near-side wheels to stop them turning. Once they were in position, vehicles could proceed slowly downhill with a guard leading

Fore Street, Hatfield, looking down the hill in Clare's direction of travel. When it was part of the Great North Road, its precipitous incline required the harnessing of extra draft animals on the ascent and the fitting of skid pans on the descent.

HATFIELD TOWN in 1841
(sketched from tithe map)

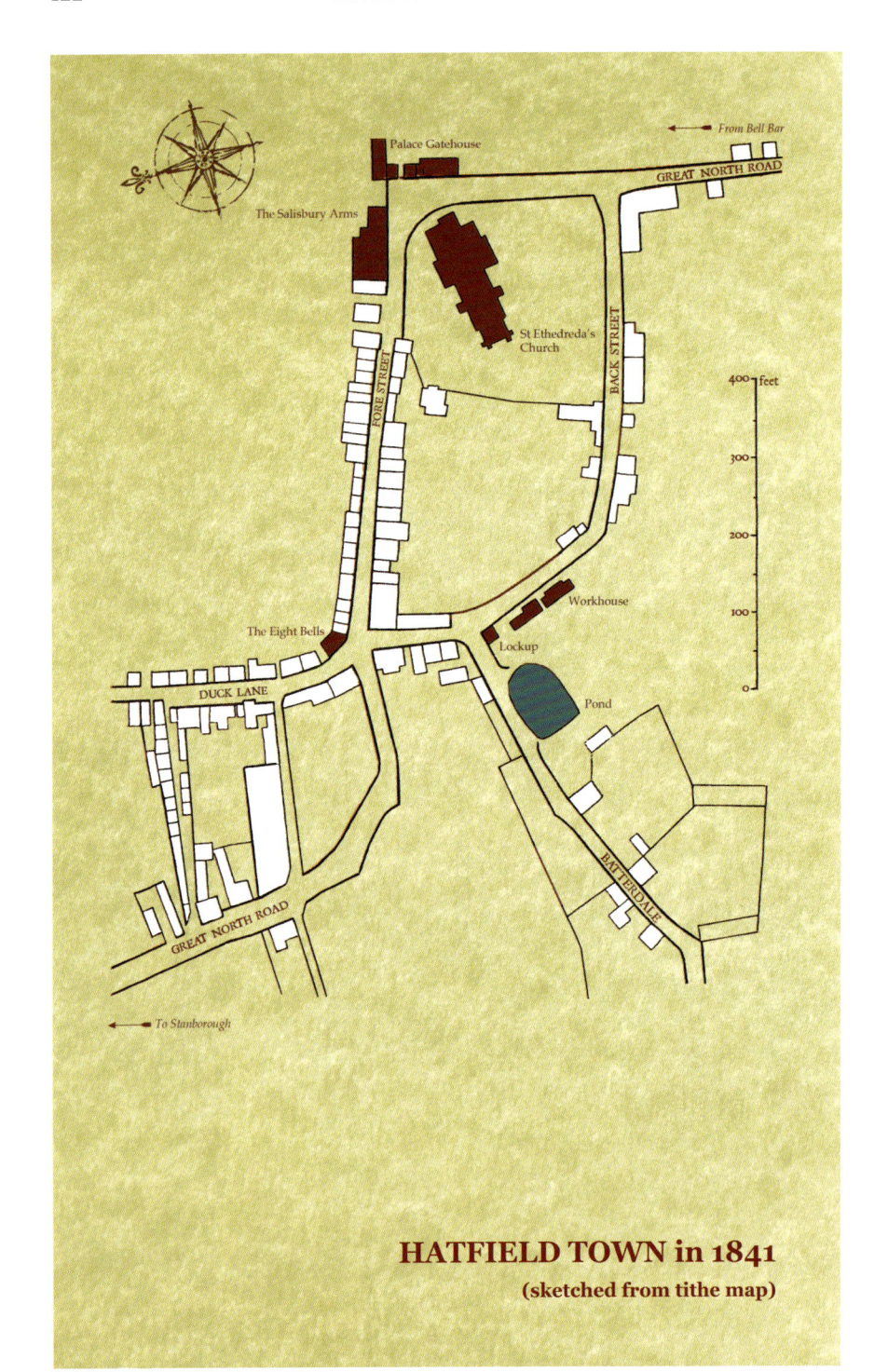

The Eight Bells public house, with Park Street on the left of the picture and Fore Street rising steeply towards the Old Palace on the right.

the horses to steady them through the awful din of braked wheels being dragged over cobbles. Climbing the street in the opposite direction was even more challenging: the York Waggon once needed no fewer than sixteen horses to struggle to the top.[11]

Standing by the grand entrance to the Salisbury Arms, Clare could look down to the houses of Hatfield clustered below the parish church of St Etheldreda, whose peal of eight bells was cast by a local man, John Brian, at his foundry in Hertford and inaugurated on June 5th 1786, just two days before his own wedding there. The inn at the foot of the hill called the Five Bells was duly renamed 'The Eight Bells' to celebrate the increase in number.

On a bitterly cold day in February, Ellis and I are standing at the top of Fore Street in the archway of the Palace gatehouse, talking to a porter. It's her job to tell visitors like us that the house and gardens are closed for the season, but she allows us into the outer yard, where workmen are renovating the roofs of the old stables. From here we have a fine view of the Great Tower, where Henry VIII secreted Elizabeth after her mother, Ann Boleyn, was beheaded, and where little princess Mary, child of Henry's divorced queen Catherine of Aragon, waved her father goodbye while he rode away without acknowledging her. Behind the Old Palace, hidden from view, is the exquisite Jacobean Hatfield House, built in 1611 by Robert Cecil, First Earl of Salisbury and Chief Minister of King James I and VI. In 1603, James, newly arrived from Scotland to take up the English throne, met Cecil here on his way to London. He needed to establish his authority over a court in which he was a complete unknown, and believed that the old queen's adviser could offer him advice and insider knowledge. On arriving in London, James created him Lord Salisbury and made him his chief councillor. Shortly afterwards, taking a fancy to Cecil's family home at Theobalds near Enfield, he suggested a swap with Hatfield House—an offer Cecil, wisely, felt unable to refuse.[12]

The Salisbury Arms, Hatfield's most prestigious coaching inn, at the top of Fore Street. It was a stopover for aristocrats both living and dead: Byron's funeral cortège paused here to change horses before descending the hill on its way north.

    The porter urges us to come back in the summer to see the House, and prompted by our interest in its history relates how in 1835 a terrible fire gutted much of its west wing. The Dowager Lady Salisbury, wife of the first Marquis, was living there at the time. Famous for her horsemanship, high spirits and strong character, she was indomitable to the end when, impatient of her failing eyesight, she demanded more candles be brought to her bedroom. Exactly what happened next is unclear, but the resulting fire brought appliances from as far afield as Barnet and London, and though her staff made frantic efforts to save her, she burned to death.[13] Ellis and I, hearing this, are so taken aback that for a moment we're speechless. Three years later Mary Joyce would also perish in a fire, and the similarity of their ends is shocking. Given that the Hatfield Cecils were cousins to the Cecils of Burghley House, news of the Hatfield fire must surely have reached Clare. He may even have read Dickens' account of it in *The Morning Chronicle*.

    Leaving the Palace gatehouse, we stand at the top of Fore Street and take in our surroundings. To our right, the old coach house adjoins the Salisbury Arms, which in 1841 was Hatfield's most prestigious inn. Perfectly placed at the top of the hill, it had a carriageway leading directly to a yard that could stable a hundred horses; Byron's funeral cortège stopped there to change teams on its long, slow journey from London to his final resting place at Hucknall in Nottinghamshire. Quite apart from catering to stage coaches, the Salisbury also served as a hotel for visitors who were not sufficiently good or great to merit lodgings at the House.

In the early morning, Fore Street is deserted. Isolated in the heart of Hatfield Old Town, away from schools and workplaces, it is elegant, dignified and tranquil; a home to the affluent childless. The houses have gracious fronts with canted bow windows and fanlit pilastered doors. Though quiet at this time of year, in summer it provides a conduit for hordes of visitors who advance on Hatfield House for their fix of history, heritage and cream teas.

Opposite the Salisbury, St Etheldreda's stands in a graveyard crowded with tombs. Some have partly sunk into the soil, and many are so weathered and lichen-encrusted that their inscriptions are illegible. Though picturesque, it has an air of neglect that makes a sharp contrast with the now fastidiously maintained homes on the street. This was definitely not the case in 1901, however, when Charles Harper remarked that Hatfield Town "touches the extremity of wretchedness, just as Hatfield House marks the apogee of late feudal splendour".[14] In those days Fore Street was still the centre of town life with its two great inns: the Salisbury here at the top, and the Eight Bells at the bottom, the latter having become world-famous after Dickens chose it in *Oliver Twist* as the place where the villain Bill Sikes goes to ground after murdering his lover Nancy.

When journalist James Greenwood reached here in 1877, he also found little to please him. Lodgings could be obtained in back-street houses that had a room or two to spare, and he managed to secure a billet in one of them for fourpence. He had to share his bed with another tramp who came in drunk at midnight, forgot to remove one boot, and kept "lunging out with it against the foot-board", waking

Victorian tombs, some resembling steamer trunks, litter St Etheldreda's churchyard opposite the Salisbury Arms.

himself up each time and yelling "Come in!" The man made amends the following morning by standing Greenwood breakfast in return for writing a letter to his wife. It turned out he was a hatter by trade, and had attached himself to a benefit society so he could get relief at its lodges along his route.

Salisbury and Gaussen's re-routing was well established by the time Greenwood and Harper passed through Hatfield, but in 1841 the Great North Road still followed the old coaching way, entering the town at the Palace gate, descending Fore Street, and continuing straight over the crossroads with Park Street—then known as Duck Lane—before making its way northward out of town.

On our first visit, confused by a change in road layout, we assume that the Great North Road rounded the bowed front of the Eight Bells and continued down Park Street, so we set off in that direction. The first landmark to catch our eye is the Horse and Groom, a survivor from the glory days of coach travel when the town boasted over 25 inns. We only give it a passing glance, however, because directly ahead of us, striding majestically across the road, is a beautifully proportioned viaduct of great rounded arches. Barring the Great House and the Palace, this is by far the town's most impressive structure, dwarfing everything around it. Hill House, a red-brick Palladian villa, sits squashed beside it on the hill. The owners must have been incensed when the viaduct was constructed so close to their home, diminishing its proud proportions and blotting out the view.

The viaduct built to carry Lord Salisbury's carriage drive from Hatfield House to the railway station, viewed from Park Street.

Salisbury's carriage drive on top of the viaduct, looking towards the station.

For half an hour, while we explore a smart new development of commuter flats beneath the viaduct, we listen out for trains passing overhead, but none do. We speculate that the line is no longer in use—a victim, perhaps, of the Beeching cuts—yet the arches look sound and well maintained. It's only the following week, when we approach the Old Town from another direction, that we make the connection between the viaduct and the grand entrance to Hatfield House facing the railway station. It turns out that the viaduct only looks like it should carry trains because it was designed by railway engineers: it was actually built to take a carriage drive directly from the station to Hatfield House for the convenience of James Gascoyne-Cecil, the second Marquess of Salisbury.

On this, our second visit, we make our way to where the 1850 section of the Great North Road runs through the Old Town. Here, a gigantic Lord Robert Salisbury, the third Marquess, sits in effigy by the wrought iron gates to Hatfield House, presiding over the railway and the station that were crucial to his parliamentary career. He was Prime Minister three times, and not only had his own train to take him back and forth to London but a private waiting room on the station platform as well.

The entrance to the House is shut, but by great good luck we find the same porter who was on duty at the Palace gate the previous week. When we relate how we mistook the viaduct for a railway structure, she tells us how it came to be built. The Second Marquess made it a condition for allowing the railway to pass through his land that the Direct Northern Rail Road Company should build a new road connecting the House with the station. Since it would have to run across a steep valley a viaduct was the only solution, and despite the crippling costs this would incur, the company had no choice but to agree. The Marquess' second condition was

The Red Lion, Hatfield's other major coaching establishment. Unlike the Salisbury Arms it was not cut off from the flow of traffic along the Great North Road following the realignment of 1850.

much less expensive but no less imperious: that the station platforms be staggered, so the common people could not stare directly across the line at their betters. Like the rest of the grounds, the viaduct is closed to visitors out of season, but the porter opens the gates for us, granting us the privilege of looking down on the town from a vantage point once reserved for the aristocracy.

Eventually, we resume our walk up the Great North Road, and come to the place where a turnpike gate guarded a junction with the old Hertford Road. Here we find the Red Lion: the establishment that became the town's principal stopover following Salisbury and Gaussen's road alterations of 1850. Nine years earlier this Georgian coaching inn witnessed Clare passing its doors, and it is therefore a must for Ellis to photograph. As so often happens when he finds a view impeded, he takes matters into his own hands—in this case by picking up two traffic cones that are spoiling the composition and popping them over a wall and out of sight. I find myself squeezing along a wire fence on the far side of the road—*in* the road, in fact—following him as he hunts for the perfect angle. There's a constant stream of traffic passing us just inches away, and I worry that he or I might get mown down at any moment.

After five heart-stopping minutes he seems satisfied, and we carefully regain the footpath, arriving at a major junction with the A1000. On the far side is what looks like an industrial estate or business park but is in fact a continuation of the Great North Road. When we cross the traffic to join it, we find ourselves at the spot where Clare walked out of Hatfield Town. The plane tree beside us, fourteen paces in girth and twice the height of the apartment block behind it, was just a sapling when he passed it by.

Musings VIII

It was different then. Droves of meat cattle,
sheep and hogs, men with sticks and diligent dogs
and watering ponds on the Great North Road,
where he could kneel and drink from his hand,
calmed by the steady quiversound of hoof-falls.

Busy, busy traders, back then before the railways,
all counted and costed at the turnpike gate:
goods vehicles with six-horse teams, London bound,
heavy with wood, wine, flour, barley and malt
and incoming loads of night soil, rags and hemp.

❧

Sixpence for a drove of sheep to pass the turnpike;
they jostle woolly backs and curly horns
and he remembers Thomson's "fearful people
urged to the giddy brink", and jumping
to the flood to swim until their wool shone white.

These sheep, shorn short, are filthy from the road
and face the butcher's knife; such is their fate
deprived of shepherd's care, like his with all friends lost
and life just an hour glass on the run
to the quicksands round Mary and his home.

He sees flies buzzing on a rat dead in the sun,
spun out with grit and dust from well-greased wheels,
and thinks of Thomson's "ten thousand tribes
of insects, God's creatures, peopling the blaze"
and how the same sun shines on him.

❧

Lions and Lambs

Ellis and I walk to the end of the road, where we find a railway cutting spanned by a narrow steel footbridge. This was built to replace Wrestlers Bridge, a Victorian construction that carried the Great North Road across the East Coast Main Line until its collapse in February 1966. On the far side we find ourselves at another dead-end—more or less a mirror image of the one we have just left—and it's here that we come across the Wrestlers: the venerable seventeenth-century pub that lent its name to the old bridge and the immediate district of Wrestlers Hill. In Clare's day a busy roadside inn, it later became a popular stop-off for motorists coming down the Great North Road. It is now a quiet, picturesque watering hole. We guess its badly dilapidated sign must date from the 1960s, when wrestling was enjoying a revival on TV and the general public were more sanguine about physical violence, as it unashamedly depicts two near-naked men, with one grappling the other in a groin-groping clinch.[15]

The Wrestlers was the first landmark to greet Clare's eyes after he left Hatfield, as in 1841 there was no bridge or cutting here. The railway line—the same one that Hatfield station was built to serve—was constructed during the 1840s and only entered service in 1850. He was reluctant to stop at inns without money in his pocket, so he likely tramped by this one without slackening his pace.

The footbridge spanning the East Coast Main Line and severing the old Great North Road at Hatfield into two quiet cul-de-sacs.

A sign of times past at the Wrestlers Inn on the old Great North Road between Hatfield and Stanborough.

View of the Wrestlers Inn on the old Great North Road, looking back towards Hatfield.

    As we walk on, we come across a row of early-nineteenth-century cottages that Clare must have seen. Built in open countryside, they have since been engulfed by repeated tides of development: an inter-war industrial park of low-built factories and machine shops, a 1950s housing estate, and row upon row of 1960s council maisonettes.

    After a quarter of a mile or so the road ends at a roundabout. This is where the Mount Pleasant toll house used to stand, with its tiny window facing north to give the collector advance warning of travellers.[16] A stone's throw away is the former site of the Olding Engineering Works: a large triangular plot nicknamed 'Caterpillar Island' where in 1938 John Olding, a Mayfair car dealer, set up the American Caterpillar company's first UK franchise. Olding built specially adapted bulldozers for the D-Day landings here, and ran, out of his own pocket, a heavy-machinery training school for the military. The works closed in 1960, and today Caterpillar Island is home to a Tesco superstore.

    It is not going to be easy to track Clare's route beyond this point. In an article for *Hertfordshire Countryside* magazine, Peter Rumley observes that between Hatfield and Welwyn the Great North Road has undergone so many re-routings, improvements and obliterations that it's now "a more fascinating study to follow the deviations than, perhaps, any other section through the country".[17] Here, where the old road ends, is as far as we go on foot. On the other side of the roundabout is a tangle of dual carriageways clustered around Junction 4 of the A1M—no country for pedestrians. We retrace our steps and continue by car to Stanborough Corner, on the way passing Stanborough Park and its lakes: two great stretches of water threaded like beads on the River Lea. Though they are still a haven for wildlife, the rural quietude that used to surround them, like Harper's "tree-shaded hamlet of Stanborough",[18] is long gone.

When Clare took his first trip to London in 1820, the Great North Road between Stanborough and Ayot Green ran through the village of Lemsford, crossing the Lea at Lemsford Mill and passing Brocket Hall on its way to the Brickwall Tollgate. It had steep gradients and was notoriously miry, so that vehicles found the going hard and often broke down altogether. In 1833 the Welwyn and Galley Corner Turnpike Trusts commissioned James McAdam to build a new road. Running to the east of the village, it was in effect the country's first bypass. Though it shortened the route by only 418 yards while costing the enormous sum of £3,200, the Trustees believed their money well spent.[19] They reasoned that a straight, well-built road would prevent traffic from snarling up and thus attract more passenger and haulage companies to their turnpikes. In the event they were proved right: surviving accounts show an increase in tolls from £1,000 in 1834 to £1,880 in 1839. From 1840 onwards, however, there was a sharp decline in takings as customers switched to using rail transport instead.

At Stanborough, Ellis and I briefly stop to look at the Bull Inn (now a Chinese restaurant) which turns out to be a rebuild dating from the 1930s. The Bull that Clare passed, long since demolished, stood in the fork of McAdam's bypass (now the B197) and the old Great North Road. The latter has been renamed Brocket Road, after Brocket Hall, at the edge of whose magnificent grounds stands the village of Lemsford.

The Hall has figured in a recent TV drama series, *Victoria*, as the place where the young queen goes in secret to test Lord Melbourne's love for her while resisting her family's attempts to marry her off to her cousin Albert. The drama's portrayal of her relationship with Melbourne throws a new light for me on lines in Clare's 'Don Juan' dealing with the same subject. Her first child, the princess Victoria, was born in November 1840, nine months after her marriage to Albert, and Clare voices the general speculation of the day when he writes:

> I wish prince Albert on his german journey
> I wish the Whigs were out of office and
> Pickled in law books of some good attorney
> For ways and speeches few can understand
> They'll bless ye when in power—in prison scorn ye
> And make a man rent his own house and land —
> I wish prince Alberts queen was undefiled
> — And every man could get his *wife* with child.[20]

In later years Victoria carved a role for herself as a figure of rectitude and domesticity; a woman so adoring of her husband that she withdrew from public life after his death. But when she arrived in London in 1837 as a beautiful eighteen-year-old, she was inevitably seen as cast in the same mould as her uncles George and William. For twenty years William IV had cohabited with his mistress, the actress Dorothea Jordan, and while leaving no legitimate heirs, was survived by eight of their ten children. His brother George IV, when Prince Regent, was a byword for depravity and excess, featuring in George Cruikshank's political cartoons as a dissolute, boorish womaniser. As Prince of Wales he often came to Brocket Hall to visit his mistress Elizabeth Lamb, wife of Sir Peniston Lamb, first Viscount Melbourne, and mother of Victoria's Whig Prime Minister. She herself had many liaisons, so that, as one commentator decorously put it, the paternity of her children was 'a matter of dispute'.[21]

Designed in 1760 by architect James Paine, Brocket Hall is an imposing pile comprising a four-storeyed central block and two similarly proportioned three-storeyed wings capped by four massive chimneys. Though undeniably impressive, its plain red-brick exterior gives it a somewhat dour appearance that, in Nikolaus Pevsner's words, inspires "more respect than affection".[22] Overlooking an ornamental lake and set in exquisitely landscaped grounds, it was the perfect home for the celebrities of the day. Two prime ministers lived here: the second Viscount Melbourne and the third Viscount Palmerston, as did two great ladies of passion: Elizabeth Melbourne, the Prince Regent's mistress, and Lady Caroline Lamb, whose affair with Lord Byron caused a society scandal.

Lady Caroline's wild behaviour was often calculated to embarrass her devoted but long-suffering husband, the Prime Minister Viscount Melbourne. One story goes that she held a birthday banquet for him at which she arranged to be transported to the table in a large silver dish, and that when the servants lifted the lid she was revealed to the assembled guests completely naked. There are sad stories too. In 1824 she is said to have learned that Byron was dead only when she saw the black carriages and plumed horses bearing his embalmed remains as they passed through Lemsford on the way to his estate in Nottinghamshire. In one version of this tale the shock leads to her falling from her horse, and in another she is driven mad on the spot. Either way, she died four years later.

The previous day, Clare had watched the funeral cortège making its way down Oxford Street, and his observations say much about the way in which Byron, an embarrassment to his peers, was loved by the common people:

> I could see it in their faces [...] they felt by a natural impulse that the mighty was fallen and they mournd in saddened silence   the streets were lind as the procession passd on each side but they were all the commonest and the lowest orders   [...]   the windows and doors had those of the higher [order] about them but they wore smiles on their faces[23]

To the nobility Byron was *persona non grata* even in death. Some sent their carriages empty while others shunned him altogether:

> it lookd like a neglected grandeur the young girl that stood by me had counted the carriages in her mind as they passed and she told me there was 63 or 4 in all   they were of all sorts and sizes and made up a motly show   the gilt ones that lede the procession were empty

Caroline was one of the few aristocrats to shed a tear for Byron, though for many at home and abroad he was a heroic figure. Greece honoured him with a 37-gun salute and three weeks' public mourning. In England his friend John Hobhouse fell into "an agony of grief" on opening the letter that carried the news, and Tennyson remembered "the whole world [seeming] to be in darkness". The Morning Chronicle waxed lyrical: "Thus has perished, in the flower of his age, in the noblest of causes,

Brocket Hall, the home of William, second Viscount Melbourne, who as Clare lewdly hinted in 'Don Juan' was the object of the young Victoria's ardour.

one of the greatest poets England ever produced", while the Morning Herald declared, "The poetical literature of England has lost one of its brightest ornaments, and the age decidedly its finest genius".[24]

During the eighteenth and nineteenth centuries Brocket Hall, like other great estates, was an island of plenty in a sea of want, under siege from a general populace barely existing on subsistence wages. At some stage during this period a wall was built around it to deter poachers, and this subsequently gave the name to the Welwyn Turnpike Trust's southernmost collection point, the Brickwall Tollgate.

We visit the neighbouring village of Lemsford at the invitation of its local studies group. Its indefatigable webmaster, Andy Chapman, has kindly offered to show us around and tell us something of the history of the Great North Road here. Standing in the car park of the Long and Short Arm public house, he shows us where the road ran out of Lemsford to Ayot Green before McAdam built his bypass. All that remains is a track that quickly disappears into a thicket of brambles, but the most striking aspect of the view is the magnificent wall of red brick beside it, which marks the boundary of the Brocket estate. In places over nine feet high, it runs alongside the old road from here to Ayot Green. Andy tells us that as a young man he traced the route on foot, climbing over the wall into Brocket Park whenever the road, long since lost to dense undergrowth, became impassable. Clare saw the wall in its full glory aboard the Stamford Regent on his journeys to and from London in the 1820s, when the tollgate stood close to the Angel Inn at Ayot Green, just where travellers, journeying south, would catch their first sight of it.

The Brocket Estate wall at the start of the old coach road from Lemsford to Ayot Green. Clare passed this way aboard the Stamford Regent during the 1820s.

In the 1830s the Great North Road around Hatfield was one of the busiest stretches of highway anywhere in the world, so it is no coincidence that the two most famous road engineers of the day, Thomas Telford and James McAdam, were working there. Telford was engaged as a consultant by the Galley Corner Turnpike Trust, and McAdam, as well as building the Lemsford bypass, greatly improved the road between Ayot Green and Welwyn. Their methods employed three innovations, the first of which had to do with road surfacing. Traditionally, road builders had heaped large stones on the top of stone foundations. This was costly and often produced poor results, as the stones were inevitably scattered by the passage of vehicles. Instead of a single layer of large stones, Telford and McAdam used two layers of smaller ones. The lower was laid to a depth of eight inches and comprised stones of less than three inches in diameter, while the upper, exactly two inches thick, was formed of stones with a diameter of no more than 0.8 inches. Being much smaller than the four-inch wheels of the vehicles that ran over them, the stones in the upper layer, instead of scattering, bedded down and compacted beneath the vehicles' weight, creating a secure and tractable surface. This method produced such a firm and stable roadbed that stone foundations proved unnecessary, and were eventually dispensed with altogether

The second innovation involved good drainage, achieved by a one-inch camber that caused water to flow into ditches on either side of the road. This solved, at a stroke, what was perhaps the most troublesome aspect of traditionally-built roads—their tendency, as at Hatfield Park, to turn into quagmires after rain. The third—and the most difficult to put into effect—consisted in eliminating steep inclines. While traditional roads took direct routes up and down hills, Telford and McAdam's followed the land where gradients were at their shallowest and, in places where this could not be done, were driven through specially dug cuttings: a technique later adopted to great effect by railway engineers. Grading the roads in this way allowed horses to travel at a steady pace with as little strain as possible. It was for this reason that McAdam re-routed the road from Ayot Green to Welwyn away from its old steep path straight over Digswell Hill, where it was known as the 'Mountain Slow', and along the gentler contours of the eastern hillside.

These techniques were applied to turnpikes across the country, and they made a huge difference to the speed and efficiency of road travel. Gentleman coachman Charles Birch Reynardson had this to say about the modernised Shrewsbury to Holyhead turnpike in the 1820s:

> The road [...] was so good, that unless you went to a stone-heap, I don't think you could have found a stone big enough to pelt a robin with; added to this, it was so beautifully planned that there was not a hill in the whole distance from Shrewsbury to Holyhead that you could not trot up and down, and, as far as my memory serves me, we never had to put on the skid during the whole of the 107 miles from Shrewsbury to Holyhead. The road when it got into Wales ran through some very hilly country, but thanks to the immortal Telford he had overcome all difficulties, and the road throughout was pretty nearly as smooth as one of Mr. Thurston's best billiard tables.[25]

Clare's onward path from Stanborough Corner can be tracked along the B197, which crosses the A1M east of Lemsford and runs parallel to it as far as Ayot Green. The B197 is in fact the remnant of McAdam's bypass, still recognisable as his handiwork, and we take it under Andy's direction to the Waggoners, a pub at the

The old coach road, looking south from Ayot Green back towards Lemsford. The Brocket Estate wall is on the right of the picture, concealed in undergrowth.

The Waggoners at Ayot Green, next to the former site of the Brickwall Tollgate.

The Red Lion on the B197—in Clare's day the stretch of the Great North Road that comprised McAdam's bypass around Lemsford and which later became the A1.

The toll house on McAdam's bypass, which replaced the Brickwall gate.

northern end of the wall where the Brickwall tollgate was situated. A couple of hundred yards further on in the direction of Lemsford, the road the pub is standing on comes to a dead end against a wooden fence. Beyond it, the wall and the vestiges of the coach road continue all the way back to Lemsford. We look around while Andy explains that the present pub dates from 1851. Prior to that, the coach road was served by an inn called the Angel. Lady Palmerston of Brocket Hall had it closed 'on moral grounds'—an act of piety that resulted, ironically, in the licence passing only a few yards along the road to the Waggoners: an establishment over which she had no jurisdiction.

There are large dressed kerb stones peeping out from the unkempt verge, and reflective road studs or "cat's eyes" embedded in the tarmac of the car park spaced in the pattern of a three-lane highway—evidence that prior to the building of the A1M in the early 1970s this cul-de-sac was part of the old A1. It is also where, in former days, McAdam's bypass rejoined the old carriage route at the top of the Mountain Slow, where horses rested after dragging their loads up the hill.

A few hundred yards along the B197 we find the Red Lion, a fine Georgian inn that in Clare's day was known as 'The Shoulder of Lamb', and in whose car park there are more kerbstones and cat's eyes. When McAdam's road was opened, the Brickwall tollgate was moved from beside the Angel to a nearby house. While its proximity to the Shoulder of Lamb made that inn prosperous, such was the general dislike of tolls that in 1877 Benjamin Esterbee, the landlord, set up a barrel of free beer on Ayot Green to celebrate the winding up of the Welwyn Turnpike Trust.

LOVE'S COLD RETURNING

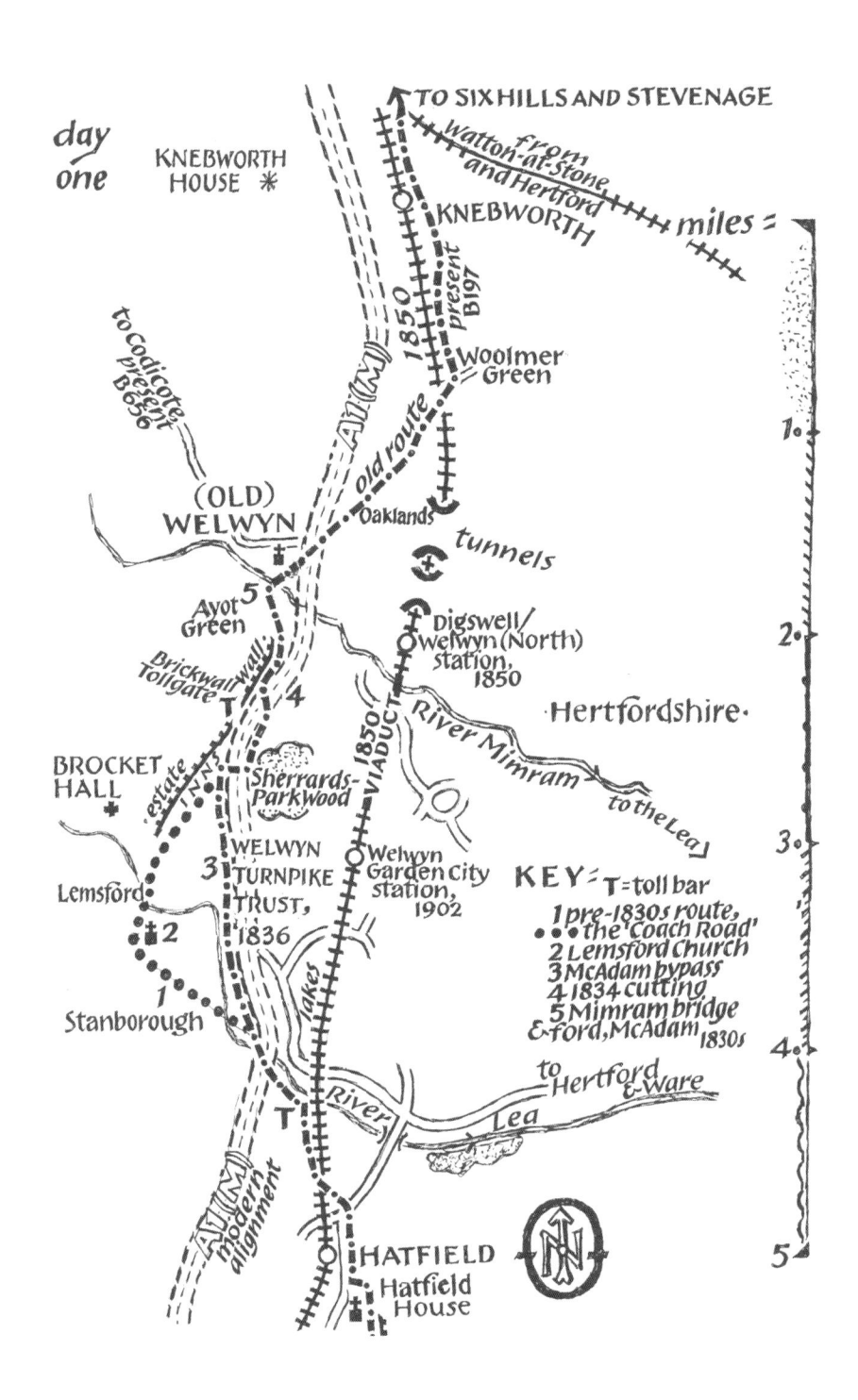

Musings IX

You can't miss the Wellington at Welwyn.
This morning three ladies are drinking red wine
just after nine. Clare will have seen the bustle
of post boys changing horses, and insiders
breakfasting on bacon, haddock and eggs.

He knew Wellington had saved the nation
from Napoleon's threatened invasion;
he may have thought back to his three weeks' training
in Northamptonshire militia and the years
of waiting to be called for active service.

It's not three months since he challenged the world
as champion of the ring, Jack Randall,
short in height but fierce and ready to fight;
proud that he never let that sneering corporal,
long ago, bully him and beat him down.

He has seen an animal trapped, a fox
defending cubs, when he surprised her
searching for a nightingale's nest;
now it is he who rushes past the crowds,
an angry dog ready to growl.

Up the hill from Welwyn, a milestone
dated 1834 displays the distance
on two sides – 25 to London,
6 to Stevenage – numbers painted black
to catch the coachman's speeding eye;

'James Loudon McAdam improved the road'
with stones broken by men with hammers,
angular to bed down firm, small enough
to fit in a workman's mouth, sized to press
smooth under iron carriage tyres.

Faded Fashion in a Rural Backwater

Ellis drives us down McAdam's road into Welwyn Old Town, nestled snugly in the valley of the Mimram. Clare would doubtless have appreciated descending this incline after so much climbing, his progress assisted by the gentle pull of gravity. I picture him passing the White Hart, where horses and coaches stand in a noisy scrum of ostlers, boot boys and smartly liveried guards; among them are the young gentlemen who will ride on the roof, hoping that for a small bribe the driver will allow them a turn with the reins, whip in hand.

For anyone coming down the hill, the White Hart jutting into the road just before it turns into the town is a disconcerting sight. Charles Harper, a keen cyclist, put it like this:

> street and houses face you alarmingly as you descend the steep hillside, wondering (if you cycle) if the sharp corner can safely be rounded, or if you must needs dash through door or window.[26]

Round the bend, the Mimram runs beneath the arches of McAdam's beautiful brick bridge. The old ford beside it no longer functions as a crossing point, as the far side has been built up with a low stone wharf, but in Clare's day it was still used by drivers and drovers alike, and provided a place for carters to soak the wooden wheels of their vehicles to prevent them from drying out and shrinking.

The White Hart, jutting into the road just before it turns into Welwyn High Street.

McAdam's bridge over the Mimram at the south end of the High Street.

From the milestone he has just passed, Clare knows that this is Welwyn Town, once the home of the poet Edward Young. Eliza Emmerson gave him a copy of Young's *Night Thoughts* when he first visited London, and in its lines can be traced a thread that runs through his own work:

> By Nature's law, what may be, may be now;
> There's no prerogative in human hours;
> In human hearts what bolder thought can rise,
> Than man's presumption on tomorrow's dawn?
> Where is tomorrow? In another world. [27]

Clare has often expressed such sentiments: the virtue of being content with one's lot; the futility of pinning one's hopes on future happiness; a submission to the will of God. But at present his resignation, fatalism and piety have deserted him. He is fixed on the morrow, with its promised reunion with Mary Joyce.

The church up ahead is St Mary's, where Young ended his years as vicar. On the other side of the High Street there's a grand coaching inn called 'The Wellington', with a wide central arch leading to a stable yard. It may put Clare in mind of the George at Stamford, where he and Octavius Gilchrist waited in the London parlour to board the Regent. With long wings stretching away on either side of the arch, the Wellington is one of the finest inns he has passed so far. The name perhaps reminds him of his good luck in not being called up to fight, back in the days when a French invasion seemed imminent and Waterloo had yet to be won. Wellington, then the darling of the nation, later became a divisive figure, supporting the butchers of Peterloo and advocating the violent repression of Radical dissent. One

The north end of Welwyn High Street and St Mary's parish church, where Clare turned right into Church Street.

The Wellington Inn, standing opposite St Mary's on the High Street.

notable and vocal critic was Lord Byron, who remarked in his 'Don Juan' how 'Vilainton' had enriched himself by drawing three pensions from the public purse.[28] Though Clare strives to emulate the poet-peer in every other way, he does not share his aristocratic disdain for Arthur Wellesley: quite the reverse in fact. As he passes

The Wellington's sign—an unconsciously ironic comment on its modern clientèle.

the market stalls and the inn, I imagine him chanting, under his breath, his 'Lines on Wellington': "Brittannia cease, For Nelsons doom / From such bewailing cries / Since he has order'd from his tomb / A Wellington to rise".[29] Their rolling metre propels him onward with the jostling traffic as it flows right into Church Street.

Just past the low wall of the graveyard is a fine old house, half-timbered and thatched, which is currently the headquarters of the town's Vestry. Mindful of the beadle standing in the doorway, Clare hurries to climb the hill. About halfway up he reaches a cast-iron milestone with the words "London 25" on one side of its triangular front and "Stevenage 6" on the other, easily visible to coaches travelling in either direction. Ahead, as it breasts the rise, the Great North Road leaves the town behind and enters open countryside once more.

At 8.30 in the morning Ellis and I are standing at the junction of the High Street and Church Street, facing St Mary's as low spring sunshine dazzles our eyes. Behind us the façade of an inn extends a cavalryman's boot that might have been stolen from Wyatt's giant statue of the Iron Duke at Aldershot. The inn's name, 'The Wellington', is painted in Olde Worlde lettering on the high-jettied gable above it, along with a date—A.D. 1352—referring to the time when, long before Waterloo, it was known as 'The Swan'. No longer a coaching stop, it now offers 'Village Pub Dining' to the green-wellied and Chelsea-tractored. Through a plate-glass window we observe a party of immaculately dressed ladies washing down a sumptuous breakfast with giant glasses of Bordeaux. As the dining room is otherwise empty, we surmise the brand new snow-white SUV at the kerb must be theirs.

The billeting returns of 1756 list the Swan as having 12 beds and stabling for 24 horses, making it a major establishment by any standard.[30] When we step into the front parlour to see how today's interior relates to those days we quickly realise there's no point: in 2009 a fire gutted the building, and any surviving historical detail was ripped out in the ensuing renovation. The interior is now a soulless parody of contemporary dining chic. Walls have been knocked through to create one long room, and with its cramped tables crammed together to maximize business, the place feels more like a hard-nosed Parisian brasserie than a cosy English pub restaurant.

Welwyn has the aspect of a rural backwater, yet we are only half a mile from the thundering traffic of the A1M. The town escaped industrialisation by an accident of road building and the opposition of local landowners, who forced the North Eastern Railway to bypass it and cross the Mimram Valley at Digswell Hill. This involved building a one-hundred-foot-tall viaduct: one of the great feats of the railway age. Just over a quarter of a mile long, and comprising forty arches of 30-foot span, it was opened in 1850 by Queen Victoria, who was so frightened by its height that on her way to the ceremony she refused to cross it, completing her journey on terra firma in a horse-drawn carriage. Still in operation today, it not only carries main line expresses out of Kings Cross but also more leisurely local services. The line narrows to two tracks, and it's not uncommon for travellers to and from Cambridge to be told their train is running late because it is "stuck behind a slow train".

THE JOURNEY – HERTFORDSHIRE – FADED FASHION IN A RURAL BACKWATER   147

St Mary's church, at the corner of the High Street and Church Street.

The bottom of Church Street with Old Church House in the foreground—in 1841 the Vestry offices, and doubtless a source of anxiety to Clare as he passed it on his way up the hill and out of town.

During the second half of the nineteenth century industrialisation naturally followed the railways, so in Welwyn's case it took place well to the east of the town. In 1927 further isolation from modernizing influences was assured when a bypass was built. This was a trend that continued post-war; not only did Welwyn Garden City, on the other side of the railway line, take the brunt of Greater London expansion,

Musical instrument shop in Welwyn High Street—a reminder of Clare and the Cremona fiddle given him by James Augustus Hessey.

but in the 1970s the bypass was itself bypassed by the A1M, which came to form a bulwark against development pressure. By 2011 the population of Welwyn Garden City had grown to nearly 47,000, whereas Welwyn Old Town was still a modest settlement of some 8,500 souls surrounded by green belt land.

Welwyn's beginnings can be traced to Roman times, when it comprised two large villas on the road from St Albans to Colchester. In 1937 the remains of the first villa were found close to Lockleys Drive, just off Church Street. Just over twenty years later the second was located by local archaeologist Tony Rook roughly 400 metres to the south, at Dicket Mead. He spent a decade excavating the site, after which it was destroyed to clear a path for the A1M. Only a bathhouse was saved, kept for posterity beneath the road in a steel vault.[31]

Clare would have been fascinated by these finds. He unearthed fragments of Roman pottery in Oxey Wood, and the excavations of his friend Edmund Tyrell Artis inspired his poem 'Antiquity', in which he wrote the following lines:

> Thy Roman fame o'er England still
> swells many a lingering scar,
> where Caesars led, with conquering skill,
> Their legions on to war:
> And camps and stations still abide
> On many a sloping hill;
> Though Time hath done its all to hide,
> —Thy presence guards them still.[32]

In December 1827, when Artis was excavating a Roman villa near Helpston, Clare wrote an account of proceedings for the *Stamford Mercury*. "The result of Mr Artis' researches," he reported, "is a fine tessellated pavement, of superior workmanship and peculiar description, which fully rewarded the labours of that spirited and indefatigable enquirer into the buried remains of ancient grandeur."[33] The article continued with an account of the archaeologist's "novel and important discoveries in the Bedford Purlieus, near Wansford, one of which is an iron foundry of the Romans with the furnace, &c. remaining entire".[34]

On making a circuit of the High Street we encounter, halfway down, a narrow shop front that presents itself as if in a picture frame. The name HILL & COMPANY is written across the fascia in light brown letters on black above two windows of small glass panes and a central door. Clamps, calipers and chisels for violin-making have been set out in the windows, and inside there are instrument cases and a grandfather clock within easy view. From just such a shop as this I picture James Hessey seeking advice for the renovation of Clare's wedding present, a Cremona violin that had been in his family for generations.

Back at the junction of the High Street and Church Street, we return to the churchyard to admire its well-kept gravestones. Whole families rest here: men of substance with their loving or dutiful wives, and their children and grandchildren. St Mary's is where, in 1730, Edward Young became Vicar and lord of Rectory Manor, having moved here to live with his new wife Lady Elizabeth Lee.[35] Her death, along with those of her daughter and son-in-law, provided the inspiration for his long poem, *The Complaint, or Night Thoughts on Life, Death and Immortality*, which appeared in instalments between 1742 and 1745.

Clare had been sent a copy as a congratulatory present when his first book was published. Admired by Samuel Johnson, and named by Goethe as an inspiration for the *Sturm und Drang* movement, it was one of the most frequently published poems of the eighteenth century. Two hundred years later the poet, author and critic Edmund Blunden would relate how it had helped him endure the horrors of the Western Front:

> At every spare moment I read in Young's *Night Thoughts on Life, Death and Immortality,* and I felt the benefit of this grave and intellectual voice, speaking out of a profound eighteenth century calm, often in metaphor which came home to one even in a pillbox.[36]

Another tome he carried about with him was a collection of poetry by Clare, who shared with Young the honour of being so constantly read that both books were eventually lost: Blunden forgot to rescue his volume of Young "when it slipped down behind the bunks" of his dugout, and realized too late that a fellow officer named Kapp had "gone away with my John Clare".

On moving to Welwyn, Young purchased Guessens House, next to St Mary's, and took up residence there. According to one source, knowing that coach companies charged by the mile, he moved the 25th milestone several hundred yards up Codicote Hill to avoid paying a higher fare to London. Such practicality in matters fiscal seems to have been just one facet of an entrepreneurial spirit, because on discovering a spring containing salts of iron in the garden of the old rectory, he set about turning Welwyn into a spa town along the lines of Bath or Cheltenham. To attract visitors, he built Assembly Rooms on Mill Lane opposite the rectory and adjacent to lodgings at the White Horse Inn.[37] The enterprise never quite achieved a life of its own, however. It enjoyed a brief period of success while he was active and in good health, but as he grew older and frailer its popularity waned, and after his death it failed entirely. The Assembly Rooms is now an apartment house, and the grounds where convalescents played bowls by the banks of the Mimram are taken up by allotments.

From Church Street we make our way down Mill Lane. There's a bridge here, and a single duck battling against the river as it rushes between brick walls vivid with moss and trailing plants. The Georgian villa that abuts the bridge is testament to the wealth of the town's miller, who built for himself the appropriately named Mill House—an elegant home complete with fanlit door and well-proportioned windows overlooking the lane. A brick wall, pocked and water-marked in tones of flaking red, runs down the lane from its grand façade to a large gate, supporting a huge swathe of clematis flung over from the garden behind it like a great white shawl. Further along the lane, we imagine coaches drawing up in front of the White Horse Inn, and well-dressed gentry alighting to lodge there while they take the waters in the rectory garden opposite.

Turning onto Mimram Walk, a narrow passage that leads back to the High Street, we find the Ebenezer Strict Baptist Chapel: a brick and stucco building painted the purest white behind a smart wrought iron fence. It was built in 1834

Mill House, a tiny brick-built Georgian villa on Mill Lane, Old Welwyn.

The White Horse, Mill Lane, which provided lodgings for gentlefolk taking the waters at Edward Young's mineral spring.

when a group of Huntingtonians broke away from Welwyn's Baptist congregation. The information board on its wall proclaims "NEXT SERVICE, GOD WILLING, LORD'S DAY". When I search them out on Google, I find that strict and particular Baptists "make a point of avoiding sacred and ritualistic excess [...] and [...] sentimental and emotional immoderation".[38] I picture them walking in sober procession down Mill Lane to immerse a new believer in the Mimram, though given the shallowness of the river there they probably use a tin bath for the job.

In 1824, Clare had considered joining the Primitive Methodists or 'Ranters'. Quoting Young to the effect that "They may live fools but fools they cannot dye", he compared his own "dark, unsettld conscience" with their "earnest though simple extempore prayers" and praised their enthusiasm, which he claimed was so overwhelming that his feelings became "unstrung" in their company. Parson Mossop's Anglican services were so dull by comparison, he said, that he could "scarcely refrain from sleep".[39] A few years later his boredom with the Church turned to outright hostility. In a draft essay of 1828, written at the height of his maturity, his anger at established religion's role in the oppression of the poor sounds uncannily like a premonition of Marx:

> Religion [...] is forced down the throats of the people to teach them patience only to bear unjust burthens the better in the shape of taxes etc. for the sole benefit of luxury and extravagance.[40]

Perhaps the studied self-abasement of Ebenezer's brethren would have mitigated in their favour, though not their fanatical strictness. Clare quickly became disenchanted with the Ranters, and later with Nonconformists generally, finding their faith too narrow and unforgiving, and their doctrine full of 'vulgar errors'.

The milestone on Church Street, Welwyn, that Clare passed as he left the town making for Stevenage. Like others erected by the Welwyn Turnpike Trust, it is made of cast iron and shows the distance to destinations in each direction.

We exit Mill Lane opposite a row of buildings that Clare hurried past as he made his way up Church Street and out of town. Among them is Rose Cottage, famous as the lodgings of Vincent van Gogh's sister, Anna, when she was teaching French and Music at Miss Applegarth's school on the Codicote Road. In 1876 Vincent was living in Ramsgate, and on two or three occasions walked all the way here to visit her—a 100-mile trek that puts Clare's own journey in the context of a time when covering great distances on foot out of financial necessity was not uncommon.

Following Clare up the hill, we come across what must surely be one of the best remaining relics of the Great North Road. It bears a prominent metal plate that announces:

> This cast iron milestone first erected in 1834 when James Loudon McAdam improved the Great North Road for the Welwyn Turnpike Trust was re-erected by WELWYN ARCHAEOLOGICAL SOCIETY a few yards down the hill from its original position in May 1999.

James McAdam's middle name was actually Nicoll; Loudon was the middle name of his father John, the inventor of macadamisation. Ellis remarks that such a slip from a bunch of historians would be inexcusable were they actually commemorating the road builder and not themselves.

I suddenly feel that Clare is very close; he would have paused to examine this stone because he used such markers to measure his progress. In the *Journey* he relates how, on the second day, he "seemed to pass the Milestones very quick in the morning but towards night they seemed to be stretched further asunder".

In 1841 the Great North Road out of Welwyn followed the line of the old Roman road. The country round about was bleak and hilly with only the occasional view across the valley of the Mimram, and the going was hard for horse-drawn vehicles, with a right-angled turn and a steep ascent up Mardley Hill. In the eighteenth century a dense wood enclosed the place where carriages slowed for the climb, making it a notorious spot for highwaymen. James Whitney, one such, is remembered from tales of Whitney's Pightle, a nearby field where he was said to have thrown trussed-up coachmen and passengers after robbing them at gunpoint. Although highway robbery ceased along this stretch of road after the mid-1790s[41] it remained hazardous to negotiate until well into the twentieth century. Only with the opening of the Welwyn bypass in 1927 could travellers avoid the lethal corner, after which it quickly fell out of use.

At the top of the hill lay Woolmer Green, a tiny hamlet that offered few amenities to travellers. It was the last overnight stop for drovers before they arrived in London, so Clare, walking out of it sometime in the early evening, is likely to have met an oncoming tide of exhausted livestock.

Up ahead, the Tudor-Gothic pile of Knebworth House would have stood out in silhouette against the evening sky. Even if he did not know what it was, he would have heard of its incumbent, the writer and statesman Edward Bulwer-Lytton, whose prolific output made him a literary colossus of the day. He was an influence on men with such diverse talents as his close friend Charles Dickens, the American writer Edgar Allan Poe, and the German composer Richard Wagner, whose third opera *Rienzi* was based on one of his novels. In 1841, when Clare plodded past his vast estate, Bulwer-Lytton had yet to reach the heights of a popularity that would last almost as long as the Victorian age itself. Today, however, he is judged unworthy of serious study, and is chiefly remembered—if at all—for the opening line of his novel *Paul Clifford*, which begins, "It was a dark and stormy night".[42] It is no small irony that Clare, on that July evening a forgotten and destitute nine-day-wonder, would come to be ranked among the great English poets, while the internationally lionized Lord would fall, almost entirely by his own merits, into obscurity.

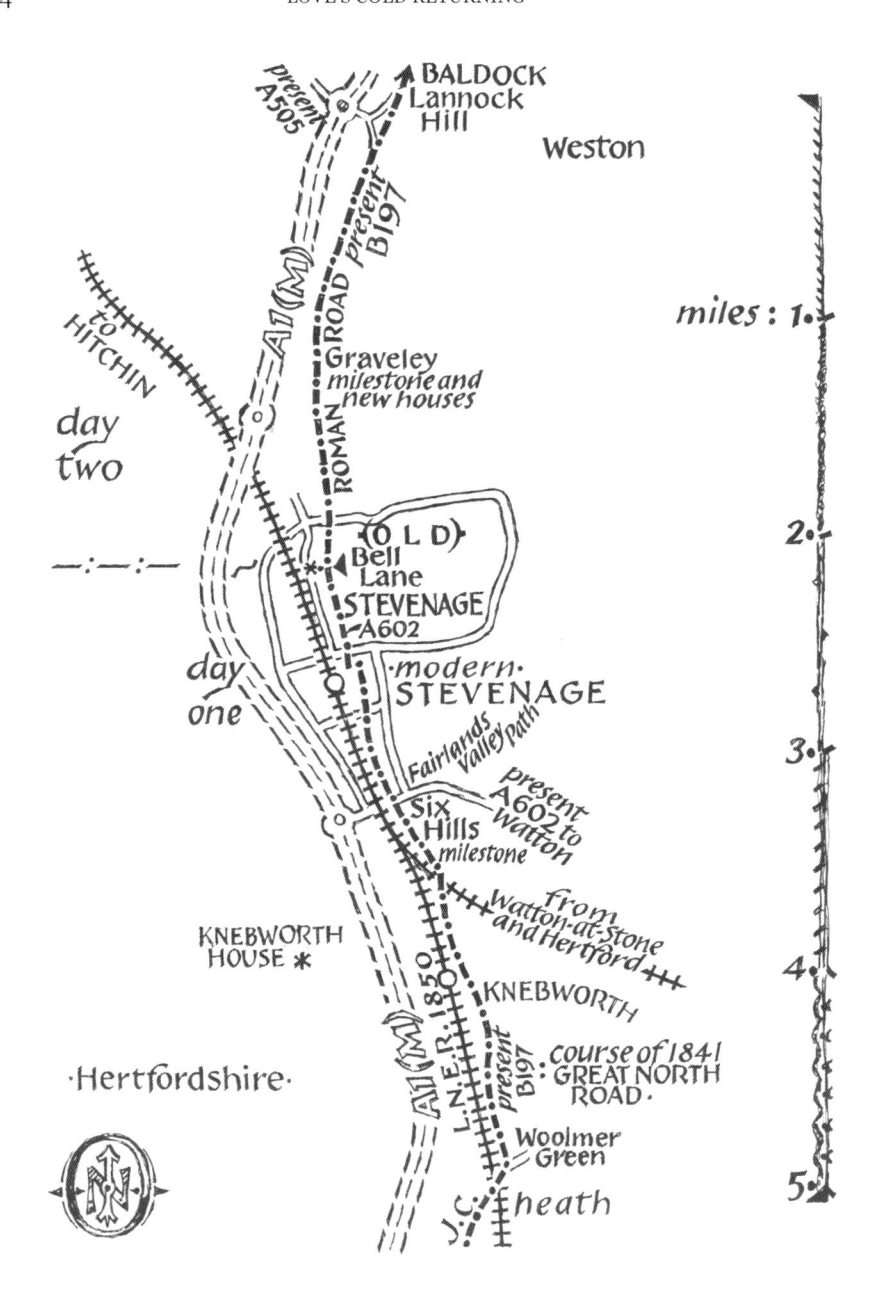

A few hundred yards to the east of Knebworth House, Clare followed another Roman road to the hamlet of Broadwater, whose principal landmark was the Roebuck Inn, where Dick Turpin arranged to meet his wife on the day he fled London for York before in due course being captured and hanged there.[43] For centuries Broadwater had given its name to a Hundred that administered over twenty local parishes.[44] The

The exuberant and slightly deranged façade of Knebworth House, captured in a hand-tinted photo taken around 1890. In 1841 the house was still under construction. Clare would have seen it outlined against the sunset as he made his way between the hamlets of Woolmer Green and Broadwater.

notion of the 'Hundreds'—the old Saxon courts of justice—was very dear to Clare, as it was not only emblematic of the pre-Enclosure idyll but also bound up with Helpston's history and folklore; in his work it appears in the guise of Langley Bush, the ancient blackthorn tree where the Langdyke Hundred met, and of which he writes:

> What truth the story of the swain allows
> That tells of honours which thy young days knew
> Of 'langley court' being kept beneath thy boughs
> I cannot tell—thus much I know is true
> That thou art reverencd.[45]

Enclosure not only brought an end to the court but also to its totem; "by Langley Bush I roam, but the bush hath left its hill", he laments in 'Remembrances', cataloguing the changes that erased the landscape of his childhood.[46]

With dusk approaching, Clare left Broadwater behind him and began to think about finding a place to rest up for the night. The land continued bare and exposed with nowhere to shelter, but as he marched on, a line of tumuli running parallel to the road presently came into view, followed by the beginnings of a town.

Musings X

He's marching in the footsteps of the Romans
past the Six Hills of Stevenage with their ancient tombs
in his legionary's identity,
without rations, carrying his standard:
a golden eagle with outstretched wings.

He'd been here before, on the Regent from Stamford
to London in 1820, buttoned up well
in his working man's coat, bright for adventure,
feeling some stranger soul had jumped into his skin,
ingénu, his publisher's peasant poet.

❦

He measures his progress by milestones
that come slowly when he's tired, quicker
as rhymes pulse in his head, marking time with his legs.
He walks in the hawk's eye, following the great ruts
where wagons churned mud in last week's storm.

Cottages, at the start of the old town,
were likely split in tenements in 1841;
maybe they remind him of home,
coming into Stevenage, fleshy face down,
balding head, shoe leather wearing thin.

❦

Dormer windows stacked along the roofs
of great houses, sleeping slots for chamber maids,
and at the door of the Swan, resplendent
in white breeches and yellow topped boots,
Thomas Cass, landlord, 46 horses always in his stables;

eight post boys, two stable lads and 'the boots'
ready to refresh each post chaise;
with Shires on call at the home farm
and even the blacksmith waiting in the wings;
Cass, courteous and jovial with his friends.

❧

At Pickworth Clare wrote a meditation
on human bones dug up in the lime kiln pit:
rich and poor are mulched in earth to nourish
future multitudes, the living walk on fragments
of the dead – soon, I too will be forgot.

In Stevenage, searching for traces of the road
he walked, we find a double row of trees,
surviving intermittently between
urban office blocks and parking lots,
and on the broken tarmac scuffed white lines.

In this sidelined quiet, birdsong and a plane
from Luton airport overtop the hum of traffic;
a mother toils over the slatted footbridge
with her child in his buggy bulked out against the cold.
We think of Pickworth – he is not forgot.

❧

The Ruins of Utopia

Ellis picks up the thread again...

Though Clare did not know it, the town in which he found himself was Stevenage. Only on the following morning, when speaking to other travellers on the road, would he learn where he had spent the night.

Stevenage is the first location he describes in any detail. The unusual clarity with which he narrates what happens to him there gives us the chance to reconstruct with some confidence the world in which it occurred, and to gauge how well his narrative fits that reconstruction. Yet of all the places he encountered on his journey, Stevenage is the one that has undergone the most change, and where unpicking the nineteenth century from the twenty-first presents a challenge of more than usual scope.

In 1841 it was a town grown fat on the custom that was daily passing through its inns. A traveller with sufficient means could take refreshment at any one of the establishments that catered to the coaching trade, from the Swan, whose clientèle consisted of the wealthy and the titled, to havens for humbler folk such as the Coach and Horses, the Old Castle and the White Lion. And if on that July evening the publicans of Stevenage were feeling content with their lot, it was only because they could not see what was awaiting them in their own future: the arrival, in 1850, of the Great Northern Railway, which almost overnight would sweep away their livelihoods and return their town to rustic obscurity.

Writing ten years after the event, Charles Dickens painted a picture of a ghost town, with the once bustling High Street now "wide for its height, silent for its size, and drowsy in the dullest degree", in which he noted

> the bareness of the little shops, the bareness of the few boards and trestles designed for market purposes in a corner of the street, the bareness of the obsolete Inn and Inn Yard, with the ominous inscription "Excise Office" not yet faded out from the gateway, as indicating the very last thing that poverty could get rid of.[47]

Stevenage made a good recovery even so, assisted ironically enough by the railway, which enabled the town's agricultural produce to reach the London markets in hugely greater volume and encouraged an influx of the well-to-do seeking refuge from the hubbub of the capital. Throughout the remainder of the nineteenth century, and half of the twentieth, it was a comfortable and prosperous place, its fabric largely untouched by two world wars and the depredations of progress. Then, on November 11th 1946, the modern world, as E. M. Forster observed, crashed down upon it "out of the blue sky like a meteorite" when it was chosen to become Britain's first New Town.

The New Towns were conceived, in the tradition of Ebenezer Howard's Garden Cities, as communities where working people could raise their families in safe, pleasant and healthy surroundings far removed from the slum conditions of their forebears. In 1945 London was a city wrecked by war and in desperate need of housing. In response, the Attlee government drew up a plan for relocating 380,000

Londoners to a ring of new settlements beyond the capital's green belt. The small market town of Stevenage, only thirty miles distant and with excellent transport links, was the natural choice to spearhead this colossally ambitious scheme.

Residents resisted what they saw as their town's imminent ruin, and mounted a successful challenge in the courts, halting the plan in its tracks. However—in the sort of reversal familiar to twenty-first-century preservationists—the initial ruling was overturned on appeal. When government minister Lewis Silkin went to Stevenage to meet the protesters in person, he had to be given a police escort, such was the size and mood of the crowd gathered to confront him. He famously told them, "It's no good you jeering. It's going to be done." To make their own point, they had replaced the signs at the station with ones reading 'Silkingrad' in red Cyrillic script. In the decades since, historians and commentators have tended to paint the citizens of Stevenage as Nimbys standing in the way of social progress, yet it's hard not to feel sympathy for them. They were, after all, facing the obliteration of a landscape they had known, lived in, and loved their entire lives. The parallel with Clare and the Enclosures hardly needs labouring. Caught up in an environmental upheaval of equal scope, they must surely have suffered a similar sense of dislocation, alienation and powerlessness.

As with the other New Towns that followed, Stevenage was planned with a view to improving the lot of ordinary people. There would be comfortable homes arranged in neighbourhoods to foster a sense of community; an abundance of green space to promote mental and physical well-being; cycle paths and pedestrianised areas to keep motor traffic at bay, and industrial zones to guarantee full employment. It was judged that along with these material advances would come a revolution in social attitudes: the breakdown of class division; a more equal, more caring society—in

Stevenage New Town circa 1960—a post-war idyll in concrete.

short, a benign and very English form of Socialism. "Stevenage in a short time will become world famous," Silkin promised, "People from all over the world will come to Stevenage to see how we, here in this country, are building for the new way of life."[48]

The new way of life was initially very successful. "The people have had well-paid regular jobs in the factories," wrote one commentator in 1963, "and this has conduced to producing a feeling of contentment. It has enabled them to furnish their homes well, to acquire television, cars, and domestic gadgets, so that many who came as habitual grousers were transformed into contented citizens in a few years."[49] This affluence also meant that workers were "not so much lacking class consciousness as seeming [...] not to need it".[50] It looked as though the attitudinal changes hoped for by the planners were also coming to pass—albeit by the back door of capitalist consumerism. By all accounts, those who first grew up in the town led happy lives. One of them, still resident, recently said of a documentary made there in 1962, "It was so much better back then, clean, excellent public transport, plenty of recreational facilities, plenty of free parking, plenty of work, excellent town centre, happier and less stressed population, lower crime".[51]

Today, however, neglect and deprivation hang about the place like a miasma. The civic buildings have aged badly—some to the point of crumbling—and the once-vibrant shopping precinct is down-at-heel and riddled with empty units. Later structures dating from the architecturally benighted seventies have fared worse; many await demolition, or 'urban regeneration' into blocks of 'stunning' apartments for flush City types. Among such surroundings, the memory of a fully-employed, classless population sounds more than just unlikely. It sounds delusional.

It's a chilly weekday morning in early spring, and Bridget and I are walking by the side of Lytton Way, one of the four-lane racetracks that festoon modern Stevenage. Cars whip by just yards away and container lorries thunder past like freight trains, raising tiny twisters of litter in their wake; just standing upright in the frigid blasts of benzene and diesel is a heroic achievement. We've left our car on an offshoot of the old Great North Road close to the Six Hills Roundabout and are making our way to the Old Town, tracing Clare's route as best we can. To follow him just this short distance we've had to negotiate the roundabout via three subways, and even now we're wide of our mark, because to follow in his exact footsteps would mean risking death beneath the wheels of a speeding juggernaut or company saloon.

In the nineteenth century we would have been treading tussocky grass, with the Great North Road crossing our present course a hundred or so metres ahead. Now, as we walk Lytton Way's footpath-cum-cycle track with the ancient and mysterious Six Hills just behind us, we can find no trace of the old highway; it has been concreted over to build Dan Dare's spaceport in the heart of rural Hertfordshire. The Hills, once thought of as Viking earthworks but now known to be the tombs of Romano-British aristocrats, are today no more than broad, flattened hummocks of grass imprisoned in a web of roads and cycleways. In Clare's day, however, they stood free on bare heathland, sufficiently tall to excite a sense of wonder in passers-by. Coaches stopped there so passengers could marvel while coachmen told them tales of ancient days and supernatural doings.

Charles Harper's 1901 pen-and-ink sketch of the Six Hills, looking south along the Great North Road.

The view from the same spot in 2015. Harper did not exaggerate the height of the tumuli—Victorian photographs show them taller and steeper than they are today.

And as it happens, Clare was there among them, aboard the Stamford Regent on a day in early March 1820. To his intense embarrassment he was travelling first class—inside the vehicle rather than on top—as his friend and sponsor Octavius Gilchrist was sparing no expense for his protégé's first visit to London. While the coach lurched through the flatlands of Lincolnshire and Huntingdonshire, a living diorama of his fellow labourers had rolled past his window. Sitting with the gentlefolk in the cab, watching it reel by, he had felt transformed: "I could fancy that my identity as well as my occupations had changed," he writes in his autobiography, "that I was not the same John Clare, but that some stranger soul had jumped into my skin."[52] On the border of Cambridgeshire and Hertfordshire

A sentimental high-Victorian view of life on the road—Myles Birket Foster's illustration to Clare's 'The Gipsy Lass' in John Law Cherry's Life and Remains of John Clare, *1873.*

the ground began to rise and swell into folds of bare downland. The labourers were gone, and with them the charms of the landscape. "I remember the road around Royston was very dreary;" he remarks, "the white chalk like hills spread all around the cir[c]le, and not a tree was to be seen."[53] A bench and a thorn bush were the only landmarks of note until the coach hove within sight of Stevenage.

At that moment Clare was far too preoccupied with the novelty of the here and now and the tantalising prospects of a glorious literary future to be much interested in antiquity. And though he had felt the seductive touch of the past among the Old Foundations of Pickworth when burning lime there, it would be another two years before he met the Steward of Milton Hall, Edmund Tyrell Artis, a brilliant amateur archaeologist who instilled in him a lifelong interest in its relics. Hence it is no surprise that he showed little inclination to astonishment when the coach drew level with the tumuli. "As we approached nearer London," he writes laconically, "the coachmen pointed out three large round hills close by the roadside and told a superstition about them which I forget."[54]

The 'superstition' was almost certainly the story of how the Devil, to stave off boredom, hurled clods of earth at travellers on the Great North Road, missing six times and creating the hills in the process. In one version, he was so disgusted by his own ineptitude that he threw over his shoulder a seventh clod, which struck and knocked down the spire of Graveley Church. Coachmen had to be tour guides as well as drivers—their livelihoods depended partly on tips—so this tale would have been told, along with other similar stories, on every journey made by the Regent. Regular passengers must have been driven to distraction by the constant repetition, but a sufficient turnover of clientèle yielded a satisfactory haul of coin.

The Six Hills generated income in other ways too. Charles Harper relates how passengers were relieved of their cash by coachmen who would make a wager with "the most innocent looking" that he could not identify which two of the Hills were furthest apart from one another. They are all, in fact, equidistant, but the luckless victim would invariably choose a pair he imagined to be fractionally further apart, "whereupon", Harper writes, "the coachman would triumphantly point out that the first and last were, as a matter of fact, the most widely divided."[55] Clare was almost certainly the most naïve passenger that day, but if he became a victim of this particular trick he does not admit to it.

His brief allusion to the Six Hills—or at any rate to half of them—concludes the account of his first journey to London. When he passed this way 21 years later, travelling in the opposite direction and on foot, he appears not to have registered them at all. In any event, the *Journey* is silent on the subject. Perhaps he was too worried about evading potential pursuers to recognise, or even notice, his surroundings. Maybe he did not see the tumuli in the gathering dark, or if he did, ignored them as being of no relevance.

But if that is the case he was mistaken, for there is a surprising connection between him and these ancient monuments. In 1902 the historian Herbert Tompkins undertook a walking tour which was to form the basis for his book *Highways and Byways in Hertfordshire*. In it, he writes of Stevenage:

> I cannot quite ignore the little town on the Great North Road, so I have wandered out this morning as far as to the Six Hills. There was one who must have often passed this way concerning whom I would gladly learn more; but his doings seem to be little known: Henry Boswell, who, as tradition states, was called the "King of the Gypsies" was born near

these hills of Danish or Satanic origin, and dying at ninety years of age in the year 1780, lies beneath the nave of the little Norman church of Ickleford.[56]

Clare never met Henry Boswell, who died thirteen years before he was born, but his descendants were a presence in his early life. They regularly camped on Emmonsales Heath, and it was there, according to Frederick Martin, that Clare met Henry's son—also called Henry—face to face. "While out on his solitary rambles," Martin writes, "John Clare made the accidental acquaintance of 'King Boswell', which acquaintance, after being kept up by the interchange of many little courtesies and acts of kindness, gradually ripened into a sort of friendship."[57] Martin is not always reliable on details, but Clare tells us, in his autobiographical writings, that about this time he formed a close attachment to the Boswell Crew which lasted well into his twenties: one that not only coloured his poetical sensibilities, but also cemented the bond he already felt with the marginalised and dispossessed. On more than one occasion he was tempted to join them, but a fear of the privations of winter and a dislike of gypsy food kept him from doing so. If not for a youthful fastidiousness, then, he might well have followed the example of his lime-burner friend James Mobbs and taken up the wandering life.

Whatever ground Clare was treading on the night of 20th July 1841 is long gone, scraped away by giant earth movers during the expansion of Stevenage. Almost a hundred and eighty years on, the fields and orchards that lined the southern approaches are not even a distant memory. We have in their place—what exactly? A New Town? The road signs would have us believe so, but it is hard to recognise anything urban about our surroundings: there are no shops, no pubs, no houses, no people. By the look of the low-rise superstores and factory outlets around us, Stevenage in the twenty-first century has abandoned its Utopian aspirations and settled instead for becoming a giant retail park.

We are standing at the place, marked by a row of lichen-encrusted bollards, where Lytton Way slices through the line of the Great North Road. Beyond this point, the course of the old highway runs ruler-straight all the way to the Old Town. Although it has been segmented into scruffy lots for car parking, a surprising amount of its surface survives; tarmac that seventy years ago bore motor cars with running boards and lorries with cargo secured by rope and tarpaulin. Beneath this crumbling layer lies a second, older roadbed that in its turn carried wagons and livestock, and latterly the stagecoaches that became the town's economic mainstay. And lower still, deep down in the soil, the stone pavement of the Romano-British.

We turn onto the old road, the soles of our shoes scraping its weathered, potholed surface. Behind us the thunder of traffic dwindles to a whisper, and we experience the onset of an unexpected calm—the sort of stillness you find in marginal urban spaces where neglect and disuse have prompted the countryside to re-invade. Here, though, the complete reverse has happened: a thin sliver of countryside has endured against the encroachment of a town. Mature trees—some a century old—flank the road for a hundred metres, interrupted solely by the boxy bulk of the Stevenage Leisure Centre, and ending only where the road itself breaks off, amputated

The old Great North Road, looking from Lytton Way towards Stevenage Old Town.

and cauterised by Swingate, a two-lane ribbon of tarmac leading to the New Town's heart. I reach for my phone to check our position, but even with the scale zoomed up to maximum the map shows us treading empty space. This remnant of the Great North Road has been purged from our collective digital memory; we are walking down a corridor of lost time.

Automotive refugees from the station car park, some half canted on the scruffy verges, sit nose to tail by the roadside, waiting for London commuters to reclaim them. By evening they will have dispersed to their own suburban habitats, leaving this unkempt corner of the town to assume a more rural character; if not of a country lane exactly—the year is not advanced enough for that—then at least of a place where beleaguered wildlife can breathe a little easier. In a couple of months, leaves on the hedges and trees and weeds by the roadside will provide enough cover to suggest how it used to look before the New Town engulfed it.

The sense of rural tranquillity does not last long. Just ahead of us looms the rear elevation of the Stevenage Arts and Leisure Centre: a building that resembles the bastard offspring of a retail distribution hub and a nuclear power plant, its white windowless walls seeming to hint at sinister processes going on within. If today this blandness makes it something of a low-grade eyesore, imagine what its visual impact must have been when it opened in 1975, covered, unbelievably, in Day-Glo-Orange plastic panels. But then this area always had its share of oddities. The ground on which the Leisure Centre stands was previously occupied by 'Our Mutual Friend', a public house built in honour of the friendship between Charles Dickens and Edward Bulwer-Lytton. Both men felt a genuine concern for less successful authors that

The rear elevation of Stevenage Arts and Leisure Centre on the old Great North Road, looking north in Clare's direction of travel towards the Old Town.

Photograph circa 1950 taken from the same spot as above, with the Our Mutual Friend public house on the left. The contemporary character of the Great North Road is well captured by the heavy goods vehicles travelling in each direction.

prompted them to found a charity whose resplendently Gothic headquarters they built just a few yards down the road. 'The Guild of Literature and Art', as they called their venture, was intended to provide impoverished writers with an annual stipend. Clare's origins would have disqualified him, though, as Dickens' contemptuous remarks on reading Frederick Martin's biography make clear:

> You read that life of Clare? Did you ever see such preposterous exaggeration of small claims? [...] So another Incompetent used to write to the Literary Fund when I was on the committee: 'This leaves the poet at his divine mission in a corner of a single room. The Poet's father is wiping his spectacles. The Poet's mother is weaving.' — Yah![58]

For Dickens, impoverishment seems to have been a condition contractable only by the middle classes, the poor being immune by virtue of their poverty. The scheme came far too late for Clare anyhow. Conceived in 1850, it did not reach fruition until fifteen years later. With unconscious irony, Lytton raised funds for it by writing and performing a play he called 'Not So Bad As We Seem'.

Lytton also built the Guild Hall, along with a row of almshouses for 'distressed' authors, on land belonging to his estate. While the Hall itself was a testament to his good intentions, the almshouses were—to put it mildly—a monumental blunder. The literary establishment, sensing high-handed condescension, took umbrage and refused to play along, one of their number memorably stating that he was damned if he was going to be 'buried alive in Stevenage'. There was resistance, too, from the wider establishment, which saw literature as an unfit object of charity; not to be "confounded in the regard of a sympathetic public with the crowd of benevolent institutions whose purview ranges from the widows of decayed Officers down to inflamed eyes and broken legs".[59] The Guild received only a handful of applicants during the thirty-odd years of its existence, and as for the almshouses, they never housed a single tenant. The whole enterprise was wound up, and the site sold off, in 1897. In 1961 the Hall and the almshouses were flattened during the expansion of the New Town.

At Swingate the western margin of the road vanishes. We exit the corridor of trees and find ourselves facing a car park under open skies. To our right there's an office block in the best seventies Brutalist tradition—all bare concrete and recessed windows—in front of which a few ivy-smothered tree trunks, the remnants of the avenue's eastern side, march on for another twenty metres, bordering a modern footpath that continues the line of the old road. To the cyclists weaving around us and the pedestrians weighed down with shopping from the supermarket up ahead, this is just a quiet byway far from the town's traffic. I find it sad that many—if not most—will never know that for hundreds of years it was one of the busiest, most important highways in the country.

Past the supermarket the path ends, and once again we're forcibly reminded that Clare's landscape is not our own. For while he is walking among fields and orchards, we are on a tarmac prairie crammed with parked cars. On it, too, there's one end of the Fairlands Way footbridge—a steel and concrete structure that joins the new town with the old, in the process leaping a four-lane artery that could happily feature in a remake of *Deathrace 2000*. Climbing its triple-decker ramp is a laborious business, and once we're there its head-high railings create the oddly claustrophobic sense of being on a prison gantry. They appear to be a later addition—presumably for deterring would-be suicides from jumping and hooligans from dropping bricks on the road below. By contrast, the bridge's simple lines speak eloquently of a time when such dark and violent acts were unimaginable in this, the Best of All Possible Towns.

The Hall of the Guild of Literature and Art, photographed in 1961 shortly before its demolition. It was situated on the eastern side of the Great North Road diagonally opposite the Our Mutual Friend public house, which was pulled down at the same time.

Standing at the mid-point, I take out the 1836 OS map. "See," I say to Bridget, pointing to where the road runs through nothing but fields, "This is where we are." It seems a far-fetched proposition. There's not a single point of reference, no landmark we can identify that agrees with the plan in front of us, save for the trees that show where the Great North Road used to run. From Clare's perspective we must be hovering, unsupported, high above the dusty highway: an inquorate conclave of baffled angels.

We fold up the map and continue down to a tiny concrete plaza. Unlikely though it may seem now, this once-pleasant little square was meant as a place for happy citizens to gather and meet—a picnic spot, even. We imagine families seated on tartan rugs, eating fish-paste sandwiches and excitedly watching the expressway below: "Look Dad, it's the future!" Now, though, the flower beds are unkempt and the shrubberies overgrown. Weeds sprout through cracks between paving slabs, many of which have been prized up and smashed to pieces. From here at least we can get a better view of the bridge, though trying to appreciate its naïvely optimistic styling amongst all this neglect quickly proves depressing, and we move on. There is nothing quaint, or picturesque, about the ruins of Utopia.

The plaza is, in any event, the only trace of the New Town on this side of the bridge. Clare's world begins to reconverge with ours as we start down Ditchmore Lane—an instantly recognisable section of the Great North Road. Its eastern side borders the grounds of the town's cricket and hockey clubs, and for this reason, most likely, the trees that grew beside the old highway are still standing. So too is a long-time companion of theirs, a solitary telegraph pole, which lists slightly to one side like a drunk. We've seen its like before, in Charles Harper's vivid little pen and ink drawings, but there they are upright, ramrod-straight and full of purpose, as yet untouched by the decades of desuetude that will rob them of their utility and self-respect.

The houses of Ditchmore Lane are expansive affairs: imposing Victorian and Edwardian villas, once the homes of the well-to-do but now in multiple occupation. Nearby builders' hoardings announce the imminent completion of new flats, or—to put it in the wildly upbeat patois of the property developer—*Exclusive, Superbly Appointed 1- and 2-Bedroom Luxury Apartments*. Pitched at professionals looking for an easy commute to London, these will change hands for fifteen times the average national salary: proof of the old adage that in matters of property, location is everything. And without doubt this is a prime area—verdant, tranquil and reassuringly old-world. Looking around, it's clear that the bridge behind us spans more than just a dual carriageway. The economic chasm of Fairlands Way runs deep and wide: a reminder, if one were needed, that the social trends of Clare's own time are repeating themselves in our own. When he laments the passing of a pre-Enclosure England in which farmers "made as equals not as slaves the poor", and where "master son & serving man & clown" could sit down together and eat at the same table, he is prefiguring a very modern regret. Herbert Tompkins, in his own Edwardian way, was just as nostalgic, commenting that Stevenage in the eighteenth century was "such [a town] as is dear to the hearts of Englishmen—a town where all sorts and conditions of men lived almost within a few yards of one another".[60]

The concrete plaza at the north end of Fairlands Way footbridge.

Ditchmore Lane, looking north towards Stevenage Old Town. The trees and telegraph pole are relics of the time when this cul-de-sac was part of the Great North Road.

South End, Stevenage Old Town, with the on-ramp to the gyratory system on the left and the pedestrian underpass on the right.

The view east over the High Street from Trinity Road to Sish Lane, with the Methodist Church on the left and the old pond on the right. Clare would have walked into this picture from the right and exited left. Photograph circa 1900.

That town lies just ahead of us, where Ditchmore Lane runs into the High Street. On our left, Gates Way gives access to the southbound lane of Lytton Way, but we ignore the break it makes in the street and keep our eyes fixed straight ahead, trying to gain an impression of the town's southern approaches as Clare might have experienced them.

In vain, as it turns out.

Our attempt is foiled by the Old Town Gyratory System, which sounds a lot more fun than it actually is, being a sort of ring road that goes through the town as well as around it. Popping up at odd places, it manifests here as a low concrete hillock decked out with steel railings. Until 1976, anyone standing at this spot would have been able to see down the High Street as far as Middle Row. Today, where Trinity Road and Sish Lane once formed a crossroads with the High Street, we find the view blocked by this elevated interchange. To our left, a vehicle on-ramp partly hides a row of cottages, and on our right a sunken underpass channels pedestrians and cyclists beneath the roadway via long, shallow-graded approaches.

Introducing a slice of seventies futurism into the Old Town's South End naturally did nothing to enhance the area's visual appeal, but its presence over the years has been more subtly deleterious in providing a focus for rampant overdevelopment, with three corners of the former crossroads being occupied by modern office blocks and apartment complexes. The fourth, thankfully, is relatively untouched and still dominated by the commanding bulk of Stevenage's Methodist Church, a rock of ages outwardly unchanged since its construction in 1876.

Musings XI

Twenty-one coaches passing through each day
with mail bags locked to the guard's brass rail.
At the White Hart, the Leeds Union
allowed two minutes for changing teams,
the grand prix pit stop of the 1840s.

We've had to get here early to see this road
without parked cars; then as now 36 paces across,
maids hurrying close to the walls,
Clare slogging at the end of his first day
too tired to mark their beauty with a wink.

❦

Tiny slippages of square ceramic tiles
have jostled this roof, over two hundred years,
into a puzzle of slip and overlap,
where today bright green cushions of moss
spawn tiny leaflet stems trembling in the rain.

This back lane's spine of cross-cut stones
may once have been a drain; did he walk here,
determined, through a press of boots and smocks
and wicker baskets, taking brief relief
from the coaches on the Great North Road?

❦

When the Lincoln Tallyho passed the Six Hills
the guard resounded his famous bugle call
and the coachman pulled the exhausted horses
close to the archway of the White Lion yard;
tired passengers climbed down, awry, on stiffened legs.

This mounting block squats on the corner
of Shepherd's Walk, under a board of bye-laws
and market day fees. Easy to imagine him
slipping past young men in riding boots,
looking for a quiet place to slink to sleep.

❧

There's no trace today of the shed where he slept
on a 6ft square-cut truss of clover.
He crossed a green field, staggering wide
of a pond for fear of falling in,
and clambered high to a safe place to lie.

A night of dreams, fingers pulling laces,
grappling with buttons, foraging their snuff-boxes
for honey. He's back in London paying
for a woman and turns in his sleep,
stretching his flesh – a man in his prime.

The woman lies by him, slim, firm and young,
and he entwines her in his arms and smells her hair
and fondles her soft breast: it is Mary,
his first wife, and he wakes to the sound of her name,
but no one is near – and she is gone.

❧

A Puzzle with a Missing Piece

Waiting for us in front of the Methodist Church is artist and architectural historian Jon Harris, who has generously agreed to be the cartographer and all-round guru for our project. His knowledge of buildings and landscapes is second to none, and Hertfordshire has been a stamping ground of his for decades. He puts away his sketching materials and together we take stock of our surroundings. Other than a few cottages dating from the seventeenth century and a late Regency red-brick house, there is little that Clare would be able to identify except perhaps for the Chequers pub, and even that has had a severe makeover. North of the junction, however, the High Street is much more recognisable as the thoroughfare down which he tramped in search of shelter.

Just where the underpass ends there's a pub sign with a picture that looks as if it's been torn from the pages of 'The Pickwick Papers'—a coach and four running at full pelt. The establishment it's advertising, the Coach and Horses, is now just another pub among many, but for over a century it was an important staging post for hauliers ferrying goods to and from London. In 1841 it had stabling for 25 horses, a blacksmith's forge, a wheelwright's workshop, and a pond for watering livestock. Sadly, the forge and workshop were demolished in the late 1920s, and the pond was drained in 1861 to make way for the flinty-faced edifice of Holy Trinity Church.

"I bet Clare would have had a good chuckle at this," says Harris as we view the grand old inn now bracketed by two stern temples to sobriety and temperance. "Just imagine the confrontations the topers must have had with the churchgoers—Established to the left of 'em, Nonconformists to the right. They'd have been outnumbered, of course, but if it came to a dust-up there were reinforcements to call on from the Marquis of Lorne over there, and the George and Dragon up the street." The Marquis of Lorne was a bakery when Clare passed it, he adds, but by the 1860s had become a popular beer house. The George and Dragon, on the other hand, had been in Stevenage "practically since the Ark."

On drawing level with the Coach and Horses, Clare was faced with a tollgate run by the Stevenage and Biggleswade Turnpike Trust. Like the one at Potters Bar, this often caused delays, giving drovers time to water their livestock and travellers the chance to down a pint or two. On Saturdays the local craftswomen peddled their wares at a weekly straw-plait market, which drew in customers from all over the district and caused even more congestion. On the evening Clare slipped through the wicket gate there would have been scant evidence of the market, or of traffic jams, save perhaps for tracts of churned-up mud where cattle had milled about, and solitary wisps of straw. In the calm of twilight he probably looked on the gate, the inn and the ponds of South End with equanimity, but its other feature, the town lockup, must surely have given him a stab or two of unease, spurring him on to seek a hiding place for the night.

Today the site of the tollgate is taken up by the junction with Letchmore Road, which marks the start of the town's High Street proper. Here, the east side is almost all early nineteenth century, while the west side offers a more varied aspect,

View north from the underpass showing Stevenage Methodist Church, and the Coach and Horses and Holy Trinity Church further along the High Street.

Looking back at the site of the tollgate and the straw-plait market, now taken up by the gyratory system interchange. The town's lockup was also situated here.

with buildings from the Regency standing next to Georgian houses and inns dating from a hundred years earlier. Barring a couple of ill-judged modern infills, the architectural outline of the town into which Clare walked is more or less intact. Remove the plastic fascias from the shop fronts, tow away the parked cars, spread a generous layer of sand on the road, and you will have a fair approximation of what he saw.

The façade of the former White Hart Inn, rebuilt following the fire of 1829.

The east side's uniformity is largely due to rebuilding that followed two disastrous fires. The first swept through the north-eastern half of the High Street and part of Middle Row in July 1807. The resulting devastation was so great that the London papers reported it in detail:

> A terrible fire broke out at Stevenage on Friday the 10th inst about noon...and burnt with such fury that by eight in the evening, when it was only got under by pulling down three cottages, it had totally destroyed 84 dwelling houses, a number of barns and outhouses, 12 large ricks of hay, a quantity of corn and malt, household furniture, clothes, tools, several fat hogs and a great deal of poultry, leaving upwards of 30 families totally destitute of habitations, food and even raiment except what they had on their backs.[61]

In 1829, the south-eastern half of the street suffered a similar fate, with the loss of ten more buildings and the White Hart Inn.

We wander on, passing the Marquis of Lorne and a couple of Italian eateries before entering territory that Clare would have recognised as townscape. A Chinese restaurant occupies the premises which in his day was the Dew Drop Inn, a spit-and-sawdust drinking den that would have been very much to his taste. With its carriageway and red tile roof, it conveys the sense of a rich former life, as do most of the properties from here to Drapers Way, among them the seventeenth-century Red Lion Inn and the town's oldest surviving shop—once a saddlery, now a picture framer's—instantly identifiable by the flight of steps leading up to its raised front door.

While these buildings are rich in history, the ones opposite present a different aspect. Many date from after the fire of 1829, with brick walls, slate roofs and staring windows that prefigure the terraces of the late Industrial Revolution. One notable exception is the rebuilt White Hart Inn. With a black-and-white façade suggestive of timber framing and a heraldic relief of its antlered namesake, it was designed to look much older than it actually is. Almost two centuries on, it has acquired some of the age to which it was aspiring when Clare walked past it, though in one important respect it is bang-up-to-date, having gone out of business and reopened as an Indian restaurant.

As Clare walked into town, in his own words "knocked up" from the day's 25-mile hike, the vista on his right would therefore have been of relatively new buildings, some less than twelve years old, plain and somewhat regimented. To his left, on the side of the street untouched by the fires, the frontages must have presented a more inviting prospect, with gates and alleys leading to stables, farmyards and outhouses. We can imagine him assessing the likelihood of finding a hiding place for the night, and making in that direction. As the third coaching stop from London after Barnet and Welwyn, Stevenage would have been busy well into the night, with plenty of folk around to take an interest in him were they so minded. This far from High Beach he probably felt safe from being collared as an asylum fugitive, but any lone stranger without visible means of support was risking a night behind bars. He badly need a bolt hole. Exactly where he found it is unclear, however. He writes:

The Red Lion Inn, Stevenage High Street, in a photograph dating from around 1870. The view through the open carriageway shows an outbuilding similar to the one in which Clare found refuge on the first night of his journey.

> I reached Stevenage where being Night I got over a gate crossed over the corner of a green paddock where seeing a pond or hollow in the corner I forced to stay off a respectable distance to keep from falling into it for my legs were nearly knocked up and began to stagger I scaled some old rotten paleings into the yard and then had higher pailings to clamber over to get into the shed or hovel

Paddocks and sheds were numerous in Victorian Stevenage, so on first inspection the tithe map of 1835 that we've brought with us gives little away. The map is a record of boundaries, fields, outbuildings and watering places—precisely the kinds of features that might help us identify the property he slept in. Change came slowly during the first half of the nineteenth century, so we can be reasonably sure that it was still accurate when he came looking for shelter six years later.

"I don't know where to begin with this," I admit, baffled by the profusion of detail. We have made the Red Lion our base of operations, and are studying the map over a pint, in the hope that some liquid refreshment will bootstrap our brains.

"A good starting point might be to establish the sequence of events as Clare describes them." Harris suggests, "He says it's night when he gets to Stevenage. What does that imply?"

"That his scope for finding shelter is limited to what he can see—close to, or just off the street." replies Bridget.

"Right," I say, "plus he's exhausted and in a hurry to disappear from view, so it's reasonable to assume that once he's through the tollgate he keeps walking straight, looking for the first chance to get off the street."

Harris nods. "So, the next question is, which properties on the High Street have ponds, paddocks and outhouses?"

We stare down at the map. It's like doing a jigsaw puzzle, but with a missing piece that could fit any number of ways. There's no identifiable candidate on the east side of the street: Church Lane runs closely parallel to its southern end, leaving no room for open spaces behind dwellings, and while there are paddocks, ponds and outhouses at its northern extremity, they lie in configurations too dissimilar to the one Clare describes.

The west side is much more promising, almost entirely given over to farmhouses backed by paddocks and yards. Most of them have outbuildings too, but only three, lying close together about halfway along, also feature a pond.

"It's most likely one of those," I say eventually, pointing them out. Harris numbers them with a pencil. "Let's call this W1, that one W2, and the last W3. What can we say about them?"

"For a start," replies Bridget, "The bottom one's no good. The pond's at the back of the paddock. Clare would have stumbled across the outbuildings first."

"That's number one out, then."

"The one above looks better." I say, "It's got a paddock and a yard next to each other."

"Just so," Harris replies, "but Clare found himself in a paddock *before* he climbed into the yard. Coming into this property from the street would entail meeting the yard first, so that doesn't fit either. Besides, if I'm not mistaken it's the White Lion—not exactly the sort of place to find a quiet hidey-hole."

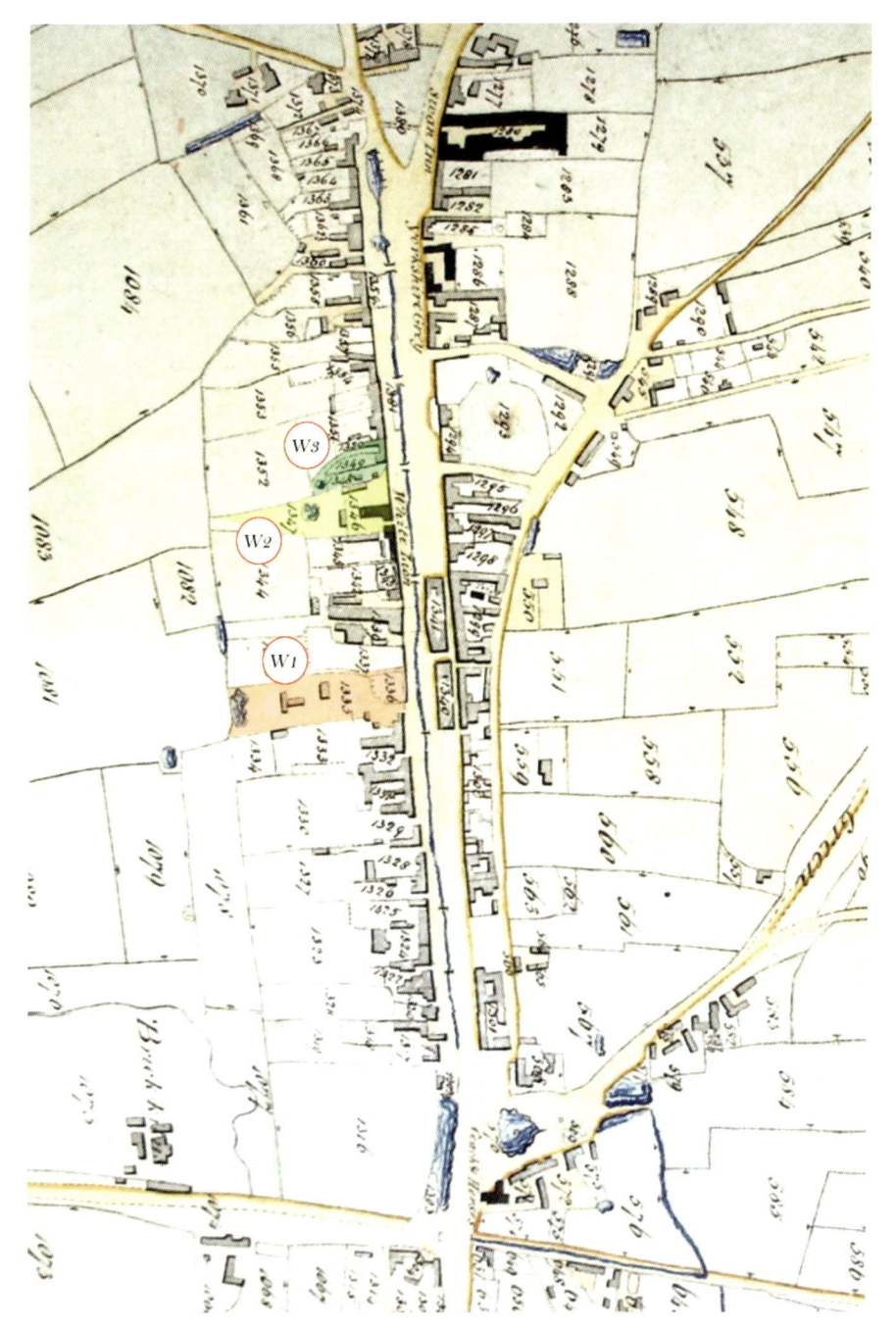

THE JOURNEY – HERTFORDSHIRE – A PUZZLE WITH A MISSING PIECE

The 1835 tithe map for Stevenage marked with three possible locations for Clare's overnight lodging on the west side of the High Street. By a process of elimination W3, shaded in green, appears to be the most likely property.

The Red Lion in 2015, with its carriage gates closed for the night. Clare may well have had to scale similar ones in order to reach the yard and shed in which he slept on the first night of his journey

When we ask why, Harris explains that the White Lion was one of the town's chief coaching inns, and an overnight stop for livestock. "What with coaches arriving and departing at all hours and the drovers watching over their beasts, the chances of him keeping a low profile would have been well-nigh zero."

"That leaves us with number three, right next door," he continues, "and this one seems to fit the bill rather better."

The map shows the carriageway of a farmhouse leading to a green area with a pond. Whether or not this area is large enough to be called a 'paddock' is debatable, but it's bounded by two other plots, one of which is a yard with an outbuilding about the size of a garden shed. So, given that Clare climbed over a fence from a place with a pond to a place with a shed, this property has all the right features in the right sequence.

"It also makes sense of his remark about having to steer clear of the pond," I point out. "The body of water looks tiny, but it's large enough in relation to the paddock to make falling in a real possibility. And his alternative description of it as a hollow also suggests a small size. You could easily imagine it evaporating in summer to leave a muddy depression in the ground."

"What about the gate, though?" Bridget asks "Where does that fit in?"

"Carriageways were generally gated," Harris replies, standing up and draining his glass, "and as I recall, this place has one. Shall we take a look?"

Out on the street, we study the Red Lion's coach entrance, which is currently blocked by a pair of black and very solid wooden gates that look like they were here in Clare's era. They're about six feet high with a couple of foots' worth of clearance at the top.

"Clare was short." I say, "About five foot. Do you really think he'd be able to climb something like those?"

"His arms were strong from doing field work at Allen's," Bridget says, "I'm sure if he could grasp the top of the gates, he'd have been able to haul himself over."

"If he did, he walked a fair distance to find them. I'm surprised he didn't try for somewhere closer to the tollgate."

"He might not have been able to," Harris observes, "given that life in a coaching town didn't stop at sunset."

As I think about this, I picture Clare slinking past groups of men drinking and smoking in the lamplit doorways of beer shops; dodging servants and tradesmen going about their business, always on the lookout for a deserted alley down which to duck. Given the crowding of pubs and inns at South End, it makes sense for him not to have stopped until he was past the White Lion, where commercial activity was diverted down the parallel thoroughfare of Middle Row, leaving the High Street to farms and residences.

"We should check out the farmhouse," Harris says, "and see what it can tell us." And as this turns out to be at the corner of Bell Lane, on the other side of the Market Place, he suggests we take a little detour through Middle Row on the way.

In 1841, Middle Row was a broad alley that offered pedestrians a refuge from the twin perils of wheeled conveyances and livestock on the march. Apart from the wares in the shops and a certain amount of inevitable gentrification, not much about it has changed: now, as then, it is mostly lined with seventeenth-century red-brick cottages, "so consistently so", remarked Nikolaus Pevsner in 1953, "that one may well feel reminded of Holland".[62] There are a few more substantial buildings scattered here and there, the largest and tallest of which—a three storey mansard-roofed affair on the corner of Baker Street—might have caught Clare's attention had he ventured this way, as it was a pub known as 'The Baker's Arms'. Today, it's a long-established Oxfam bookshop.

The far end of the alley opens onto the Market Place, close to a building that in Clare's day was a coaching inn called the Old Castle. Though unusual enough in having no carriageway—meaning horses had to be led through the parlour to be changed—it was more famous for accommodating the coffin of its first landlord, Henry Trigg, in the rafters of an adjacent barn.

Trigg was a wealthy grocer who in 1774 astutely saw that coaching was going to be the Next Big Thing and turned his house into a staging post. The story goes that late one night, coming home from an evening carousing with friends, he witnessed a party of Resurrectionists disinterring a body in the graveyard of St Nicholas's Church. Fearing a similar fate might befall him, he drew up a will stipulating that upon his death his coffin should not be laid in the churchyard, but placed instead "to the west end of my Hovel, to be decently laid there upon a floor erected by my executor on the purlin for the purpose".[63] Since this was the strict condition of a large bequest, his beneficiaries did not put up much of an objection. And if for their part the Old Castle's landlords ever harboured doubts about keeping a corpse on their premises, they never acted on them. Henry quickly became the town's chief tourist attraction, drawing in thousands of punters throughout the nineteenth century and well into the twentieth—until 1929, in fact, when the inn gave up its licence. The Old Castle (whose name is a total mystery, since there never was a castle in Stevenage) then became a branch of the Westminster Bank. The new owners arranged for Trigg's remains to be removed, but by all accounts there were precious few, as over the years visitors had pilfered most of his bones as mementoes. And while a coffin sits in the rafters to this day, it is rumoured to be a replica, the original having been stolen by souvenir hunters during the 1970s. His ingenious plan for thwarting grave robbers therefore turned out to be somewhat self-defeating: a victim of its own success.

The White Lion—now the Mulberry Tree—in the Market Place, close to where Clare most likely found his bed for the night.

Middle Row, looking north from the High Street end.

The corner of Bell Lane, redeveloped since Clare's time. The core of the building in the foreground remains, and behind it the small paddock and yard where he most likely found refuge for the night.

In 1841 the Market Place was still used for cattle trading, and the paddock belonging to the White Lion regularly filled up with livestock. From 1793—the year of Clare's birth—to 1814, it also served as a stopover for captured French combatants on their way to the prisoner-of-war camp at Norman Cross. Had he been aware of this, Clare might well have felt the stirrings of a fellow feeling he'd already expressed in verse,[64] and drawn some parallels between their situation and his own.

Crossing the Market Place, we arrive at Bell Lane. The two premises on the north corner are eighteenth century, and though they share a frontage belonging to the Cinnabar café, look almost unaltered. Unfortunately, the same cannot be said of the property next door—the farmhouse we suspect Clare broke into. Its southern half has been refaced with red brick and converted into retail premises—currently occupied by Boots the Chemist—while the carriageway arch has been demolished along with the rest of it. A three-storey red-brick edifice called Elmes Arcade occupies the vacated space, testifying to a redevelopment of the site that took place in the 1930s. This is a real blow, considering how well many of the properties in the street have been preserved, but when I get out my phone to check the satellite view I discover that against all odds the paddock is still there; a triangle of lush green hemmed in by roofs of tile and concrete. So too is the carriage entrance, in the form of a boarded-up gap between the buildings.

"Any chance of getting in?" Harris asks.

"From here? Not without a sledgehammer." I study the phone again. "But it looks like there's a gate off the loading area round the back."

The gate turns out to be padlocked, and after drawing suspicious looks from passers-by while we take turns to peek through it, we slink off back to the High Street. When I go into Boots to ask if we can take a look out the back of the shop, I receive a basilisk stare and a blank refusal. "Only staff are permitted," says the lady pharmacist icily.

"I'm not sure what we expected to find anyway," Bridget says, as we make off before the constabulary can arrive. "Nothing could have survived."

"Graffiti, maybe?" suggests Harris, "You know the kind of thing: 'JC loves MJ' in a heart with an arrow through it."

We laugh, a little ruefully. As it happens, Clare left his initials carved into the arch of a bridge at Lolham, so the idea is not that far-fetched.

"Surely it's not so much the *finding*," I say, "as the *being*; occupying the same space. The headmistress of my prep school used to visit Antioch every year to walk in the footsteps of St Paul. Aren't we doing the same kind of thing?"

"Ah," says Harris, nodding, "*Thanne longen folk to goon on pilgrimages, and palmeres for to seken straunge strondes.*"

"Stevenage isn't *that* strange," Bridget says, then looks doubtful as a man with a Mohican passes us walking his miniature poodle. It has streaks of pink and green in its coat, and a spiked collar.

We've reached the Bowling Green, and the end of the High Street. Before the Town Hall was built, this was the location for civic gatherings. Nowadays it's chiefly a dog-walking facility. The Gyratory System makes another appearance here, channelling traffic through a series of junctions and mini-roundabouts that lasso the Green in a noose of unidirectional dual carriageway. No such triumph of urban planning would be complete without a pedestrian underpass, of course, and here it is. Modest, almost bashful, in comparison with its counterpart at South End, it could easily be overlooked by strangers trying to reach the northernmost part of town.

Elmes Arcade, the the 1930s shopping parade built next to the site where Clare spent his first night on the road. To the left of it is the boarded-up alley where the carriageway stood down which he sought shelter.

The shops behind it, Harris tells us, date from the middle ages, though they've been so altered down the centuries they're no longer recognisable as such. Victorian brick and modern plate glass have conspired to disguise timber-framed structures that in Chaucer's day were the first substantial homes in Stevenage.

A few steps further on there's an imposing red-brick building with a tell-tale arch in its frontage. Now an apartment block, this was once the Swan: the town's largest and most exclusive hostelry. As the posting house it was patronised by the upper echelons of society who habitually travelled by post chaise—a form of transport so costly that the chance of having to mix with the lower orders was virtually nil. Charles Harper writes that the postmaster of Clare's day, Thomas Cass, "kept post-horses only, and his customers ranged from princes and dukes down to baronets and wealthy knights".[65] Rather appropriately, he was a superior sort of host who conversed with his guests in Latin, composed verses in Greek, and quoted the classics at every opportunity. The last of a line of innkeepers dating back to the sixteenth century, he cannily shut up shop in 1850—just as the railways arrived to steal his trade—and sold off the premises, which were duly converted into a school.

We are now at the northernmost limits of the town as it was when Clare passed through, so after briefly viewing the Old Maltings, with its half-timbered upper storey, we slowly make our way across the Bowling Green and back down the High Street, stopping one last time outside the property in which he most likely took shelter. We think of him waking up there on the morning of July 21st 1841 in the

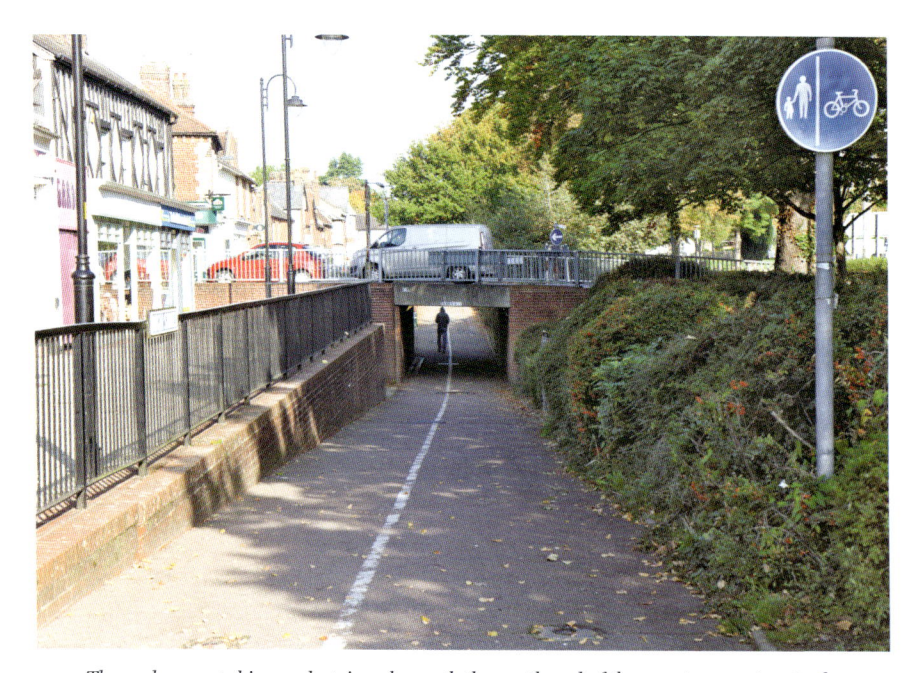

The underpass taking pedestrians beneath the north end of the gyratory system to the Bowling Green. Despite appearances, the buildings here are among the town's oldest.

The Swan, Stevenage's posting house, now an apartment block.

light of an early dawn, having taken his last proper rest before reaching home, some sixty hard and painful miles down the road.

"When I awoke," writes Clare, "Daylight was looking in on every side and fearing my garrison might be taken by storm and myself be made prisoner I left my lodging by the way I got in." He had spent the night stretched out on some bales of clover "piled up about 6 or more feet square", soundly asleep and dreaming of Mary. The dreams were not easy: "I thought that my first wife lay on my left arm," he recalls, "and somebody took her away from my side which made me wake up rather unhappy." As he woke, he heard a disembodied voice speak her name.

We imagine him clambering over the gate and dropping deftly into the street in the grey dawn light. Stevenage is at its quietest, the populace still sleeping. The mild damp air is fragrant with scents of the town, loud with the chattering of waking birds. Perhaps a cock crows in one of the yards and is answered from the far distance by a rival. Maybe, in the paddock of the White Lion, a heifer lows quietly. Clare knows which way to go because he lay down to sleep with his head pointing north. So he passes the shuttered houses and inns to find himself at the Bowling Green, where the road forks in two. Here he pauses, pushing back his hat as he decides which route to follow. There is no fingerpost to help him, but the rutted track that passes by the Swan clearly shows where the Great North Road runs into the countryside. He pats his pockets for his pipe and lucifers, shrugs once to settle his knapsack on his back, and trailing blue tobacco smoke strides confidently out into the wide morning.

Musings XII

He has slept with his head to the north,
pointing the way. Now in case of capture
he hurries on his troops, and learns from vagabonds
like him, man and boy coiled together asleep
under the bank, that the next town is Baldock.

He's free, a full day's march away from the women
who tore their clothes to rouse him
to forbidden lust; away from fear
of booted and belted keepers, hypocrites
who had the women locked away for their own play.

❧

He has a practised walking habit,
bikes hardly known in his day. Soldier-like,
with swinging gait and kitbag on his back,
he looks neither to left nor right.
A quarter hour from one milestone to another.

Today at the Granby, the 32-mile stone stands waist high
on a mown grass verge. We crouch, exploring
where morning sun guides our fingers into lichen-crusted cuts.
Moved in wartime to hide its message from invaders,
it's restored to where it was, more or less here, for Clare.

At Graveley, 33 miles to London,
the squat stone's roughened by lichen
like silver fractal etchings. He walked here
when these houses were new-built, dropping to the pond
past drovers herding geese and sheep to drink.

At the George and Dragon Inn, did he remember
his friend Rip's painting – 'The Stage Coach Breakfast' –
showing him as a young man at the wall clock,
anxious to board on time, and Dorothy Wordsworth
pouring tea for Charles Lamb and her brother?

❧

Clare sees lime-burners, reminders of himself,
as he walks the road twenty years on.
Breaking the stone, and stacking it layered
with well-packed coal, is work for young men
surplus to village needs once the land's enclosed.

First, a day priming the kiln; then three of flame
tended close to keep constant the flow of air;
two days to cool; and one to unpack and sift
and sort and shovel the quicklime on carts.
Today, hiding shy in a gentle Rutland hill,

obscured behind a 'Keep Out - Private' sign,
the Pickworth kiln is decked about
with buddleia and oak, blackthorn flowers
and long meadow grass.   Clare and his mate
uncovered human bones digging this pit.

On the road he remembers himself at twenty-four,
walking to Tickencote to slake lime dust
with beer, aching from labour and wet with sweat;
and how, setting eyes on Patty, he climbed a tree
to celebrate her beauty and seal his destiny.

The 32nd milestone, which still stands close to the public house that Clare would have known as 'The Marquess of Granby' and is now called simply 'The Granby'.

Notes Scribbled under a Dry Hedge

Though Clare started his second day's march on an empty stomach he was in good spirits, grateful to have found a decent shelter for the night. As he left Stevenage he thanked God "for his kindness in procuring it", because, "any thing in a famine is better then nothing and any place that giveth the weary rest is a blessing". The ability of Providence to deliver was a recurrent theme of his, especially in the early poems, and while to modern readers it can come across as a touch sententious—just like his lapse into a liturgical register with the phrase 'giveth the weary rest'—there is little doubt it was wholeheartedly meant. When he was feeling buoyant, as on this fine summer morning, his contentment with his meagre lot and conviction that 'the Lord would provide' were undeniably genuine.

Not far from the town, just beyond the 32nd milestone, he passed an inn called 'The Marquess of Granby'. It was not a coaching establishment *per se* but had grown in tandem with the coaching trade from small beginnings as a roadside alehouse. In 1756 Robert Thurgood, a Baldock brewer, took out a mortgage on the property at the same time as the Stevenage and Biggleswade Turnpike Trust was setting up a tollgate more or less next door. Such was the business resulting that Thurgood was able to pay off the mortgage within a few short years. The inn was renamed at about this time—probably by Thurgood—in honour of John Manners, the Marquess of Granby, who was then the Member of Parliament for Cambridgeshire. He was also a colonel in the Royal Regiment of Horse Guards, and popular with his men, many of whom he set up as innkeepers on their retirement.

Negotiating the tollgate, Clare was now on the turnpike to Baldock. He had no idea where he had stayed the night, nor where his next destination lay. The gypsy's map had long ceased to be of any use and he was now travelling by dead reckoning. The fact that he'd turned himself into a compass by sleeping with his head pointing north shows how few resources he had for navigating by, the sun being his only constant guide. That morning the weather continued wet and overcast, however, and he was on the only available road which was, just now, crossing sparsely wooded heathland.

It was still early when he came across two travellers taking their overnight rest: "on the left hand side the road under the bank like a cave I saw a Man and boy coiled up asleep," he writes, "which I hailed and they woke up to tell me the name of the next village." The name they gave him was Baldock. He had already passed through Graveley, with its two large inns, nestling below the steep rise of Jack's Hill.

Today Graveley has been bypassed by the A1M, but its history as a stop on the Great North Road is commemorated by its village sign, which features a stage coach at full gallop. The inns that witnessed Clare marching by are still here, standing side by side and remarkably untouched by time: the red-brick George and Dragon, with its grand Regency door case and fine sash windows—the very image of a golden age coaching establishment—and its humbler neighbour, the seventeenth-century white-stuccoed Waggon and Horses. If their names are anything to go by they had very different clientèles, with coachmen and passengers taking their meals in the former, while waggoners and drovers huddled in the latter over mugs of pearl and beer.

The Census of 1841 lists 350 residents in the village, a large number of whom were engaged in roadside provisioning. Like those of many isolated settlements along the Great North Road, Graveley's fortunes were closely bound to this artery, whose travellers acted as blood cells bringing it the oxygen of trade.

Clare's description of Graveley comes after his account of meeting the man and boy, but in all likelihood the episodes were reversed. The *Journey* is not a strictly linear narrative. As a case in point, Clare mentions Graveley while relating events that will take place in Potton on the evening of the same day, the reason being that he has just found, in the middle of the act of writing, a note he made on the road. He says:

> On searching my pockets after the above was written [i.e. his account of Potton] I found part of a newspaper vide 'The Morning Chronicle' on which the following fragments were pencilled soon after I got the information from labourers going to work or travellers journeying along to better their condition as I was hopeing to do mine...
>
> 1st Day – Tuesday – Started at Enfield and slept at Stevenage on some clover trusses – cold lodging
>
> Wednesday – Jacks Hill is passed already consisting of a beer shop and some houses on the hill appearing newly built – the last Mile stone 35 Miles from London   got through Baldeck and sat under a dry hedge and had a rest in lieu of breakfast [66]

Clare's account is so fascinating precisely because of moments like these, when we not only read his recollections but can witness him in the act of putting them down on paper. This passage (which he probably intended to insert in correct chronological order but never did) is particularly informative. It tells us that the weather was bad, that he walked as far as Baldock in the first part of the morning, and that the road was busy with itinerant workers. Most interestingly of all, it reveals that he did not know precisely where he was; the 'information' he gleaned from the other road users concerned local place names—'Stevenage' and 'Jacks Hill'.

He scribbled the note somewhere between the 35th and 36th milestone, while going over Jack's Hill: the mention of Baldock suggests the final sentence was added later. The village he calls 'Jacks Hill' has to be Graveley; in his day there was nothing on the hill itself apart from a windmill, and in any case Graveley, standing at the foot of the rise, was the only settlement between Stevenage and Baldock.

Today there is a pub-restaurant a short distance from where the mill used to stand. Called 'The Highwayman', it post-dates Clare by over a century, having grown out of a transport café that thrived on long-distance motor haulage before the A1M reduced this stretch of road to a byway.[67] Its name, and the name for the spot, relate to the same individual, a figure of folklore known as Jack O' Legs.

The George and Dragon and the Waggon and Horses, two former coaching inns side by side on the old Great North Road at Graveley between Stevenage and Baldock.

According to legend Jack O' Legs was a giant who lived close to the village of Weston during the early Middle Ages. The story goes that following a bad harvest the bakers of Baldock raised their prices disproportionately. Incensed by their greed, Jack ambushed them on the road and distributed their flour to the poor. The bakers took their revenge by capturing and blinding him before putting him to death. As a last request, he asked to be pointed in the direction of Weston so that he could shoot an arrow to show where they should bury him. They handed him a huge bow that no-one had ever managed to draw, and with it he shot an arrow three miles into the churchyard of Holy Trinity Church.[68] As Herbert Tompkins relates, in the manner of a rustic storyteller, "when they had slain the giant, like good men and true they remembered their word and digged the grave full twelve feet long at the spot where the arrow had fallen."[69]

The tale was widely known as far back as 1521, when it was mentioned by John Skelton in his delightfully titled polemic against Cardinal Wolsey, *Speak Parrot*, and was later recorded in full by the eighteenth-century antiquary Nathanael Salmon in a book on the history of Hertfordshire. Its roots lie somewhere in the period between the founding of Baldock in the twelfth century and Skelton's own time—more likely earlier than later, as executing a felon without recourse to trial, known as *Infangthief*, was permitted under feudal law. Comparisons with Robin Hood are inevitable, but in Jack's case there is evidence that he really existed. Like those of Henry Trigg in Stevenage, his remains provided a source of income for locals. Visitors came to view his grave, which was marked by two stones in the churchyard placed 14 feet apart, and generations of Parish Clerks made beer money by bringing

LOVE'S COLD RETURNING

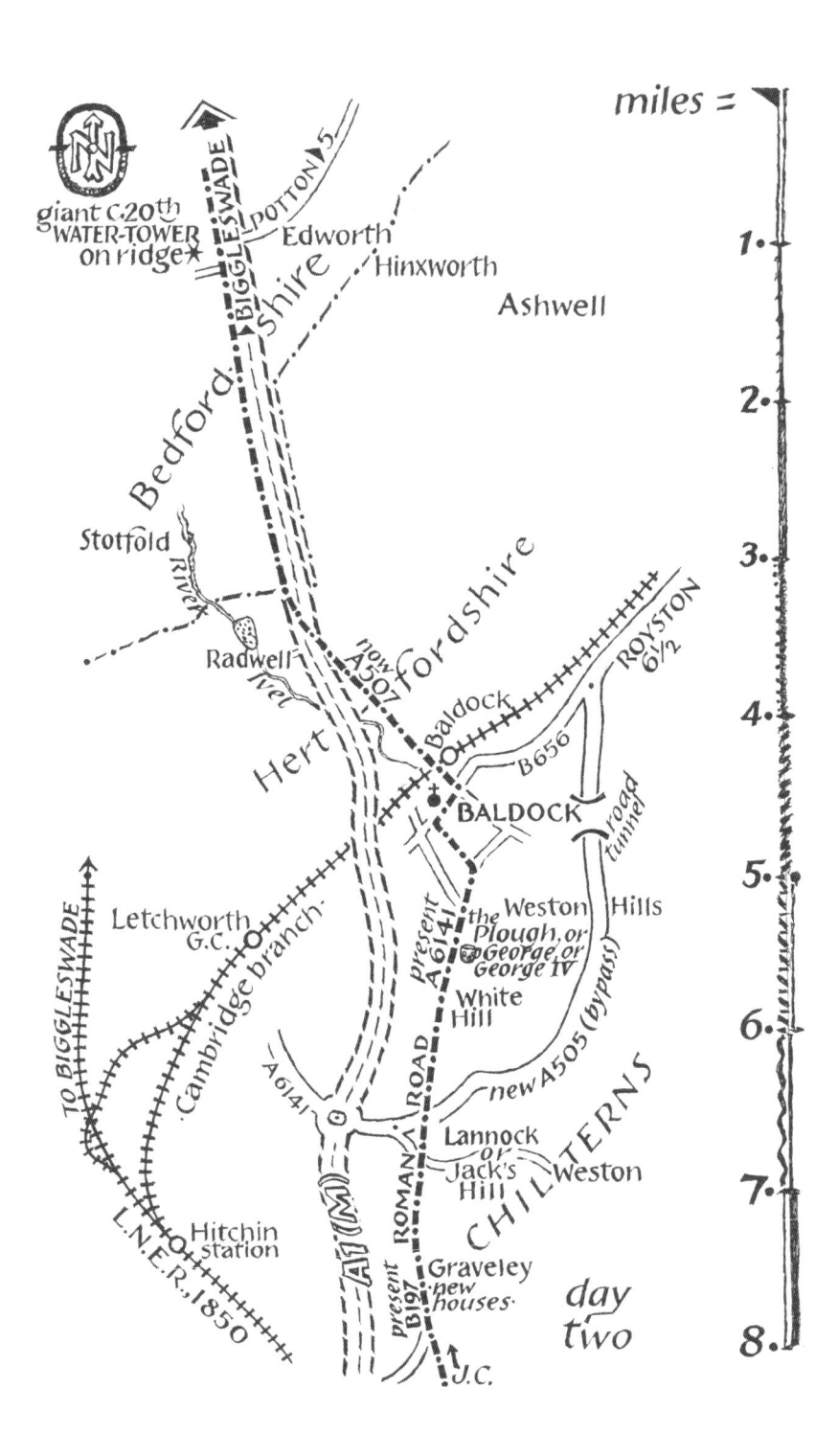

out, for a small consideration, what was claimed to be his thigh bone. The antiquary John Tradescant the Elder, who was Gardener at Hatfield House from 1609 to 1614, bought the relic to add to his 'Closet of Rarities', which eventually formed the nucleus of Oxford University's Ashmolean Museum.[70] Clare almost certainly knew the legend, if only because he would have heard it aboard the coaches he took to and from London during the 1820s, and it may even have been this familiarity that made him seize on the name 'Jack's Hill' for Graveley.

As so much else in his account, the portrayal of the village—"a beer shop and some houses on the hill appearing newly built"—is frustratingly incomplete. The houses are the only ones between Stevenage and Baldock dating from the 1830s or 40s, and they still stand on the slope that descends to the village from the south (and not, as Clare appears to imply, on Jack's Hill rising away to the north). But of the beer shop there is no sign. There are records of a pub called 'The Windmill' that began trading sometime around 1840—a date that fits well with the new houses—so this may be the establishment he is referring to.[71]

The other watering hole he mentions on this section of road is a pub he calls 'The Plough' which, as things turned out, was to be the scene of an event that would colour the rest of his journey. Shortly after speaking to the man and the boy, he had another encounter. "Somewhere on the London side the 'Plough' public house," he reports, "a man passed me on horseback in a Slop frock and said 'here's another of the broken down haymakers' and threw me a penny to get half a pint of beer which I picked up and thanked him for." Quite clearly a day and a night on the road had taken their toll on him, and the rider—by his garb no man of means himself—had

Clare's "newly built" houses at Graveley, one of which may have been the public house known as 'The Windmill'.

Elmwood Park gatekeeper's lodge, now a private residence. The manor house it served was destroyed by fire in 1916, and the parkland was subsequently levelled to make way for a photographic processing plant.

donated his ale money to a stranger who looked more in need of it. Clare retold the incident in the letter he sent to Allen on returning home: "I had travelled from Essex to Northamptonshire without ever eating or drinking all the way," he wrote, not entirely truthfully, "save one pennyworth of beer which was given me by a farm servant near an odd house called the plough."[72]

By 'odd' Clare meant solitary or isolated, and the Ordnance Survey map of 1836 shows an inn fitting his description at the 36th milestone, on the side of White Hill where the road descends into Baldock. But if this is the establishment he is referring to, its name was not the Plough but the George.[73] He continues: "when I got to the plough I called for a half pint and drank it and got a rest and escaped a very heavy shower in the bargain by having shelter till it was over." It may have occurred to him then and there, while he was enjoying more warmth and comfort than he'd experienced since leaving Lippitt's Hill Lodge, that the benevolence of strangers could be relied upon. If so, he was soon disabused of the notion. "Afterwards," he writes, "I would have begged a penny of two drovers who were very saucey so I begged no more of any body met who I would."

Even though Graveley lay well behind him by the time he'd reached the 'Plough', at this point in the narrative he describes the village in terms very similar to those in the scribbled note: "I passed three or four good built houses on a hill and a public house on the road side in the hollow below them." This muddled timeline is consistent with his account of the rest of the day, which reads as an impressionistic blur. He recalls how the milestones seemed to be increasingly far apart the further on

The Cock, standing opposite the former gatekeeper's lodge—Clare passed by its door as he made his way along Baldock High Street.

he toiled, and remembers going through a 'village'—most probably Baldock—though not its name. He calls to mind, most vividly of all, sitting on a dry patch of ground beneath some trees and wishing for breakfast. The lack of incident, the accumulating tiredness of limb and mind, and the gnawing hunger have all merged into a single half-memory. Only at Potton, where he interacts with people once again, will his recollections snap back into focus.

But those encounters are still some twelve hours away. Now, smarting from the drovers' scorn, he continues down the hill and into Baldock. At the southern end of the High Street he passes the grounds of a large house which, though marked on the 1836 map as 'Place House', has by now become known as 'The Elms' or 'Elmwood Park', a red-brick Regency manor house set in grounds that contain—amongst other things—a walled garden, a formal Italian garden, hothouses, a croquet lawn and 50 acres of parkland.[74]

Opposite the gatekeeper's lodge on the High Street stands a fine terrace of cottages and an inn called 'The Cock', while a little way further on, where the street broadens out, a long marketplace is dominated on one side by the White Lion Inn and its maltings, and on the other by a large brewery. It is around nine o'clock on a Wednesday morning in late July, and Clare, happily, has arrived in a town devoted entirely to the manufacture of beer.

Musings XIII

"How great are my expectations!" Clare wrote
in a letter, two years before he went to London.
But even then he feared being just a farthing
rush light, soon to be forgotten. Like Dickens' Pip
his coach ride was a rite of passage.

He said he lost his sense of self, lolling
on cushions, sheltered from rain and sun,
watching men of his kind digging ditches
and ploughing the fields. He rolled into London
on a ribbon of lamps tapering into stars.

As he tramped the road in 1841,
up against pounding hooves and grinding wheels
covered in dust, did he remember
the promise and thrill of that first trip,
sweeing along the road on reeling springs?

how he rushed from the coach to hear Madame Vestris
sing his song at Covent Garden ... and missed it;
next day to Taylor's, his advocate,
pernickety editor and friend, to savour
heady writers' talk and his first cup of wine.

Evenings with his brothers in the muses
from the *London Magazine* – playing at punning
extempore, Coleridge hunched in his chair;
off to see Keane strut the boards at Drury Lane
and test the lights and pleasuring of Vauxhall.

He jokes that peasant poets are stray cattle
in the field, but they dress him in a fine green coat
and yellow silk cravat, to have his portrait painted.
The oil's an excellent likeness, though he prefers
the watercolour copy Hilton gave him.

The swell of the Chilterns behind him,
he drops to Baldock, past shire horses
heaving sweet, dark barley to the breweries;
still today, houses are set on raised pavements
where the turnpike trust eased the road's gradient.

There's a small, square window on the second floor
of the White Lion Inn, where a boy is set
to watch for the coach from London clattering
faster-than-intended down the hill;
a man goes purposefully past, white with dust.

Clare liked watching crows. This morning there are six.
They fly-jump across neat rows of Georgian pots,
strutting and ducking on the chimney stacks,
tail feathers jerking to balance each hop.
Down here in the street we watch in the wet.

Boom Town

As he walked up the Market Place, Clare, the keen amateur antiquarian, may have thought about the Romano-British settlement buried beneath the twelfth-century foundations of the town, which the Knights Templar founded and christened 'Baldac' after the Norman-French name for Baghdad. Like their more peaceable brethren who founded Stevenage, these warrior monks looked on their creation as a purely financial proposition—a means of raising tithes for their military campaigns in the Holy Land. Today, Baldock is a far cry from those feudal beginnings; a handsome town, rather, with Georgian houses standing prominent and proud among its whitewashed cottages and half-timbered inns. A clue to the wealth behind this elegant ostentation can be found in the High Street which, as Herbert Tompkins remarked, is "unusually wide"—wider, in fact, "than any in the county except St. Peters Street, St. Albans, or High Street, Berkhamstead".[75] It accommodated the medieval markets and fairs that brought merchants from as far afield as Brabant in the Low Countries, and in Clare's day provided room for horse-drawn traffic to pass and turn into the town's inns and breweries. Writing in 1902, Tompkins described it as "a fine street, shaded on either side by elm and lime", and—with the exception of the elms, sadly lost to disease in the 1970s—it is a picture that still holds true today. Having escaped the worst excesses of twentieth-century redevelopment, it is one of the few places on Clare's itinerary to have preserved the general aspect of his time.

Baldock was a major stop for coaches running between London and the towns of Stamford, York, Boston, Leeds and Hull—coaches with colourful names like 'The Regent', 'The Rockingham', 'The Perseverance' and 'The High Flyer'. All halted either at Peterborough or Stamford, and at least one carried Clare back and forth on his youthful visits to the capital.[76]

Baldock High Street, looking north. In medieval times this unusually wide thoroughfare hosted fairs that drew merchants from all over the country and northern Europe.

As befitted a coaching stop, Baldock had a large collection of inns. Most were relatively recent in origin, with only two dating from the Middle Ages. In those days north-south traffic passed along Ermine Street some miles to the east, and Baldock saw few outsiders apart from the merchants attending its markets and fairs. This situation changed in Tudor times with the rapid growth of London, which led to more westerly routes in and out of the capital being sought and used. By 1622 the road through Baldock was being described as:

> A Great Road [...] the higheway for the great part of the Northe parts of this Realme of England towards the Cittie of London by the contynuall drifts and droves of Catell driven towards the said cittie for the serving thereof and by means of the frequent passages of Waynes Carts and Carriadges.[77]

Passing through Barnet, Hatfield, Welwyn and Stevenage, this was in fact the embryonic Great North Road that Samuel Pepys took when travelling to his family's home in Huntingdonshire in the 1660s, and which Daniel Defoe, in his 1724 *Tour Through the Whole island of Great Britain*, referred to as the "Coach Road".[78]

Just like the one from Hatfield to Welwyn, the stretch that passed through Baldock was pieced together from existing highways. From Stevenage it followed a surviving section of Roman road before running the length of Baldock High Street and taking another out to Biggleswade—a piecemeal arrangement that is still in place today, so that travellers making their way north have to turn right into Whitehorse Street and then left onto Station Road, completing an awkward dogleg that would never have featured on a planned highway.

By 1621 the Baldock to Biggleswade section had become so crowded with carriages, wagons and livestock that the parishes charged with its upkeep petitioned Parliament for help with keeping it in good repair.[79] The parish system was never designed for such volumes of traffic, and there were similar complaints from overburdened vestries the entire length of the road. By the middle of the eighteenth century the problem had largely been resolved, with a turnpiked Great North Road providing faster, more reliable access to and from the North than the frequently waterlogged Ermine Street.

The George, at the corner of Hitchin Street and Church Street, was one of two coaching inns with roots in the medieval past. Converted from a church outbuilding, it was first recorded in 1466 as "le George", possibly because it formerly housed props for morality plays featuring St George and the dragon. Even in those days it was a large establishment, owned jointly by two manorial lords from the nearby settlement of Clothall. A second inn, 'The Tabard', belonged to a wealthy town guild known as 'The Brotherhood of the Name of Jesus', but by the mid-sixteenth century it too was being leased to a lord of Clothall, who renamed it 'The Talbot' after the breed of hunting dog that appeared on his coat of arms. Other establishments were operating at around this time too; there are records of a 'Swan', a 'Crown' and an 'Angel', but whether these were inns offering rooms and stabling or merely taverns is not known.

The George, on the corner of Hitchin Street and Church Street, started life in the fifteenth century and was expanded and rebuilt at the end of the eighteenth.

    The new road from London prompted an expansion of the number of inns. Round about 1600, the White Horse opened next door to the Crown and opposite the Talbot, creating a cluster of them where the London road met roads from Hitchin, Royston and Biggleswade. By the end of the century more had opened their doors—the Falcon (also at the crossroads), the Bell, the Cock, the Boot, the King's Head (later renamed 'The White Lion') and the Rose and Crown—some sited on the High Street, others in Whitehorse Street and Bell Row. They were small, with limited overnight accommodation, but even so the diarist Samuel Pepys found much to commend in one of them—sadly not identified—on 6th August 1661: "Got to Baldwick," he wrote in his diary, "and there had a good supper by myself. The landlady being a pretty woman, but I durst not take notice of her, her husband being there."[80] The following month he was back, this time with his friend John Bowles, but the visit was not a happy one: "We took horse and got early to Baldwick; where there was a fair, and we put in and eat a mouthfull of pork, which they made us pay 14^d for, which vexed us much."[81] The fair had evidently pushed up prices—an aggravation for Pepys, perhaps, but a sign to historians that business in Baldock was booming. Certainly, the population had grown to the high hundreds when George Fox, founder of the Quaker Movement, visited the town.

    In 1655 Fox was staying at the George while on a nationwide preaching tour. He relates how, after curing a mortally sick Baptist woman, he repaired to the inn, where he found "two desperate fellows fighting so that none durst come nigh them to part them". With characteristic courage, he capped one miracle with another:

The White Lion—originally the King's Head—was one of the many inns founded in Baldock during the seventeenth century as the Great North Road grew in popularity.

The Stamford Regent at an inn on the Great North Road, in an illustration from 'Down the Road', Charles Birch Reynardson's memoir of a gentleman coachman.

> I was moved in the Lord's power to go to them, and when I had loosed their hands, I held one by one hand and the other by the other hand; and I showed them the evil of their doings, and convinced them, and reconciled them each to other so that they were loving and very thankful, so that people admired at it.[82]

So impressed were the townsfolk with his feats that "many hundreds" were converted, starting with the revived Baptist and her husband. Baldock owes much to Fox. The descendants of those newly-minted Quakers, whose faith valued practicality and good business sense, would secure its prosperity for the next two hundred years.

Improvements in road building from 1750 led to the introduction of 'flying' coaches and wagons, and speed of travel became a priority—even more so when mail coach services were introduced in 1784. During the next twenty years, journey times fell by half and kept on falling: in 1836 the 194-mile journey from London to York took 24 hours instead of the four days it had taken in 1750. Better roads also led to a proliferation of services; that same year around 350 coaches were leaving London daily, and Baldock was receiving ten 'up' and ten 'down' coaches every day.

Reliant as they were on a continuous supply of fresh horses, the flying services created an unprecedented demand for stabling. In Baldock this was met not by building more inns but by enlarging existing ones. Over the course of the eighteenth century the White Horse absorbed its less prosperous neighbours, so that by 1820 it covered three quarters of an acre, and not only provided stabling for 150 beasts but also operated its own brewhouse and a separate pub called 'The White Horse

Tap'. The George's options for expansion were more limited, bordered as it was on two sides by the churchyard, but at some point it began leasing part of the yard and erected barns and stables there. In 1790 the main building was replaced by a larger one in the Georgian style.

Many other inns did not have room to grow, and either closed or played a reduced role in the town's economy. By 1800 just three establishments were taking the lion's share of trade, each with its own clientèle: like the Swan at Stevenage, the White Horse was a post house servicing mail coaches and chaises, while the Rose and Crown, somewhat more down-market, catered to stagecoach passengers. The George, at the bottom of the heap, was even less salubrious because of its popularity with waggoners —the long-distance lorry drivers of their day.

As a class these men did not enjoy a good reputation. One historian remarks that they "lacked the dignity and skill that was usually associated with the stage and mail coach drivers", the main cause being their habit of "taking rather liberal quantities of liquor at the frequent stopping places along the route", so that "hard drinking was almost a symbol of a waggoner".[83] This being so, the fight that Fox broke up was probably nothing out of the ordinary in the George's long and no doubt colourful history.

Today it is difficult to imagine it ever being a rough house. Time, and the modern inclination to associate anything Georgian or Regency with the decorous world of Jane Austen, has ennobled it and lifted it clear of its gritty, hard-nosed roots. Promotional copy for its current incarnation as "Baldock's Newest Boutique Hotel" and "Modern Eatery Showcasing Contemporary British Cuisine" makes much of its past as a coaching inn, but absolutely nothing of its less savoury role as the haunt of boozing, brawling proto-white-van-man.

A carrier's wagon of the type serviced by the George and driven by notoriously drunk and disorderly waggoners. Aquatint by J. B. Pyne.

It is, as Bridget and I discover, a very smart building in a town full of smart buildings. Walking up the street to take a look at the White Horse—that *nonpareil* of Baldock's coaching era—we find instead a pub called 'The Old White Horse', and though it dates from the same period as the rebuilt George, its pitched roof, heavy proportions and outsize quoining make it look positively vulgar by comparison: to our twenty-first-century eyes a much more likely place for ruffians and low types. We later learn that it used to be the White Horse Tap—the separate pub built on the site of the Falcon following that inn's amalgamation into the White Horse empire. Sadly, it's all that's left; the rest went up in flames soon after shutting in 1864—like other staging posts a victim of the railways.[84]

The Rose and Crown still stands in Whitehorse Street, though it has seen better days. We hover on the pavement and look doubtfully into the former stable yard, now an ill-kept space where smokers can sit at a rickety table with their pints. The façade is tired and grubby, and the elaborate glass canopy over the entrance smeared with birdlime. It looks like a place on the way out. In 2016 the poet John Gallas, at the end of his first day following Clare on foot, fetched up in Baldock and stayed there. He writes:

The Rose and Crown—once Baldock's premier coaching inn—in 2016, fallen on hard times and within a year of closing for good.

The stable yard of the Rose and Crown in a drawing from 1907, when it was still catering to horse traffic.

> It was Baldock Rock weekend. I took a room at the Rose & Crown; small, shabby and directly above the main door, the street, and the Rock room. 'I hope,' said the landlady, 'you're not thinking of getting any sleep'.[85]

In 2017 the pub was boarded up; a planning notice fixed to the wall spoke glibly of 'luxury one- and two-bedroom apartments'.

We're in Baldock to visit the museum, which is situated on the ground floor of the old town hall. This hasn't been as straightforward to arrange as we'd expected. It closes for the winter and reopens at the beginning of March, but this year it has stayed shut. Last summer a rainstorm of tropical proportions swept through the town, flooding the exhibition space, and renovations are still ongoing. Despite this, we have been allowed inside by kind invitation of its director, Brendan King. The exhibit room stands empty and there's an all-pervasive smell of damp plaster. Display boards are stacked against one wall and decorators are moving about with pots of paint, putting things right, 'making good'. Brendan says he has material to show us on the Great North Road and its role in the town's economy during the early nineteenth century.

The three of us stand in the bare, echoing space around a plaster model of a hillside with two roads running along its flank. Brendan explains that the route between Graveley and Baldock was difficult for horse-drawn vehicles. Following the Roman Road straight over White Hill, it was so steep that it put horse teams

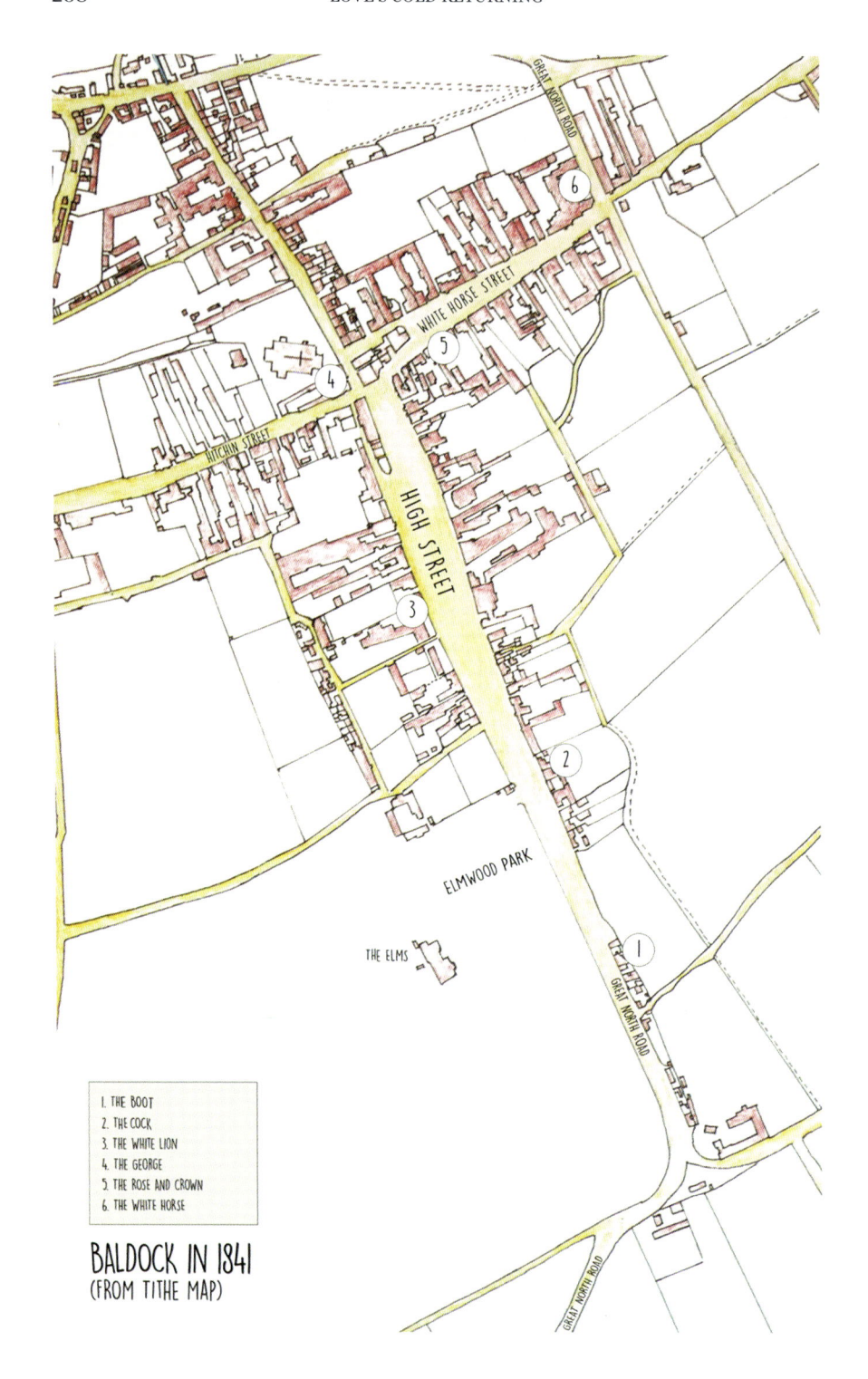

1. THE BOOT
2. THE COCK
3. THE WHITE LION
4. THE GEORGE
5. THE ROSE AND CROWN
6. THE WHITE HORSE

BALDOCK IN 1841
(FROM TITHE MAP)

under strain when climbing and damaged shoe-braked wheels on the descent. In icy conditions extra horses had to be harnessed as a matter of course. It was, in short, an atrocious stretch of road. By 1823 the Stevenage and Biggleswade Turnpike Trust had sufficient funds to improve it, which they did by digging a cutting across the summit of the hill, moving the descent eastwards to where it presented a gentler incline, and then raising the way with spoil from the excavations. Brendan's model shows the original route and its replacement, along with the public house that Clare called the Plough, which had to be moved from the old road to the new one. The Trust compensated the pub's owner handsomely for the cost of the relocation, but given that the man in question, local brewing magnate John Izzard Pryor, was a trustee, such uncommon generosity is entirely understandable.

The Trust also improved the road north to Biggleswade, as this suffered from a steep gradient at Pear Tree Hill near Radwell. The story goes that the embankment raised there to level the road was so high that the inmates of Radwell's Poor House, which stood beside it, were unable to climb its slope and became marooned.

For Baldock's businessmen, though, these improvements were a boon— especially for Pryor, who by the time of Clare's visit controlled most of the town's industry. To show us the extent of his empire, Brendan unfolds an OS map—a genuine 1836 edition, no less—on which Pryor had marked the locations of his assets. Using crimson ink, he had created a pattern like the spray of blood from a wound, with a dense carmine mass centred on Baldock, where his breweries manufactured his beer, and out-flung flecks of red where his tied houses sold it. If this grotesque work of action painting shows anything, it is the importance of a good transport network. Hauling product to widely distributed outlets required wagons, and wagons needed navigable routes. Reliable turnpikes were therefore vital to Pryor, as they were to other local gentry: the farmers and the manufacturers of foodstuffs and cloth whose goods also went by road.

A significant part of Pryor's business involved malting—the process of conditioning barley for brewing. This was done by soaking it in water, spreading it on a drying floor to germinate, and heating it in a kiln. The procedure transformed a tasteless and indigestible seed into a grain with a soft, crumbly consistency—one that readily released its flavour and nutrition and was easily milled. It also gave beer a colour that could range from a light amber through shades of brown to a lustrous black. Along with the nearby town of Ware, Baldock was a major centre of malt production, and during the eighteenth century three things happened to give its business a huge boost. First was a fashion for London Porter, a dark beer best compared to today's Guinness, which was made with scorched or 'black' malt. Baldock's maltsters seized on the opportunity to produce it because it sold at a premium the brewers were happy to pay while the fashion lasted—which it did well into the following century. Second was the opening of the Lea Navigation, which had its northern terminus at Ware and whose barges were able take the product to London in bulk and hence more cheaply. And third was the modernisation of the turnpikes, which led to a rise in the frequency and speed of wagon services. The rapid growth in malting that followed these innovations paralleled almost exactly that of the coaching trade, making late-eighteenth-century Baldock a boom town on two fronts.

Simpson's Brewery in Baldock High Street, photographed in 1965 shortly before its closure and demolition.

Fifty years on, in 1841, the signs of that boom were everywhere—in the handsome houses of those who had prospered from it, in the maltings and breweries that crowded every street, and in the pubs and inns that jostled between them. Clare plodded through a town that economically speaking was riding high: Hertfordshire's answer to Burton-on-Trent, where brewhouses and malting sheds loomed over streets reeking of malt and beer, and the smoke from kilns and chimneys choked the air.

We take our leave of Brendan and spend an hour exploring the town, trying to imagine how it looked in those days. Clare left no record of what he saw as he reached the end of the High Street, dodged down Whitehorse Street, and re-joined the Great North Road climbing away towards Radwell. We do get a hint from Herbert Tompkins, though, for on leaving the town in 1902 he described a view that had not changed substantially in sixty years:

> As I go up the hill towards the Compasses I turn to look back upon the town. It is almost screened from view by the smoke from the many chimneys, [while] high over all, and to the left, in a clearer atmosphere, two malting kilns are conspicuous objects.[86]

We can guess that when Clare passed this spot, he did not look back.

Bedfordshire

(with a brief excursion into Cambridgeshire)

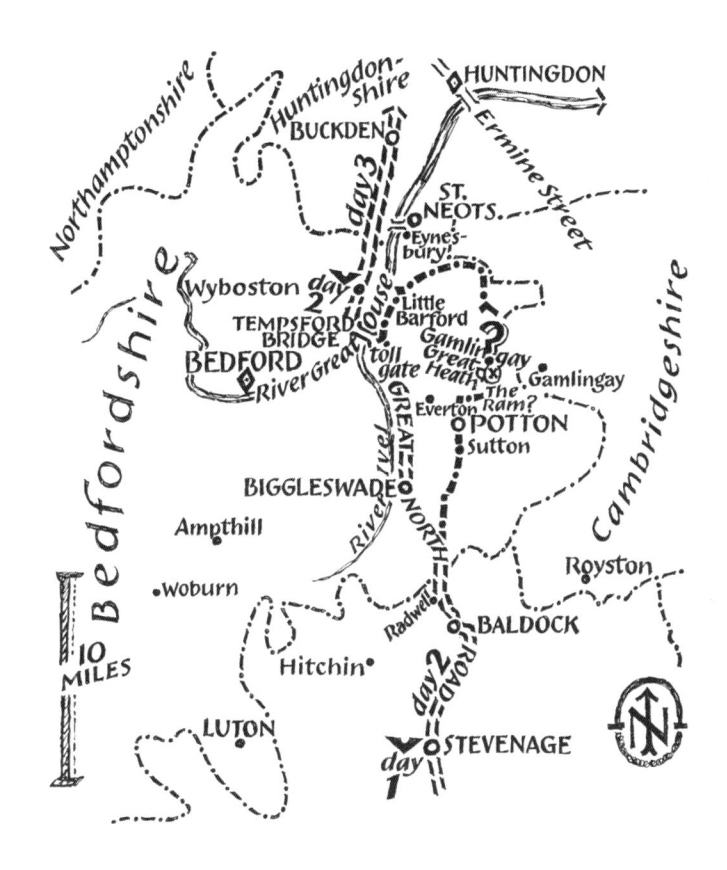

Day 2, 21ˢᵗ July 1841, Potton to Wyboston
Day 3, 22ⁿᵈ July 1841, Eaton Socon to Crosshall

Musings XIV

Mid-morning, late July, the sun's hot
after the rain and he's been up since dawn;
thick trees shelter the road, so he sits
for half an hour in the dry,
yearning for breakfast.

Hunger gnaws his gut and saps his courage,
bringing horrible imaginings
of bread and succulence; he's weak
but dare not rest, pounding on the miles,
inventing waymarks – the next great tree or spire.

The road is lonely. After each hectic clatter
of hooves and wheels, he listens
to his footfalls, watches the land change:
swathes of woodland – and then bare fields
where scarlet poppies stood before the hay was mown.

A cottage garden with a golden russet
apple tree reminds him how he used to climb and pick;
there was a robin watching new-turned earth for worms
and a thrush fetching pootys to the door,
one by one, to crack them open on the step.

She speaks:

'He wanted his pipe lighting and stood timid
at the door, dusty from the road, his face
shining with sweat; he'd been walking all day.
My brother fetched a taper from the fire
and Nana smiled, not quite hearing him right.

'I had my hands clean, busy with the lace,
all my bobbins in place across the pillow,
the threads taut. "Where does the overseer live?"
he asked. Was it the workhouse he meant?
We couldn't say, so he went away.'

Nowhere in Particular

If Clare intended to follow the coaches that had ferried him back and forth to London, then so far he'd done a good job. His next waypoint should have been the market town of Biggleswade, whose neighbourhood, according to Charles Harper, was "interested wholly in cabbages and potatoes, and other highly necessary, but essentially unromantic, vegetables".[1]

Biggleswade was notorious for the parsimony of one of its innkeepers, Mr Crouch of the White Swan. Charles Birch Reynardson, who drove the Stamford Regent during the 1820s and 30s as an amateur 'gentleman coachman', remembers the dismal service provided by "that long, sour old beggar". It was a common practice at coaching inns to keep service slow so that passengers could not eat too much during their brief stopover, and Crouch had it down to a fine art. Here's Birch Reynardson's description of stopping at his hostelry on a winter's day:

> Only twenty minutes was allowed for dinner; and by the time [...] you had got one quarter of what you could have consumed had your mouth been in eating trim, and your hands warm enough to handle your knife and fork, the coachman would put his head in, and say: 'Now, gentlemen, if you please; the coach is ready.' After this summons, [...] having paid your two and sixpence for the dinner that you had the will, but not the time, to eat, with sixpence for the waiter, you wished the worthy Mr. Crouch good day, grudged him the half-crown he had pocketed for having dined so miserably, and again mounted your seat, to be rained and snowed upon, and almost frozen to death before you reached London.[2]

The Swan catered to 'up' coaches only; travellers heading for Stamford stopped elsewhere for their dinner and presumably fared better.

As far as Harper was concerned, beyond its inns—the White Swan and the Crown—Biggleswade did not have much to offer the visitor except "an extraordinarily broad and empty market place" and a church "with a spire of the Hertfordshire type".[3] Not a memorable place, then, which could be why Clare missed it altogether. Directly after noting how he wished in vain for breakfast, he writes, "I forget here the names of the villages I passed through but reccolect at late evening going through Potton in Bedfordshire". This places him, at the end of the second day, some four miles east of the Great North Road and seven miles north-east of Biggleswade. He has either lost his way, or deliberately abandoned the coach road home. While he has strayed from the obvious route before—winding up in Enfield Highway instead of Enfield Town—on that occasion he made a mistake, and admits as much. Here he offers no reason. But intentional or not, his foray into Bedfordshire's hinterland is also a journey into the surreal, where things take on the aspect of a dream, or more properly a nightmare.

Potton, with a population of 1,800 engaged in farming and handicrafts, was typical of the country towns he'd already passed through, the only difference being its

Charles Harper's pen-and-ink sketch of Biggleswade market place with its two coaching inns: the White Swan in the background, and the Crown at foreground right. Both were shadows of their former selves when he drew this in 1901.

dearth of coaching inns. For if it was not on the road to nowhere, it was certainly on the Road to *nowhere in particular*. Standing where the flood plain of the Ivel meets the Sandy and Gamlingay Heaths, it had a foot in two agricultural camps, with cereals and market-garden crops flourishing in the rich alluvial soil to the south, and sheep grazing on the sparsely wooded hills to the north. It was placid, prosperous and self-contained, as yet untouched by the changes afoot in the wider world. Pigot's Directory of 1839 describes it as "a neat little town [...] pleasantly situated beneath gentle eminences", consisting of "a good market place with a number of tolerably spacious streets branching from it". Kelly, equally complimentary, notes its "fine, fruitful and healthy neighbourhood" which has led to "many [..] inhabitants having attained a great age", and Slater remarks on the "great number of handsome residences, occupied by opulent individuals, who contribute largely to [its] traders' prosperity".[4] If these descriptions conjure up a Regency town along the lines of Bath or Cheltenham, that's probably because most of Potton was rebuilt following a fire in 1783, which conferred upon it an architectural elegance it might otherwise not have enjoyed.

Along with its 'opulent individuals' there were humbler folk, as Clare relates:

> I called in a house to light my pipe in which was a civil old woman and a young country wench making lace on a cushion as round as a globe and a young fellow all civil people — I asked them a few questions as to the way and where the clergyman and overseer lived but they scarcely heard me or gave me no answer

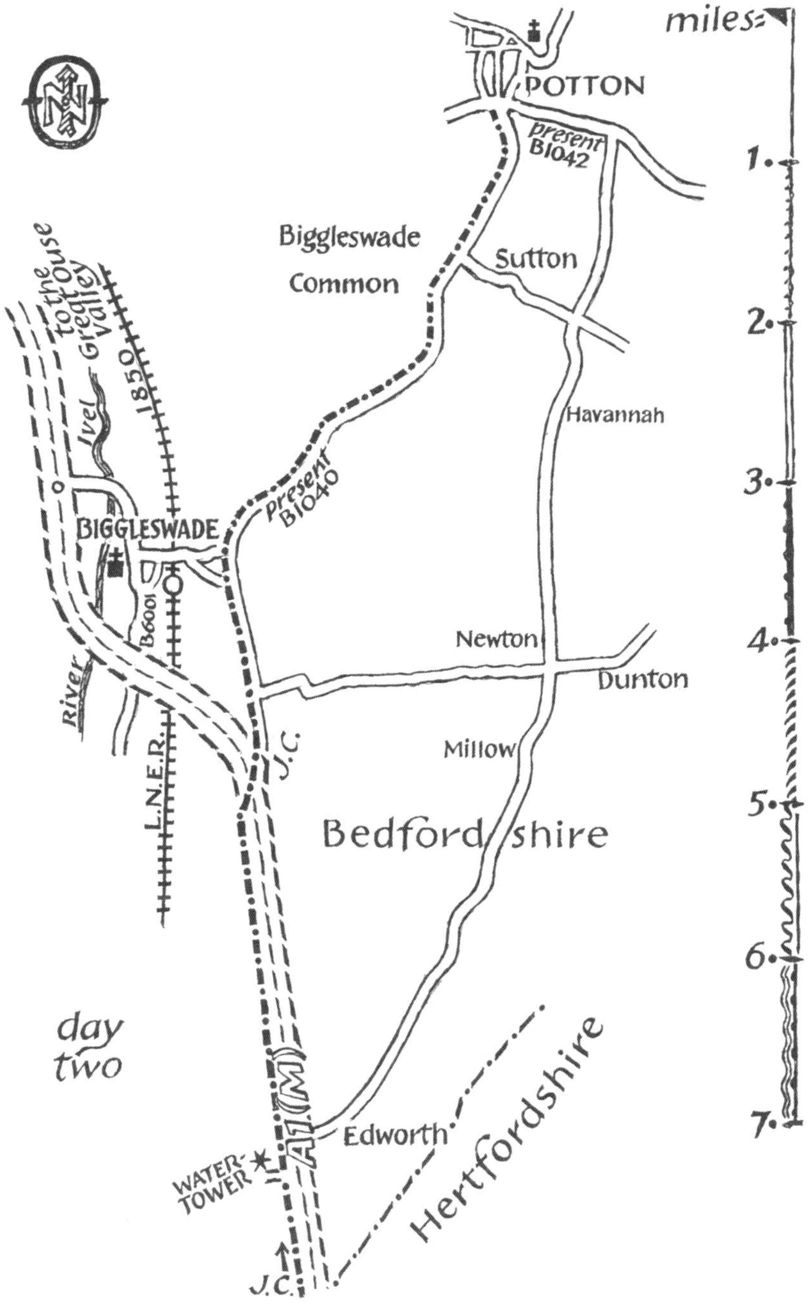
miles
1.
2.
3.
4.
5.
6.
7.
POTTON
present B1042
Biggleswade Common
Sutton
Havannah
to the Great Ouse Valley
Ivel
1850
present B1040
BIGGLESWADE
B6001
Newton
Dunton
River
L.N.E.R.
J.C.
Millow
Bedfordshire
day two
A1(M)
Edworth
Hertfordshire
WATER-TOWER
J.C.

None the wiser, he carried on through the town and into the countryside beyond. Presently he met a "kind talking country man" who told him that "the Parson lived a good way from where I was or overseer I do'nt know which". This news must have come as a blow, for two days' marching had exacted a heavy toll, and he was now so tired and footsore he had changed his mind about not asking for money. "Had I found the overseers house at hand or the Parsons," he says, "I should have gave my name and begged for a shilling to carry me home." Not least of his problems was a crippled foot "for the gravel had got into my old shoes one of which had nearly lost the sole", but as there was no immediate relief in prospect, he was "forced to brush on penniless and be thankful I had a leg to move on".

He must have looked pitiable even by the standards of the day, when the roads were thronged with indigents—the "broken-down haymakers" and their ilk—because the countryman, evidently concerned for his welfare, was reluctant to leave him. Clare must have been recalling his previous night's lodging at Stevenage, because he asked if there was a farm nearby where he could spend the night on some dry straw. The man replied that there was a public house "on the left hand side of the road at the sign of the 'Ram'" where he could find shelter, but at this point, overcome by the pain in his feet, Clare was forced to sit down and rest on a stone heap. This proved to be a disaster, because instead of going with his companion to the pub—and possibly, with his help, obtaining food and drink and permission to

View south along Sun Street, Potton, showing the seventeenth-century former Sun Inn, which was still trading in 1841.

The George and Dragon, on King Street, was Potton's posting house in 1841. The kind-talking country man with the hamper and lockup bag was very likely taking letters and provisions from here to Tempsford, there to be picked up by one of the mail coaches plying the Great North Road.

sleep in an outbuilding—he insisted that the man carry on ahead of him. "The good fellow lingered awhile," he writes, "as if wishing to conduct me and then suddenly reccolecting that he had a hamper on his shoulder and a lock up bag in his hand cram full to meet the coach which he feared missing—he started hastily and was soon out of sight."

With his friend now lost in the dusk, and the weather beginning to turn, Clare was alone in hostile territory. When he was sufficiently rested he carried on in the direction the countryman had gone, but exhaustion overtook him and he lay down between a shed and a line of densely suckered elms—in what, as it turned out, was a natural wind tunnel: "I lay there and tried to sleep," he says, "but the wind came in between them so cold that I quaked like the ague and quitted the lodging for a better at the Ram which I could hardly hope to find."

By now it was completely dark. He looked into cottage windows that showed "the inside tennants lots very comfortable and my outside lot very uncomfortable and wretched", but hobbling on, he eventually succeeded in finding the Ram. Had the countryman been with him, he might have had the courage to enter. As it was, the timidity that had seized him earlier in the day on being rebuffed for begging returned in force:

THE JOURNEY – BEDFORDSHIRE – NOWHERE IN PARTICULAR   219

A street plan of Potton in 1832 based on the Enclosure Map of that year. Clare almost certainly arrived along the Biggleswade Road and left via the Everton Road, but it is impossible to know the route he took through the town. Given his impulse to keep travelling north, however, he most likely took Back Street and Horslow Street, missing the centre entirely.

Gamlingay Great Heath at midwinter—a view west along the Everton Road from the crossroads where Clare became disoriented and lost his sense of direction. The kind-talking countryman most probably took this route after leaving him.

> At last [I] came to the Ram the shutters were not closed and the lighted window looked very cheering but I had no money and did not like to go in there was a sort of shed or gighouse at the end but I did not like to lie there as the people were up — so still I travelled on

Now the road "was very lonely and dark in places being overshadowed with trees", but there was just enough light for him to pick out milestones, including one at the point where the road branched. Rather than sending him reassured on his way, however, this led to the second disaster of the night.

On seeing the stone, he "heedlessly turned back to read it to see where the other road led too and on doing so [...] found it led to London". He knew he had come from the direction of the capital, and this made him panic so much he could no longer remember which way was north. Turning around to look for clues in the dark only made things worse, as he could see "no tree or bush or stone heap" he could remember having passed. Completely disoriented, he carried on, hoping against hope that the road would lead him in the right direction.

Eventually, he says, "I saw a lamp shining as bright as the moon which I found was suspended over a Tollgate". At last he was able to ask the way, for the gatekeeper "came out with a candle and eyed me narrowly"—as well he might, given his rough appearance and the lateness of the hour. For his part, Clare had regained his courage. He asked the man whether he was going northward. "When you get through the gate you are," came the reply.

With his internal compass reset, his spirits quickly revived, and as he made his way along the road he hummed 'Highland Mary'—a tune he'd learned from his gypsy friend Wisdom Smith.[5] And though he had not yet solved the problem of where to sleep, his luck was about to change:

> I at length fell in with an odd house all alone near a wood but I could not see what the sign was though the sign seemed to stand oddly enough in a sort of trough or spout there was a large porch over the door and being weary I crept in and glad enough to find I could lye with my legs straight the inmates were all gone to roost for I could hear them turn over in bed as I lay at full length on the stones in the porch

There he slept until daylight, when he awoke "very much refreshed".

Of all the episodes in the *Journey*, the one dealing with the second night must be the most intriguing, and the most perplexing. Its fusion of dream-like incident and vivid description reads like the visions of a fever-wracked opium addict. Clare, it should be remembered, was an admirer of both Coleridge and de Quincey. It also has distinctly literary qualities. The cottagers who cannot hear his questions; the eerie moon-like lamp and squinting toll-keeper; the strangely-signed, solitary house whose inhabitants are known only by the creaking of their beds—all these possess a decidedly Gothic air. Added to which, there is also the stuff of Romantic adventure: the hero's struggle against the elements; his exile from comforts of hearth and human contact, and the change of fortune, when all seems lost, that turns despair into joy. There's even a gag to lighten the mood, when the kind-talking countryman suddenly realises the obvious—that he's holding two large and heavy objects he needs to be rid of—and makes a hasty exit.

The question thus arises as to how much of this is genuine recollection, and how much is embellishment. We know the *Journey* was written with an audience in mind; Mary Joyce, for certain, but also, very probably, a wider readership. Clare was collecting material for an autobiography as early as 1820,[6] and though it was never published, the resulting work, produced during 1825, sprang from a self-declared wish to leave behind an accurate account of himself. The same impulse must surely have been operating sixteen years later, causing him to write with at least one eye fixed on posterity.

Though he does not describe the town, he is very clear about its identity—"Potton in Bedfordshire"—and the time he arrived there—"late evening"—which gives his account a solid geographical and chronological context. On reaching the other side he found himself on Gamlingay Great Heath—Pigot's "gentle eminence", which was in fact a dreary and exposed tract of waste standing some 200 feet above the floodplain of the Ivel.[7] The sense of desolation conveyed by his writing fits well with the aspect of the place, as does his description of the climate. Standing at a higher elevation, the Heath was cooler and windier, and night-time drops in temperature correspondingly lower: quaking "like the ague" would have been entirely reasonable behaviour for someone crossing it at night, even in summer.

He also reports that as night descended, the road was dark where it was "shaded by trees", implying a sky that was bright enough to cast shadows. Light levels would have been dependent on cloud cover, and in the absence of local weather records we can only note that he refers to showers earlier in the day so that a partial or intermittent overcast seems likely.[8] We know from ephemeris calculations that a sickle moon had slipped below the horizon just as dusk was falling, leaving only stars to light his way.[9] By his own account his night vision was poor—he famously records how on poaching expeditions he could scarcely see a thing—but had the weather been clear, he would have walked, in a world free of air and light pollution, under a resplendent sky of the kind immortalised fifty years later by Van Gogh.

Musings XV

Trees stand guard in the dark, roots burrowing
under his step, the breath of leaves in the breeze,
a rustle as snails and hedgehogs weave through dried mud
and matted twigs; a child again, his heart shivers
for fear of terribles with saucer eyes.

Fear keeps him walking in the dark,
nowhere to lie down and sleep; cottage windows
flicker, but he dares not knock
or even lie in the outhouse shed,
just huddles in a dyke and wakes wet to the skin.

A Fearfully Open Sky

Overall, it looks as if we can place our confidence in Clare's account of conditions on the second night of his journey. But what of the locations he describes? Aside from an empty landscape and some cottages with lighted windows, he mentions just four —the Ram public house, a fork in the road with a confusing milestone, a tollgate, and an isolated house.

As far as the Ram is concerned, earlier Clare scholars tended to the view that it stood at Crosshall, near Eaton Socon. There's a map, which crops up repeatedly in the literature, showing the route of the *Journey*, with a tiny zigzag where this establishment was located, just west of St Neots.[10] As an inn on the Great North Road it makes a good candidate, but its location ten or so miles north of Potton means that if Clare's account is to be trusted, he could only have met the countryman who offered to walk him there much later than he reports—not before dusk, in fact, but early the following morning.

Then, in 1980, an alternative was revealed in a newly-published collection of Clare's prose, which contained a photograph above the caption:

> This old house, over a mile from Potton on the road to Gamlingay, can almost certainly be identified as Clare's 'Ram'. It was a public house within living memory and is still known locally as 'The Ram'[11]

The photo shows a narrow red-brick building in the Gothic style, standing end-on to the road and fronted by a large ground-floor bay window. Its position on Gamlingay Heath, within half-an-hour's walk of Potton, not only makes it an excellent fit for Clare's timeline, but also places it on the circuitous route we deduce Clare must have taken on that dark and confused night. Visiting a building he apparently saw with his own eyes—and especially one with such a prominent role in his story—is an irresistible prospect. So, on a dull and overcast August morning, Bridget and I set off in search of Gamlingay Heath, and the Ram.

For most of its passage through Bedfordshire, the A1 has wiped out all trace of the Great North Road, which means we can only make a partially faithful approach to the spot where Clare parted from the old highway. We leave the motorway a mile or so to the south, at the Biggleswade exit, which immediately lands us in a sprawl of shiny steel warehouses branded with corporate logos. This is the A1 Retail Park: a sort of hugely metastasised service area that sucks in shoppers and their cash from far and wide without contributing anything to the local economy. "Man is born free, but is everywhere in chain stores," Bridget observes as we pass Next, H&M, Matalan, Laura Ashley, and just about every other high-street purveyor of mass-produced objects of desire. It takes several roundabouts to escape, but presently we're back in the real world, driving through a leafy suburb of detached houses, trimmed lawns and manicured hedges. When we reach the junction where Clare went awry, we find it marks a transition to something altogether less salubrious: streets of mid-Victorian semis and terraced cottages dating from the arrival of the railway—never prime housing stock, and now decidedly down-at-heel. To add to the general air of decline, there's a second-hand car dealership in the fork of the road, with its tired merchandise parked out on the forecourt. "Low mileage," I say, noting the fluorescent cards propped up on the windscreens, "Low prices. Low expectations. Low prospects. Low. Low. Low."

When Bridget asks me what I mean, I tell her I'm not really sure, beyond the fact that Biggleswade adheres to a truth about many British towns. The further in you go, the less prosperous their neighbourhoods become. Unlike, say, continental Europe, where it's the reverse—something that accounts for why we associate French *banlieues* with deprived immigrant communities, not plump, self-satisfied stockbrokers driving Jags.

I park a few yards up from the garage to consult the maps we've brought with us—an up-to-date Ordnance Survey Explorer, and a reprint of the first edition of the One-Inch Series, circa 1860. A bit late for Clare, one might think, but the notes that come with it say it was based on surveys made in the 1830s. Comparing them, we can immediately see that the road layout at this spot has stayed the same. Except for a tiny kink just before the junction, the road to Potton—technically a right turn—could easily be mistaken for a continuation of the London Road (the old Great North Road). Conversely, keeping to the London Road could look very much like taking a left. "If the junction looks misleading now," I say, "imagine how much worse it was in an age without road markings or reliable signage."

We've already talked through with Harris the question of why Clare headed for Potton. When we met with him to discuss it, he'd already given the matter some thought and offered up a possible explanation we'd not considered—that the gypsies had given Clare some inside information regarding Potton's vestry—"Soft touches, maybe."

One of the issues I'd been grappling with was how Clare managed to miss the turn into Biggleswade. Even if the junction was confusing, the weight of traffic heading there should have steered him in the right direction. If he'd been intending to go to Potton all along, however, that would no longer be a problem. Gypsy families undoubtedly shared information about which places were good to camp at, which to avoid, and so on, and perhaps Potton was known to have a sympathetic—or gullible—parson. The idea that the gypsy who told Clare the route home also instructed him on where to obtain help is intriguing. Clare's repeated questioning of Potton locals about vestry men who might give him "a shilling to carry me home" could well be evidence for this, as could his unusually precise naming of the town as "Potton in Bedfordshire", as if he had noted it down before setting out. But to advance it as a serious possibility requires more textual evidence than we have, so, reluctantly, we must set it aside. The simplest explanation—and the likeliest, given the configuration of the roads at this point—is that tiredness and inattention caused him to plod on in a straight line and veer off the Great North Road without realising. As for seeking financial help to get home, he might equally well have attempted that at Biggleswade had he stuck to the highway.

Bridget pointed out that northerly traffic would have been lighter at Biggleswade, with some already siphoned off down turnpikes to Wales, the North West and the Lakes. Railways had also begun to carry freight between London and the Midlands, resulting in fewer stage wagons taking the route. These things considered, the Potton road might not have differed much in appearance from the Great North Road, especially as it was the major droving route through Bedfordshire.

"But surely," I said to Harris as we talked around the subject, "Clare must have been aware that Biggleswade was close by. He would have seen the church and so on."

"I think you're just too much up on the hill there," he replied, "and the church is actually almost at river level, down by the mill. Although it's big, it wouldn't announce itself, and there would have been trees and so on in the way. Line of sight, there wouldn't have been much of a clue."

On balance, then, Clare probably took the road to Potton believing he was still on the Great North Road. And by the time he realised something was wrong, he could no longer retrace his steps—he was lost.

From the junction, Bridget and I follow the route Clare took off the Great North Road, which is still called Drove Road: an incongruous-sounding name now that it's lined with mile after mile of housing. As I drive I try to visualise the cattle, sheep and geese that thronged it in their hundreds of thousands when all this was open country. After a while, though, the houses run out, and we're in rural Bedfordshire—at this time of year strikingly beautiful, with flat fields of shining golden stubble and trees in their dusky late-summer foliage. We glimpse the perfectly kept lawns and fairways of the John O'Gaunt Golf Club—probably the closest thing to a natural environment in this intensively farmed area. Then, almost instantaneously it seems, we're on the southern outskirts of Potton.

It's a town of narrow, picturesque streets, mercifully spared the vandalism other market towns suffered during the 1960s mania for traffic schemes. The downside of

View down Warden Hill in the direction of Tempsford. This is the road Clare would most likely have taken had he not tried to seek shelter for the night at the Ram.

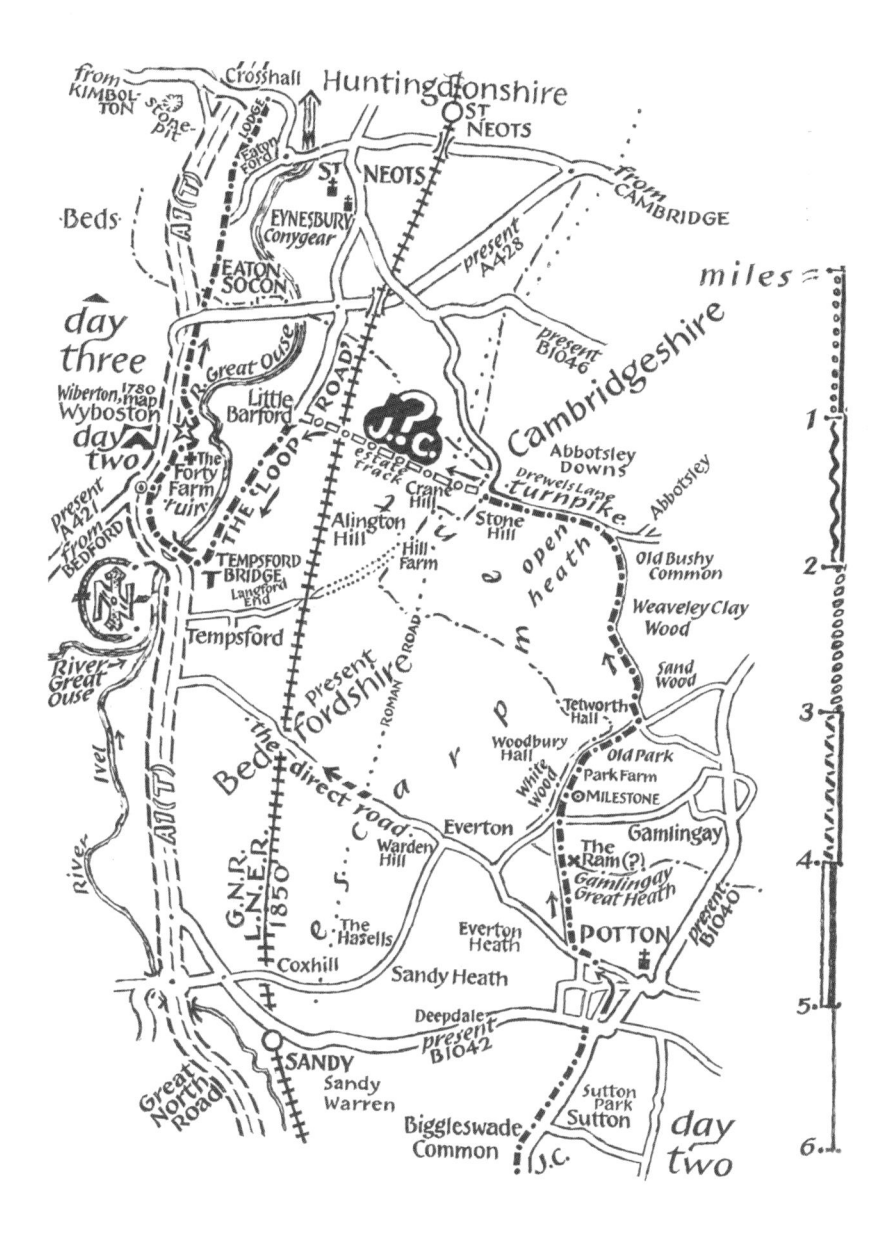

THE JOURNEY – BEDFORDSHIRE – A FEARFULLY OPEN SKY 227

this is that negotiating it in a car takes time. We drive slowly around the Market Square, past the elegant front of the Coach House Inn and on towards the north end of town. Here the streets run out, and once again the view ahead is of nothing but hedges and fields. The road is skirting the southern edge of Gamlingay Great Heath and heading west on a course which, if followed to its end, will take us off the escarpment and down to the village of Tempsford, close to where the A1 crosses the Great Ouse. By rights Clare should have followed that route, with its steep

The former Ram public house on Gamlingay Great Heath, which ceased trading in 1960. The brickwork clearly shows the location of the door that led to the saloon, and though the windows have been modernised the bay still retains its original proportions.

descent down Warden Hill and easy walk along the south side of Tempsford Hall. And who's to say he wouldn't have, but for meeting the countryman with his offer of shelter? We're guessing that this must have happened soon after he left the town—somewhere along here in fact—because we've come to a minor T junction with a road on the right, signed 'Potton Road, The Heath'. It used to be known as 'Drove Road' and, if we've read his account correctly, it's the one he hobbled down with his new-found friend.

We make the turn and follow it as it climbs to a high plateau, and then—like Clare before us—we're out on the Heath. There's no mistaking the bleak emptiness, the sensation of exposure, the fearfully open sky. I roll down the window and feel the air rush in sharp and cool, but when I check the dashboard I find there's been no drop in temperature; it's still a close and cloying 22° C.

The pub—or rather *ex-pub*—we're making for was known as the Ram for a good reason, but it's one that has been irrelevant for generations. At some point after Clare was here, the flocks that grazed on the Heath were driven off so that its thin, unproductive soil could be enriched—first with guano and coprolite, and then with phosphates—and harnessed to grow cash crops. On either side of us are hedges and trees, and, beyond them, a never-ending succession of farmers' fields. "Brassicas," Bridget declares flatly, as she stares out at endless rows of dull-green *somethings* receding to the horizon. Once this place had a character and ecology all its own.

Now it's indistinguishable from the rest of Eastern England; we might as well be in deepest Lincolnshire but for the needle of the Sandy Heath transmitter, way over in the distance, piercing the dull overcast. Suddenly Bridget points straight ahead, drawing my attention to something I recognise from the maps—a thin, dark line where land meets sky. Something Clare, too, might have seen in the fading twilight: the trees of the White Wood, standing patient guard around Woodbury Hall.

Before we can reach it, however, we arrive at our destination—a thin drift of Victorian houses lining the road. I park on a strip of well-tended grass (hopefully no-one's pride and joy) and gather up my cameras while Bridget finds her notebook. We try to appear nonchalant as we exit the car, surreptitiously watching for the twitching curtains of the Neighbourhood Watchers. Sure enough, there's a pale face at the window of one of the cottages—featureless at this distance—but before I can alert Bridget it's gone. I'm reminded of Clare's narrative poem 'The Lodge House', which relates how vigilant servants foil an attempt by ne'er-do-wells to rob an isolated farm. Some of the old country customs, it seems, are still alive and kicking.

We are reasonably sure that the identification of the house in front of us is correct; that it was, in fact, the pub that Clare encountered on that confused and muddled evening. Not only is it where our estimated timing of his movements place it, but it's eminently recognisable from his terse description. Bridget fishes a copy of the text from her bag and reads aloud the relevant passage: "The shutters were not closed," she recites, "and the lighted window looked very cheering." Here, for

Workers' cottages opposite the Ram. Clare's report that the pub was on his left as he made his way up the road might suggest that in 1841 it was housed in one of them.

certain, is the big bay window Clare describes. I can picture it casting a fan of lamplight onto the road, picking out the lines of his face as he stands looking in from the edge of the dark. And as she says, "There was a sort of shed or gighouse at the end", my eyes dart to the building's rear, where it descends to a kind of outhouse or scullery; surely once a shelter for a small two-wheeler or bales of hay for livestock. "Well," I say to her, when she finishes, "*I'm* sold."

"Only..." she replies, looking up from her book and slowly turning a full circle, "...it's on the wrong side of the road."

"Sorry?"

"It states here," she says, holding up the book, "that it's on the left, not the right. Clare reports the countryman saying: 'It's a public house on the left hand side of the road at the sign of the 'Ram'."

Now she's pointed this out I can see the problem. The Ram is standing opposite where it ought to be. "So the man got it wrong?" I suggest.

"Unlikely. He's obviously local."

"Or maybe they're walking the other way?"

"You mean *towards* Potton?"

"Yes, so our right would be their left and their left would be...okay, okay, it's a stupid idea." And then I do what she's just done—I turn fully 360 degrees, looking hard as I go. "But I wonder, could the Ram have moved across the road from *there*?" And I point to a two-storeyed cottage standing opposite the old pub. She follows my gaze. "Are you suggesting *that* was the local when Clare came through?"

I nod. "And then afterwards, when the landlord needed larger premises, he made the switch."

We go over and take a look. The cottage has been semi-modernised, with double-glazing and some sort of pale render, now heavily weather-stained, plastered over the original brick. A sign hanging from a small gibbet by the gate identifies it as a cattery. "That'd explain things, perhaps," she says without conviction, "though it doesn't look like a pub, does it?"

I agree, but remind her that it doesn't have to. In the 1840s any licensed householder could sell beer in their front parlour. But Bridget is doubtful, and if I admit it so am I. The cottage simply doesn't look right. The Ram does. After talking round the subject for a while we settle on the likeliest explanation: that Clare must have muddled his left with his right. He was, after all, labouring under more profound misapprehensions on the day. "And anyway," I add as I start taking photos, "Who *hasn't* been guilty of misremembering something at some time or another?"

As I finish up and stow away my gear, I ask her whether the place seems at all familiar.

"In what way, exactly?" she asks.

I shrug. The whole scene reminds me of something, only I can't think what. "Never mind," I say as we climb into the car, "All this Victoriana must be getting to me—I'll be seeing it in my sleep." I turn the key in the ignition and ease off the handbrake. Bcfore moving off I crane my neck to look at the watcher's window. The face is back. I give it a wave but there's no reaction. As the buildings dwindle behind us in the rear-view mirror I wonder what its owner made of us.

THE JOURNEY – BEDFORDSHIRE – A FEARFULLY OPEN SKY 231

The milestone on Drove Road by Park Farm and Woodbury Hall. This is the only waymarker that Clare could have encountered between the Ram and the Waresley turnpike, and is therefore likely to be the one that caused him to lose his way.

The road is taking us towards Clare's second landmark—the place where he became lost. We've identified two points where this might have happened, and the first is only a couple of hundred yards away: a crossroads where the Drove Road meets the road coming in from Everton. What makes it such a strong candidate is a nearby milestone, which prominently features the distance to London.

From a comparison of maps, it seems that not a lot has changed. The White Wood runs up to the western boundary of the junction as it did in 1841, and the land continues to stretch away all around, flat and featureless. There's a 1930s cast-iron signpost—a joy to see, and quite rare; the fact that it hasn't been replaced speaks volumes about the remoteness of this spot. The only other addition is St Silvester's, a red-brick church, now deconsecrated, which was raised in the 1870s to bring the Word of the Lord to, literally, the Heathens. Originally made of corrugated iron, it continued to be called 'The Iron Church' long after its reconstruction, and is still known by that name today.

The milestone is within sight of the junction, and by a happy coincidence—or maybe no coincidence at all—it's under a hedge. "50 Miles from London," I read aloud, kneeling by it. The name of the capital comes across as slightly unreal here, in a place where all around is brassicas. I try to imagine how it must have appeared to Clare as he bent down to read it in the middle of a wild and windswept heath. Did he know he was lost? That he'd unwittingly left the Great North Road behind him? I think he did. And perhaps the realisation was recent, so that when he found a stone which he took to be pointing towards London, his new-born anxiety flared into a full-blown panic attack.

Roger Burgoyne's milestone is now situated at Park Farm. It is unclear whether this was always so, as all waymarkers were removed at the outbreak of WWII and then returned—with varying degrees of accuracy—at the conclusion of hostilities.

Behind the hedge is a house belonging to Park Farm, which stood here even then, and just up the road there's a cottage of similar vintage belonging to the Woodbury Estate. So if this was the spot, why didn't he knock on a door for help? Why blunder around, alone and fearful, in the awful dark? When I frame the question aloud, Bridget replies with the answer I've already come to: "For the same reason he didn't enter the Ram; he was afraid of rejection, of verbal abuse, and possibly worse."

In 1782 the German writer Karl Philipp Moritz embarked on a walking tour through the Home Counties and found himself the target of what he judged to be a peculiarly English prejudice: "A traveller on foot in this country seems to be considered as a sort of wild man, or an out-of-the-way being, who is stared at, pitied, suspected, and shunned by every body that meets him," he wrote in his journal, "and [is] considered as either a beggar or a vagabond, or some necessitous wretch, which is a character not much more popular than that of a rogue."[12] After 36 hours on the road, a haggard and travel-stained John Clare would undoubtedly have provoked such a reaction from people even in broad daylight. Knocking on a stranger's door in the dead of night would have been entirely out of the question.

"Okay, so there's a milestone here," I say, "but does the lie of the land put you in mind of what he wrote? I mean, he doesn't mention a farm, or a cottage, and the stone isn't where the roads actually meet."

"No," she answers, "But he's forgotten to mention bigger things than farms, and milestones do get moved. Bear in mind, too, that this is the first reference to London he would have come across after passing the Ram." She's invoking Occam's Razor, of course, and it's a compelling argument.

There's an inscription on the stone, but much is illegible and part has sunk into the ground. When I later contact the Milestone Society about it, they email me a transcription they made when they renovated it some thirty years ago:

> 50 Miles from London. The Six Miles Stone from ye 44 Mile Stone in Baldock Lane to this place was set up by Rog. Burgoyne Bart in 1751.

Roger was the 6th Baronet of Burgoyne, one of a long line of aristocrats who had their seat at Sutton Park (now the John O'Gaunt Golf Club), and the Member of Parliament for Bedfordshire from 1735 to 1747. It's more likely that he erected the stone with a view to memorialising himself than helping lost travellers, and the fact that he chose this method over others strongly suggests that such waymarkers were vanishingly rare on the Heath.

If Clare missed it he would have carried on to Gamlingay Cinques where the road forked, with one branch heading straight on towards the Waresley tollgate and the other—to use Clare's own phrase—"going right about" in the direction of Gamlingay. The map shows it as being a good match for his description, but when we get there we find that the passage of time has pulled it out of shape; the Gamlingay turn is gone, its curve reduced to a field boundary—the result, perhaps, of the rise of the internal combustion engine. I suspect that not even Mr Toad would have subjected his motor car to what was likely to have been a rough and rutted surface. Like his more circumspect be-goggled brethren, he would have carried on to the wider, better-paved turn at the nearby crossroads.

At exactly a mile from Park Farm, this was where Drove Road met the road running from Gamlingay to Eynesbury and then to St Neots, a significant meeting of ways that would have merited a fingerpost and also—given the precise distance—a milestone. But over the years it has been comprehensively landscaped and provisioned with signs for Toad's teeming descendants, and the stone, if it was ever there, is gone. After a couple of minutes wandering about and failing to find anything of interest in the long grass, we return to the car to consult our maps.

As I try to make sense of the web of tracks that made up the nineteenth-century Heath, Bridget re-checks Clare's account. "He sees a milestone, gets confused and doesn't know which way's north any more," she says, "so he's got three choices—he can go back towards the Ram, right towards Gamlingay, or straight on to the Waresley tollgate. Which do you think he took?"

I've already thought about this. If he'd gone back, he'd have stumbled on the Ram again, which would have told him he was retracing his steps. So that left the road to Gamlingay and the one to the tollgate.

"The tollgate," I say.

"Even though he doesn't mention it?"

"He doesn't mention a village either," I reply. Gamlingay would have been noteworthy enough to record, even if he couldn't remember its name. It was large —something he'd have referred to as a 'town'.

"He does talk about looking at lighted cottage windows, remember."

"But that's *before* he gets lost, and besides, he refers to the cottages as 'odd'; so, isolated, not standing together—not in a settlement."

It's a moot point, anyhow, because we've already considered the cottages at length and suspect they were most likely an embellishment. Single homesteads were rare on the heath, and Clare may have invented the lit windows to heighten the atmosphere. The theme of tenants sitting snug by their fires with storm-lashed travellers at their door occurs elsewhere in his work.[13] I'm about to say as much when I see something on the map I've not noticed before—a tiny lane, running north-west, which joined the road next to the now-vanished fork. "Or he might have taken *this* way," I say, showing it to her.

"Where did it lead?" she asks.

I trace it with my finger. "Waverley Woodgate..., Cold Arbour..., and then, if he took a left *there*, all the way to Langford End and the Tempsford tollgate." Precisely where we think he ended up, in fact.

"Can we see if it still does?"

I switch maps. "No. It's a private road now. But if you like, we can take a left up Tetworth Hill, and work round to Tempsford from further north." This is a route we'd already considered but rejected, as it would have taken Clare too far out of his way. The road climbs through a landscape that even today looks heath-like —*heathen*, as the ministers of the Iron Church might have said. Windswept trees stand in bald, bare fields, and aside from the red-brick outline of Low Farm—which Bridget tells me is marked on the 1860 map—there's not a sign of human habitation. The countryside feels overwhelmingly like the one we imagine Clare traversing for "mile after mile" before finally finding the tollgate and, despite being well to the north-east of Waverley Woodgate and Cold Arbour, we take this to be a good omen. We pass Weaveley Clay Wood, whose hilltop profile hasn't altered in two hundred years, and the copses of Old Bushy Common, still miraculously intact among cultivated fields. When we arrive at what looks like a T junction I hit the brakes, unsure if I have right of way. Then I realise that it consists of a sharp left turn with a narrow, neglected-looking lane leading off it to the right. We later discover that this was part of the Waresley Turnpike and must once have taken a fair amount of traffic.

Bridget tells me to follow the road round to the left, where it becomes 'Drewels Lane'—a name used by the locals of Clare's day. Today it broadens out into the B1046 about halfway along, dropping us down into the valley of the Great Ouse and the old settlement of Eynesbury. There's no transition here between countryside and town, just a sudden zone of drab inter-war suburbia squeezed between the river and the east coast main line. A couple of roundabouts further on and we're in the *Blade Runner*-esque landscape of Little Barford Power Station: a row of huge steel buildings from which lines of pylons trail away like giants hauling fire buckets. And, although we can't see it, somewhere to the right of us the river is sliding placidly through water meadows by the side of Wyboston Lakes.

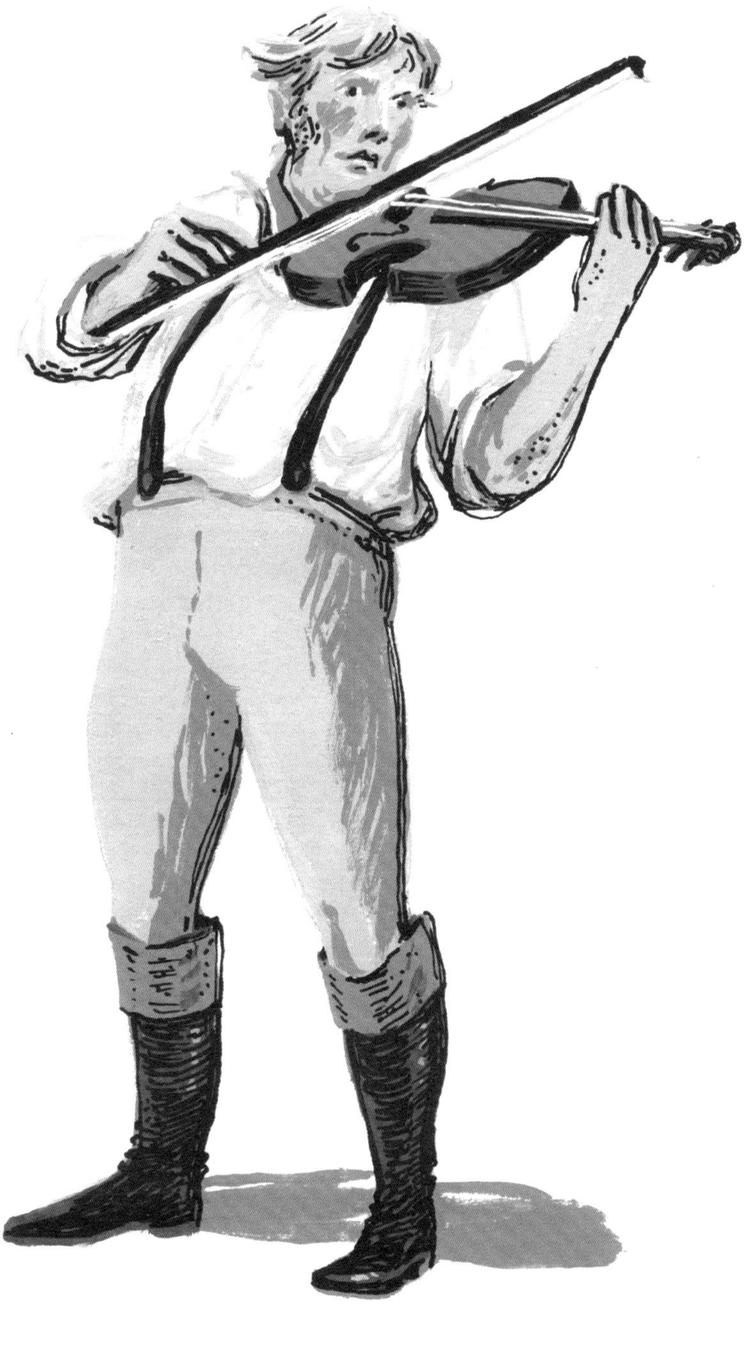

Musings XVI

It's in his blood, the wild swing of violin
with his grandfather's abandon, fired up
by the open hearth and smoke at Langley Bush,
where he learnt from the gypsies how to fly
the bow high, and was soon 'a desent scraper'.

There in the Bluebell, he's playing by ear
to a gaggle of neighbours, fingers skidding the strings,
bow arm swinging, body bent like a sapling
towards his father's singing face, pink with sweat
and the good cheer of John Barleycorn.

Here he hums the air of Highland Mary
to cheer him on the road… Who took away
his Cremona violin that made a rare noise –
and plenty? Music might have saved him
as Farinelli's singing cured the mad king.

The Beacon Moon

We're now heading south, approaching Tempsford on the end run of a detour that's taken us around the western side of the former Heath. Clare, on foot, was able to go directly across; or maybe not so directly. He was walking at random, increasingly desperate and despairing of finding his way. Footpaths and droves criss-crossed this wilderness, but none is likely to have been well tended. The few turnpikes were the only roads in the area with good footings and definite destinations, and it is tempting, because it makes for a tidy narrative, to suggest that he stuck to them. Unfortunately, the time frame of the events he describes—leaving Potton at sundown and settling to sleep in the dark somewhere north of Tempsford—simply does not permit this.

Before we took this trip, we'd talked to Harris about how Clare may have made his journey during the hours of darkness. If his broken shoe was giving him as much trouble as he says, he would have been too slow for a route that kept to turnpikes. Hobbling along at, say, 1.5 mph, it would have taken him about eight hours to complete, and this at a time of year when darkness lasted less than seven. In any event, he would have had to go as far north as Eynesbury before taking a turning south along the eastern side of the Great Ouse valley. "From that turning," Harris said, "Clare would be able to see St Neots: the towers of the two churches and the chimney of the mill would have been clearly visible against the night sky. Given his circumstances, I can't imagine him shunning the town, and carrying on aimlessly until he found the tollgate, which, after all, was much further south."

So even if Clare had started out on the St Neots road, at some point he would have left it and wandered west across the Heath, following pathways as he found them. He might even have been forced to negotiate stretches with no paths at all: local byways often petered out at sheep pastures or shepherds' huts. Little wonder, then, that as he says, "doubt and hopelessness made me turn so feeble that I was scarcely able to walk".

He must have been frightened as well. In a fragment of his autobiography he describes an incident that took place while he was at Casterton and courting Patty. Having escorted her home, he lost his way on the common that ran beside the river Gwash:

> twilight with its doubtful guidance overtook my musings and led me down a wrong track in crossing the common and as I coud not correct my self I got over a hedge and sat down on a baulk between a wheat field when the moon got up I started agen and on trying to get over the same hedge again as I thought to cross the common I saw somthing shine very bright on the other side I fancyd it to be bare ground beaten by the cows and sheep in hot weather but doubting I stoopd down to feel and to my terrord surprise I found it was water and while in that stooping posture I saw by the lengthy silver line that stretchd from me that it was the river if I had taken a step without this caution my love [would have met a sudden end][14]

But as he stumbled over the Heath, a fear of drowning would not have been the only thing oppressing him. Night-time in open country held other terrors for a man in a society where the supernatural was taken for granted. His childhood was spent working in the fields, listening to the old women of the village tell stories of "Jiants, Hobgobblins and faireys", and by the time he took his first job as potboy of the Bluebell public house those tales had taken firm root. On short winter days the 13-year-old Clare dreaded his weekly journey to the neighbouring village of Maxey to collect flour for his mistress because he had to pass two or three reputedly haunted spots along the way. Making a detour was not an option, for "it was impossible to go half a mile any were about the Lordship were there had nothing been said to be seen by those old women or some one else in their younger days". Instead, he told himself stories to bolster his courage and "keep ghosts and hobgoblings out of the question". This could only go so far in quelling his fears, however, "for as I passed those awful places, tho I dare not look boldly up, my eye was warily on the watch, glegging under my hat at every stir of a leaf or murmur of the wind", so that "a quaking leaf was able to make me swoon with terror".[15] And if on growing up he gained a more rational view of the world, it was one that could not withstand the onset of darkness; "tho I always felt in company a disbelief of ghosts witches etc," he confesses, "yet when I was a lone in the night my fancys created thousands and my fears was always on the look out every now and then turning round to see if aught was behind me."[16]

In 1824, just as he was turning 31, those fears were still with him. Recounting his visit to London that summer, he writes:

> When I used to go any were by my self [...] I used to sit at night till very late because I was loath to start [...] for fear of meeting with supernatural [apparitions] even in the busy paths of London and tho I was a stubborn disbeliever of such things in the day time yet at night their terrors came upon me ten fold and my head was as full of the terribles as a gossips — thin death like shadows and gobblings with soercer eyes were continually shaping in the darkness from my haunted imagination[17]

The following year, his rational inclinations were dealt a further blow by an eerie phenomenon he witnessed at Eastwell Green just south of Helpston. He wrote up the incident in an appendix to his journal, which he entitled 'The Will O Whisp or Jack A Lanthorn'. In it, he describes how he saw columns of marsh gas behaving as though they were conscious, self-directed beings—so convincingly, in fact, that in his own words they "robd me of the little philosophic reason[in]g which I had about them I now believe them spirits".[18]

Given his description of himself as a sceptic in the daytime and superstitious by night, it seems inconceivable that the terror he experienced on previous occasions did not return as he struggled on in the pitch dark. The sight of a tollgate lamp "shining as bright as the moon" must have come as a huge relief on more than one level—a sign he had not just been saved in body but also in soul.

The image is one of the most visually evocative in his account. From someone else it might be dismissed as cliché, but Clare was a writer of accurate and detailed observation, and the simile therefore repays some scrutiny—especially when considered in the context of a time when producing artificial light was a difficult business.

In 1841 the poor, and particularly the rural poor, mostly relied on smoky, malodorous rush lights for household illumination. The better-off could afford beeswax candles, or Argand lamps, which burned vegetable oils such as Colza,[19] but even these gave out a relatively modest light, so that the cosy glow of cottage windows that Clare reports seeing would have looked distinctly dim to modern eyes. Brighter-burning fuels such as paraffin wax and kerosene were still some twenty years off, awaiting the technologies to extract them from coal and rock oil.

As for exterior lighting, this was virtually unknown outside towns and cities. In London, street lamps lit by coal gas had become commonplace following their introduction in the 1810s. Clare remarked on them when first visiting the capital with Octavius Gilchrist, from which we know that by 1820 they had proliferated from the city proper to its fringes:

> I had read in my reading [made] easy of the worlds seven wonders but I found in london alone thousands   as we approachd it the road was lind wi lamps that diminishd in the distance to stars   this is London I exclaimd   he laughd at my ignorance and only increasd my wonder by saying we were yet several miles from it.[20]

Excepting carbon arc lamps, which were rarely used until the 1870s, nothing could rival the moon for brilliance. So, in making the comparison, Clare is indicating that by the standards of his day the tollgate lamp was very bright indeed. We can rule out the idea that it was an arc light, and we can likewise discount coal gas, as gas works were confined to towns. The lamp must therefore have run on oil, and while we might speculate about the effect of a relatively dim light on Clare's dark-adapted eyes, there is a simpler explanation for its brilliance; namely, that it was burning a type of fuel harvested from the sperm whale. 'Sperm oil', as it was called, fetched a high price, not just because it was extremely bright but also because—unlike other fuels—it produced a pure white light. While it was commonly burned in coach lamps to illuminate the way ahead, its use at a tollgate suggests that the gate in question was on a major route or at a junction of turnpikes, and the one at Tempsford was both. Even so, the toll keeper came out with a candle to inspect the lone traveller, indicating that it acted more as a beacon than a floodlight.

The brief exchange of words that took place beneath it, as Clare reports them, is curious. He did not inquire where he was; rather, he wanted to know whether he was heading north. And the answer he received—"When you get through the gate you are"—has proved puzzling. To see why, we need to understand the geography of the Tempsford gate. It was situated north of the village, at the meeting point of the Great North Road and a turnpike—sometimes referred to as the 'Loop Road'—which diverted coaches like the Stamford Regent away from the high road and towards St Neots and Huntingdon. Both branches of the junction therefore led in a northerly direction, with one taking an easterly bearing and the other a westerly one.

"My point is," I say to Harris when we consider the question together, "that both routes can be said to be 'going north', and in any case Clare's already walking north

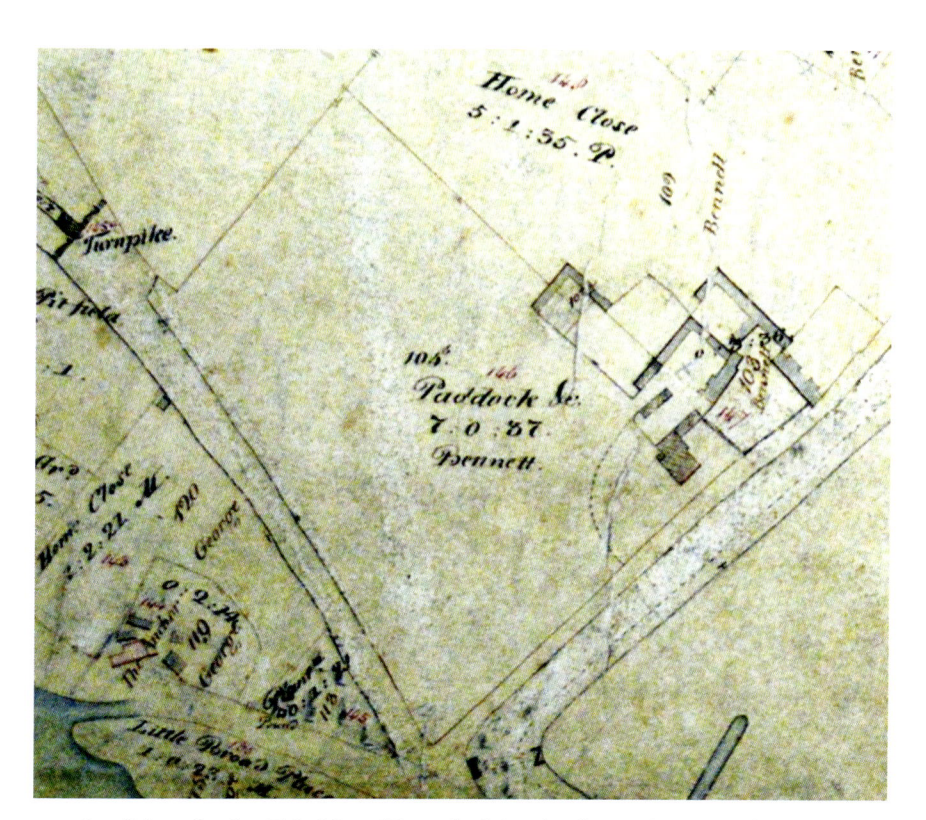

Detail from the 1829 Tithe Map of Tempsford showing the meeting point of Langford End and the Great North Road. The toll house is clearly shown flanked by two gates, the left leading to the Great North Road and the right to the St Neots Loop Road.

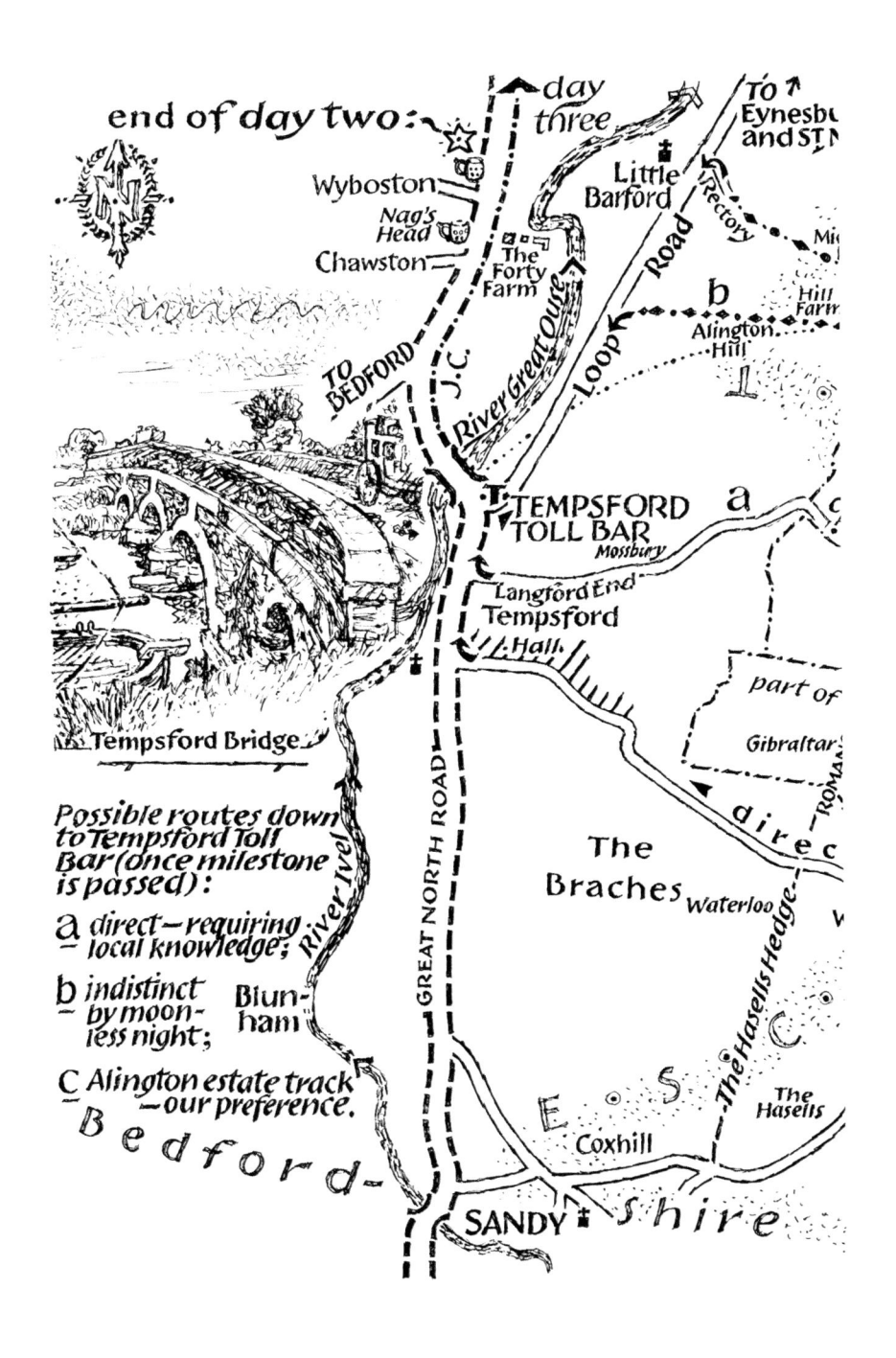

end of day two ❀ *day three*
Wyboston
Nag's Head
Chawston
TO BEDFORD
J.C.
The Forty Farm
River Great Ouse
Little Barford
Rectory
TO Eynesb[ury] and ST N[eots]
Hill Farm
b
Alington Hill
Loop Road
TEMPSFORD TOLL BAR
Mossbury
a
Langford End
Tempsford Hall
part of Gibraltar
Tempsford Bridge
GREAT NORTH ROAD
River Ivel
The Braches
Waterloo
direc[t]
ROMAN
The Hasells Hedge

Possible routes down to Tempsford Toll Bar (once milestone is passed):

a direct — requiring local knowledge;

b indistinct — by moonless night;

c Alington estate track — our preference.

Blunham
Bedford-shire
E S
Coxhill
The Hasells
SANDY

THE JOURNEY – BEDFORDSHIRE – THE BEACON MOON   243

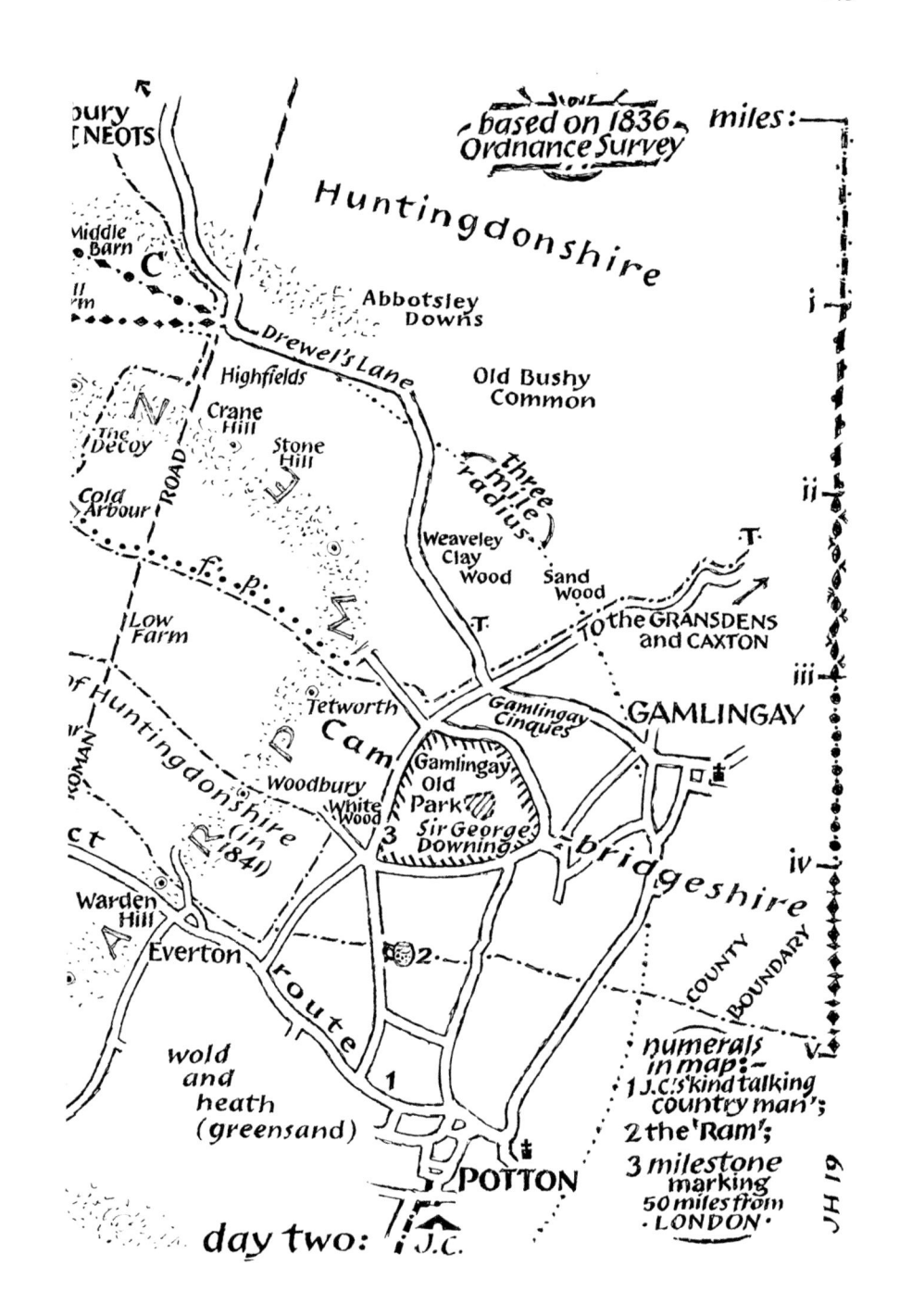

[Map based on 1836 Ordnance Survey showing the area around Gamlingay, Potton, and Everton. Key features labelled include:]

- *bury / ~~N~~EOTS*
- *Middle Barn*
- *Huntingdonshire*
- *Abbotsley Downs*
- *Drewel's Lane*
- *Highfields*
- *Crane Hill*
- *Stone Hill*
- *The Decoy*
- *Cold Arbour*
- *Old Bushy Common*
- *three mile radius*
- *Weaveley Clay Wood*
- *Sand Wood*
- *to the GRANSDENS and CAXTON*
- *Low Farm*
- *Tetworth*
- *Gamlingay Cinques*
- *GAMLINGAY*
- *of Huntingdonshire (in 1841)*
- *Woodbury / White Wood*
- *Gamlingay Old Park*
- *Sir George Downing*
- *Cambridgeshire*
- *Warden Hill*
- *Everton*
- *COUNTY BOUNDARY*
- *wold and heath (greensand)*
- *route*
- *day two:*
- *POTTON*
- *J.C.*

numerals in map:—
1 J.C.'s 'kind talking country man';
2 the 'Ram';
3 milestone marking 50 miles from LONDON

JH 19

when he arrives at the gate—he's approaching it from Tempsford village—so the toll keeper's comment makes no sense."

I bring out a tithe map I found in the Bedfordshire Records Office. Dating from 1829, it shows the position and layout of the tollgate. "You can see from this there are two gates standing side by side, with the left one leading to the Great North Road and the right one to the Loop Road."

"Yes," he says, after studying it carefully, "And that, in fact, suggests a rather intriguing possibility."

"Which is?"

"That he was *not* walking north when he encountered the gate, but *south*, down the Loop Road."

We'd discounted the turnpikes because there was simply not enough time for Clare to have taken them. I remind him of this.

"Ah," he says, "But suppose he stumbled across the Loop Road while cutting west across the Heath, well south of Eynesbury. That might work in terms of the schedule, mightn't it?"

I'm doubtful. As I recall, there were no paths or tracks meeting the Loop Road. "He'd have to trek across country a fair way to reach it, then."

"Well, not necessarily. Suppose he *was* on the road to Eynesbury, and then left it on the stretch called Drewels Lane."

"Why would he do that?"

"Why indeed, if there was no road or track to follow, but I'm pretty sure there *was*, even though it's probably not marked on your map."

I get out the 1836 map. As I thought, there's no sign of anything leading west. "You see," Harris says, pointing, "All that land over there by Little Barford—below the power station—was part of an estate owned by the Alington family, and around the time Clare was doing his walk they were expanding their operations, with a lot of building going on. There was a track leading through the estate for moving construction materials, and it linked up with the Loop Road on the other side."

"So, you're saying Clare followed this track all the way to the Loop Road and then turned south?"

"Exactly, so when he reaches Tempsford he is coming *south* through the right-hand tollgate, where he's met by the keeper. He then goes *north* through the left-hand gate to get onto the Great North Road. When you see it like that, the keeper's statement makes perfect sense."

"*If* there was a track there," I say.

"Oh, it was there all right, and still is. It's been tarmacked over and turned into a proper road. The only question is, when was it built? The workers' cottages look to be 1840s, but there are no records to say when building started on the farm proper."

Bridget and I can't recall seeing a road leading off Drewels Lane, but when we check Google Maps it's there—narrow and single-tracked to be sure, but evidence that Clare might have reached Tempsford entirely by road. Though it's far from conclusive, Harris's suggestion fits both the written account and the timeline. Clare could have walked it in six hours, maybe less.

Musings XVII

You are humming Highland Mary
as you climb the flood plain's causeway,
the long night's tension ebbing with each breath.
In the dark the river slides through water meadows
cleared for grazing after Lammas tide.

As the road rises on the arches of the 1820 bridge,
ripples sucking round its cutwaters,
perhaps you remember your fright that other night
when lost in rhyme you nearly stepped to death
on a moonlit river's lengthy silver line.

Then as now, the Great Ouse slowly snakes
to the Wash through flat East Anglian land;
in a timeless moment, under the weightless fluff
of clematis vitalba, the old ford fills with Roman chariots
and farm carts from medieval times.

You missed the Anchor when you passed the turnpike gates,
but in this June light, its Victorian veranda,
riverside terrace, willow trees and lawns
remind us of de Wint, whose sketches that breathe
with living freshness you so admired.

Ever-present Whispers

Tempsford in the twenty-first century is a village divided. During the 1960s the A1 trunk road—four lanes of dual carriageway—was driven straight across it along the line of the Great North Road. And while that too had been a through route, it had at least connected the village to the rest of the world. Now, accessible only via slip roads, Tempsford is invisible; cars and lorries thunder through it in seconds, oblivious to its presence.

Bridget and I have been following the Barford Road down from Eynesbury, past Little Barford Power Station and the farm buildings of the Alington estate. Now that we're on our final approach, the road has started to run parallel to the motorway—so closely, in fact, that from the air it looks like a third carriageway. The settlement's partition is brought home by a sign that reads "For Tempsford Village Hall Follow Tempsford (Church End)", meaning, in effect, "the centre of your village is on the other side of the motorway; you'll have to negotiate two roundabouts and a flyover to reach it". Church End, where the village hall is located, makes up the western half. Its eastern counterpart, on our side of the A1, is called 'Tempsford (Station Road)', and comprises—as well as the road—the village cricket ground and Tempsford Hall. Prior to the arrival of the railway, it went by the name of Langford End—a loose agglomeration of shops, pubs and farms straggling Tempsford Hall's northern boundary.

Stonebridge Farm, close to where the tollgate stood in Clare's day. This magnificent house was the most opulent in Langford End—today's Station Road.

Tempsford's village sign on the A1, in the shadow of the footbridge that links its two halves. Pedestrians wishing to walk between them must brave the speeding traffic of the northbound carriageway, limited—but only in theory, alas—to 60 mph.

I turn left and park by a surviving section of boundary wall, where a sign indicates that the house is now the corporate headquarters of a nationally-known building contractor; one more case, as Bridget remarks, of big business appropriating the trappings of aristocracy. "Meet the new boss," I reply, as we turn back and wander up the road, "Same as the old boss."

The street is tranquil, almost suburban. The old shops and pubs have been transformed into handsome upmarket homes, with little cul-de-sacs of modern terraced dwellings shoehorned in between them. If Clare arrived by way of Cold Arbour he would have walked down here straight off the Heath. There were fewer houses then, more sparsely distributed. In the dark he might have sensed the outlines of the Wesleyan Chapel, the bakery and the butcher's, and—depending on how late it was—seen lights in the windows of the Black Horse and the White Hart.[21] At the end of the street he'd have passed its most imposing house, the Georgian Stonebridge Farm, before turning right onto the Great North Road. There he would have found the tollgate, with its great moon of a lamp, directly in front of him.

There are no shops here; the last of them—the village general stores—closed in 1989. It makes me wonder, not for the first time, how those who do not drive manage to survive in places like this. Perhaps, as I suggest to Bridget, the village's western splinter might have some amenities for the locals. But even if it does, getting there is not simple. There's a huge steel gantry of a footbridge to cross, followed by several minutes' walk against the oncoming traffic of the A1 behind flimsy-looking barriers; not the most pleasant of outings for the young and fit, and for the elderly, one imagines, positively daunting.

The former Anchor Hotel, purpose-built in 1830 as a coaching inn and now—in keeping with its colourful history—a private members' club for swingers.

On the far side of the bridge there's a bus stop, and behind it, the imposing bulk of the Anchor Hotel. At first glance this magnificent pile, with its heraldic decoration and ornate chimneys, looks to date from Tudor times, though it is in fact a late-Regency pastiche that owes its existence to a re-routing of the Great North Road across the Great Ouse. Until 1820, the road had forded the river just west of Langford End, but the completion that year of a stone bridge a few hundred yards downstream prompted the construction of a new section of highway to meet it. The old section, with its now less attractive crossing point, was quickly abandoned. As a result 'The Anchor', an alehouse that had served travellers for over two hundred years, suddenly found itself marooned from the Great North Road and cut off from its principal source of income. The Anchor Hotel, which opened on July 4th 1831, was its replacement, specifically built to catch the trade it had been progressively losing over the previous decade.[22]

Both establishments belonged to the Tempsford estate, then owned by the Stuart family. They designed the hotel to be large and lavish, a testament to the prevailing mood of optimism about the growth and longevity of coaching. An auction catalogue from 1913 lists it as having a tea room, a kitchen, a tap room, a smoke room, a private office, a sitting room, a dining hall, eight bedrooms, a larder and a dairy, as well as sheds, stables and other outbuildings.[23]

If its design was glorious, its history has been less so. Its anonymity as a purveyor of beds on a major trunk road made it a natural place for assignations, and it acquired a certain reputation in the village. As for its economic fortunes, these waxed and waned over the years, but overall the trend was downward. In 1927 a surveyor's report described it as a free house operating a six-day licence,

THE JOURNEY – BEDFORDSHIRE – EVER-PRESENT WHISPERS 249

The gable end of the Anchor Hotel was decorated lavishly in stone, testifying to the builders' conviction that coaching would thrive and flourish.

The Great Ouse flowing past the Anchor Hotel towards Tempsford Bridge.

with water laid on and electric light from its own plant. The landlord kept no books, and takings were estimated to be around £800 to £900 per year, which the surveyor thought rather low. It remained part of the Stuart family estate until the 1970s, when it was sold off to Hamilton Taverns, who in turn sold it to Scottish & Newcastle Breweries.

It finally closed in 2010 but almost immediately gained a new lease of life for the very reason it had acquired its former notoriety, as a local newspaper reported with the jaunty headline, "Swingers' Club is in the Right Place, say Owners".[24] In 2011, locals were up in arms about its conversion into 'The Vanilla Alternative', a private members' club that would, in their view, "change the image of the village". Their online petition garnered only 30 signatures, however, and the Parish Council, bowing to the inevitable, looked the other way. It was a sort of apotheosis, after all.

Today the place looks down-at-heel. The original entrance—a Gothic oak door facing the direction of the village—has been retired from use, replaced by a modern hotel reception tacked onto the back of the building, discreetly out of sight. Weeds grow everywhere, and a general air of neglect is compounded by an outbuilding constructed from naked breeze blocks. It's as if the owners do not wish to attract attention, or—God forbid—have the place mistaken for a *bona fide* hotel. To that end, perhaps, the old pub sign has been replaced by one that shows a woman sitting demurely on a couch with her legs spread wide. Fortunately she's wearing a long dress, so, as Bridget jokes while I take photos, it's all in the best possible taste. Unfortunately this assumed air of sophistication is somewhat punctured by a poster advertising a camping event on an adjoining meadow. Sid James and Barbara Windsor instantly spring to mind, and I wonder what it is about the idea of the British engaged in sex that's so intrinsically hilarious.

The Anchor Hotel is a strictly nocturnal habitat, and desolate in the naked light of day. The patrons have all stolen away under the cover of darkness, leaving the glass-fronted reception abandoned and the car park empty. All that's needed to complete the scene is a tumbleweed rolling by.

The meadow at the building's rear sweeps down to the Great Ouse, which slides past in a graceful arc like something out of a Corot painting. It draws us down as we follow a tree-shaded track to the cottage that was once the old Anchor Inn.

When the Anchor began trading is uncertain, but we do know it was operating in 1794 because John Byng mentions it in his journal entry for September 15th of that year, the day he undertook an angling expedition with a group of friends:

> This morning I had appointed my generals to assemble at early day upon the banks of the Ouse – to secure the ford leading to Wroxton […] before nine o'clock, I was at the Anchor alehouse; but where are my troops? None arrived!!

And then later:

> We were now anxious for departure, but as F and Finch were not come in I and O took another turn for an hour – upon the rivers bank – opposite our public house, where we caught some fish.[25]

In 1810 it appeared in a valuation as "a public house near the bridge, a stable and a close at the back of the house, a meadow by the river, ozier bed and a narrow slip over the river". Four years later it was offered for sale "with stabling and outbuildings, yard, garden and sundry pieces of meadow, pasture and arable land and ozier ground containing ten acres, three roods and ten perches".

The former Anchor Inn, now a private residence, and the old section of the Great North Road that led to a ferry crossing over the Great Ouse.

Tempsford Bridge, built in 1820 to replace the old ford and ferry crossing a couple of hundred yards upstream.

The track we're following is in fact the old redundant section of highway, and beyond the former inn it vanishes, sunk by time and disuse into the long meadow grass. We trace its route as far as the ferry crossing. There used to be a wooden footbridge here, presumably for travellers who didn't want to pay to be rowed across, but after the road was re-routed it fell into disrepair and was eventually demolished. The bridge for the new section was built only a couple of hundred yards downstream, close to where Byng and his friends caught their fish.

If Clare reached Tempsford by Langford End—the street on the Hall's northern boundary—he would have passed the Anchor Hotel as he neared the toll bar. Whichever way he made his approach, the moment he passed through the gate the village was behind him. Ahead lay lush green country, prime grazing land that would have given no hint of the misery it inflicted on travellers during the long months of winter. Standing, as Charles Harper puts it, "where the Ouse and the Ivel come to their sluggish confluence",[26] it invariably flooded to a depth that could easily drown livestock and bring the unwary traveller to a watery end.

Some coaches, including the Stamford Regent, left the Great North Road at the tollgate and took the Loop Road to St Neots and Huntingdon: a route that led them across low-lying land, and often into danger. Harper reports that on one occasion, "two old ladies were given a terrible fright, the road being deeply flooded and the water coming into the coach, so that they had to stand on the seats". He adds that had the driver been less experienced the vehicle might have ended up in a ditch, whereupon "it would have been 'all up' with the 'insides' for certain and perhaps for the 'outsides' as well".[27]

The Great North Road above Tempsford stood on higher ground, and the new bridge had adjoining causeways across the meadows of the Great Ouse where floods were at their most extensive. Spanning the river on three broad arches, it was about fifty yards long and ten wide; at the time able to take vehicles in both directions. Today it carries the A1's northbound lanes, while traffic heading south is routed over a modern crossing nearby.

The bridge can be reached from river level by a flight of wooden steps bolted to its western flank. At the top, a wicket gate gives access to a narrow strip of pavement, but with vehicles flashing past just feet away at 70 mph or more, only the suicidal would want to use it. The pavement recedes away in both directions, presumably for the benefit of those hardy—or foolhardy—souls who prefer hiking the A1 to driving it. If we chose, we could return to the car on it. Instead we decide to take the scenic route back after we've explored the bridge's bridle tunnel.

Round-arched and narrow, this short passage is eerily dark and claustrophobic even by day, and at night, one imagines, positively Gothic with menace; it has the sort of entrance you expect bats to issue from. On the other side there's a marina of cabin cruisers and caravans sprawled around the southbound bridge of the A1.

There's no evidence of a staithe here in Clare's time, but one next to a bridge carrying the Great North Road would have made perfect sense. Though the Great Ouse was shallow, it was navigable in broad, flat-bottomed barges known as Fen Lighters. Roughly fifty feet long, and with a cargo capacity of twenty-five tons, these were the principal means of moving goods around the Fens. Empty, they could float on a depth of two feet, and for every ton added they settled an inch in the water, giving them a draught of just over four. A strictly local design, they were built at boatyards in Cambridge, Ely and Upwell.[28]

Lighters must have been familiar to Clare, sailing in 'gangs'—groups of craft coupled head-to-tail moving under a combination of wind and horse power. A gang usually comprised four lighters worked by a skipper and his mate, along with a boy called the 'knocker' who was in charge of the horse. The second craft in the line had

The bridle tunnel through Tempsford Bridge on the river's east bank. As its name suggests, horses were led rather than ridden through this confined space.

a cabin for the men, while the one behind that—called the 'hollip'—was fitted with a small shed where the boy could sleep when permitted. The rear lighter towed a 'butt boat' where the horse could be stowed when the gang was under sail.

Manoeuvring a gang was arduous. The front lighter had no rudder, only a long pole linking it to the craft behind. On approaching a bend the skipper would adjust the steering ropes that allowed it to follow the line of the bank. The trailing lighters were then eased round, each in their turn, by sheer muscle power. Much of the work fell to the knocker, so boys who did the job had to be exceptionally tough— accustomed, if nothing else, to treading muddy banks in bare feet for up to twenty miles a day. They also slept rough, only being allowed on the hollip when goods were not being carried. Along with the men, they lived on a diet of pickled beef and pork, and drank vast quantities of beer. In many respects lighter crews had the same social status as waggoners—looked on as outcasts; the lowest of the low.

Lighters were prevalent in the fens from about 1700 to 1850. Had Clare seen them at Tempsford Bridge they might have reminded him of his boyhood journey on the Nene to Wisbech. As a principal shipping artery from the East Anglian farmlands to the Wash, this river was thronged with gangs carrying all kinds of cargo, from coal, salt and agricultural produce to construction materials such as timber, brick and stone. During the Napoleonic Wars, they even carried captured French combatants destined for the internment camp at Norman Cross.

A gang of two fen lighters being hauled by a boy, or 'knocker', on a horse. Location and date of photograph unknown.

St Peter's at Church End, Tempsford's western half. Like the rest of the village, church and graveyard are kept in immaculate condition.

Returning from the bridge, we get back in the car and cross the A1 to Church End, Tempsford's western half. Like Station Road it's a backwater, but this was not always so. Church Street—the backbone of the old settlement—used to be part of the Great North Road, and for two centuries there was not an hour in the day when traffic of one sort or another wasn't passing the parish church at the heart of the village.

When the A1 arrived in the 1960s, it clipped the south-western corner of Tempsford Hall, necessitating the compulsory purchase of part of the park and marooning the main gates. For almost forty years the thin wedge of land between the dual carriageway and the former entrance was a wilderness, neglected by the Highways Agency and unloved by the locals. Its eventual purchase and rehabilitation into a 'nature reserve' by those same locals suggests a gung-ho community spirit at odds with the notion of a fractured village.

Collective action can arise from necessity when there's no money to be had, or from a surfeit of leisure—and the material ease with which to enjoy it—when there's plenty around. In Tempsford the latter was definitely the case, because in defiance of all logic, having its geography wrecked and being withdrawn from the road network has turned it into a desirable place to live. A glance at local estate agents' windows will reveal existing properties changing hands for half a million to a million pounds each, with developers promising more. In light of this, the question I posed about amenities for the locals seems embarrassingly naïve. Of course Tempsford doesn't have any. It doesn't need any. Just to *be* locals, people will have the means to take the A1 to work, or to the superstore.

The 51st milestone on a remnant of the Great North Road at Church End.

There's a sense, too, that the A1 has become such an established part of the village that it no longer registers. It curves away from Church Street and back again in the shape of a longbow, never more than 75 metres distant, yet the street's calm and orderly demeanour suggests there's nothing around for miles but bucolic idyll. Certainly the seventeenth-century Wheatsheaf, Tempsford's last remaining pub, and the old timber-framed White Hart Inn—now a private residence known as Gannock House—both conform to that rustic ideal.

We pass by them as we walk north, towards the parish church of St Peter with its striking medieval tower and nave of banded clunch and ironstone. Like the rest of the village it's picture-postcard perfect. The churchyard lawn is beautifully manicured, the headstones scrubbed up to a golden glow, and ivy drapes itself across the tombs so artfully that one half-glimpses the hidden hand of a stage dresser. It's a painting of Clare's own time come to life: a vision of Picturesque neglect—the Platonic Ideal of St Etheldreda's churchyard at Hatfield.

This is as far as we can get from the A1. Beyond the church, the street begins its long, slow convergence with the highway. A little further on there's a crossroads with the lane which, on the A1's far side, leads past the southern edge of the Hall, making for Warden Hill and the village of Everton. On a small green nearby, we find a recently raised memorial to the agents of the Special Operations Executive, who parachuted into Nazi-occupied France from a nearby airfield.

As we walk, the ever-present whisper of the A1 gradually rises like static on an untuned radio. Where the houses run out and give way to close-set trees, we find a relic of the Great North Road—a milestone telling us we're 51 miles from London. Directly opposite is Tempsford Hall's old gateway. This now admits visitors to the Millennium Garden Sanctuary, the local eyesore turned tranquil woodland retreat (if such a thing can exist just yards from a dual carriageway).

The entrance—stone columns, lions rampant, wrought-iron gates and all—is a modern replica of the long-since-demolished original. Behind its imposing façade there are bark-chip paths winding among mature trees and wooden benches for the weary or the merely contemplative.

The entrance to Tempsford's Millennium Garden Sanctuary now occupies the spot where the gateway to the Hall used to stand unguarded by bollards.

The old White Hart Inn at Church End, now a private residence known as Gannock House.

There is also a notice explaining how this all came about. In the spring of 1999, it says, locals proposed to turn "a very neglected, run down and overgrown site" into "a wildlife sanctuary and a village feature". With an estimated cost of £22,500, the final bill came in at £37,000—an overspend to make even the most brazen cabinet minister blush—yet with donations from various quarters, public and private, the job was done. A real note of justifiable pride is struck by the statement that it took "approximately twenty months of hard work carried out by the residents of Tempsford Village" to bring about.

I can't help wondering, though, as we wander its pristine paths, whether all this tidying up has benefitted the wildlife quite as much as it has the villagers. Were I a shrew or a vole, or just a plain old crow, I might have preferred things the way they were, no matter how unsightly to human eyes.

In most respects Church Street is a clone of Station Road: a mixture of farms, handsome old residences and twentieth-century housing. For sheer visual impact, though, it's the structures that were here in Clare's time which stand out, from the great Tudor half-timbered houses to the barns and sheds of Ouse Farm and Church Farm: even a wooden outbuilding that reminds us of the 'hovel' he slept in at Stevenage. Like Station Road, too, it becomes sparser the further on it goes, until finally it kisses (without embracing) the A1, and runs out completely.

Musings XVIII

We stand beside the drovers' road on Gamlingay Heath,
then nowt but a track, wide to encompass
sheep in motion, weaving close-cropped flanks
through sun and shade in a wave of dust,
like the sea billowing between high banks.

Opposite the imposter Ram of 1850
we conjure a tiny pop-in beer shop
with a lighted window, where working men
enjoy their penn'orth of ale on the road to Smithfield,
Defoe's 'greatest meat market in the world'.

Clare might have found shelter here, but had no cash
and remembered those saucy drovers from the morning.
He dared not go in. Beds were probably ready,
pushed close in a back room – and makeshift truckles
in the gighouse – but our wanderer pressed on.

A Shot Fox

About a week after our expedition to the Heath, I receive an email from the Gamlingay Historical Society: a response to my request for material on the Ram. Ominously headed "Probably not what you were expecting", it bears quoting here in full:

> People who have tried to work out the route of John Clare's 1841 walk from the evidence of his confused recollection have all made the reasonable assumption that the Ram he mentions after leaving Potton must be the beerhouse of that name on Gamlingay Heath, and that when Clare says it was on his left he must have been mistaken, because coming from Potton it would have been on his right.
>
> The problem with this assumption is that in 1841 there was no Ram beerhouse on Gamlingay Heath, which was then, as it had always been, Common land. In 1844 the first steps were taken to enclose the parish. A map was made that year showing how the land would be divided up among the landholders, with separate fields awarded to individual owners in proportion to their previous holding of strips in the open fields.
>
> On the Heath two blocks of land were given to the Reverend William Wilkieson of Woodbury. By 1848 the changes were complete, and the Enclosure Award was confirmed. Wilkieson immediately set to work building sixty dwellings in the Gothic style on his land, one of which became the Ram. Building work may have started straight away in 1844, more probably in 1848.
>
> The Royal Commission on Historical Monuments in 1968 dated these buildings, which it described as a colony, as 'c 1850'. There are no buildings in that area of the parish on the 1836 OS map, the 1844 Enclosure map or the 1850 Tithe map. The Ram therefore cannot pre-date 1844, and had probably not been finished in 1850. By the 1851 Census there are some 40 or so cottages on the Heath listed as occupied but it is not possible to locate each one.
>
> Certainly, at the time Clare undertook his epic walk in 1841 there was no Ram on Gamlingay Heath. The earliest known reference to it by name comes from the *Cambridge Independent Press* of 27 Feb 1864 which reported an inquest held there.

The society has helpfully attached reference documents, including copies of the enclosure and tithe maps, presumably by way of apology for having, as they put it, "shot our fox". The text, they explain, is for an article in their forthcoming newsletter.

It goes without saying that this comes as a shock, not least because the Ram on the Heath has been an accepted part of Clare scholarship for the best part of four decades. Our first move is to double-check the supplied references; they are, of course, rock solid. Our second is to consult Harris, who proposes we should revisit the site together and reassess the evidence for ourselves.

Autumn is well advanced by the time we park outside the Ram again. The morning air is chilly but Harris is prepared for it, togged up in his all-weather gear and woolly hat. He has a sketchbook to hand and Bridget has her notepad at the ready, but I've not bothered to unpack my cameras. I've been thinking about how,

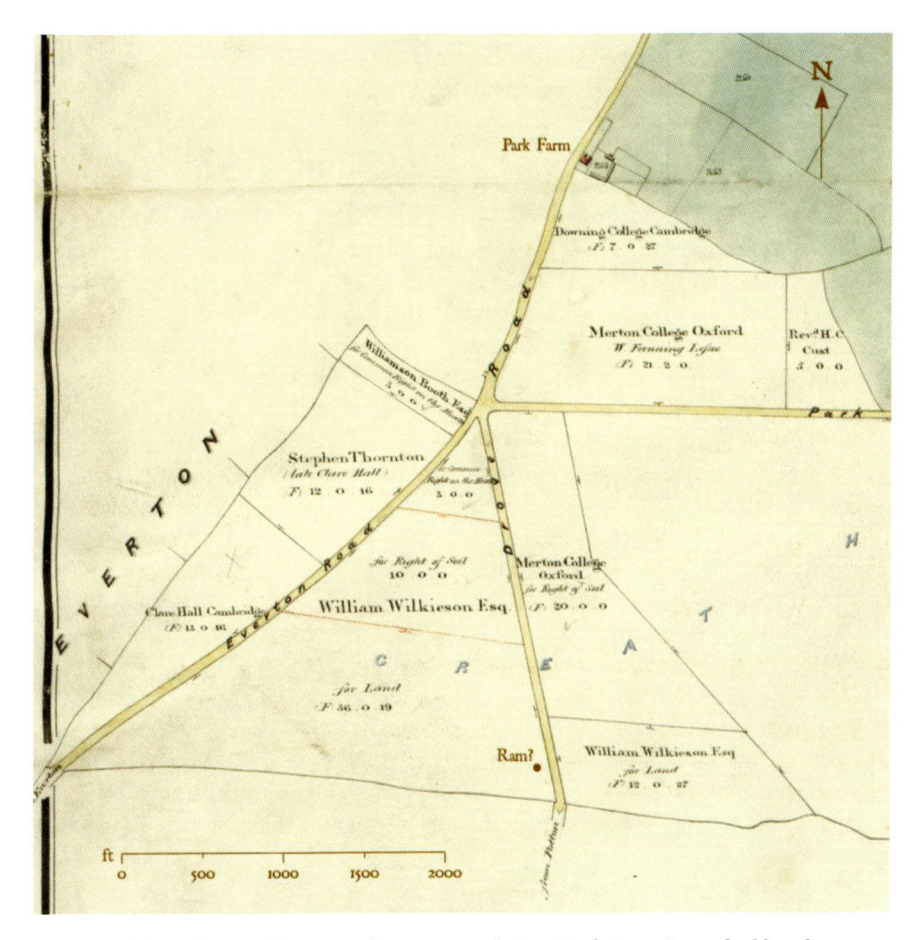

Detail from the Gamlingay Enclosure Map of 1844. Park Farm is marked but there are no buildings where the Ram should be. This may suggest Clare saw a drover's beerhouse on an encroachment on the west side of Drove Road that was later replaced on the east side by the house still known locally as 'The Ram'.

when we were last here, the evidence of our eyes was so convincing, and so wrong; or to put it more honestly, how easily we had convinced ourselves of evidence that was simply not there.

"The Gamlingay lot are right," Harris says after studying the buildings around us. "All these houses date from around 1850, including your pub here."

"So it didn't exist in 1841?"

"Couldn't have. The style's a clincher. It'd be like coming across a Regency building at the time of George the First."

He points at the house next door. "See the cowling above the first-floor window? That's your classic fifties Gothic right there—rather charming in its own way, though a bit extravagant for an out-of-the-way-place like this. The chap who built it obviously liked his architecture. Any idea who he was?"

"The owner of Woodbury Manor." I reply, "A man called Wilkieson. A bit of a mover and shaker in these parts, apparently. When the area was enclosed he got a large tract of land on that side of the road,"—I point to the cottages opposite the Ram—"and most of this side was awarded to Merton College Oxford, though he did receive a parcel just here where the houses are."

"Well that's all very satisfactory," Harris says, "Because there's no doubt in my mind that the whole colony was put up at the same time and by the same builders, and all on this chap Wilkieson's land."

I ask him why he calls this place a 'colony'. He explains that landowners in receipt of enclosure grants often built settlements for agricultural workers on their newly acquired property, and since those settlements tended to be remote—on previously common or 'waste' land—they were referred to, half jokingly, as 'colonies'.

"Like Botany Bay," Bridget says.

"In New South Wales?" asks Harris, sounding doubtful, "Well I suppose so, by analogy."

I shake my head. "Not that one. Bridget means the Botany Bay on Enfield Chase. This place is identical—built for the same purpose; no wonder it felt so familiar the last time we were here."

"Well," Bridget says, "Given all that, I think we have to conclude that before the enclosure there was nothing here but empty heath."

Harris looks thoughtful. "Yet the name of the pub is so suggestive, considering we're on a drove road. Just think, you've got sheep and cattle and Lord knows what else passing along daily. Your man Wilkieson's just up the road; and when he's awarded the land he puts up a pub to catch all that trade. Let's suppose for a moment that by doing so he's just legitimising something that's already been going on for years."

"On an encroachment?" asks Bridget.

"Just so. This would've been the ideal place to set up a trading post for drovers to have a drink and get their animals foddered. I can't imagine no-one ever thought of doing it."

The idea of an unsanctioned, pre-enclosure alehouse doesn't strike me as very likely. "Structures weren't permitted on common land, were they?"

"Well, that depended on the structure. Permanent buildings, no, but temporary ones—shepherds' huts and what-have-you—those were all right, and it's a small step from them to something larger, like a wooden shack. And then if you wanted to build a proper house you could do so, provided you put it up, roof and all, within 24 hours. Then you'd have squatters' rights."

If I understand Harris correctly, he's proposing that a Ram stood on this spot before Wilkieson built the colony—very likely on the left-hand side of the road, where he was granted land. "A timber house," Harris suggests, "a shack or whatever, thrown up by the estate workers and roofed with prefabricated trusses so the thing's structurally complete inside a day."

So, then, a wooden building—a sort of 'Ram-shackle'? With maybe a single room and a hayloft or hovel on one side? Later, when I put the idea to the Gamlingay

Historical Society, they say it's not impossible. Such places existed all over the area without ever being recorded on maps or documents. In an email, Jim Brown of the Society outlined the challenges involved in tracking them down:

> One thing to bear in mind is that Gamlingay's Ram was a beerhouse, and beerhouses only appeared after the 1830 Act allowing them to be set up. Some of them consisted of little more than a room in a private house where beer was served, and many of them didn't exist for very long. I've been researching Gamlingay for 40 years and just discovered one in Gamlingay I'd never heard of before, called the Bricklayer's Arms. It was described as well-established when it was sold in 1862, but the last I can find of it was in 1877 when the license was transferred. It's quite possible that the Ram you are looking for was also a beerhouse and will be equally difficult to track down.[29]

"And," Harris says, "somewhere like that would be exactly the kind of place where Clare could doss down. I'm guessing your average pub wouldn't have wanted a tramp in the outhouse. Perhaps that's why the chap with the hamper recommended it."

Musings XIX

There is a sense of disconnect.
We sidle on a verge of beaten grass
between the flow of A1 traffic pounding south
and nettles glistening in the April damp;
then veer left through budding hawthorn.

Beyond a broken fence the building looms,
a roofless ruin. There is no visible door,
but lilac flowers from the former owners' garden
overhang the larder window, where stacks
of shelves stand open to the weather.

Is this the house where John Clare came
in the early hours of a moonless
July night? Was it here he heard
the sound of inmates gone to roost
and stretched out in the porch to sleep?

We've waited what seems ages to explore this house
but it's been left to rot; no blue plaque here.
A self-seeded sycamore pushes up
through the foundations like a strangler fig
invading the abandoned temple of a forgotten god.

But there's no sign there ever was a porch
and we settle on another roadside house instead.
Outside, a flowering cherry cascades pink for spring;
and as Harris says, 'a good ruin is a rare thing'.
So in the end we do connect.

A Very Odd House

Ellis hands the narrative back to Bridget…

I take over again at the point where Clare, just having found his way off Gamlingay Heath, passes through the tollgate at Tempsford. While my earlier writing was based on circumstantial evidence supported by local historical records and the evidence of surviving roads and buildings, I now have Clare's first-hand account as my primary source. Inevitably this raises new questions. Exactly what kind of text is it? How did he decide what to include and what to leave out? How much is invented? How did his state of mind over the remaining 36 hours of the walk affect his memory when he came to write? Most importantly, perhaps, how did he want to present himself? He had already produced autobiographical pieces for public consumption, so was the *Journey* more of the same?

From this point on there is no question about the route he followed, which means we have a yardstick against which to gauge the accuracy of his account: the fit between the narrative and the road. Ellis and I decide, as a first step to answering my questions, to undertake a close reading of the text while tracking his every move—as far as is possible—on the maps of the time.

Once Clare was through the tollgate, his spirits revived; as his doubts vanished he "soon cheered up and hummed the tune of highland Mary". His optimism was soon rewarded:

> I at length fell in with an odd house all alone near a wood but I could not see what the sign was though the sign seemed to stand oddly enough in a sort of trough or spout   there was a large porch over the door and being weary I crept in and glad enough I was to find I could lye with my legs straight

Our 1836 map shows a group of buildings between Tempsford and Eaton Socon, near the 53rd milestone and a little north of the Nag's Head Inn. On paper at least 'Forty Farm', as it's labelled, looks to be a good candidate for Clare's stopover. When we check it out on Google Maps we find it standing close to a patch of long-established woodland, which fits well with his description; equally promising is an old photo on the British Listed Buildings website showing a farmhouse partly surrounded by trees.[30] It's clear from the satellite view that the farm is now a ruin. On doing some further research, Ellis discovers that it has also been the subject of a YouTube video by a group of urban explorers. When he tries to contact them online, however, there's a deafening silence at their end followed by the swift withdrawal of the video. Their paranoia appears to stem from a fear of being prosecuted for trespass, as among other things the video documents a close shave with the owner. When we debate with Harris the wisdom of making our own little foray to the place, we conclude it's the only way to test our hypothesis, possible confrontations with the management notwithstanding. "There's a McDonalds right next door," Ellis says, not very helpfully, "If we're caught we can always say we were looking for a short cut."

The Forty Farm, just south of Wyboston: a prosperous concern in 1841, when it had recently been enlarged and extended. Evidence for this can be seen around the doorway, where gault bricks supplant the older red.

    The farm entrance lies directly off the southbound A1. From Google Street View it's clear that parking beside it won't be an option because it's too close to the road. Driving in is also out of the question: the track beyond it has vanished beneath hummocks of grass and scrubby undergrowth, and, as Ellis points out, his Volvo may have four-wheel drive but it's hardly a Chieftain tank. McDonalds' car park would be the ideal place, but we'll be making our approach northbound, on the wrong side of the A1 to reach it. We consider doing a loop around one of the interchanges but in the end decide to leave the car at Wyboston on a by-passed stretch of the old Great North Road, and walk to the farm along the southbound carriageway.

    As we park, we have moment of a *déjà-vu*. Wyboston is Tempsford in miniature, sliced down the middle by four lanes of tarmac and held together only by a metal footbridge: too insignificant a place for a bypass. The eastern side, where we've fetched up, has an odd collection of buildings, two of which, Harris assures us, were in existence when Clare passed through. The rest, he says, mostly date from the 1850s or 60s. In particular he points to a pebble-dashed house called South Corner, which looks to me as if it could have been put up at any time in the last hundred years. Only when Harris directs our attention to the window frames and roof do I realise it must be seventeenth century; the render has utterly ruined what otherwise might have been a characterful, even charming, building. Ellis, disgusted by the sight, pulls a face but takes a few photos anyway.

He and Harris debate the merits and demerits of pebble dashing while I take in our surroundings. We're standing in the middle of what was once the main highway and is now a quiet cul-de-sac. Next door to South Corner there's a black timber garage of the type that was common on major highways during the early twentieth century; a combination of filling station and repair shop. It seems to be in use because parked outside it are several vintage cars awaiting renovation. Pre-war advertising on the front wall instructs me to buy "Redline, for Spirit", and informs me that "Dominion Motor Spirit" is "Always the same, always Good". I can't decide whether these adverts are original to the building or just a kitschy attempt to conjure up the golden days of motoring.

There's no more time to explore this oddity because the others, still deep in conversation, have set off ahead, striding down to the end of the road and onto a narrow strip of pavement by the A1. This is even more unnerving than the roadside path at Tempsford, because there's no barrier between us and the traffic. Luckily, we only have a short walk, and for once we're going faster than the cars. It's rush hour and both southbound lanes are repeatedly edging forward, stopping, and edging forward again. There's the familiar stink of exhaust, the susurrus of idling engines, and I'm unpleasantly aware of the mass of canned humanity squeezed together along the road's narrow confines while the rest of the world, on this mild April morning, is empty of people and breathing free.

When we reach the farm we find that the front yard has indeed fallen to scrub, but the real surprise is the farmhouse. From the satellite view we could tell it was derelict, but the full extent of its ruination is only apparent up close. The frames

The ground floor interior of the Forty Farm, with its carpet of collapsed ceiling joists.

have gone from the windows, which stare blankly back while we peer inside to find that the upper storey has collapsed. Joists lean jaggedly down from the ceiling, or lie heaped, like disused railway sleepers, among other detritus on the floor—a blue-painted door, and a sheet of corrugated iron like the ones blocking up windows on the other side of the house. Ellis ventures through the gaping doorway and climbs over the trash to take photographs. I warn him to be careful; the whole interior looks dangerously unstable.

 Harris meanwhile has been taking a turn around the farm with his sketch pad. When he joins us he says he's come across a seventeenth century dovecote, "very picturesque, but falling apart". It's the one we found a photo of on the Historic England website when planning our expedition, but on checking the picture again using Ellis's smartphone we realise that it bears about as much resemblance to what Harris has found as a healthy body does to a skeleton. Despite its Grade II listed status, it's been left to rot like the rest of the farm.

 Harris also insists on poking about inside the farmhouse, and much to my dismay disappears into a dark passage for what seems like an eternity. When I call out to him he cheerfully informs me he's found the pantry. After he re-emerges we take a wander round the garden, and he finds it again, this time from the outside. It's crammed with sagging shelves that are slowly dissolving under the onslaught of weather coming in through a hole where the window used to be. From the size of the room, and the yards and yards of shelf space, this must have been a productive farm, and the tenants comfortably provisioned. They were also keen horticulturists: as we go round the garden Harris points out, among the tangles of self-seeded weeds, the flowers and shrubs they had planted before they moved away or died. I imagine that in a month or two this straggly waste will bloom, like an accidental firework display, in spasmodic echoes of that long-vanished domesticity.

 The real point of our walk around the farmhouse is to find the porch in which Clare slept. It quickly becomes apparent that it's missing, but given the state of the building as a whole this hardly comes as a surprise. Instead, we start to look for signs of it at ground level. After making two more circuits we are forced to admit that while the foundations of the house are plainly visible, those of a porch—even a tiny one—are not. I ask whether they would have been needed, and Harris reminds me that Clare mentioned solid flagstones, so "yes, very definitely". We are faced, therefore, with the rather vexing prospect that we've been following a red herring; Forty Farm cannot be the place where Clare lay down to sleep.

 Harris is apparently unfazed by this turn of events. He cheerfully remarks that the last hour has been time well spent. Ruins are always rewarding, he says, and this one particularly so. We follow him glumly back to the car while he stops every so often to point something out—a flowering roadside weed, an insect, some lichen on a log. Unaccountably he's in great good humour, but we're unable to reciprocate. We're both grappling with the fact that we're back at square one. If Clare did not stop at the farm, then where?

 It's only when Ellis is by the car fishing for his keys that Harris lets us in on his secret. He indicates South Corner with a flourish of the hand. "There you are," he says, a conjurer pulling a rabbit out of a hat. He watches us expectantly as he points to what at first glance is an elongated bay window. I look hard, trying to spool it

South Corner, Wyboston, whose pebble-dashed walls and concrete roof tiles disguise a seventeenth-century cottage with a porch (right) wide enough for Clare to have slept in.

back in time, and suddenly I'm very excited. I realise that pebble dash and French windows are disguising what would otherwise be obvious: a porch about a third the width of the house, built to foil the prevailing east wind. I have the prickly sensation, as I did at the milestone in Welwyn, that Clare is very close. I look over at Ellis, who has also made the connection. "Harris does it again," he says, grinning, and moves in with his camera. I ask Harris how old he thinks the porch is. He points to a tiny square window high up on the right, and says, "judging by that, early nineteenth century". He explains that he noticed it when we were parking up but decided to reserve judgement until we'd explored the farm. Ellis comes over and asks about Clare's description of an odd house standing "all alone", because this one is firmly attached to a terrace of workers' cottages. "Those are later," Harris replies, "1850s or so." In 1841 South Corner was isolated, exactly as Clare says.

This prompts me to recall that he also made a point of calling his house "odd" in the sense of strange or unusual, so is there, I wonder, any clue as to why that might be? The exterior is modern-day, so there's none there, and the ground plan seems conventional enough. Ellis points out that Clare made much of a sign standing in "a sort of trough or spout"—something he found strange in its own right—and that this might be the reason.

What exactly did he mean by such a description? In his day a 'spout' was either a pipe for dispensing liquid, or a chute for delivering dry goods such as coal or grain. To modern minds Clare's other noun for it, 'trough', might suggest that water was involved. Piped water was not common in the 1840s unless pumped by hand, and while this does not rule out an animal watering station, if Clare meant such a thing why didn't he just come out and say so? And in this connection, his use of the equivocator "sort of" tends to suggest he was struggling to explain what it was he was seeing. There's no mental image any of us can conjure up to make sense of his report, and perhaps that is unsurprising: if the thing was bizarre to him, it would be even more so to us. Harris, characteristically, turns the problem on its head by thinking about the sign. "If it was standing in a chute," he says, "it could have been there to tell people what came out of it—turnip seed, or nutty slack, or grain, or whatever." South Corner might therefore have housed a feed store, or a seed merchant's. We can never know of course, but in any case no such speculation is needed to connect the house with Clare. The evidence is there before us: an enclosed porch, easily capable of accommodating a man lying down fully stretched.

He could only have caught about three hours' sleep there, but it seemed to do him good: "I slept here till daylight and felt very much refreshed as I got up," he reports, adding that

> I blest my two wives and both their familys when I lay down and when I got up and when I thought of some former difficultys on a like occasion I could not help blessing the Queen

These words have a jokiness about them that suggests he is enjoying telling the tale of his scrape with destitution. Hunting through his autobiographical writings for 'a like occasion', we come across his account of sleeping rough as a young lad, when he was sent to fetch Burghley's head kitchen gardener home from drinking in Stamford "at all hours in the night":

> and as I [was] very often fearful of going instead of seeking him I used to lye down under a tree in the Park and fall a sleep and in the Autumn nights the rhyme used to fall and cover me on one side like a sheet which affected my side with a numbness [31]

And though there is only a single reference to Clare being locked out by Patty (when Herbert Marsh dropped by to see him unannounced),[32] it seems highly likely that more than once during their long marriage he was forced to doss down out of doors, drunk and in disgrace.

But none of this helps to explain why he blessed the Queen. Had the homonym, 'quean', with its meaning of "harlot or strumpet" been used among the *London Magazine* set for prostitutes? If so, is he recalling a night spent in the London stews with his dissolute friend Rip? And, by association, does this remind him of the harsh innuendos about "little Vicky and her snuff-box", which he had written in 'Don Juan' just a month or two previously?

Or, looking at it in a different light, might this be one of the clearest indications that he is in fact mad? Or is it just, in the spirit of the rest of the sentence, a joke? Whatever the reason, the Queen was very much on his mind as he set out again on this, the third morning of his long walk home.

Musings XX

She speaks:

'I saw him soon as I came out the gate,
my bag as heavy as ever, for I'd made
no trade with my willow pegs, split neat
and bound tight with tin. Sat on a flint heap
nursing his feet, he caught my eye and smiled.

'A *gaujo*, I thought at first, strong but burnt out
from marching three days without wittles;
said he was escaping from a madhouse,
away home. He pulled a Romani hat
from his pocket, all squashed and splashed with ink

'and shoved it well down, till he looked fair rough.
I thought he might be noticed and locked up,
so I give him rags to stuff in the crown
and show him a shortcut,
but he was afeared to miss the road.'

❧

Eyes fixed on the dust trampled by his feet,
he remembers huddled benders camped round Langley Bush:
King Boswell's crew standing their ground on the site
of the Hundred Court – bearing witness
to the rape of common land.

What if he'd taken his chance and gone with James Mobbs
to join the gypsy race, wandering free
without care of king or country,
field folk of mystic powers to read the future
from runes of palm and cup, lines and leaves?

A hard life, though, creeping under hedges
against the driving rain, in wooden clogs
and evil-smelling mackintoshes;
eating hedgehogs smoked and roasted in a pit,
mending broken-bottomed chairs and whittling pegs.

❧

King of the Heap

There are no paragraph breaks in the *Journey* to indicate whether events follow on from one another immediately or are separated by periods of time, but we can surmise this from other textual cues. When, directly after describing how he blessed his family and the queen, he writes, "— Having passed a Lodge on the left hand within a mile and a half of [St Neots][33] I sat down to rest on a flint heap where I might rest half an hour or more", the long dash and following capital suggest that he has walked a few miles and an interval has passed.

The fact that he knows the heap to be a mile and a half from St Neots suggests that he has asked someone, or more likely seen a fingerpost. If the latter, this would place him just north of Eaton Ford at Crosshall, which, as the name suggests, was a crossroads where the Great North Road met a major road joining Kimbolton to St Neots. Not only was Crosshall exactly a mile and a half from St Neots, but it would almost certainly have had a sign showing destinations and distances.

As for the 'Lodge' Clare writes about, it must have been significant in some way for him to spell it with a capital 'L'. On our 1836 map there's a building marked at Crosshall's south-west corner, on his left as he walked up the Great North Road and thus in exactly the right place. Just as intriguingly, there's a stone pit about a hundred yards away on the Kimbolton Road. The flint heap on which Clare rested was one of many placed at regular intervals for maintenance gangs repairing potholes, and this pit almost certainly supplied the one at Crosshall, which would have served both roads.

The straight-line distance from Wyboston to Crosshall is about three miles—an hour's walk for a fit person but perhaps as much as twice that for Clare, who was suffering the effects of his previous night's ordeal and the damage to his shoe. After finishing up our exploration of Forty Farm, Ellis, Harris and I do the same journey in a matter of minutes, though of course not along his route, which despite being slower was at least direct. As we're on the southbound side of the A1, we have to double-back to the Black Cat roundabout before joining the northbound carriageway and taking the exit to Eaton Socon.

Now on the old Great North Road, we pass several landmarks that Clare would also have seen: the Crown Inn, situated at the start of a long, straight stretch of road through the town; the superb Tudor half-timbered house that for centuries was the Old Plough and is today—as will come as absolutely no surprise—an Indian restaurant, and the White Horse, which Clare may well have recalled from his coaching days. This staging post for the Stamford Regent also caught the eye of Charles Dickens, who gave it a cameo role in *Nicholas Nickleby* as the inn at 'Eton Slocomb' where the eponymous hero is thawed out and given a hot dinner after riding for hours in freezing weather on the Yorkshire coach.

In Clare's day the two Eatons—'Socon' and 'Ford'—were separate settlements. Today they have merged into a single suburb about a mile and a half long, with the hamlet of Crosshall situated at the northern end. The first thing we notice on reaching it is Clare's 'Lodge', which Harris instantly dates to 1810. Today it's a pub-hotel called 'The Eaton Oak' but, as a nearby information board makes clear, it was a farmhouse until the 1970s. In the early stages of our research, Clare's term for it caused us no small amount of head-scratching. We were convinced that 'Lodge' meant it was a gatehouse to some larger building, our prime candidate being a nearby Regency fishing lodge on the banks of the Great Ouse. Standing here now, it seems entirely possible that Clare mistook it for a similar sort of place, its size and general aspect being more in keeping with a rich man's sporting retreat than a farm.

Diagonally opposite stands Crosshall Manor, a magnificent red-brick seventeenth-century residence that in Clare's day was another farmhouse. Until 1840, the year before he passed through here, it had been the inn that was initially and erroneously identified as the 'Ram' of his account. There is of course no trace of the flint heap.

It seems that by the start of his second day's march, Clare was thinking seriously about turning his great escapade into some sort of literary work. He began recording events as soon as they happened—or as soon after as was practicable. The longest and strangest of the notes he made reads as follows:

> The man whose daughter is the queen of England is now sitting on a stone heap on the high way to bugden without a farthing in his pocket and without tasting a bit of food ever since yesterday morning — when he was offered a bit of Bread and cheese at Enfield — he has not had any since but If I put a little speed on hope too may speed to morrow — O Mary mary If you knew how anxious I am to see you and dear Patty with the childern I think you would come and meet me.[34]

The Eaton Oak at Crosshall—Clare's 'Lodge'—in 1841 a large and prosperous farm.

Two road signs at Crosshall where Clare's 'Great York Road' has been bypassed and turned into a dead end, as at so many other points along its route.

The editors of *John Clare by Himself* suggest this was written late on Wednesday 21st,[35] but its jauntiness is totally at odds with the fatigue he was feeling on the way to Potton and the despair that overcame him as he wandered over Gamlingay Heath. Moreover, Buckden is the next town on the Great North Road after the Eatons, so being "on the high road to Bugden" places him north of Eaton Ford, very possibly having seen a milestone or fingerpost with 'Buckden' or 'Bugden' inscribed on it. In the light of this and our time-and-distance calculations, he is almost certainly writing this note at Crosshall on the morning of Thursday 22nd. As for believing he ate at Enfield 'yesterday', it is easy to see how, following the trauma of the previous night, he could have become confused about how long he has been on the road.

He dramatizes the father of the queen of England as a comic figure sitting on a stone heap—himself in the third person—suffering without coins in his pocket or food in his belly, until the 'he' morphs into an 'I' as he begins to see the end of his journey in sight. Might this hint at a retreat into fantasy as a means of coping with stress? We've already seen that as a child he invented imaginary scenarios to ward off terror when passing supposedly haunted places, and it turns out that he adopted similar strategies when feeling lonely and unhappy:

> I got into a habit of musing and muttering to ones self as a pastime to divert melancholy, singing over things which I calld songs and attempting to describe scenes that struck me   tis irksome to a boy to be alone and he is ready in such situations to snatch hold of any trifle to divert his loss of company and make up for pleasenter amusments [36]

The note can easily be explained in these terms, though the repetition of his most persistent delusion that he has two wives makes it impossible to brush aside the craziness of his claim to be the father of the queen—especially when we consider that on the same morning he blessed her in the same breath as blessing his wives and their families. Was he really mad enough to believe that she was one of his children?

When Ellis and I made some investigations prior to coming here, we discovered that the Kimbolton Road stone pit has survived down to the present day. On Google Maps it's a large, white depression in the middle of a farmer's field filled with scrub and trees. It's impossible to gauge its depth from the satellite image, and we're curious to know how far down it goes, inspired by Clare's description of a similar place:

> The passing traveller with wonder sees
> A deep & ancient stone pit full of trees
> So deep & very deep the place has been
> The church might stand within & not be seen
> The passing stranger oft with wonder stops
> & thinks he een could walk upon their tops
>
> ...
>
> The boy that stands & kills the black nosed bee
> Dares down as soon as magpies nests are found
> & wonders when he climbs the highest tree
> To find it reaches scarce above the ground [37]

Clare was writing about a pit local to Helpston that dated from Roman times, and we're keen to see if ours might be of similar age. So, in a spirit of adventure and inquiry, we set off down the Kimbolton Road to find out. As so often happens on our expeditions, however, things do not go quite to plan. Ellis takes the lead, tracking our progress on his phone, while Harris and I follow. After a hundred yards or so he raises his hand like a tour guide, commanding us to stop. On our left, the field with the pit is bordered by a thick hedge, difficult to see through let alone pass, but we've halted at a place where there's a break in it wide enough to wriggle through.

What greets us on the other side is unexpected, though given the time of year it shouldn't be—a sea of flowering oilseed rape, beaming its dazzling Chrome Yellow at the sky. The plants are waist-high, and so densely packed it's hard to see how we can get to the pit without leaving a trail of destruction in our wake.

The air is thick with a sweet, musky stink, and I'm suddenly aware that beside me Ellis has started to cough. His eyes are streaming and his breathing has turned fast and shallow. He goes back through the hedge and squats down, retrieving an inhaler from his camera bag and taking several doses from it. His eyes are alarmingly bloodshot. I ask if he needs medical attention but he shakes his head and assures me it's just an asthma attack and will soon pass. "Ah," says Harris, gravely, "I have a sovereign remedy for that. What you need, my boy, is a pint," but as the Eaton

LOVE'S COLD RETURNING

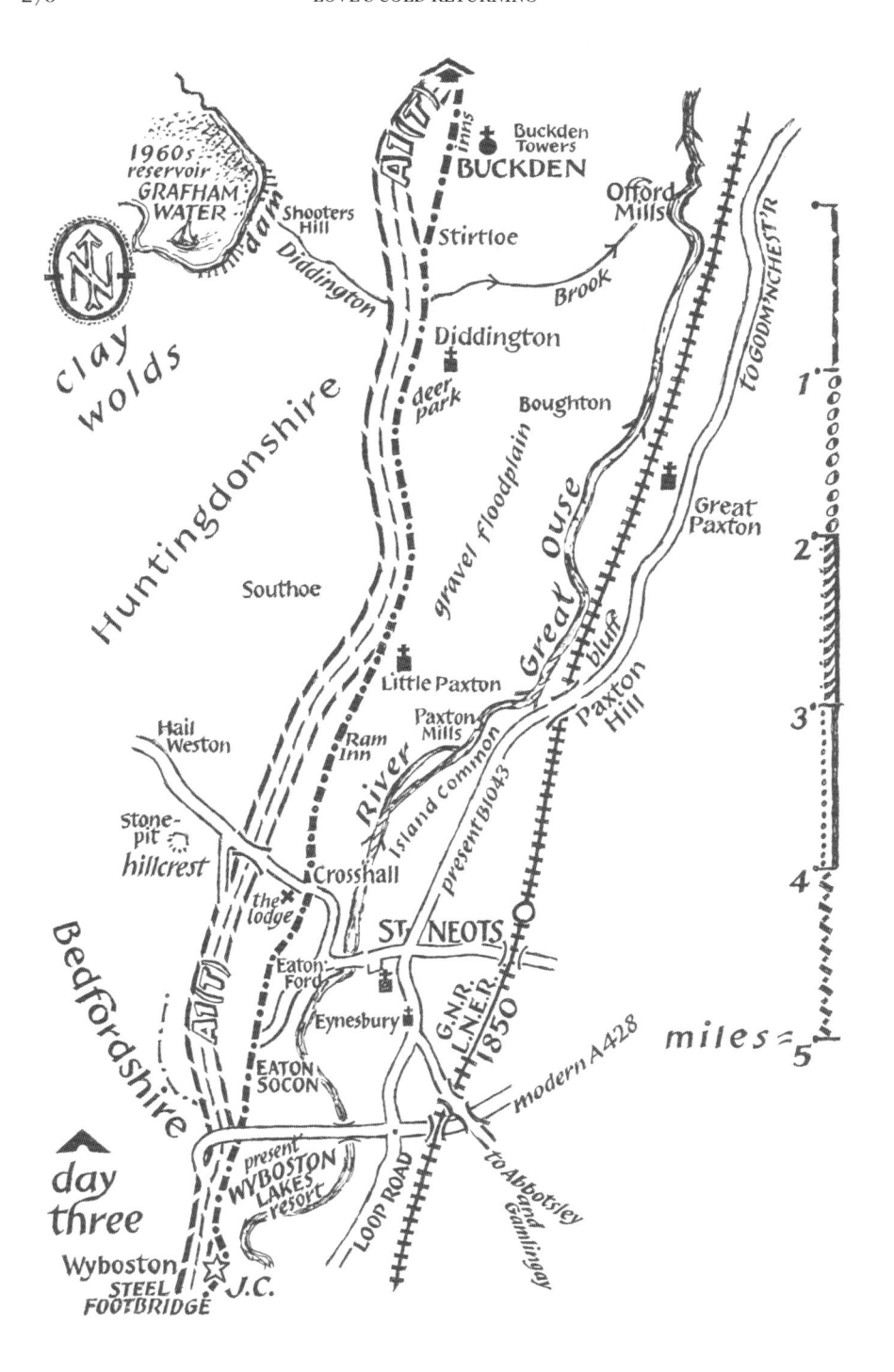

At Crosshall the northern stump of the Great North Road turns into a paddock—a tiny oasis of calm by the side of the A1.

Oak does not open its doors for another half hour, his nostrum must wait. We fill in time by wandering down to the end of the Great North Road, where there's a row of newly built homes. The freshly-tarmacked road comes to a stop at a wooden gate guarding the entrance to an overgrown paddock. It might be there for keeping animals penned up but looks more decorative than functional. Beyond a line of trees, the A1 hisses and roars like a thing alive.

When we're installed at the bar with our drinks, we tell Harris the story of how Clare, while resting on his flint heap, noticed someone leave the property we're currently sitting in. He writes that "a tall Gypsey come out of the Lodge gate" and

> when she got up to me on seeing she was a young woman with an honest looking countenance rather handsome I spoke to her and asked her a few questions which she answered readily and with evident good humour so I got up and went on to the next town with her

It would seem that the sores and blisters on his feet were instantly forgotten. This was the old Clare turning on the charm, engaging a pretty girl in conversation, and her response suggests that she was pleased to have him walking beside her. He goes on:

> she cautioned me on the way to put something in my hat to keep the crown up and said in a lower tone 'you'll be noticed' but not knowing what she hinted — I took no notice and made no reply

When Ellis and I first examined this part of the narrative, we wondered about the reason for the young woman's concern. As a gypsy, she would have known that her dark hair and brown skin, along with her distinctive head scarf, skirt and apron, marked her as an outsider,[38] and perhaps she feared that Clare would draw the attention of Vestry officials to them both. In any event, her comment implies that he was looking disreputable after two nights' sleeping rough—probably more so than he realised. The hat was the one he'd found the previous Sunday at the gypsies' abandoned camp: a "wide-awake", which the Shorter Oxford English Dictionary records as meaning in 1837, "a soft felt hat with broad brim and low crown, without nap or pile". He had squashed it into his pocket on picking it up, and very likely had been using it as a writing desk ever since. The young woman was clearly thinking that its flattened state made him look like a vagabond.

Clare relates how they continued on, until

> at length she pointed to a small tower church which she called Shefford Church and advised me to go on a footway which would take me direct to it and I should shorten my journey fifteen miles by doing so

How far had they walked before the gypsy drew his attention to the church? And where were they when she did so? As Frederick Martin points out, they could not have been at the village of Shefford, as this lay between Bedford and Hitchin, half a day's walk south of Crosshall.

The first settlement they passed together was Little Paxton, just over a mile from where they met. There the parish church of St James' was set back from the road at a distance of roughly 500 yards and so would have appeared 'small', just as Clare describes. But he also states that he and the gypsy walked and talked "at length" before she pointed out the tower, which suggests that by then they had covered a rather greater distance. The church of St Lawrence on the Diddington Estate, two miles further on, was both close to the road and physically little—factors which, along with its greater distance from Crosshall, make it the likelier candidate. Today, standing just east of the A1, it is still a very striking landmark with its flint nave and castellated red-brick tower. What's more, our 1836 map shows it connected to the road by a narrow path, marked in white, for which 'footway' would have been an apposite description.

But why did the girl suggest leaving the road and striking out east? This makes no sense given that the Great North Road was literally the most direct route Clare could have taken to Northborough. For a moment Ellis and I considered the possibility that she was trying to waylay him, but then realised the blindingly obvious: that she could only have suggested a short cut if he'd told her where he was headed.

Since he must have been navigating at least in part by the memories of his coach trips to London, there is the strong likelihood that he thought he would soon be passing through Huntingdon, a stop on the Stamford Regent's itinerary. Not only was the town memorable to him for its Civil War connections, but also because it had been the home of one of his most beloved poets. Describing his first experience of travelling by coach, he wrote:

The diminutive church of St Lawrence, Diddington, which the gypsy girl pointed out to Clare when recommending a short-cut home.

> When we passd thro Huntingdon Mr [Gilchrist] shewd me at this end of the town where Oliver Cromwell was born and the parsonage with its mellancholy looking garden at the other were Cowper had lived which was far the most interesting remembrance to me tho both were great men in the annals of fame I thought of his tame hares and Johnny Gilpin [39]

If he'd told the gypsy he was heading for Huntingdon, then her suggestion would make some sense, though not to the tune of 15 miles. On that particular point he may have misheard her, or she could have been under the misapprehension that they were indeed close to Shefford—she was, after all, constantly on the move. He writes:

> I would gladly have taken the young womans advice feeling that it was honest and a nigh guess towards the truth but fearing I might loose my way and not be able to find the north road again I thanked her and told her I should keep to the road when she bade me 'good day' and went into a house or shop on the left hand side the road.

When we first read this passage we didn't fully understand his anxiety, but now, having tracked his walk across Gamlingay Heath on the long detour from Potton to Tempsford, we can appreciate the terror he must have felt at the possibility of losing his way a second time.

He and the girl must have parted at Buckden, since he says he "went on to the next town" with her. She'd met him as she was exiting a large residence and was now leaving him to go into a house or shop, so she was likely hawking small wares such as pegs: work that gypsy women commonly undertook at the time.

Huntingdonshire

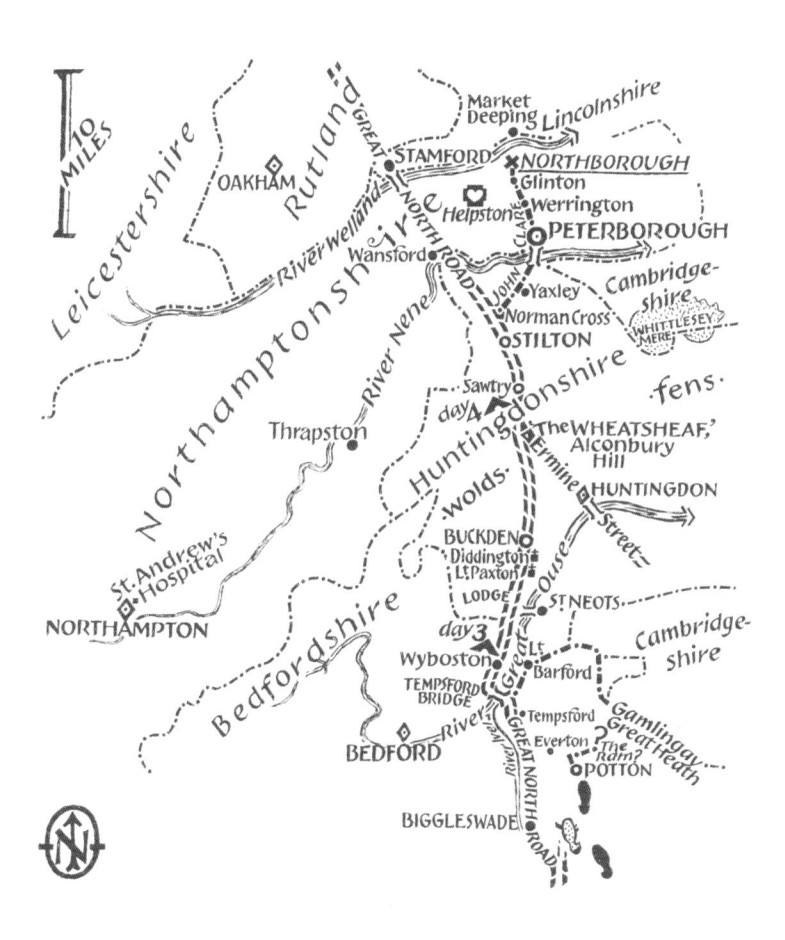

*Days 3–4, 22nd July–23rd July 1841:
Buckden to Yaxley*

Musings XXI

When his foot hurts, he remembers the toil
and tenacity of birds: a blue titmouse
fetching a hundred caterpillars
in twenty minutes from white pear blossom
and the leaves of a plum, to feed her young;

and the nightingale building her nest
from dried oak leaves, lined with velvet moss
and little scraps of grass. Like her he sings
unceasing till he senses danger near;
then quietly puts up with pain, to sing again.

❧

When I stop to empty from my shoe a tiny chip
I think of him, leather wearing thin,
one shoe breaking, positioning each step
so that the loose sole doesn't catch
on the Great North Road's uneven flints.

He concentrates on his feet, raw rubbing
where blisters have burst, skin flaps stuck with blood
to the wool of his socks, a hole working his heel
to fret on coarse stitching. How did he stand the pain,
again and again, loose gravel working in?

He was a strong enough tramp when he started out
stocky and fit from Matthew Allen's garden
and days of compulsive rambling in the forest.
Now, he sees the road blurred and stupid
as himself, losing sense of time and place.

❧

Hessey dreamed to make him Helpston's
Gilbert White, writing letters for a book
on his botanising and birding;
"biographies of birds and flowers"
Clare called it, particular and personal.

He doesn't mention birds in the account
of his escape, not seeing any friends;
but carries in his thoughts footnotes of his book –
the flycatcher's nest in the thatch, larks
and thrushes in Royce Wood, high in song.

The Stupid Road

In 1841 Buckden—or 'Bugden'—was a thriving settlement with a population of 1,291. Today it has doubled in size, mostly through the construction, during the 1960s and 70s, of dormitory housing for commuters using the A1. Despite this, the centre of the village, strung out along the High Street, still retains much of its old character. It's here that the old Great North Road crosses the road running east to the Great Ouse and Offord Cluny, and where in times past the Bishops of Lincoln periodically took up residence in their grand Palace. Its castellated red brick walls still stretch away on two sides of the crossroads, while a pair of former coaching inns, the Lion and the George, face each other on the sides opposite.

In 1839 Pigot's Directory noted that coaches passed through Buckden "almost hourly", and Robson listed over a dozen—including the Stamford Regent—that stopped there twice a day. Though Clare witnessed the village just two years later, he tells us nothing of the coaches that rattled through the archway of the George, or the stables and paddocks at the Spread Eagle, or the Vine Inn and its on-site brewery.

When Ellis and I make our visit we appreciate the conscious irony of a nail bar called 'Nails at the Forge', which occupies the building where blacksmiths once hammered out horseshoe nails in a rage of heat and dust. The original door has been preserved behind glass like a museum exhibit, its low lintel reminding us of the small stature of nineteenth-century working men due to their poverty and poor diet.

The Lion, left, and the George, right—the two principal coaching inns on Buckden's High Street when it formed part of the Great North Road. Clare walked up the street towards the spot where this photograph was taken, passing the Vine Inn (visible beyond the George) on his left, and exiting on the right of the picture.

St Mary's parish church stands just outside the grounds of the Bishops' Palace, now Buckden Towers. It was heavily endowed by the Bishops of Lincoln down the centuries and underwent repeated rebuilding in consequence.

Buckden's close connections with the Church meant it had prosperous residents too, though today they are cast in a decidedly more secular mould: a fur-coated, mini-skirted lady parks her convertible outside a lingerie shop next to the old Lion Inn, and goes inside, while across the road, where a *hacienda*-style bungalow lurks behind high walls and electric gates, a bald man with the build of a boxer gone to fat stares truculently through the bars while he talks on a phone and jabs the air, his chunky gold bracelet winking in the sun.

We wander along the High Street and into the grounds of the Palace. Now known as Buckden Towers, this twelfth-century fortified manor is home to a community of Claretian Missionaries. According to signs planted among the flower beds they are happy for visitors to walk around the grounds and take in the atmosphere, which is heavy with the weight of history. There's a centuries-old redwood in the outer court, and an inner court decked out with information boards listing famous visitors: Catherine of Aragon 1533-4; Henry VIII and Catherine Howard 1541; Samuel Pepys 1667. It is April, and the statue of 'St Hugh, Bishop of Lincoln and Lord of Buckden Palace, 1186-1206' stands serenely in a drift of daffodils.

Close by is the parish church of St Mary: a magnificent building that for centuries enjoyed the patronage of the bishops of Lincoln. Like most other English churches it is an agglomeration of eras and styles, with a thirteenth-century tower capped by a later spire and a castellated nave that echoes visually the palace keep behind it. The windows are plain, their original glazing having suffered the attentions of Cromwell's men. Only a couple of tiny panels survive, showing brightly coloured angels that once

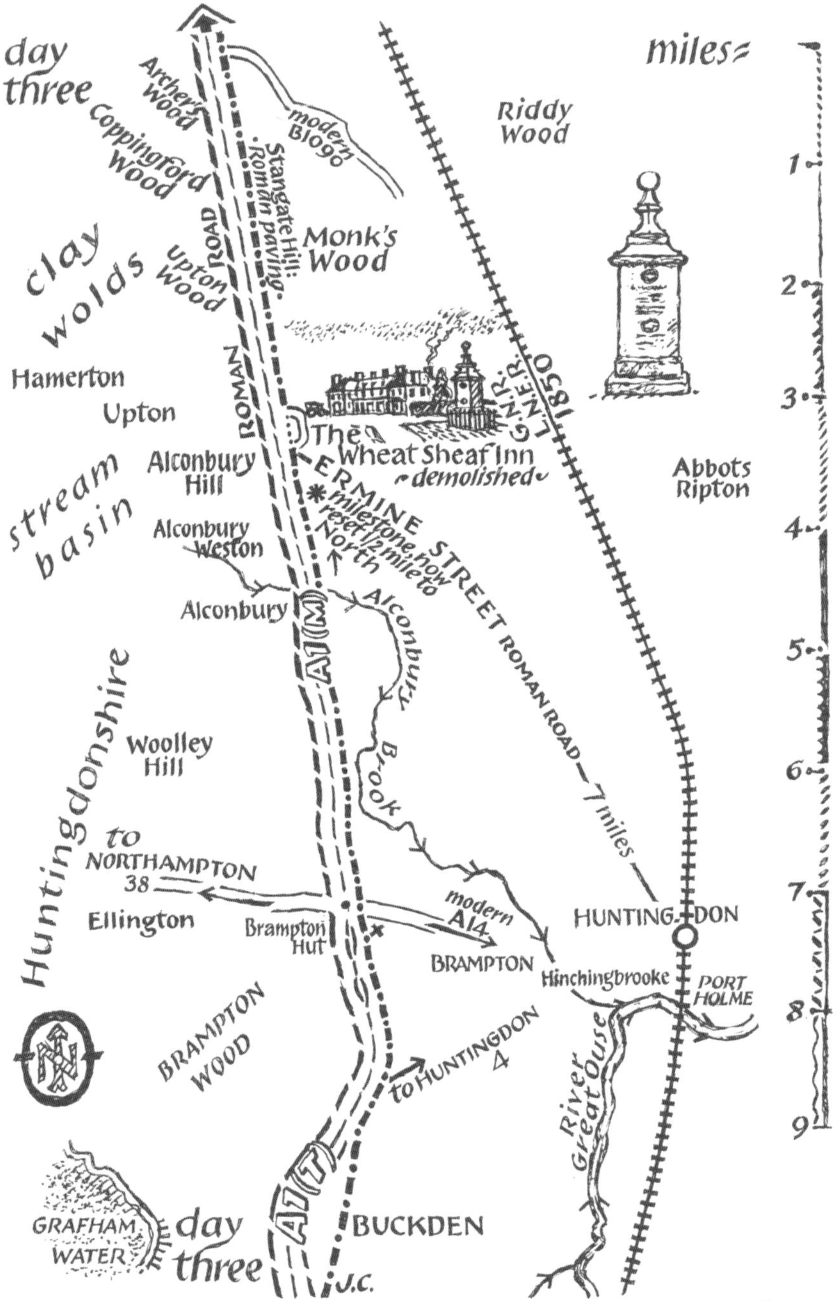
day three
miles
Archer's Wood
Coppingford Wood
modern B1090
Riddy Wood
Stangate Hill: Roman paving
ROAD
Monk's Wood
clay wolds
Upton Wood
ROMAN
Hamerton
Upton
The Wheat Sheaf Inn
demolished
G.N.R. L.N.E.R. 1850
Alconbury Hill
stream basin
ERMINE STREET
milestone, now reset 1/2 mile to North
Abbots Ripton
Alconbury Weston
Alconbury
A1(M)
Alconbury Brook
ROMAN ROAD — 7 miles
Huntingdonshire
Woolley Hill
to NORTHAMPTON 38
Ellington
Brampton Hut
modern A14
HUNTINGDON
BRAMPTON
Hinchingbrooke
PORT HOLME
BRAMPTON WOOD
to HUNTINGDON 4
River Great Ouse
A1
GRAFHAM WATER
day three
BUCKDEN
J.C.
1
2
3
4
5
6
7
8
9

adorned scenes of the Annunciation and the Coronation of the Virgin. There's a fine font, too, and an oak door with a huge iron handle that was forged by the village blacksmith over five hundred years ago, but the building's real glory is the choir with its fifteenth-century wooden angels gazing down from the ceiling.

Buckden is an unusual place with one foot in the spiritual and the other in trade and commerce, yet Clare makes no mention of it beyond saying that he and the gypsy parted there. This suggests a withdrawal into the self, a retreat from external stimuli under the combined assault of hunger, pain and exhaustion—something that is also indicated by the ensuing breakdown of his narrative into a sequence of disjointed memories, beginning with the statement:

> one night I lay in a dyke bottom from the wind and went sleep half an hour when I suddenly awoke and found one side wet through from the sock in the dyke bottom so I got out and went on

When we first read this we wondered whether this was a re-telling of events that had taken place the previous evening when he lay down to sleep north of Potton, but the reference to a 'dyke' appears to locate him in the wetlands south of Stilton rather than the drier, naturally drained environment of Gamlingay Heath. He continues:

> I remember going down a very dark road hung over with trees in both sides very thick which seemed to extend a mile or two

Our 1836 map shows an area of woodland called Monk's Wood stretching for more than a mile to the east of the Great North Road near the 69th milestone, and two lesser ones, Upton Wood and Coppingford Wood, to the west. Their position just over twelve miles from Buckden would be consistent with him travelling at night, given that he was slowed up by his broken shoe and was probably walking at little more than a mile or so an hour.

There follows a passage of sequential narrative more firmly anchored in time, though at first sight it reads more like a hallucination:

> I then entered a town and some of the chamber windows had candle lights shining in them – I felt so weak here that I forced to sit down on the ground to rest myself and while I sat here a Coach that seemed to be heavy laden came rattling up and stops in the hollow below me and I cannot recollect its ever passing by me

We know that Clare used 'town' for settlements of all sizes, but there is not even a hamlet between Buckden and Stilton. Sawtry St Andrew, west of the Great North Road, might have fitted this description, but getting there would have required him to make a detour—extremely unlikely given his stated reluctance to leave the highway. So did he write this passage purely for effect?

As Ellis and I puzzled over this, his mention of the coach suggested a possible explanation. At Alconbury Hill, Clare reached the most important junction of the coaching age, where two major roads from London merged to continue north: the Great North Road, which he had been following, and the Old North Road, or

The meeting-point of Ermine Street and the Great North Road as painted by Charles Dickinson Langley in 1840—just a year before Clare passed by.

Ermine Street, the road on which he'd started but left in order to reach Enfield Town. He appears not to have noticed the junction, but given he arrived there at night, when all but the long-distance stage and mail coaches had come to a halt, this is perhaps understandable. It was marked by a stone obelisk, shown in a contemporary painting as standing close to a large establishment called 'The Wheatsheaf'—a major posting house that also catered to stage coaches, wagons and droving teams. At a time when exterior lighting was unknown in the countryside, Clare may have mistaken this enormous building, with its long rows of lit windows, for a grouping of houses, and though this presupposes that he encountered the tree-lined section of road afterwards and not beforehand, a note he added to the text suggests it as a strong possibility:

> The Coach did pass me as I sat under some trees by a high wall and the lamps flashed in my face and wakened me up from a doze when I knocked the gravel out of my shoes and started.[1]

A high wall in otherwise open country could only have belonged to a large building, and the Wheatsheaf was the only one of any size in the vicinity. We imagine Clare propped against the wall of one of the yards, woken by lights sweeping across him as a coach arrived to have its team changed.

In 1901, Charles Harper wrote of the obelisk:

The obelisk has been reset about half a mile north of its old position, on the B1043—the original Ermine Street—which today runs alongside the six-lane A1M.

This monumental milestone, now somewhat dilapidated, railed round, and with some forlorn-looking wallflowers growing inside the enclosure, is a striking object, situated at a peculiarly impressive spot, where the left-hand route by Huntingdon is seen going off on the level to a vanishing point lost in the distant haze [...]; the right-hand road diving down the hill to Alconbury Weston and Alconbury at its foot.[2]

On an early visit to explore Clare's route, Ellis and I had to search hard to find it. It lost its imposing position on the A1 in the 1990s, when the A14 from Cambridge was re-routed via a bridge and slipways to feed directly into the newly constructed A1M, but it is still impressive: three metres high, with a chess-pawn finial and the distances to various towns and villages carved into two of its faces. It stands, enclosed within the same iron railings that Harper saw, beside the motorway on a wide grass verge cleared of trees.

At Alconbury Hill the task of imagining Clare's experiences is almost impossible. Simply too much has been lost. Even Harper, writing barely sixty years after the great age of coaching, seems to be describing a mythical world:

> in the bygone days [the Wheatsheaf] possessed a semi-circular approach from the road, and afforded all the year round, and round the clock of every day and night, a busy scene; with the post boys whose next turn-out was, sleeping with spur on heel, ready to mount and away at a minute's notice, north, south, east, or west.[3]

It had been replaced, he tells us, by a "mere public house", but at least he was able to see the obelisk in use and in its proper place.

All trace of the Wheatsheaf has gone—even its mean replacement was demolished to make way for the A1. Gone too is the thrill of stagecoaches changing teams with precision timing, the mail coaches setting off with red-and-gold-liveried guards toting their blunderbuss and pistols, and the rumours of highwaymen lurking in ambush at nearby Stangate Hole.

Given Clare's fear of the supernatural it was perhaps fortunate that he did not meet any locals, as they might have told him the tale of the Drummer Boy of Alconbury. This involved a murder that took place at a bridge over the River Wey, a mile or so from the Wheatsheaf. In 1780 a young soldier called Gervase Matcham was sent with his regiment's drummer boy from Huntingdon to Diddington to collect money for supplies. Instead of returning home directly, the pair stayed overnight at Alconbury, and in the morning Matcham slit the lad's throat and made off with £7 in gold coin. To escape justice, he fled to the nearest port and joined the navy under the assumed name of Robert Waters.

After six years' hard fighting at sea he returned to England believing himself safe from prosecution. On the day of his discharge, however, while crossing Salisbury Plain in a thunderstorm with a friend, he began to see a grisly apparition following him. The incident is recorded in *The Ingoldsby Legends*:

> Cried Bill, whose short legs kept him still in the rear,
> 'Why, what's in the wind, Bo?—what is it you fear?'
> For he saw in a moment that something was frightening
> His shipmate much more than the thunder and lightning.
> 'Fear?' stammer'd out Waters, 'why, HIM!—don't you see
> What faces that Drummer-boy's making at me?'
> ...

> 'Keep him off, Bill—look here—Don't let him come near!
> Only see how the blood-drops his features besmear!
> What, the dead come to life again!—Bless me!—Oh dear.'[4]

Matcham was so terrified he immediately confessed his crime to a magistrate, who arranged for him to be taken in chains to Alconbury assizes where he was convicted and hanged. His corpse was left to rot on what became known as Matcham's Gibbet, close to the bridge where the boy was killed. As with tales of the supernatural that Clare heard as a child, this one held a warning: "It is said that if you walk down the road between Alconbury and Alconbury Weston at sunset you can still hear the footsteps of the drummer boy walking behind you, and if you listen carefully you can even hear the tapping of his drum."[5]

We should pause here to consider whether it is worth continuing to track Clare's account against the 1836 map. While we can present evidence for where he lay down in the "sock" (in the wetlands south of Stilton), where he walked under "overhanging trees" (by Monk's Wood, north of Alconbury Hill) and where he dozed against a wall and was woken by a coach (at the Wheatsheaf), these three events are not recounted in the expected sequence but in reverse order. Yet does this matter? Might it not be, in fact, an example of Clare striving for effect: the kind of 'art in artlessness' that John Goodridge and Kelsey Thornton detect in his poetry?[6]

He says that "between [Buckden] and Stilton I was knocked up and noticed little or nothing" and, apart from one use of the word 'then', makes no attempt to present memories in the order in which they happened. Perhaps he is consciously and 'artfully' presenting himself as suffering from a state of mental and physical exhaustion—almost, one might say, from the pains of heroic endurance—when he writes:

> I then got up and pushed onward seeing little to notice for the road very often looked as stupid as myself and I was very often half asleep as I went

The reputedly haunted Matcham's Bridge sketched by Charles Harper in 1901.

It is thus possible to argue that he is going out of his way to construct a text designed to illustrate his sufferings. In his book, *Night Walking*, Matthew Beaumont makes precisely this case, noting the "phantasmagorical intensity" and "self-conscious attention to dreamlike detail" of Clare's account, in which the poet is characterised by a "strange half-absence", so that

> both the road and his mind feel stupid, stupefied. The nightwalk has collapsed almost completely into a sleepwalk, the noctambulist into a somnambulist.[7]

An interesting sub-question is whether Clare has also lost his grip on the passage of time. His reference, in the note written at Crosshall, to "not tasting a bit of food ever since yesterday morning [...] at Enfield" strongly suggests that he has. On the other hand his assertions that "on the third day" he ate grass, and on "the next and last day" he chewed and ate tobacco are precise, and accord with our own time-and-distance calculations. This discrepancy between these two cases can be accounted for by the fact that he wrote the note on the road in a state of befuddled exhaustion, while the other incidents are being reported in retrospect after a night's rest at home, during which time he has had a chance to put his recollections in order.

Before bringing his account of heroic suffering to a close and returning to a coherent narrative, Clare repeats his claim to be in a state of amnesic confusion between Buckden and Stilton, almost like a closing bracket:

> I remember passing through Buckden and going a length of road afterwards but I don't recollect the name of any place until I came to stilton where I was completely foot foundered and broken down.

From Alconbury Hill onwards the Great North Road ran ruler-straight, betraying its Roman origins. The legions laid their roads along an embankment, or *agger*, with broad scoop-ditches on either side.[8] Major highways were also given a stone surface, and Harper quotes Defoe's observation in 1724 that at Stangate, just north of Alconbury, some parts still had Roman paving.[9] The road had almost certainly been resurfaced by 1841, but continued on Roman foundations through Monk's Wood, which Harper described as a desolate place where a lonely churchyard was all that remained of St Andrew's Church and the dissolved monastic foundation of Sawtry Abbey, after which the wood was named.[10]

Clare could not recall the names of towns or villages between Buckden and Stilton because there weren't any: just a tollgate belonging to the Stilton Turnpike Trust a little north of the 70th milestone, and an inn called the Crown and Woolpack at the 73rd, described by Harper as "a very large red-brick posting house" partly occupied by a pub and partly turned over to cottages.[11] The 1836 map shows a network of dykes, lodes and fens to the east of the road between Sawtry St Andrew and Stilton. It was likely there that Clare slept for half an hour in a dyke bottom and was, quite literally, *soaked*.

Musings XXII

Mary and Martha, it's strange his two wives
have these names –
one he would hold and hammer
in a flow of sparks to ecstasy,
housewife and cook, his children's mother;

the other, the flower his soul enjoys for ever.
Martha he loved at first sight, his Patty,
who ran to meet him in her gingham dress,
damp from airing on the hedge;
                                      and Mary,
his love since the kingcups were shining like flame.

He first saw Mary in the vestry schoolroom
of Glinton church, a little lass with rosy cheeks
and sweetest smile learning her ABC
and how to sing the hymns and say the prayers,
a farmer's daughter, apple of her father's eye;

and across the room with the noisy boys,
he was sometimes there and sometimes away
if it was a sunny day or harvest time;
though poor, he was his mother's only son
and she scraped and saved for him to go to school.

He ran in the fields with the village lads,
hunting birds' eggs, and collecting pooty shells
ribbed with rings of colour to hang above the hearth;
but sometimes wandered and wondered alone,
carrying paper and ink in the crown of his hat.

And as he grew, Mary was always there.

Out Cold on the Causeway

From the moment he arrives in Stilton, Clare's narrative regains focus. The dream-like quality of the Romantic wanderer struggling to keep a hold on reality is replaced by a clearly delineated sequence of events and encounters. He writes:

> When I had got about half way through the town a gravel causeway invited me to rest myself so I lay down and nearly went sleep

On our map the causeway can be seen running alongside the Great North Road from Alconbury Hill to Stilton, and from there to the inn at Norman Cross. Its position and alignment strongly suggests it was part of Ermine Street's *agger*. Writing in 1967, Ivan Margary said of Ermine Street that "in places where the *agger* can still be observed it is often four of five feet high and up to 45 or 50 feet wide", the central carriageway being metalled with stones, and the sides forming "a gravel causeway used by pedestrians and animals".[12]

Its relatively dry surface must have been inviting to a man who had travelled as far as Clare had on so little rest. From South Corner, close to the 53rd milestone, where he had slept three hours on the second night, he had walked for a day and a night to Stilton at the 75th, only dozing a little at the Wheatsheaf Inn and catching half an hour's sleep in a dyke.

The Bell, with its massive sign, was Stilton's most prestigious coaching inn.

The Angel, facing the Bell across the High Street, was its rival, only surpassed in the traveller's imagination for not being the 'true' home of Stilton cheese.

Though the route by which he arrived in Stilton is still called the Great North Road, it has been severed from the road network. There's a cul-de-sac at the southern end of the village and an all-too-familiar interchange at the northern end connecting it to the A1. The place itself is relatively unspoiled—a reprieve that began when Clare's neighbour and patron, the Marquess of Exeter, refused to allow the railway through Burleigh Park and forced it to loop east by Peterborough, well away from the Great North Road. As was the case with Welwyn, keeping the trains at arm's length preserved Stilton's rural character.

When Ellis and I visit the town, we are struck first by two great inns, the Bell and the Angel, facing one another across a broad High Street. In the heyday of coaching, these establishments were busy round the clock, with blacksmiths shoeing horses, ostlers changing teams, servants loading and unloading luggage, and passengers embarking and disembarking.

Outside the Bell there is an enormous copper sign suspended on an elaborate wrought iron frame, perhaps the village's most arresting feature. When Charles Harper saw it at the start of the twentieth century, he was so impressed by its size and the "mazy quirks and curls" of its ironwork that he declared it to be "incomparably the finest sign on the road". Like the Six Hills at Stevenage, it provided coachmen with a valuable source of extra income, being "the subject of many wagers [...] with unwary strangers who did not, like those artful ones, know its measurements. It measures in fact 6 ft. 2 ¾ inches in height".[13]

The Bell was Stilton's pre-eminent coaching inn, and the focus of the village's fame. Now an upmarket country hotel, it still trades on those old associations. A vintage signboard inside the entrance announces 'Finest quality blue Stilton cheese sold here', reminding visitors of where this gourmet foodstuff started life. It's a well-known tale: in 1730 Cooper Thornhill, the landlord of the Bell, came across a blue cheese he particularly liked while visiting a farm near Melton Mowbray in rural Leicestershire. He struck a deal with Frances Pawlett, the maker, which granted him exclusive marketing rights, and having christened the cheese 'Stilton' began to serve it at the Bell, giving customers the impression that it was made in the village. As the coaching trade grew, they also bought it packaged up as a gift for friends and family, making it famous throughout the country and eventually the world.

This at least is the authorized version, which celebrates Thornhill's marketing prowess and makes a claim for Stilton being the first 'invented' cheese—the Lymeswold of the eighteenth century. But it is not entirely true. In 1724, six years before Thornhill's marketing campaign began, Daniel Defoe wrote:

> We pass'd Stilton, a town famous for cheese, which is call'd our English Parmesan, and is brought to table with the mites, or maggots round it, so thick, that they bring a spoon with them for you to eat the mites with, as you do the cheese.[14]

Whatever this might have been it was not Pawlett's creation, as Trevor Hickman explains:

> During the seventeenth century [travellers] were expected to obtain, 'cheese at Stilton'; this became 'the Cheese of Stilton', and eventually 'Stilton cheese'. The early cheeses were obtained from a variety of sources, all were pressed cheeses, and as they aged they developed 'blue veins'. Eventually a blue-veined cheese was expected to be supplied. Cooper Thornhill [...] standardised an unpressed cream cheese with blue veins with Frances Pawlett. They marketed her Stilton cheese, and this cheese developed into a type of Stilton cheese similar to what is available in the twenty-first century.[15]

Irrespective of its origins, by 1820 Stilton was a highly-prized delicacy. When Clare first visited London in March that year, it may well have been on the menu of the dinner party given by John Taylor in his honour.

Across the road from the Bell is the former Angel Inn. The younger and smaller of the two establishments, it was founded in the seventeenth century. The present building, constructed of brick rather than the Bell's more expensive stone, was erected in 1741, a date commemorated on its carriageway entrance. Today it is an Indian restaurant, though trappings of its glory days survive, including a mounting block and an outbuilding, complete with picturesquely ramshackle roof, that once housed its smithy.

Some of this we learn from Roy Baines, the owner of a bar called 'The Stilton Tunnels', which occupies the Angel's old stable block. Roy is something of a rarity; while out and about on our expeditions we tend to arouse the suspicion of locals with our photography and note-taking, but when he noticed us looking at the inns he came over to ask if we would like more information about them.

The Stilton Tunnels—formerly the Stilton Country Club—still has the original stone floor over which carriage horses were led, and its brick walls bear the iron rings to which they were tethered while being groomed and foddered. The bar is

The carriageway of the former Angel Inn, with its mounting block still in place.

The entrance to the Stilton tunnels beneath the old Angel Inn. No-one knows exactly when this village-wide network of passages was built, or what its purpose was.

named for a network of underground tunnels linking the inns and the parish church of St Mary Magdalene. Most are inaccessible now, blocked off by cave-ins, but Roy has cleared a short section which he takes us down the stable cellars to see. He has plans to open up more of them, he says, and turn them into a tourist attraction. We trudge a short way into a long, narrow brick-lined vault. The air is damp and chill, and we're wearing polythene overshoes against the puddles of water that have collected from the dripping ceiling. Roy says that no one knows who built the tunnels, or for what purpose, but one source suggests they were used to store the large quantity of manure generated by the coaching trade, which was then collected by farmers at the tunnel ends for dressing their fields. It's as good an explanation as any, though it doesn't account for the church being connected to the network.

When we resurface, the conversation turns to Clare and his love of the Fancy, prompted by the picture hanging above the bar. It shows the great bare-knuckle bout between Dan Mendoza and Richard Humphries that took place at Stilton in 1789. Clare would undoubtedly have known about this legendary contest: his father had been an amateur wrestler with an interest in boxing, and he himself developed a passion for the sport while sampling London's loucher attractions with Edward Villiers Rippingille:

> I caught the mania so much from Rip for such things that I soon became far more eager for the fancy than himself and I watch'd the appearance of every new Hero on the stage with as eager curiosity to see what sort of a fellow he was as I had before done the Poets.[16]

Roger Sales observes that by putting his enthusiasms for prizefighters and poets on an equal footing Clare was consciously buying into a construction of Regency literary identity: in the 1820s he felt "very much part of the London Magazine coterie that gained pleasure from laddish rambles and sprees around the metropolis, which included going to boxing matches."[17] Sales argues that by adopting the persona of Jack Randall at Lippitts Hill Lodge twenty years later, Clare was returning to the kind of sly, mischievous comedy which had characterised that golden period of his life. While at the Lodge, he wrote—and subsequently crossed out—the following:

> Boxer Byron
> made of Iron, alias
> Box-iron
> at Spring-field [18]

At first sight these four lines seem nonsensical. What, if anything, could they mean, beyond braiding together his three obsessions of pugilism, Byron and women? The first, taken on its own, holds no mystery: 'Boxer Byron' was taught the noble art by champion prizefighter 'Gentleman' John Jackson, and has the eponymous hero of his 'Don Juan' take it up on returning to London.

The association by rhyme of 'Byron' with 'Iron' in the second line is also obvious, famously used by Isaac Cruikshank in his cartoon of 1815, 'The Separation: A Sketch from the Private Life of Lord Iron who panegyrized his wife, but satirized her confidante', which alludes to verses the peer had circulated privately, claiming that he was the injured party in the breakup of his marriage. Clare was probably familiar with the work, but regardless of a possible reference, there is also a deliberate allusion to hardness (and thus, knowing Clare, an element of sexual innuendo) in the image.

The last two lines are the most difficult to fathom. A box-iron was a smoothing iron filled with hot coals, but by deliberately hyphenating "Spring-field" Clare actually seems to be alluding to box-iron springs, which were commonly used in Victorian beds. Putting all this together, we can surmise that he was fantasising about what he could do, in his adopted Byronic persona, with the women being kept up the road from his billet at Lippitts Hill Lodge.

But much more important than the piece's sentiment is its form. Pithy, teasing and aphoristic, it appears to validate Sales' contention that Clare was attempting a return to the "playful and frolicsome" identity of a Regency writer.

Shortly afterwards, on May 1st, Clare wrote "Jack Randall's Challenge To All The World":

> Jack Randall The Champion Of The Prize Ring Begs Leave To Inform The Sporting World That He is Ready To Meet Any Customer In The Ring Or On The Stage To Fight For The Sum Of £500 or £1000 Aside A Fair Stand Up Fight half Minute Time Win Or Loose he is Not Particular As To Weight Colour Or Country   All He wishes Is To Meet With A Customer Who Has Pluck Enough To Come To The Scratch.
>
> Jack Randall [19]

It's a delightful coincidence that with his passion for boxing and recent adoption of Randall's persona he spent his third night of travel close to the site of one of the most famous fights of all time—especially as it was won by the underdog, Mendoza, a working-class Jew from the East End of London. It was the second time the opponents had fought. 'Gentleman Boxer' Humphries had won the previous bout after a penalty against him for 'diving' was overruled, which so enraged Mendoza that it gave Humphries the psychological advantage.[20] At Stilton, Humphries was again declared to have fouled after faking a fall, but this time the decision was upheld, the fight continued, and Mendoza proved his superiority. Clare might have seen something of himself in the winner—an outsider of slight physique who relied on quick wits, agility and skill to overcome more powerful opponents.

As Roy tells us the story, I imagine a boxing ring set out in the High Street between the Bell and the Angel, but as Luke Williams relates:

> Humphries-Mendoza 2, in the grounds of Henry Thornton, Esq.'s county estate in Stilton, Huntingdonshire, was a huge affair. To accommodate the insatiable demand among fight fanatics for a ringside view, an octagonal amphitheatre was constructed which held around 2,000 spectators, while the number of carriages that descended upon Stilton for the contest was "beyond belief."[21]

A contemporary cartoon celebrating Dan Mendoza's victory over Richard Humphries at Stilton in May 1789, which praises Mendoza for his 'spirit and liberality' in giving his opponent a second chance despite the latter's attempt to cheat.

Resting on the gravel causeway in the middle of the village, Clare, down and very nearly out, looked nothing like the prizefighter he professed to be. And as the gypsy had feared might happen on the previous day, he was being 'noticed':

> a young woman (so I guessed by the voice) came out of a house and said 'poor creature' and another more elderly said 'O he shams' but when I got up the latter said 'o no he don't' as I hobbled along very lame   I heard the voices but I never looked back to see where they came from

This brief snatch of dialogue has the ring of a painful memory rather than a fiction to generate sympathy in the reader; Clare was a connoisseur of young ladies' charms, and it can only have been shame at his condition that caused him to struggle to his feet and limp away without so much as glancing at this one's face. His retreat is reminiscent of a sonnet he wrote about an unkempt vagrant, who "talks to none but wends his silent way",[22] and perhaps this image, or something like it, was in his mind as he limped along the causeway out of Stilton.

Musings XXIII

Sheep and cows eat grass, so why not he?
It's growing lush, sheltered by a rosemary bush
from the dust: a tentative nibble at first,
then substantial bites, tearing the strong green
with his teeth, slightly sweet from July's sun.

Something like bread, chewed into lumps
and churned and rolled between his cheeks and tongue
to make a kind of cud without the benefit
of five stomachs. They died in Ireland eating grass,
corpses with green stains around their mouths.

❦

With his lucifers exhausted he cannot smoke.
So he takes a wodge from his pouch and chews;
pungent and dry at first it softens to gum
and works his mouth till, all flavour gone,
he swallows the desiccated quid.

❦

This old wide-awake might come in useful
he thought, and squashed it in his pocket –
and it turned out so; he'd years of practice
making a desk from the crown of his hat
and now he sat on a stone pile and wrote

using the tools of his trade, a thin pen
with a metal nib, dipped in a screw-top jar
of portable ink. In his cursive handwriting
he summoned the sweet breast of Mary,
his poetical fancy, to be his love.

He brought her close, as he is close to us,
through the intensity of empathy and thought;
and yet, four years without a woman in his arms,
without a wife, contrary to Christian law,
or paid-for woman, left his aching longing growing.

In March he wrote to Patty, 'my affection
is unaltered'; in June he wrote to first and second
wife together, 'I'm determined
to keep you both for ever'; now his pen draws
Mary closer as his feet bring Patty nearer.

An Eagle for a Slave

Clare reports that there was an inn at the end of the causeway, where

> I met two young women and I asked one of them wether the road branching to the right bye the end of the Inn did not lead to Peterborough and she said 'Yes' it did so   as soon as ever I was on it I felt myself in homes way and went on rather more cheerfull though I forced to rest oftener then usual

The phrasing of his question, "wether [...] the road *did not* lead to Peterborough" (our italics) indicates that he has recognized the establishment and knows he is on the final stretch home. It stood on the western side of the Great North Road, opposite the Yaxley Road where coaches turned off to Peterborough, Lincoln and Louth. Clare had encountered it on eight separate occasions when travelling to and from London, and must have passed it many times more on his habitual walks around the fen country.

In after years it was a familiar landmark on the Great North Road called the Norman Cross Hotel. In what is by now an all-too-familiar tale, it was swept away in the 1960s by the arrival of the A1. A replacement of sorts—not a hotel but a *motel*—was built in the form of a futuristic doughnut-shaped structure that would

The Norman Cross Hotel circa 1920, more or less unchanged in appearance since Clare's time. View south along the Great North Road.

Detail from an Ordnance Survey Map of 1819 showing the size and extent of the Norman Cross Depot compared with the settlements of Coldicote, Stilton and Yaxley.

have looked more at home in an episode of *Thunderbirds* than the Cambridgeshire fens. When it was absorbed into the larger complex of the Norman Cross Premier Inn in the 1990s, its atomic-age profile was disguised with brick cladding to harmonise it with other buildings on the site. It now looks like a squat brown biscuit barrel—proof yet again that visions of the future rarely survive contact with their eventual present.

Norman Cross was famous for its 'Depot'; a prisoner-of-war camp established during the Napoleonic Wars for captured French combatants. Constructed in 1796 and in use until 1814, it was huge, covering ten acres and at its peak housing almost 7,000 men. Built to the design of a contemporary artillery fort, it was formidably secure, with a 27-ft-deep ditch to prevent tunnelling, a high perimeter wall, and a sophisticated system of surveillance involving hidden guards, regularly spaced watch towers and a central panopticon blockhouse. Prisoners were billeted in double-storeyed wooden sheds distributed across four quadrangles. As a child George Borrow saw them at first hand, and later wrote this vivid description:

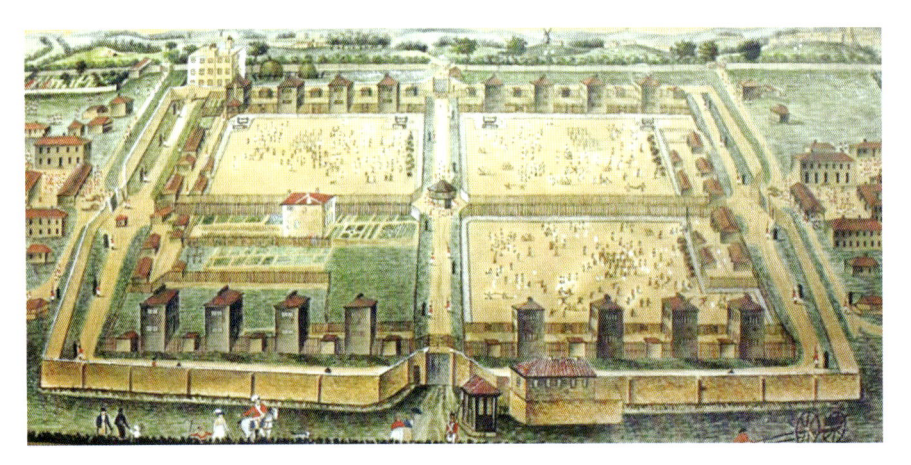

The Norman Cross Depot, circa 1797.

> What a strange appearance had those mighty casernes, with their blank blind walls, without windows or grating, and their slanting roofs, out of which, through orifices where the tiles had been removed, would be protruded dozens of grim heads, feasting their prison-sick eyes on the wide expanse of country unfolded from that airy height. Ah! there was much misery in those casernes; and from those roofs, doubtless, many a wistful look was turned on lovely France.[23]

For modern readers Borrow's narrative is redolent of twentieth-century gulags. It is generally accepted that the first concentration camps were built during the Second Boer War of 1900 to 1902, but on the evidence of his testimony the Depot must surely have the prior claim. Conditions were squalid, and the prisoners malnourished — given, as he says, "carrion meat, and bread from which I have seen the very hounds occasionally turn away". But the most striking parallel with later camps concerns the brutality of the guards:

> And then, those visits, or rather ruthless inroads, called in the slang of the place "straw-plait hunts," when, in pursuit of a contraband article, which the prisoners, in order to procure themselves a few of the necessaries and comforts of existence, were in the habit of making, red-coated battalions were marched into the prisons, who, with the bayonet's point, carried havoc and ruin into every poor convenience which ingenious wretchedness had been endeavouring to raise around it; and then the triumphant exit with the miserable booty; and, worst of all, the accursed bonfire, on the barrack parade, of the plait contraband, beneath the view of the glaring eyeballs from those lofty roofs, amidst the hurrahs of the troops, frequently drowned in the curses poured down from above like a tempest-shower, or in the terrific war-whoop of "Vive l'Empereur!"

Though it may have been hell for those inside, the Depot gave the local economy a huge boost, providing carters, farmers, merchants and craftsmen with extra business.

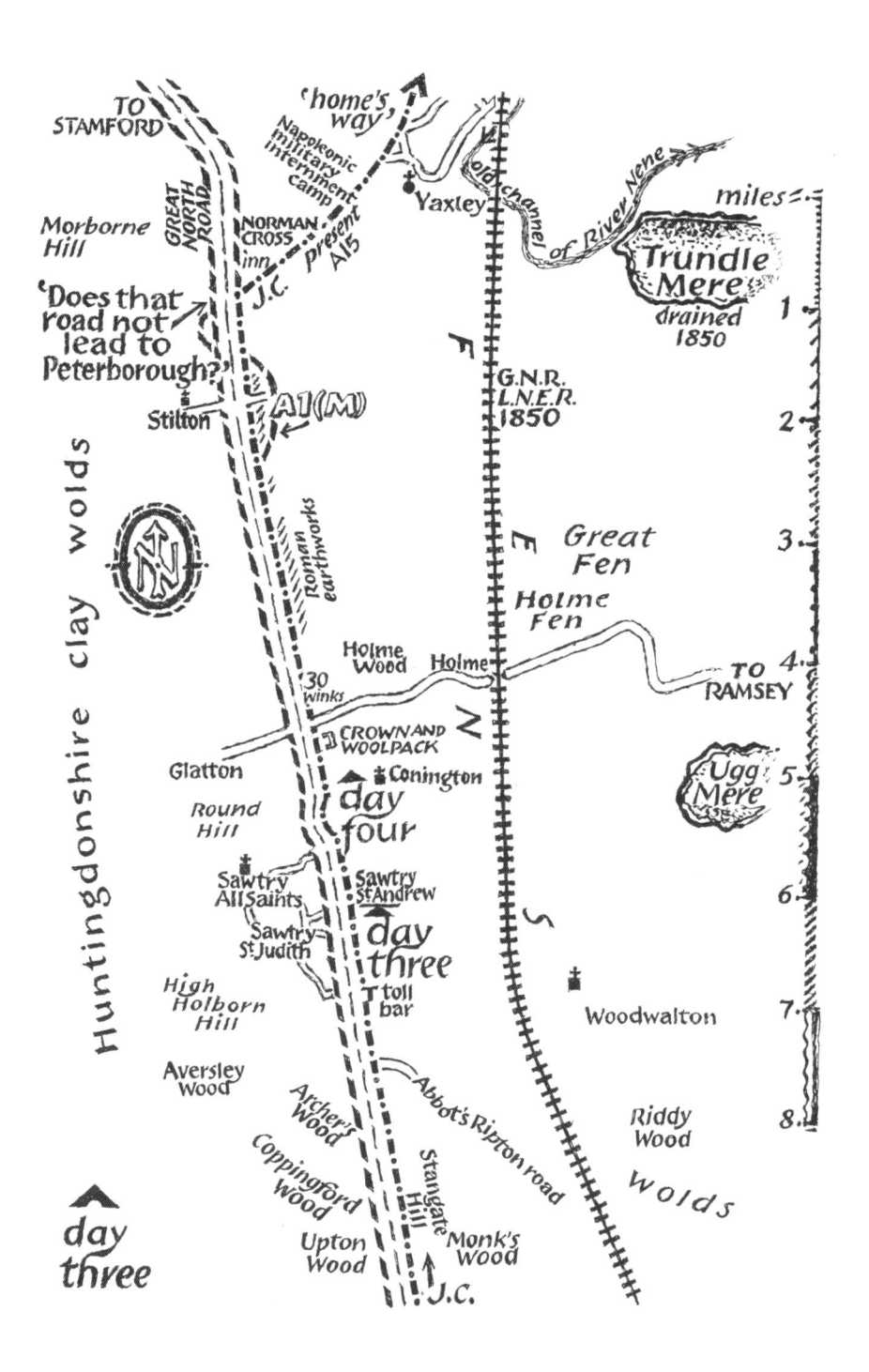

THE JOURNEY – HUNTINGDONSHIRE – AN EAGLE FOR A SLAVE   307

The Norman Cross Memorial, with its replacement bronze eagle, now situated on the road to Peterborough close to the Depot's administrative buildings.

Hostels and inns as far afield as Peterborough also benefitted, as officers and French civilians on *parole d'honneur* were permitted to take private rooms within a five-mile radius, and could mix freely with the local gentry.

The place must have loomed large in Clare's adolescence, when the threat of a French invasion was never far from the nation's thoughts. A belligerent Gallic principality in the neighbourhood—albeit a captive one—would doubtless have preyed upon the anxieties of a young man who had joined the Northampton Militia and was retained until Napoleon's defeat to defend his county at a moment's notice. Yet we find in his references to it a compassion for the inmates and an acknowledgement of their common humanity. In one sonnet composed after 1832 he describes the desolate field where the Depot once stood—a place, though apparently unremarkable, "that may well claim / A place with glory by the side of fame":

> Yet there the warrior rests that longed to tell
> By their own homes how valour fought & fell
> They had their glory & their wounds to show
> Yet weeds not laurels oer their honours grow

and contrasts his own sympathy with the attitude of a passing coachman,

> Who laughed & said tis there [the] frenchmen lie
> They fought for tyrants their reward was slaves
> & england was their prison & their graves.[24]

In another sonnet from the same period he addresses a "fair maid of france" —perhaps the sweetheart of a paroled officer—whom he encounters in the locality and whose beauty captivates him. There is nothing new in Clare writing about a pretty face, but in this case his infatuation serves the more general point that attraction between individuals is more powerful than the enmity of nations:

> Thy countrys honour on thy face attends
> Man may be foes but beauty makes us friends.[25]

The camp was pulled down in 1816. The ghost of its perimeter, etched in the soil, is still visible in aerial photographs, but at ground level there's no sign: just a large paddock dotted with mature trees.

Two of its administrative buildings are still standing—the handsome three-storeyed Governer's Residence, now called Norman House, and the Sessions House where the camp's legal work was done. For almost a hundred years they provided the only physical evidence that the camp ever existed. Then, in the summer of 1914, a memorial was raised on the Great North Road close to the Norman Cross Hotel. The date of its inauguration lends it a symbolism far weightier than could have been wished for by its patrons, the Entente Cordiale Society, whose belief in the commonality of British and French interests was immediately and tragically realised in the unfolding of the Great War. In 1990 the monument—a stone column capped by a bronze imperial eagle—suffered the attentions of a group of less high-minded individuals, who stole the eagle for its scrap value. A replacement was cast following a public appeal, and in 2005 the entire memorial was moved to its present site near the Depot buildings on the road to Peterborough.

A mile or so down the same road lies the village of Yaxley, which in 1841 was still an inland port surrounded by waterlogged fens. These were not drained until almost a decade later, when the Great Northern Railway Company laid its line from London to York across them. When operations to empty out the water were finished, the land had fallen by almost eight feet.

The road ran past the village rather than through it, but Clare would have been able to see the tower and steeple of the church, some half-a-mile distant. It was somewhere along this stretch of road that he sat down for one of his rests and experimented with eating tobacco:

> I recollected that I had some tobacco and my box of lucifers being exhausted I could not light my pipe so I took to chewing Tobacco all day and eat the quids when I had done and I was never hungry afterwards

Quoting him like this is perhaps unfair, because it makes the falsehood of the final statement very evident—after all, he will shortly be telling us that he is begging for food—but it illustrates a change of style. The hyperbole of "never hungry afterwards" is very different from the careful exactitude of the earlier passage, "I felt myself in home's way and went on rather more cheerful though I forced to rest oftener then usual". His recollection of having tobacco but no light, then realising he could chew and so could eat, is precisely sequenced. He was, after all, experienced in writing narrative, and the *Journey's* structure, focus and pacing reflect this expertise—something its lack of punctuation can mask, even from experienced readers of his work.

Musings XXIV

They speak:

'We were up early to catch the cart home.
Six of us, counting the driver
and two farm hands with picks and rakes,
so hardly room for our grips. And what do you know?
just at the Nene bridge we overtook John Clare.

'Poor bugger, what was he doing struggling
to walk home all that way, such a famous man –
feet torn to bits and nothing to eat for three days?
The carter wouldn't stop, but we looked
what we'd got and threw him five pennies for grub.

'Patty was baking when we came,
her fingers clagged with dough. The Poet's Cottage
is goodly, but they say she'd had a hard time
and was glad to have him gone. No matter... she rushed
with racing pulse to hire a cart to bring him home.'

A Fistful of Pennies

After describing his encounter with the young women at Norman Cross, Clare continues with a vivid account of a meeting, told with the power of understated emotion:

> Before I got to Peterborough a man and woman passed me in a cart and on hailing me as they passed I found they were neighbours from Helpstone where I used to live – I told them I was knocked up which they could easily see and that I had neither eat or drank any thing since I left Essex   when I told my story they clubbed together and threw me fivepence out of the cart

This succinct statement allows readers to form their own understanding of the emotional impact of the encounter. Frederick Martin, by contrast, gives us a highly charged, melodramatic version of the same events:

> The wanderer, in a faint voice, told those friends his tale of woe; but even they were not Christians enough to lift him into their vehicle and take him home. All they did was give him a few pence; not even placing the money in his hand, with, perhaps a kindly greeting, but throwing it at him from their cart.[26]

There is no doubt about the dynamics here: Clare is a victim, and the old neighbours uncaring—even disdainful—of his situation. His suffering at the hands of others is a constant theme in Martin's book, which must bear some responsibility for the widely held notion of 'Poor Clare' that dogged his posthumous reputation for almost a century.

From Clare's account it is not immediately apparent how events played out. He says that "a man and a woman passed me in a cart". Does he mean that the cart was travelling in the same direction as he was and so overtook him from behind, or was it, instead, coming at him head-on? Martin has Clare collapsed at the roadside in a dead faint, starving and near death, so the only clue he gives to the neighbours' direction of travel lies in his report that they later stop at Northborough to alert Patty to her husband's imminent arrival.

If he writes this because Patty, apparently forewarned, later met Clare on the road, then he has made a reasonable assumption. But he makes others that are less warranted: that the neighbours could have lifted Clare into their cart and taken him home but chose not to; that their gift of five pence was mean-spirited and insufficient for his needs, and that the act of throwing him the money, rather than placing it in his hands, was an expression of indifference or contempt. Perhaps Martin is telling the story as it has been told to him, second or third hand, and this is partly the reason for its high emotional colouring. Certainly, it would appear he did not get sight of the manuscripts—or, at least, not the octavo notebook in which Clare immediately set down half the narrative the night he got home—for he claims, wrongly, that on arriving at Northborough Clare was "utterly exhausted", and only started writing the following morning in "an old bank ledger, in which he formerly entered his poems".[27]

Other biographers and commentators have steered clear of placing any interpretation on the episode, and if they address it at all quote Clare verbatim. An exception is Oscar Turnill, a direct descendant of the Helpston family who helped the young Clare with his education. In an article published in the *John Clare Society Newsletter* of December 2000, entitled 'Clare's Journey – Who were the 'Old Neighbours' on the road?',[28] Turnill suggests they were two of his forebears returning home to Sawtry All Saints after making a visit to friends in Helpston.

His take on the encounter is radically different from Martin's. Most obviously, he has the cart and its passengers coming south, against Clare's direction of travel, claiming that Clare's use of the verb 'passed', "surely means 'met', not 'overtook', in which event he might have clambered on board". Having already decided on the identity of the travellers and their destination, Turnill is of course forced to reach this conclusion because otherwise his whole line of argument will collapse.

The problem for him is that Patty came looking for Clare, a circumstance that makes perfect sense if the neighbours—heading towards Helpston and not, as he insists, away from it—paused at Northborough to alert her. He visibly wrestles with this point to no satisfactory effect: "The fact that later on Patty Clare met her husband at Werrington makes one wonder whether by then she had been warned of his likely arrival; certainly, it seems more than chance. Even so, without some general hue and cry, the people he met earlier were hardly likely to have known."

Martin's and Turnill's contradictory interpretations are only possible because Clare's own account is so brief and terse, but even so it is capable of yielding insights that can stand up to scrutiny. The first is that the encounter must have lasted some minutes. Clare had time to tell his old neighbours why he was on the road and in such bad shape, and for them to pool their money together. They may have stopped the cart to talk to him, but had they done so, it is reasonable to imagine at least one of them stepping down and greeting him face-to-face, which apparently did not happen. It is therefore more likely that they slowed their pace to match his, which suggests they were travelling in the same direction. If we set aside Martin's contention that they were hard-hearted (in which case why did they help Clare at all?), their failure to stop must relate either to their schedule—they had urgent business to attend to—or their status—they were not in charge of the vehicle.

Clare's statement about there being "a man and a woman in a cart" does not necessarily indicate that they were the only people in it, and his choice of the verb 'to hail' over, say, 'to greet', in describing how they accosted him may suggest that the cart was in a state of continued motion which was not in their power to stop. So, therefore, might they have been paying passengers?

For most working folk in the eighteenth and nineteenth centuries, travelling by cart was the only alternative to walking. Carters and waggoners took passengers to supplement their income, allowing them to 'ride along' for a few pennies. This practice is well described by Tobias Smollett in his 1748 novel *Roderick Random*: "A hundred guineas?" complains one of the protagonists, "If I had so much money, d'ye think I would be found travelling in a waggon, at this season of the year?"[29]

If the old neighbours had been hitching a ride, it is possible that others were too. Clare's description of them 'clubbing together' to find him some change is an odd choice of words, and could suggest the sum was the product of more than two pockets. In any case, the five pence raised was not as niggardly as Martin would have us believe. It procured Clare "two half pints of ale and two penn'orth of bread and cheese", after which—given the price of beer at the time—he still had a penny left. Nor was the way it was handed over in the least bit brutal; like "the man on horseback in a slop frock" near Baldock, who gave Clare a penny for a half pint of ale, the old neighbours threw their contribution not *at* him, but onto the ground *beside* him, from where he could pick it up. And as for not taking him home themselves, this would not have been possible aboard a cart whose owner had his own schedule to keep.

Northamptonshire

Day 4, 23rd July 1841:
Peterborough to Northborough

Musings XXV

Who was the man who brought Patty to fetch him?
and what of Charles when his poet father,
legendary for botanising and birding,
seemed not to recognise his mother –
and what of the struggle to get him in the cart?

Clare's thoughts were full of Mary,
longing for his lost home, soul mate, poetic muse;
and now, slumped against the wooden boards,
he's face to face with Patty who grasps his hand,
and berates him lovingly. And suddenly is angry.

❧

When the July light dims on that first night
does she draw him to her bed, warming to the touch
of his thigh, his breath, flesh of his flesh?
Does he glory in remembered passion
for this woman whose body was his graven habit?

A monolith between them, his madness
impedes what might have been,
his dream of ease in the arms of his wife
is scythed away like poppies dying
in a harvest of betrayal.

❧

He speaks:

'The cart brought me to this desolation,
a prisoner again, shackles tight on my breath.
Not free. This is no home to me.
I set my heart on Glinton spire where Mary
waits. But Patty stole me away.

'Scorpions lurk among the unkempt yews
that my sons once clipped to shape,
hissing and grinning at my derelict hopes
in this fevered fenland
where the nightingale never comes.

'I blessed sweet Mary every night before I slept
beside the road, and bless her still,
so strong when I saw her not twelve months since
and fair and delicate as a hare bell.
They lie to spite me when they say she's dead.'

❦

'Four years I've yearned for my two fancies,
to hold soft flesh in close embrace, salving
my loneliness in penetrating warmth.
Now Patty looks askance at me, as she's afeared,
and blights my hope with hesitating smiles.

'That first night when I stopped to write
I climbed the stair and found the bedroom
barred against me; locked out from my rights,
nowt but a lodger in Lord Milton's
tenancy, his trust to me, the Poet's House.

'Asleep on the settle by the open hearth,
I dreamt I was back on the road and Mary,
my poetical fancy, rose of the world,
came with Patty to embrace me both,
their children ranked behind.'

❦

'Yesterday, taking my old stick, polished
by years-in-hand spent proggling briars and starting
landrails from their meadow holes, I walked
across the fen and up the gentle rise
to Helpston, nestled in beside Royce Wood.

'The cottage where I and my children were born
stands by the Bluebell, fragrant with John Barleycorn,
where oft I scraped my fiddle for my father's singing;
and there I wept to see Glinton's spire, standing still
mid clouds feathering the blue, pointing to heaven.'

❦

Where is Angel Mary Now?

Oscar Turnill suggests that the small public house where Clare broke his fast was at Fletton, but Clare himself tells us it was "near the bridge", which places it unequivocally at Peterborough, a mile further on.

Clare was spoilt for choice when it came to obtaining refreshment; that year Pigot listed no fewer than nine taverns close to the bridge. If Clare's account is accurate he most likely ate at the Boat or the Rose and Crown, at the foot of Bridge Street on the northern bank of the Nene. Crossing the river, he would have seen them immediately on his left, with the Customs House on his right, and behind that, at a distance of maybe a quarter of a mile, Peterborough Cathedral. His friend Marianne Marsh, the wife of the Bishop of Peterborough, had been living in the cathedral close when he was admitted to High Beach. It is uncertain whether he knew of her husband's death in 1839, but in any case he was unlikely to have been dwelling on old friends as he threaded his way through the city's streets: he had enough to cope with fighting the pain and exhaustion that was threatening to overwhelm him.

Anyone who has ever hiked a long distance and sat down to eat and relax will recognize his description of how difficult he found starting out again. His legs would have stiffened up, and blood from blisters would have stuck to what was left of his socks. By the time he'd eaten it was late morning, or possibly early afternoon, and Peterborough was thronged with vehicles and pedestrians. This added to his

Peterborough's medieval town bridge, which Clare crossed as he made his way to the nearest alehouse, having just received 5^d from his former neighbours. Photograph circa 1860.

Bridge Street, Peterborough, viewed from the bridge. Stepping off it, Clare had the choice of entering the Boat or the Rose and Crown. Photograph 1910.

discomfort; the cobbles were making it hard for him to manage his broken shoe with its flapping sole, and the social awkwardness that had first assailed him at Stilton returned, driving him on:

> when I had done I started quite refreshed only my feet was more crippled then ever and I could scarcely make a walk of it over the stones and being half ashamed to sit down in the street I forced to keep on the move and got through Peterborough better then I expected

With the city behind him, he resumed his strategy of sitting awhile on every stone heap he came across; away from the public gaze he could nurse his pain without fear of being pitied by strangers.

North of Peterborough the high road forked at a tollgate belonging to the Leicester and Peterborough Turnpike Trust. Taking the left-hand branch, he was now on the Lincoln Road heading for Northborough. The village of Walton lay two miles ahead, and that of Werrington less than a mile further on. It was there that his walk unexpectedly ended:

> bye and bye I passed Walton and soon reached Werrington and was making for the Beehive as fast as I could when a cart met me with a man and woman and a boy in it

The woman was Patty, the boy most probably Clare's youngest son Charles, and the man almost certainly the cart's owner.

Clare's mind was on a half-pint of ale when they accosted him; he still had a penny left after paying for his meal, and was heading for somewhere to spend it. Past attempts at locating his goal—'The Beehive'—have met with no success. The best guess anyone can make is that he was confused and drawing on memories of his walks to Stamford, where there was a pub of that name.[1] Yet his use of the phrase 'making for' suggests somewhere close by—in or near Werrington, which, as a relatively large settlement, would have had several alehouses not listed in official records. The Beehive was very likely one of those, known to him from his regular walks to and from Peterborough.

The High Street ran at right angles to the Lincoln Road, so 'making for' may also indicate he was about to turn into it when Patty appeared, meaning she was within a whisker of missing him. On the other hand, the report in his letter to Matthew Allen that "one of my fancys […] meet me on this side Werrington with a horse & cart"[2] places him past the turn, in which case the Beehive was not in the village proper but on the Lincoln Road. However, given his propensity for over-dramatization (writing to George Reid that he had been "3 Nights & 4 days on the road without food & lodging"[3]) he may have been exaggerating how far he'd managed to walk in order to suggest that he very nearly reached home under his own steam; something that fits with other inflated statements about triumphing over adversity.

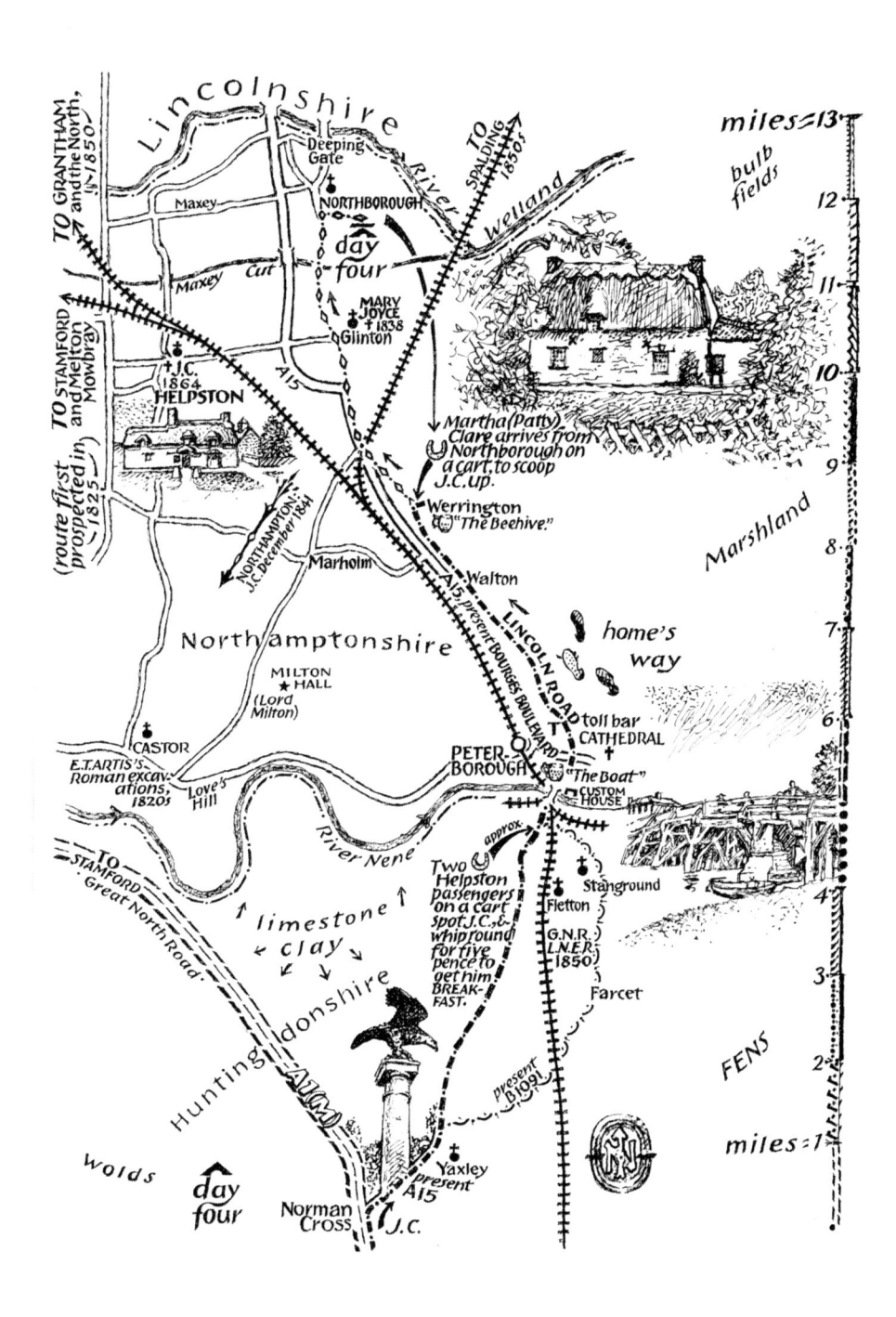

THE JOURNEY – NORTHAMPTONSHIRE – WHERE IS ANGEL MARY NOW? 321

St Benedict's church, Glinton, where Clare first met Mary Joyce, and whose spire came to symbolise her enduring presence in the life of his imagination.

The former neighbours who passed him on the road almost certainly went straight to Northborough and told Patty they'd found him walking home, famished and exhausted—something Martin states as fact, calling them with intended irony, "*charitable* Helpston people" (our italics).[4] Given the time frame of events, she must have acted with great haste, either hiring a cart or persuading a neighbour to take her to meet him. Clare continues:

> When nearing me the woman jumped out and caught fast hold of my hands and wished me to get into the cart but I refused and thought her either drunk or mad but when I was told it was my second wife Patty I got in and was soon at Northborough

Once again, the narrative is fast-moving and succinct, presenting us with the drama of the meeting without embellishment. There is an energy about Patty's actions at the moment she sees him, jumping out and catching fast hold of his hands. She must have been shocked to hear he was coming, but Clare's narrative conveys the sense that she gives him an excited welcome. By contrast he describes himself not recognising her and thinking her "either drunk or mad", which is poignantly ironic in the light of the note he penned at Crosshall: "O Mary mary If you knew how anxious I am to see you and dear Patty with the childern I think you would come and meet me." There is also something odd about the phrasing of "when I was told it was my second wife Patty": a curious detachment, and one that only makes sense if there has been a fracture in the process of writing the narrative. Up to this point Clare has been working with the memories of his time on the road. Now he is writing in the light of his experience of returning to Patty, and of her reaction to him. He appears to have composed the *Journey* over a period of days, starting on July 23rd and ending on the 27th, the date of the letter he appended to the finished text. There is hostility, violence even, in his saying he thought her either drunk or mad. He has been away for four years and his return has been a shocking disappointment, not least because—as is evident from his letter to Matthew Allen—she has not granted him his conjugal rights. Sex was a major motive for his escape from High Beach, and Mary was its focus. Any pleasure Patty felt on his return must have been quickly dispelled by his desire for his 'first wife'. A month later, writing to Allen, he makes explicit the breakdown of any physical relationship with her: "I look upon myself as a widow or bachelor I don't know which – I care nothing about the women now for they are faithless & decietfull."[4]

He was also, however, a Romantic poet writing about the return of a wanderer after a long separation. The Ancient Mariner had to tell his story to assuage his sin, and Odysseus returned to a wife who did not recognize him.[5] Claiming he did not realise that Patty was his 'second wife' evokes such literary analogies, and calling her mad skilfully turns attention away from her long-standing accusation of insanity that led to his confinement in the asylum.

The greatest shock of all was arriving home to find Mary absent. It must have begun when the horse and cart passed through her home village of Glinton, two miles down the road. We can imagine him asking why she hasn't come to meet him, and Patty's hurt and anger at this talk only of Mary, and his relegation of her own position to that of 'second wife'.

Three stanzas from one of the songs he wrote that evening hammer out his pain, and they refer specifically to Glinton:

> The church spire still attracts my eye
> & leaves me broken hearted
> Though grief hath worn their channels dry
> I sigh oer days departed
>
> The church yard where she used to play
> My feet could wander hourly
> My school walks there was every day
> Where she made winter flowery
>
> But where is angel Mary now
> Loves secrets non disclose 'em
> Her rosey cheek & broken vow
> Live in my aching bosom[6]

Mary Joyce's headstone in St Benedict's churchyard. Despite Clare's continued insistence that she was alive and well, he could not possibly have missed this conclusive proof of her death, placed as it was beside the path to the south door.

The *Journey* continues:

> was soon at Northborough but Mary was not there neither could I get any information about her further then the old story of her being dead six years ago which might be taken from a bran new old Newspaper printed a dozen years ago but I took no notice of the blarney having seen her myself about a twelvemonth ago alive and well and as young as ever

Clare's state of shock is strongly indicated in the uncontrolled emotion of this passage, so different from any other in the text: "the old story" suggests that he has been told of her death before, possibly by Allen, who may even have been sent a copy of a local newspaper; "six years ago" doubles the actual passage of time since Mary's death, and "a bran new old Newspaper printed a dozen years ago" doubles it again, camping the story up as a load of old nonsense—a contemporary meaning of "blarney" being 'wild Irish cajoling talk'.[7] He also has the evidence of his own eyes that she is alive and well, though this is belied by him saying that "a twelvemonth ago" she was "as young as ever".

Clare's belief that Mary was his first wife, and that he would find her with Patty and the children, underpins the whole of the *Journey*. It is the single fixed, unwavering delusion that might suggest he was seriously disturbed. The personae of Byron and Jack Randall were, by contrast, confined to the asylum, and ceased when he left it, suggesting a knowing—or partly knowing—charade to keep at arm's length the horrors he experienced there. And as for seeing Mary, Oliver Sacks notes that hallucinations in the sane were well recognized in the nineteenth century.[8] Patty would not have seen it that way, however: she must have insisted with some bitterness that he was mad to think he had ever had two wives.

What is certain is that Mary was the muse who inspired Clare to write about love. She was his ideal to such an extent that he saw her face in all women, and her imagined presence was his constant companion in the loneliness of his years at High Beach.

The *Journey* ends on a tragic note of isolation and endurance:

> so here I am homeless at home and half gratified to feel that I can be happy anywhere
>
> > 'May none those marks of my sad fate efface
> > For they appeal from tyranny to God'[9]
> >
> > Byron

As is his habit, Clare refuses to despair. He openly quotes from Byron, indicating that taking on the persona of the poet-peer was never more than a playful guise. In selecting these two lines from the *Prisoner of Chillon*, he likens the *Journey's* account of his sufferings to the marks of Bonnivard's feet worn into the stone floor of his castle prison. He invites us to see him, like Bonnivard, as an "eternal spirit of the chainless mind". It is a triumphant ending, claiming a place alongside Byron in the literary canon of his day.

The Man

Authors' Note

During the last few months of writing this book we came to realise that our understanding of John Clare's life and achievements had undergone a profound change, and that our appreciation of him had deepened more than we could ever have anticipated. It seemed a kind of bonus for our work.

To celebrate, and to present him as we now see him, Bridget has written eleven poems that attempt to do justice to his complexity. These are intended to be read in parallel with the short articles that accompany them, which summarize our thoughts on some of the key issues in Clare studies: Clare's supposed madness; his relationship with Eliza Emmerson; his political engagement; his drive in writing about the Enclosures; his place among the English Romantic poets, and the nature of *Journey out of Essex* as a literary text.

EH

Father of the Queen of England

It's a splendid joke. High on a heap of stones
to bung into holes in the road, Clare presides,
refigured as Edward Duke of Kent,
the old reprobate who married late
and begat a queen, a rake in a Cruikshank cartoon.

At last light and first dawn he blesses his two wives
and all their swarming, overflowing progeny,
and adds a special blessing for little Vicky,
whose snuff box he guessed, not two months since,
was being defiled while Albert was in Germany.

He is still John Clare of the *London Magazine*
flaunting his wit: the man wot rites the werses
and burns up lies like summer mist;
imperious in the wide-awake hat like Byron
in his turban, a wry punster but not Byron – poh!

Lunatic, Lover and Poet

John Clare was committed to the lunatic asylum at High Beach in 1837—in another age, when definitions of madness and assumptions concerning how to treat the insane were very different from our own. Madness is, at heart, a culturally constructed diagnosis. As a psychiatrist friend of mine put it, "If people around you find your behaviour incomprehensible, you're called mad and get taken for treatment or containment. This happens throughout all ages and all cultures. Only the diagnosis differs".[1]

Clare was fortunate that the asylum his publisher, John Taylor, chose for him was a benign establishment that followed the latest methods. There, he was treated with respect, encouraged to talk about his problems, and given good food and the freedom to walk in the grounds and surrounding forest. He was, however, a committed inmate, and when, in early 1841, he was moved to a house with a harsher regime and denied female company, he felt abused and imprisoned.

When we started work on this book we assumed that Clare's madness was incontestable. This seemed to be confirmed by the very first entry of the *Journey*, where he promises a gypsy fifty pounds to help him escape: a sum wildly out of proportion at a time when half a pint of ale cost a penny and he was promised 5[d] a day for field work.

Very quickly, however, a tone of comic innuendo emerges from the text. Describing the first moment of his escape on July 20th, he writes, "having only honest courage and myself in my army I led the way and my troops soon followed". It's a brave joke: there is no army, but there is great courage, the more so in the light of the effects of institutionalisation after four years in the asylum.[2]

When he was seventeen, Ellis and his friend, Martin Phillips, wrote a novel called *The Great Spaghetti Scandal*,[3] in which the characters from their A level texts had bizarre adventures narrated in the hyperbolic language of Monty Python and the Goons. They might equally have drawn their inspiration from Clare; there is something in his self-portrayal as a general at the head of a non-existent army that is in the same maniacally surreal vein. And when, midway through the *Journey*, he writes, "the man whose daughter is the queen of England is now sitting on a stone heap on the highway to Bugden without a farthing in his pocket", a statement that could easily be construed as insane seems to us no more than a joke to buoy up the spirits in the face of suffering.

Roger Sales' account of Clare's transformation on joining the literati of the *London Magazine* in 1820,[4] and J. H. Reynolds' caricatures of them, including one of Clare as a man with "ten little children all under the age of four years",[5] both confirm that Clare had been assimilated into and become part of a comic literary tradition. In this context, his self-portrayal as a royal rake turned vagabond, his writings in the persona of Byron and his claim to be Jack Randall all seem less like the products of madness and more like elaborate jests.

Again, we find Sales persuasive when he suggests that Clare found, in Allen's asylum, a release from the controls put upon his writing by patrons and publishers. After fifteen years of being required to write for the market as a Peasant Poet, Clare was able to return to the irreverence of the London literati of the 1820s, and in this connection it is hardly surprising that he adopts the guise of another poet: pseudonymous writing was, after all, a key feature of the *London Magazine's* house style.[6]

Using other voices allowed him to experiment with other styles of writing and other ways of being. In 'Don Juan' he broke more social taboos than Byron himself, particularly in the insinuations about the young Victoria's relations with Lord Melbourne. Though the poem could never have been published in his own day, it enabled him to break new satirical ground and lay claim to elements of his own persona that had been too long repressed.

When Theseus, in Shakespeare's *A Midsummer Night's Dream*, declares that "The lunatic, the lover and the poet are of imagination all compact", he construes imagination as visionary power. Clare, in regarding Mary Joyce as his "poetical fancy"[7] and writing so many poems about her, drew on a source of imaginative energy that was not available to him without the stimulation of a love affair. Eliza Emmerson perceptively remarked that he seemed to need to fall in love in order to write, and he found continual inspiration in reliving the fantasy of his relationship with Mary. As a poet and a lover—never mind a lunatic—Clare's imaginative life with her during his four years in the asylum seems to have become at least as real as his memories of Patty and the children.

Of course, the *Journey* is a literary as well as a biographic text, and Clare was a master of narrative. The exile overcoming loneliness and hardship to return to his lady is a classic trope of chivalry and romance. It could transform the simple story of an escape from a lunatic asylum into a tragic odyssey. It could justify the offer of an exaggerated sum of money, £50, to buy a safe path.

During the months spent preparing to write this book, in particular reading and rereading the *Journey*, we have come to the view that Clare was never mad. Even his denial that Mary is dead and his claim of "having seen her myself about a twelvemonth ago alive and well and as young as ever" seems tragic rather than manic. Perhaps he is simply angry when he writes this, or has been subject to the notorious unreliability of memory. Deprived of his family and friends, he may have experienced a hypnagogic hallucination similar to the voice that he hears saying 'Mary' as he woke up from his night's sleep in Stevenage. Or perhaps he was locked away in solitary confinement at Lippitts Hill Lodge, and saw one of the brilliantly vivid 'prisoner's cinema' hallucinations experienced by those held in isolation.[8]

As Roy Porter observes, Clare may ultimately have been a sane man kept in a place where insanity was the norm, and where his actions were judged accordingly: "Behaviour which, in the wider world, would be read as socially acceptable, becomes, in the context of the asylum, further confirmation of psychosis. [...] What contemporaries stared upon as symptoms of madness, we could easily read as Clare's subversions, fantasies of poser, private performances."[9]

BS

Emma and Johnny

After Madame Vestris sang 'The Meeting' at Drury Lane
he was the talk of the town: small of stature
but of startling physical allure with blue eyes
and a sunburst smile, she thought him like the robin
in his poem singing of lost golden days.

In 'The Vow' he expressed palpable delight
in an educated woman's sympathy of thought,
declaring with tremulous joy that 'I was born for thee'
and arguing ... if and if ... against heaven's rules of trespass;
and around that time she gave him her picture.

She was a woman of style and independent mind,
who shared his writer's passion, herself a poet.
At her townhouse in Stratford Place, Clare
enjoyed flirtation and his own Skylight Room –
when decorum allowed, her husband being at home.

Later, he wrote a song enticing her
to leave the dinsome city to enjoy
the exquisite pleasure of meadows
and bubbling springs, and take home memories
to treasure of a summer's day together.

She understood his penury and loved
to send him gifts: after that first London visit
Patty's wedding gown; and later
two neckerchiefs of Indian silk shot through
with woven light to set off his ardent eyes.

Emma and Johnny to each other, theirs
was the trusted love of intimates. In letters
written over twenty years she was his confidante
and poetry advisor, buoying his spirit
with unfailing reassurance of his genius.

"Beautious Emma"

Clare arrived in London three months after the publication, in January 1820, of his first collection, *Poems Descriptive of Rural Life and Scenery*, in which his publisher John Taylor presented him as a poet worthy of serious consideration. He was accompanied by Octavius Gilchrist, whose article, 'Some account of John Clare, an Agricultural Labourer and Poet', had also appeared the same month in the first issue of the *London Magazine*. During the interim, Clare had been invited to visit Lord Milton and his father Earl Fitzwilliam at Milton Hall, and the Marquess of Exeter at Burleigh House. He had presented all three with copies of his book, and they in turn had congratulated him and given him encouragement with cash and promises of patronage. These experiences, though somewhat disconcerting, led to what he called his 'great expectations'. He was nervously awaiting reviews in the London magazines when Gilchrist suggested a visit to Taylor with his coach fare paid. He arrived to find his fame had gone before him: that very evening the foremost operatic singer of the day, Madame Vestris, was billed to perform a setting of one of his songs at the Theatre Royal. Unfortunately, the coach arrived too late for him to attend.

Eliza Emmerson was one of the first people Clare met in London. Several weeks earlier, she had given a copy of *Poems Descriptive* to the influential Christian evangelist Admiral Lord Radstock, accompanied by a poem of her own entitled 'Lines—Written by a Lady, and presented with a volume of "Clare's Poems"—to a Noble Friend'. She had also written to Clare, praising the collection, and sending him a copy of Edward Young's *Night Thoughts on Life, Death and Immortality*.

Clare's visit lasted only a week, but Eliza moved quickly. She and her husband, the picture dealer Thomas Emmerson, were near neighbours of Radstock. They lobbied him on Clare's behalf and gained his support in advance of the poet's arrival. By the time Clare returned to Helpston, he had been encouraged to count Eliza as his friend and depend on her for support.

For more than two decades thereafter they corresponded, and also met face-to-face during his four visits to London and her own visit to Helpston. At first Eliza played the role of patron and eager recipient of new poems, providing critical feedback and encouraging Radstock and Taylor's continued support. Over time, Clare was able to provide her with assistance in furthering her own career as a poet, in particular helping her to publish under the pseudonym E. L. E. in the Stamford newspaper *The Bee*, where, according to Alan Vardy, she published more poems than Clare himself.[10] Then, during the early 1830s, when Clare was unable to gain sponsorship for his huge projected collection, 'The Midsummer Cushion', Eliza assisted him in selecting and editing poems from it for *The Rural Muse*.

Eliza was, in Jonathan Bate's words, "Clare's most intimate and indefatigable correspondent",[11] so it is sad that there appears to have been no contact between them during his time at High Beach. She wrote to Patty in November 1837 when she heard he had been confined, thinking at first, incorrectly, that he was in the asylum at York. She said she had been ill, but asked to be kept informed of his progress, and wrote again the following year, reporting that she had paid Taylor five pounds towards "the medical & kind care of our dear Clare".

When we first started work on this book, we were captivated by the puzzle of Clare's inclusion of a tender love song in his otherwise bawdy 'Don Juan'. Who was the Eliza Phillips to whom he wrote, shortly before he escaped from the asylum, "Come dear Eliza set me free / & oer the forest roam with me"? There was, as far as we knew, no Phillips in Clare's life at the time, but there had been an Eliza, and the poem seemed to be addressed to a former acquaintance.[12]

A year or so later, we came across Emma Trehane's article in the *John Clare Society Journal*, which asserted that Eliza and Clare "came to know each other as Emma and Johnny".[13] Shortly afterwards Roger Rowe sent us some of Clare's notes about Eliza, which confirm that the nickname started from an allusion to the love of a grand lady for an aspiring young man:

> I fancyd it a pretty [thing] to correspond with a lady & by degrees I grew up into an admirer sometimes foolishly when I could not account for what I did & then after requested her portrait & then I recollect ridiculously enough alluding to Lord Nelsons Lady Hamilton she sent it & flattered my vanity in return [14]

Her importance to Clare as a frequent correspondent and literary mentor, and as the godmother to Clare and Patty's second daughter—christened Eliza Louise after her—made us wonder if there might be any private poems shared between them. We searched for any mention of 'Emma' in the Clarendon edition of *The Early Poems of John Clare* and came across two, shown on the facing page.

A week after Clare returned to Helpston he was married to Patty. The day before the wedding Eliza wrote to him, thanking him for a poem he had sent her: "I shall *treasure* it in *my heart*, where it shall be kept *secret and secure from the world*."[15]

The first poem we found, 'The Vow', which was addressed to "beautious emma" looked like it had to be the one: given its ardour it would certainly have needed to be kept secret. But we wanted more evidence, and so sought out Emma Trehane's doctoral thesis.[16] In it, she brilliantly documents the speed of development and the intimacy of Clare and Eliza's friendship. In June, shortly after Patty gave birth to their first child, Eliza wrote that she was about to send him her portrait: "Your 'Guardian Angel' as you are pleased to call her, shall shortly wing her way to your peaceful cottage."[17] When the portrait arrived, it was accompanied by sugar tongs engraved with the name 'Emma'.

Trehane relates how, by July 1820, Eliza and Clare had started sending each other poems in their letters. One in particular delighted Eliza, which she called 'The Invitation to Emma'. She offered to copy it out for John Taylor and suggested that Clare should include it in his second book of poems, or publish it in the *London Magazine*. In response to it she wrote an 'echo', which she entitled 'Answer to the Invitation':

THE VOW

If feelings that fond bosoms move
In sympathy our thoughts coud prove
Then might thou know my only love
That both our hearts agree
If theres a power exists below
That secrets of the soul coud show
Soon beautious emma shoudst thou know
That I was born for thee

& if theres aught beneath to dread
& if a heavens oer my head
Then strike the rash deluder dead
If falsity is mine
May heaven deny its bliss to me
& all to take revenge be free
If ere a beauty face I see
Seems half so sweet as thine

Upon the dewy wings of even
From lovers hearts there neer was given
A vow more worthy room in heaven
Then this Ive breathd the while
& how ere favourd in thy sight
If true love there can give delight
I know ere now my vows to night
Has met an angels smile

Early Poems II, 93.

SONG

Emma leave the dinsome city
Where the coaches bustle down
Where trade yells its daily ditty
Wend wi me to country town
From the noise that taste abuses
Bid a summer days adieu
Where thro moss the fountain oozes
Sit we me & nature view

Song of birds & clowns at labour
Where theyre all the noises made
Where sweet bends the rosey arbour
O'er its silence & its shade
While the bubbles breezes meeting
From the spring head float & flee
Warning us that pleasures fleeting
Emma share the hour wi me

There we'll walk the meadows gaily
Marking scenes that please the eye
& as sunbeams waxeth paley
Ah – we'll greet 'em with a sigh
here we'll wander flowers to gather
Clover bottles on the lea
Emma now tis summer weather
Natures beautys trace wi me

& as even dulling dreary
Chills her moisture on the flower
Parting us before we're weary
Emma – thens the gloomy hour–
Fare thee well & at thy leisure
'Gen while noise environs thee
Think when ye, in guiless pleasure
Spent a summer day wi me

Early Poems II, 445.

Two poems by Clare to Eliza Emmerson.

Edward Villiers Rippingille's 1824 painting 'The Stage Coach Breakfast', which shows the London Magazine's *contributors and their social circle. The figure standing by the window examining the clock is generally accepted as Clare, and the woman on the extreme right looking in the glass is thought to be Eliza Emmerson.*

> Could "Emma" fly the noisy city,
> Where folly dwells, with riot rude
> How pleased, she'd list, thy Rural ditty,
> Sung, in sweetest solitude: –
> To all, which now her heart refuses
> She would bid a glad Adieu!
> And where purling fountain oozes,
> Sit with thee, and nature view! [18]

In her thesis Trehane comments that Clare's original 'Invitation' has been lost. However, Eliza's 'Answer' mirrors exactly the sentiments, narrative focus and even two thirds of the line endings of 'Song', the second poem we found. This makes it certain that 'Song' is, in fact, 'The Invitation to Emma', which has been hiding in plain sight within the pages of the Clarendon edition since 1989.

Eliza wrote to Clare in April 1825, asking him to exclude her letters from any correspondence to be sold on his death, because "It is my wish, should I be your Survivor, to give to the World for the benefit of your family – our mutual Letters, published at my expense and under my own Name and arrangement". Specifically, she asked him to include a clause in his will—viz "All Letters—recd from my early friend —Eliza Louisa Emmerson —most of which are signed "Emma"—shall immediately on my decease, be deliverd to her, for her entire arrangement & disposal—& in case of her death—to be deliverd to her Husband T—E."[19] In the event she died ten years before Clare, and most of their correspondence has been lost.

It is impossible to know whether writing to each other as Emma and Johnny was solely a matter of using loving nicknames. It can be argued that, in excluding 'The Invitation to Emma' from *The Village Minstrel*, Clare or Taylor may have wanted to avoid public speculation. Certainly, if 'The Vow' was the poem Eliza promised to keep secret, the use of nicknames would have been a useful safeguard. It surely cannot be coincidence that the Song to Eliza Phillips in 'Don Juan' issues an invitation which mirrors exactly the 'Song' that so pleased Eliza Emmerson in 1820. By giving her the surname of a patient at the asylum, Clare throws a shawl of obfuscation over the poem, which he teasingly calls "entirely new" and "entirely true":

>Eliza now the summer tells
>Of spots where love and beauty dwells
>Come and spend a day with me
>Underneath the forest tree
>Where the restless water flushes
>Over mosses mounds and rushes
>And where love and freedom dwells
>With orchis flowers and fox glove bells
>Come dear Eliza set me free
>And oer the forest roam with me
>
>Here I see the morning sun
>Among the beachtree's shadows run
>That into gold the short sward turns
>Where each bright yellow blossom burns
>With hues that would his beams out shine
>Yet nought can match those smiles of thine
>I try to find them all the day
>But none are nigh when thou'rt away
>Though flowers bloom now on every hill
>Eliza is the fairest still
>
>The sun wakes up the pleasant morn
>And finds me lonely and forlorn
>Then wears away to sunny noon
>The flowers in bloom the birds in tune
>While dull and dowie all the year
>No smiles to see no voice to hear
>I in this forest prison lie
>With none to heed my silent sigh
>And underneath this beachen tree
>With none to sigh for Love but thee [20]

Poet with an Oaken Bludgeon

You wrote your poem, 'Shadows of Taste',
on the back of a tract urging electors
to vote in the *Interests of True Religion*.
Your poem contrasts the styles of Pope's
regularities of rhymes and John Donne's broken feet

and extols the fashion for gravel walks
to offset nature's wild beauties: with no cash
for paper, what a brilliant use of a handbill
of no possible interest to poor men like yourself
who had no rights to vote.

You recognised in the politics of your own time
Shakespeare's 'mob impulse of the moment'.
Two Stamford papers sought out your contributions
for the force of your pen and independent mind,
though you subscribed to the politics of neither.

The Champion ran your 'Apology for the Poor'
ridiculing the hypocrisy of tax reforms
that only benefitted middle men. *The Bee* took poems
to bring your name and fame on board
until you withdrew when they failed to pay.

Once when riots became all the fashion to support Reform
and even villagers, fired up with passion for Queen Caroline,
took a stand against the king, you prepared an oaken bludgeon
to defend your windows and refused to hang out lights
for Peterborough's grand illuminations night.

Your political writings strike a fearless tone
with heavy irony and innuendo,
and the ease and confidence of style
of the *London Magazine*. Unpublished, they have the worth
of a working man's experience.

An old-fashioned 'king-and-country' man, your weapon
was your pen lambasting self-interest in the powerful,
especially the hypocrisy of one-time Tories
turned brawling Radicals. You burned with the distress
of your father's increasing rheumatic incapacity.

A Man of No Party

In December 1820, Queen Caroline of Brunswick was the darling of the people, an unofficial patron of the Reform movement, and a figurehead for Radicals and their sympathisers. On the first of that month, popular support for her efforts to be acknowledged as rightful queen alongside George IV, her estranged husband, was to be shown by the placing of lights in windows. Clare, however, vowed that his window would stay dark. He wrote to his publisher James Augustus Hessey that neighbours had advised him to change his mind for the sake of his safety, but he would stick to his principles. He was prepared to bludgeon anyone who attacked his home in the cause of Radicalism.[21]

This is a perplexing incident. Behind the marketing-driven image of the Peasant Poet as simple rustic was an intelligent, perceptive and compassionate individual who recognised social injustice and condemned it roundly in his work. How could a man who wrote so eloquently and damningly about the oppression of the poor set his face against a protest for social equality?

The answer is complex, having to do with his unyielding stance on honesty in human dealings and his belief in common sense over partisanship. It also involves his outlook on the society of the time, which, informed by his upbringing among the rural poor, was more conformist than might be imagined. A fear of the mob, instilled in him as a child growing up on tales of the Terror and the threat of French invasion, meant, too, that his championing of the downtrodden—his Radicalism with a small 'r'—could never translate into support for popular revolt. "God forbid," he wrote to John Taylor in 1831 following a local outbreak of rioting and arson in support of Captain Swing, "that I should live to see a revolution."[22]

Clare was as suspicious of the Radicals as he was of the established political parties, and in this he appears tainted with the prejudice of his peers. As an urban movement founded by artisans unfettered to the land, Radicalism was in general regarded by the rural working class as an interloper out of sympathy with its needs and aspirations. The only country voices calling for revolution belonged to those farmers—the "Tory Radicals", as Clare called them—who hoped to profit from the chaos that might ensue at the fall of Britain's *ancien régime*.

As a common feature of rural political discourse, such naked opportunism was all too familiar to Clare, and it caused him to suspect prominent Radicals of being driven solely by personal advancement. "Politics may be said to be an art of money catching," he wrote, "the terms Wig & Tory & Radical are only distinctions between the actors in the play — their discourse is of their country but when their parts are done we see they only meant themselves." And while Whigs and Tories could line their pockets, "Radicals having no share in the harvest grow clamorous in mobs & raise a hue & cry against laws & property which prevents them from possesing it themselves."[23] In 'The Parish' he depicts Young Brag, the son of a Tory farmer and a false-flag Radical, as a rabble-rouser on the make with no social conscience or respect for order. Yet Cobbett fares no better, being in Clare's view nothing more than "a timeserving polotician (sic) and a restless adversary of what hangs about every lover of their country",[24] and though a powerful writer, a man "with no principles to make those powers commendable to honest praise".[25] Tom Paine he simply dismisses as "a low blackguard".[26]

Given Clare's anxieties about the collapse of social order, it is perhaps not so surprising that he expressed support for the class system in general, and the aristocracy in particular. From childhood he had absorbed from his peers a deference to the nobility that was later reinforced by the patronage of Lord Milton, Admiral Lord Radstock and the Marquess of Exeter. The historian E. P. Thompson observes that during the eighteenth century, titled landowners increasingly distanced themselves from the people by placing the day-to-day business of administering their property in the hands of estate managers, gamekeepers and tenant farmers. This enabled them, through occasional interventions and acts of charity, to appear sympathetic to the very workers they were exploiting.[27] Tellingly, it was these intermediaries whom Clare identified as oppressors, and such charitable acts— especially Lord and Lady Milton's solicitude for his father's health—that informed his view of aristocrats as considerate, if lofty, friends of the poor.

So what are we to make of the attack on "accursed wealth" in 'Helpstone', the opening poem of his first collection, which so incensed Radstock for its Radical tone? Again, Thompson is able to provide us with an insight. In trying to resolve the apparent contradiction of a late-eighteenth-century rural working class that was deferential and conservative on the one hand, yet also rebellious on the other, he points to the effects of the Agrarian Revolution, which withdrew ancient rights, swept aside traditional ways of working and killed off time-honoured customs. Unrest among the English rural poor, he argues, was curiously reactionary—driven less by a hunger for revolution than a desire to return to the *status quo ante*.[28] Clare shared this sentiment: writing to William Hone about old country customs, he remarked of one that "inclosure came and destroyed it with hundreds of others —leaving in its place nothing but a love for doing neighbours a mischief and public house oratory that dwells upon mob law as absolute justice."[29] In light of this, it is possible that the wealth he was railing against in 'Helpstone' belonged not so much to Milton, Salisbury or Radstock as the members of the newly ascendant bourgeoisie who had destroyed the settled order: the farmers, the squires and the hunting parsons, all of whom were prominent beneficiaries of 'inclosure', cruel exploiters of those below them, and despoilers of the sacred past.

Radstock also objected to a line in 'Dawnings of Genius', another poem in the collection which, in recognisably Radical terms, referred to the "rough rude ploughman" as the "necessary tool of wealth and pride".[30] As Sam Ward points out, in the febrile atmosphere whipped up by Caroline's supporters, such an image could easily be misconstrued as encouragement to those wishing to bring down the establishment.[31] In the event, however, the young, politically naïve Clare may have been thinking less about the national debate and more about the social realities on his home turf—aiming the barb, as he did a year or so later, at those "mongrel clowns, low as their rooting plough", who were arrogating authority to themselves over and above the law of the land, so that every village "owns its tyrants now / & parish slaves must live as parish-kings alow".[32]

THE MAN – A MAN OF NO PARTY

George Cruikshank's 'The Radical Ladder', which shows a revolutionary mob bent on the destruction of the State hanging onto Queen Caroline's train as she attempts to gain the throne. It sums up elegantly the widespread fear—strongly shared by Clare—that general anarchy might result from Radical agitation.

Provided it excluded such upstarts, Clare appears to have had no problem with the notion of 'the rich man in his castle, the poor man at his gate', taking on trust that each of their estates, like the monarch's, was divinely ordered. For him, monarchy was the lynchpin of a nation—remove it and chaos would ensue as it had in France. This he regarded not as a credo, but as self-evident truth: "Common sense", he wrote, "will teach you that a king is better then no king."[33] The nobility, in their turn, he thought essential to social stability—the "props of a nation."[34] Writing to Taylor in 1831, he expressed the hope that "the unbearable oppression of the labouring classes" could be lifted by one of their number, the Whig MP for Northamptonshire and friend of Lord Milton, Lord Althorp, whom he judged to be an "excellent sample of honest intentions".[35]

The handbill that urged opposition to Reform in the name of piety was useful to the disenfranchised Clare only as writing paper. Yet given his deep-rooted faith, its message might have elicited a degree of sympathy from him, despite standing in the way of improvements to the conditions of his class. "Religion is not only necessary for the interests of the individual," he wrote in notes he made towards an essay on political religion, "but useful for the better order & government of the community at large [...] were there no religion there would be no law & were there no law there would be no living."[36] Yet if he was in favour of the Church as a moral force, he was no friend of the clergy, whom he came to regard with pre-Marxist prescience as agents of social control.[37] Nor, in later years, was he against the principle of political reform. While in 1820 he viewed it as synonymous with violent revolution, by 1832 he had moderated his position, possibly in the knowledge that Lord Milton was a supporter of the Bill then being debated in Parliament. He wrote to Marianne Marsh:

> I am no politician but I think a reform is wanted — not the reform of mobs where the bettering of the many is only an apology for injuring the few — nor the reform of partys where the benefits of one is the destruction of the other but a reform that would do good & hurt none [38]

As for Queen Caroline, it was not her supporters against whom he had set his face, but the woman herself. Having spent six years in Italy, reputedly in an adulterous relationship, she returned to Britain to assert her rights as Queen the moment she learned of her husband's coronation. In August 1821, on hearing she had died, Clare wrote:

> I hated her not as a woman or as a queen but as the vilest hypocrite that ever existed [...] Im of no party but I never saw such farcical humbug carried on in my life before & I never wish to see it again for its launched me head over ears in politics for this last twelvemonth & made me very violent when John Barleycorn inspired me

He added, but then crossed out:

> who made me side for the king & a little true subject though I was formerly as I was touchd with the stain of radicalism [39]

Many hold to the view that Clare was a Radical who only ever made statements against Radicalism to appease his more conservative patrons and supporters.[40] There is of course no question that his instincts were in close alignment with the Radical agenda insofar as it touched on the condition of the poor. Neither is there any doubt that he could—and often did—slant his views towards those he was engaging with. Yet to categorise all his 'Radical' utterances as genuine and all the 'conservative' ones as mendacious is to ignore the psychology of the man: his often self-contradictory nature and his obstinate refusal to take sides. In matters of politics he was proud of his independence and made a point of judging arguments on their own merits, and in doing so found himself in different camps at different times: "I hate party feudes," he confessed to Eliza Emmerson, "& can never become a party man but when I have friends on both sides there I am on both sides as far as my opinions can find it right."[41]

His response to Caroline's bid for the throne brings us about as close as we can get to pinning down his political temperament—born of an independence of mind he termed 'common sense', focussed not on ideology but on moral (i.e. Christian) conduct, ever on the lookout for hypocrisy and 'humbug', and profoundly suspicious of the broader sweep of political debate. Notwithstanding the "radical stain" on show in so much of his work, these aspects of his outlook could only bring him so far in supporting progressive social reform. In this respect, at least, he appears to have been as much a Tory with a small 't' as a Radical with a small 'r'.

EH

Lament

The Act imposed a straightness on the land.
A new road of statutory width cut a ruler line
from Glinton through Helpston's clustered cottages
and market cross and out to King Street's Roman bank,
where it ripped unthinking through antiquities.

A straight drain known as Maxey Cut and a second,
Fenland-style in parallel, were dug across the north.
Springs where water bubbled from the rock
were blocked. Swordy Well was not just stopped
but sacked by road builders for flints and stones.

Where you learned to cut a furrow in the horse's hoofprints,
ploughing the whole furlong's length and leaving
curving darksome bawks of muddied grass,
in a craze to free the land from inefficient waste
everywhere was hedged and ditched.

Where working men and milkmaids once walked the eddings
and horses rested while the plough was turned
and ploughboys proggled from their shoes the heavy clinging mud,
you took paid work to fence the new allotments,
stringing straight rails between bleak new posts.

And everywhere the axe was laid to roots of trees
in a mania to turn new acquisitions into gold.
The right to roam was lost as ancient footpaths
were criss-crossed with fences. Village animals
disappeared with the loss of rights to graze.

You were the muse of Round Oak Waters and Swordy Well,
embodying their living springs, prising water
from the pressured depths of limestone caves
to nurture yellow iris, long purples,
mare-blob marigolds and ragged-robin pinks.

Your genius inhabited the willow's grey-green boughs,
became the pebble in the brook, mused on Nature's
sympathy for a child separate from the throng
who in later youth became a senseless wretch
paid to pour out his body's sweat;

paid by an Act that loosed the greed of men,
your arm ached from swinging the weight of the axe
to the willow's root in a crisis of self-destruction;
you became the muse of the broken land and cried out
your forgiveness and your lamentation.

"Inclosure like a Buonaparte"

Parliamentary Enclosure reached Clare's home village of Helpston in 1809. In the February of that year the area's landowners met to petition Parliament for a Bill to bring the commons into private ownership and redistribute land that was already under the plough. The reasons given were that

> Some Parts of the said Arable, Meadow, and Pasture lands are intermixed, and otherwise inconveniently situated for the respective Owners and Occupiers thereof, and the said Commons and Waste Grounds yield but little profit, and in this present State are incapable of any considerable improvement.[42]

That last word, 'improvement', was a general rallying cry that enabled Enclosers to claim the moral high ground in the fierce political debate surrounding the practice. It was synonymous with 'Progress', suggesting better land management, greater efficiency, larger crop yields leading to more abundant food, the promise of lower prices, and a reduced reliance on imported grain—an especially desirable outcome during time of war. There were some who believed it would bring benefits to all; Lord Milton, who chaired the meeting, was one. But for most of its proponents the prime motive was financial advancement. Those who stood to gain most were not, as a rule, the owners of the great estates but gentlemen farmers. James, the father of Mary Joyce, was one; he was also a signatory to the petition.

Work began that year as soon as the Bill was passed. A Commission of Enquiry was appointed to assess the claims of landholders and decide their new allotments. At the same time, new roads were built and watercourses rerouted. Over the next decade, springs were stopped or culverted, trees were felled in large numbers, and commons placed in the hands of individuals who already had holdings of their own.

The transformation of the landscape could not have been starker. Instead of sitting at the centre of a circular arrangement of fields and commons, Helpston was now fractured along a rectilinear grid of holdings. Its orientation to the outside world was also changed—turned through a hundred and eighty degrees by a new road that replaced Stamford with Peterborough as the principal local town.[43]

The commons were gone, and with them the villagers' rights to graze and glean, but Clare did not suffer as a result. As the son of a casual labourer he held no right of commons, and so had nothing to lose. For a while he even benefitted, taking a much-needed job as a fencer and ditcher. Yet the transformation of his environment distressed him greatly. He returned to the subject again and again, amassing a body of work that lamented the despoiled landscape of his childhood—a landscape he knew and loved intimately, to the extent that for him each wood, field and stream was a living thing, and each tree a friend. He looked on 'Improvement' as an act of savagery—even murder. In the poem 'Helpston', he sees "the woodmans cruel axe employ'd" in its pursuit; in 'Helpston Green' he tells how "the uplifted ax no mercy yields" but "strikes the fatal blow"; in 'Remembrances', "the axe of the spoiler and self interest" lays low beloved local spots, and in 'The Lamentations of

Round-Oak Waters' those responsible are "Hard as the ax" that fells the brookside willows. In the latter poem the *genius loci* of the brook cries out in misery, recalling when shepherds and cowboys brought beasts to be watered, and trees, bushes and wild flowers flourished along its banks:

> But now alas my charms are done
> For shepherds and for thee
> The Cowboy with his Green is gone
> And every bush and tree
> Dire nakedness oer all prevails
> Yon fallows bare and brown
> Is all beset wi' post and rails
> And turned upside down [44]

And in 'The Lament of Swordy Well', Clare gives a voice to an ancient stone pit that in his youth was a quiet haven for wildlife. Now, in private hands, it has been reduced to a sterile quarry for road builders and a parched, overgrazed field:

> I've scarce a nook to call my own
> For things to creep or flye
> The beetle hiding neath a stone
> Does well to hurry bye
> Stock eats my struggles every day
> As bare as any road
> He's sure to be in somethings way
> If eer he stirs abroad [45]

Clare is not content to dwell fatalistically on the passing of the old world, but goes out of his way to attack the architects of the new: those whose "greedy mind" and "greedy hand" have destroyed places like this pit, levelling its "mossy hill" into a bare "russet land". Yet for him this environmental catastrophe, like the others he documents around his parish, is not just a crime against Nature: it is also the outward manifestation of a profound social evil. Swordy Well continues its lament thus:

> There was a time my bit of ground
> Made freemen of the slave
> The ass no pindard dared to pound
> When I his supper gave
> The gypseys camp was not afraid
> I made his dwelling free
> Till vile enclosure came and made
> A parish slave of me [46]

This link between the rape of the land and the exercise of tyranny is at the heart of Clare's quarrel with the Enclosers, as readers who had grown up during the Napoleonic Wars would readily have realised, when he wrote in 1832:

> Inclosure like a Buonaparte let not a thing remain
> It levelled every bush & tree & levelled every hill
> & hung the moles for traitors though the brook is running still
> It runs a naked brook cold and chill [47]

For Clare the sterile post-Enclosure landscape with its persecuted wildlife mirrors perfectly the mindset of those who have produced it, and moles are not their only victims: those at the lower levels of rural society are also suffering. Their independence and self-sufficiency has vanished along with the commons and the strip fields, rendering them totally reliant for survival on a cash economy controlled by the Enclosers. In 'To a Fallen Elm', written in 1830, Clare exposes the hypocrisy of one of their number who hails 'Improvement' as the ally of liberty while knowing full well it "[devours] freedoms birthright in the weak":

> With axe at root he felled thee to the ground
> And barked of freedom—O I hate that sound
>
> It grows the cant terms of enslaving tools
> To wrong another by the name of right
> It grows the liscence of oerbearing fools
> To cheat plain honesty by force of might
> Thus came enclosure—ruin was her guide [48]

Lord Milton was the instigator of the 1809 Enclosure Act, yet he takes no blame for the ensuing calamity. Instead, Clare sets his sights on Enclosure's most conspicuous beneficiaries, expressing the resentment felt by his class against the farmers who, having grown fat on protectionism while squeezing the wages of hired labour, are now being rewarded with even greater wealth. He also knows that, a generation or two previously, the divide between rural classes was far less pronounced. Then, there was a sense of community uniting employer and employed, who worked the fields together and ate at the same table. Now, bloated by wartime profiteering, the farming class is aspiring to the status of gentry:

> That good old fame the farmers earned of yore
> That made as equals not as slaves the poor
> That good old fame did in two sparks expire
> A shooting coxcomb & a hunting Squire
> & their old mansions that was dignified
> With things far better than the pomp of pride
> At whose oak table that was plainly spread
> Each guest was welcomd & the poor was fed
> Were master son and serving man & clown
> Without distinction daily sat them down
> Were the bright rows of pewter by the wall
> Se[r]ved all the pomp of kitchen or of hall
> These all have vanished like a dream of good
> & the slim things that rises where they stood
> Are built by those whose clownish taste aspires
> To hate their farms & ape the country squires [49]

These lines are taken from the long satirical poem 'The Parish', in which Clare pours out his contempt for this new aspirational class, which has broken its covenant with the land and turned its back on its fellow men—a class of "upstarts that usurp the name / Of the old farmers dignity & fame".

He mercilessly lampoons its members, among whom we find 'Farmer Cheetum' who lives the life of a country squire without the means and takes on loans he has no intention of repaying to sustain the sham; and 'Mistress Peevish Scornful' who—"tho her fathers gain / Depend[s] still on cattle and on grain"—affects such a ladylike disdain for all around her she repels her suitors, and—"Husband mad" —must run away with the serving man. Other targets of Clare's wit include Young Farmer Bigg, a "proud conceited fellow [...] Wise among fools & with the wise an ass", who makes mothers of peasant girls before concealing his guilt with hush money; and Young Headlong Racket, a sexual predator without Bigg's discretion, whose only other occupation is killing animals for sport, and who, preparing "by turns to hunt & [whore] & shoot", is "Less then a man & little more then brute."

These grotesques, and the many others encountered in the poem, underscore Clare's view of 'Improvement' as the product and upholder of a class of venal, morally bankrupt tyrants. The harmony that used to prevail between farmer and labourer has degenerated into the brutal dichotomy of master and slave. While the smallholder and farm worker—thrown off the commons and left to sell his labour for a pittance —finds his freedom utterly curtailed, that of the landed farmer has grown through the wealth and power granted him by the very agricultural system he has conspired to introduce.

EH

The Education of a Man of Taste

You were drawn to the music of imagination,
to a secret separation from ordinary chores,
living in Thomson's 'sultry hours
and ever-fanning breezes' and the tormented struggles
of Satan's fall in Milton's dark sublime.

Knowingly different yet choosing to conform
to intellectual trials, indeed to strive
always to win the teacher's prize,
you never fell behind when necessity
kept you working in the fields.

You had ambition to be a poet
from the earliest age before you knew the world;
and from the first your natural talent
for recognising gold from dross
hinted your destiny as Man of Taste.

As a teenage garden boy at Burghley House
you found a blue poppy growing as a weed
between two rows of vegetables
and in a moment of Romantic rapture
hailed it a miracle.

Eager, experimental reading refined
your sensibilities, heightened your longing
for poetic ecstasy. The beauty of birds
and flowers sparked your fervour to understand
God's creatures of whom you were one.

You saw in nature Burns' 'wee, modest daisy'
and Wordsworth's 'lesser celandine', entwined
with your creative self in a poetic interplay;
and woodland flowers that scarcely saw the light
were rapturous truths in Nature's book.

As poet and expert on native flora
the lawns and gravel walks of Milton Hall
were yours to roam. You revelled in the Picturesque:
delighting in a fish pond with a single island topped by firs
bent under this year's pile of heronshaws' nests cranked high.

Clare's Science of Sensibility

In the autumn of 1821 John Taylor called on Clare at Helpston and published an account of his visit in the *London Magazine*. In it he not only painted a vivid picture of the locality and its landmarks, but also, and more importantly, presented the poet to his public in a new light. Up to then Taylor had been peddling the image of an unlettered 'natural' genius, "a day-labourer in husbandry, who has had no advantages of education beyond others of his class",[50] yet the vogue for labouring-class poets was fast passing, and it was time to give his rural bard a makeover. After describing Clare's cottage, which he judged "no whit superior to the poorest of the peasantry", he related how his host

> opened an old oak bookcase and showed me his library. It contains a very good collection of modern poets, [...] Burns, Cowper, Wordsworth, Coleridge, Keats, Crabbe, and about twenty volumes of Cooke's Poets.[51]

Most, he noted, were gifts from well-wishers; and there were more—among them works by Scott and Chatterton and Allan Cunningham. Here was a side to Clare that must have been wholly unexpected to his public: a man who, rather than living in ignorance of prevailing cultural trends, had at his disposal the works of the 'modern' poets in a collection that was likely equal—if not superior—to their own.

By the end of his life Clare had amassed over 300 books covering—among other subjects—poetry, prose, drama, literary criticism, biography and history, philosophy and theology, and mathematics and natural history. By 1824, three years after Taylor's visit, he felt entirely at ease passing judgement on the articles he was reading in the *London Magazine*, for example approving of Lamb's review of De Quincey's life of Goethe. (By then, he had read the German poet in translation and composed a verse treatment of the final chapter of *The Sorrows of Young Werther*.)[52] His education continued throughout the 1820s with visits to London and correspondence with the luminaries he met there—the *London Magazine* set and their artistic hangers-on.

He also found intellectual stimulation at Milton Hall, becoming close friends with the steward, Edmund Tyrell Artis, and the head gardener Joseph Henderson. Artis was the archaeologist who unearthed the Roman town of Durobrivae at Castor, close to Helpston, and Henderson a noted botanist with links to Cambridge University, whose local researches uncovered new species of fern. Clare frequently accompanied them on hunting expeditions for fossils, buried artefacts, insects, plants and fungi. With typical modesty (and a sly nod to his "run-a-gate of a grandfather") he characterised himself as:

> not wonderfully deep in s[c]i[e]nce nor so wonderfully ignorant as many may have fancied from reading the accounts which my friends gave of me   if I was to brag of it I might like the village schoolmaster boast of knowing a little of every thing a jack of all trades and master of none[53]

He counselled his children to study the disciplines in which he had taken an interest when young: "I would advise you," he wrote to his youngest son Charles, then 15 years old, "to study Mathematics Astronomy Languages and Botany as the best amusements for instruction."[54] At a similar age he had absorbed a diverse range of subjects—"Mathematics Particulary Navigation and Algebra Dialling Use of the Globes Botany Natural History Short Hand with History of all Kinds Drawing Music etc etc"[55] —though never in a thorough or systematic way:

> I puzzled over such matters at every hour of leisure for years as my curosity was constantly on the enquiry and never satisfied and when I got fast with one thing I did not despair but tryd at another tho with the same success in the end yet it never sickend me I still pursued knowledge in a new path and tho I never came off victor I was never conquored[56]

But if the acquisition of knowledge fascinated him, systems of knowledge irked him greatly. An early irritation was grammar: "a jumble of words classd under this name and that name and this such a figure of speech and that another hard worded figure", so alien a concept for the young Clare that he "turned from further notice of it in instant disgust".[57] A little later, Botany, a discipline then striving to classify as well as catalogue its objects of study, presented a similar challenge. He read James Lee's introduction to Linnaeus but found it "a dark system",[58] and was at a loss when it came to applying binomial labels to the plants and flowers he collected —something his lack of Latin must in any case have hindered. He was also conscious of a distinction between the poet's response to Nature and that of the scientist:

> to look at nature with a poetic feeling magnifyes the pleasure yet Naturalists and Botanists seem to have little or no taste for this sort of feeling they merely make a collection of dryd specimens classing them after Lienneus into tribes and familys as a sort of curiosity and fame   I have nothing of this curosity about me tho I feel as happy as they can in finding a new spiecies of field flower or butterflye which I have not before seen[59]

Yet if he initially found the systematisation of knowledge sterile and unprofitable, he later seems to have come to the view that it plays a role in the poetic sensibility. From his reading of eighteenth-century poets and essayists he was familiar with the notion of 'Taste'—a topic given new urgency in his own time by the Romantics' preoccupation with how beauty is perceived in the natural world.[60] It was a subject to which he returned on several occasions, his first foray being a sonnet that begins "Taste is from heaven / A inspiration Nature can't bestow", and goes on to cite the "curious eye" as instrumental in bringing "the very senses in the sight / To relish what it sees". He contrasts the Man of Taste with the "gross clown" who, with his awareness stunted by ignorance, is unable to appreciate beauty in the world:

> —Natures unfolded book
> As on he blunders never strikes his eye
> Pages of lanscape tree and flower and brook
> Like blank leaves he turns unheeded bye[61]

He further developed the theme in his unpublished essay 'On Taste', in which he notes how "the man of dissernment" is enraptured by the sights and sounds of Nature because he brings to bear on them an organising faculty and a body of knowledge. "There is happiness," he writes,

> in contemplating the different shapes of leaves of the various kinds of trees plants and herbs there is happiness in examining minutely into the wild flowers as we wander among them to distinguish their characters and find out to what orders they belong in the natural and artificial systems of botany [62]

For him, 'Taste'—unlike its antithesis 'Fashion'—was a universal constant that can even be observed in the natural world: "not mind alone the instinctive mood declares / But birds and flowers and insects are its heirs", he writes in 'Shadows of Taste', where he suggests that species choose their respective habitats for aesthetic as well as practical reasons. (On the face of it a fanciful notion, but one that fits well with his perception of creatures as individuals with their own 'biographies'.)

Yet even while proposing an innate drive towards beauty, he returns to knowledge as being the lynchpin of its discernment:

> The man of science in discoverys moods
> Roams oer the furze clad heath leaf buried woods
> And by the simple brook in rapture finds
> Treasures that wake the laugh of vulgar minds
> Who see no further in his dark employs
> Then village childern seeking after toys
> ...
> But he the man of science and of taste
> Sees wealth far richer in the worthless waste
> Where bits of lichen and a sprig of moss
> With all the raptures of his mind engross
> And bright winged insects on the flowers of may
> Shine pearls too wealthy to be cast away
>
> The heedless mind may laugh the clown may stare
> They own no soul to look for pleasure there
> Their grosser feelings in a coarser dress
> Mock at the wisdom which they cant possess [63]

He was clearly thinking of his expeditions with Artis and Henderson when he wrote these lines, as he would have done more generally when contemplating 'science' as the factor that elevated him above his forebears.

EH

Laying Out Plans for an Iron Railway

In May 1825, Clare found an orchis
of a pale rusty tinge with a root like pile wort
thickened and curled: a rare 'Bird's Nest' orchis it proved;
and the same day he heard a clap of thunder
strike an ash tree, ejecting lethal splinters fifty yards.

For the Romans it would have been an omen.
Clare harked back to their legions on forced marches north;
once, in a new dyke dug deep in King Street's bank,
he had found pooty shells preserved and clarified in sand,
buried for two thousand years by Roman slog.

The next week, he was crouching to observe
purplish spikes of orchises in a boggy spot
in Royce wood. He counted their stigmas and leaves
and noted the markings of their petals
to write a marginal note in Henderson's *Guide*.

Water gleamed in the long grass, and shadows
fell across his face from three fellows
laying out plans for an iron railway.
Portents blocking out the sun. Clare wrote a note
that this boggy spot for orchises would be despoiled.

Guilt for Steam

On our search to trace your journey
you walk with us just like a friend.
So intimate has been our effort
to inhabit your experience that we feel guilty
when steam trains fascinate and distract us.

You crossed one single iron track built within a twelvemonth
but otherwise there was no overlap
between your journey and the railway's encroachments
that brought disruptions to natural solitudes –
as bad as the Enclosures.

But for us the impending revolution
throws a golden glow over your journey
of a world passing, before iron rails ravaged the orchards
around Ponders End and graced the gentle valley
of the Mimram with a Victorian brickwork bravura.

Further on, we stand beneath another viaduct
designed by railway engineers for the grand new avenue
to Hatfield House. We relish its Roman arches
and imagine its construction, swarming with men
once unemployed itinerant labourers.

Nine years after you walked the old road
railway money paid McAdam to build the new,
on newly-acquired land, between implacable new railway tracks.
Fine wrought-iron gates opened direct on the new stone station
with Lord Salisbury's personal waiting room.

Sent by Train

They box him up and send him by regular train
with a tall funnel and great spoked wheels
and it pulls into Helpston with a whistle-blast and fuss.
No one is waiting. Four porters shoulder
the good oak coffin to the new stone waiting room.

The Asylum Secretary, in a tall black hat,
checks the peep-hole of thin glass to view his dead face
and understands the body's not expected.
Messages have gone awry. Clare's been 'put away'
and hasn't seen his wife for twenty years.

He spends the night, left luggage in The Exeter Arms.
Next day the family rally to bury him, but not son Jack
away in Shropshire. Clare rode his first train
as dead freight, but Jack's a railway carpenter
earning money beyond his father's dreams.

Clare and the Railways

When Clare died on 20th May 1864, a message was sent to Helpston to inform Patty of the time his coffin would arrive at Helpston Station, but she lived at Northborough, three miles away, and the message did not reach her in time.

Clare's meeting with railway engineers in Royce Wood, on Saturday 4th June 1825, was an extraordinary occurrence. The world's first steam railway, for hauling coal wagons from collieries near Shildon to Stockton and Darlington, was to open three months later. George Stephenson and his son Robert, who had been involved in surveying the line, developed their first engine for it, which they named 'Locomotion No I'. It was men employed by George who had run into Clare and told him they were "laying out the plan for an 'Iron rail way' from Manchester to London".

Clare's prediction, recorded in his journal, that a railway would cause major disruption to the countryside showed great foresight, but he cannot possibly have imagined the scale of industrial and social change to come. When he escaped from High Beach in 1841 he crossed a single-track line at Ponders End that ran from London to Broxbourne. It had been in operation for less than a year, but demand for services meant that work had already started on doubling its capacity with a second track.

Within five years, two lines had pushed through from the capital to the north of England, decimating coaching traffic. A whole world was being swept away, often for the worse but occasionally for the better: building the infrastructure for this new transport system—its stations, bridges and viaducts—and running and maintaining it created an employment boom that went some way to alleviating rural poverty.

BS

Helpston railway station in 1970, six years after its closure.

Writing a Song,
the Evening He Returned

From his table in the window
the apple tree with four years' new growth
has closed a declivity in the view.
He brushes a fly from the sill, fleshless and crisped,
and hears the oak stairs creak under adolescent feet.

He imagines a room within a room
and through the window watches Mary plant roses
and kingcups by his orchis collection;
her likeness has gone from the wall, but the real Mary
presses his lips with an insistent kiss.

He can only tell of his lonely heart in song.
He hummed an old song on the road to ride hope high
for Mary – now in a new song he weaves
lost hope and love for Mary in a sweet refrain.
Through song his lonely heart is free to fly.

Romantic Sensibilities

It was a wondrous stroke of luck that such a book,
of folio size, untouched by pen and ink,
was waiting for him. It was as if the gods
had set him up to write his story.

So, let's guess…

Since his departure for the madhouse
many, knowing of his fame, had trekked
to Northborough and been directed
to 'The Poet's House'.
So Patty had set out a 'Poet's Room'.

A table in the window and the book –
someone's gift in lieu of cash donation –
were waiting idle. And then he came
shockingly unexpected and mad for Mary
who he wouldn't believe was dead.

So, in a state of frenzy he claimed
the 'Poet's Room' and started writing.
'I've escaped after four years locked up
in a place of appalling depravity
deprived of the comforts of my wives and family.

'I gathered my troops like Wellington
and walked three days suffering hunger and pain
in control of my destiny. The world shall know
my story, the pinnacle of my biography.
A poet's life is a work of art in making.'

MS 8, John Clare Collection, Northampton Library

It has been rebound, but its weight lies in my hand
just as it did in his. Inside, in faintest ink,
John Clare Poems, Feb. 1841; and then Child Harold's
howl at the spring blotted out, capitalising word-shouts,
quicksands of madness befuddling his hopes.

The first gathering is edged with tiny rips
where he cut its folds, in haste, with a blunted knife;
and here two pages opened flat have been spattered
with wet and closed damp, doubling a blot;
and here he's turned it landscape and used a thicker nib.

But wherever ... the words roll out across the page
in handwriting that's clear to read, with loops
on Ls and Gs, and sit-up-and-beg Bs,
and Ss doubled, long and short, and high curls
completing every D, sometimes looped back to cross a T.

Inside the binding, page corners are scuffed
from rubbing in his pocket. Here, like old friends
are Jack Randall's Challenge; Don Juan's vitriol
at "little Vicky" and her snuff-box; and
the very first draft of *Journey out of Essex*.

Our meeting is one-to-one. On this page,
pen poised, John Clare spun out his fancy
and it's my fancy that I watch him writing this note:
king of the castle, sitting on road-menders' flints,
he smiles at that pretty gypsy from the lodge and winks.

John Clare, Writer and Man

John Clare wrote *Journey out of Essex* with single-minded focus. Disregarding his physical exhaustion after three and a half days on the road, he wrote the first half on the evening he arrived home. The following day, despite having plenty of blank pages left in the notebook he'd carried with him, he copied the draft into a new book and continued writing. We have come to understand this extraordinary creative process as an act of self-vindication. Clare was confined to the asylum at High Beach for just over four years. Perhaps wanting to let him enjoy family celebrations, Patty had sent him away a day or two after his birthday in July 1837, and would commit him again, to Northampton General Asylum, less than a week after Christmas 1841.

Institutionalisation has the effect of taking away the life-affirming qualities of independence and responsibility,[64] and Clare's deficit in life skills was manifest in his setting out without money or food, and lacking even a serviceable pair of shoes. But it appears that over the long hours of walking he was buoyed up by a belief in himself as a writer, making notes along the way and beginning to plan by picking out the events that would make a good story. Everything points to him arriving home with the narrative bursting to be written down.

His decision the next morning to copy what he had written into a brand-new folio-sized book demonstrates the importance he placed on the *Journey*. The cost of books of this kind made its use exceptional for a man who habitually wrote on any available scrap of paper, and it is surprising that he had one in his possession. Publication was clearly in his mind when he copied the two poems to Mary into the front cover. The note that they "were written directly after my return home to Northborough last Friday evening" casts him in the role of a Romantic hero who has endured great privations for the sake of his mistress: he is claiming Mary as his Beatrice.

We know that in 1822, Henry Cary, a fellow *London Magazine* writer, gave Clare an inscribed copy of his translation of Dante's *Divine Comedy*, and in his poem, 'The Winters Come',[65] Clare relates how his spirits soared as he sat by the fire reading it. He may have been remembering afternoons spent with Eliza Emmerson, who was a Dante enthusiast,[66] and with whom he was staying when he and Cary first met.

Emma Trehane suggests that Clare wrote his poems to Mary in conscious imitation of Dante's to Beatrice, and cites an anonymous contribution to the *English Women's Domestic Magazine* in 1867 that claimed, "Not Petrarch's Laura nor Dante's Beatrice was more faithfully and fondly worshipped than the Mary of John Clare."[67] This endorses our view that when he placed the two songs to Mary at the head of his account, he was doing so deliberately and self-consciously. Rather than being the rambling journal of a confused lunatic, the *Journey* is a finely crafted piece of literary biography.

The successful completion of Clare's escape was hugely empowering for a man who had been deprived of taking action for four years. He seems to have been driven, like the Ancient Mariner, to tell his story, and here was a chance to publish a stirring autobiographical piece. During the mid 1820s there was a decline in the market for poetry that coincided with the death of Byron and the rising popularity of Walter Scott's novels. Jonathan Bate records that Clare's medical advisor in London, Dr Darling, "suggested that he should make alternative plans to a career in poetry. There just wasn't going to be enough money in it".[68] Prompted by his publishers to write a Helpston version of Gilbert White's *Natural History of Selborne*, Clare embarked upon an epistolary work to be called 'Biographies of Birds and Flowers', which unfortunately he never finished. He also wrote works of criticism—most notably 'Popularity in Authorship', which was published in *The European Magazine* for November 1825—and various works of religious and political commentary, including the 'Apology for the Poor', which appeared in a local newspaper.[69] More particularly, Taylor and Hessey encouraged him to produce autobiographical writings over many years. In preparing a fair copy ready for an editor, he appears to have intended the *Journey* to be the culmination of this work.

While working on *Love's Cold Returning*, we have been astonished at the *Journey's* narrative power and careful structuring. Clare's habitual lack of punctuation has not served him well with readers of his prose; whereas his poems are tightly bound and framed by the creativity and fluidity of his rhymes, the prose flows unbroken even by paragraph divisions. Yet the *Journey* is by far his longest single piece of autobiographical writing and its power comes alive in the reading aloud.

The opening is beautifully constructed: starting on Friday July 23rd with the bleak arrival home to find no Mary,[70] then flashing back to Sunday 18th with his disappointment at being abandoned by the gypsies, followed by the suspense of Monday's terse entry, "Did nothing", and the comic irony of setting out the following day "having only honest courage and myself in my army".

He is selective in what he includes, paying little attention to the places he passed and none at all to modern wonders such as the railway at Ponders End. This is in marked contrast with his account of his first coach trip in 1820, when he remarked on the street lamps at the edge of London dwindling like stars into seeming infinity.[71] Instead of giving an account of each stage of his journey, he shapes his story through vivid incidents, focusing on his interactions with people on the road and narrating them with an eye for the Gothic. Dialogue is suggested vividly and succinctly without stage directions, and emotions are unstated but powerfully implied, as in the passage where, after a night wandering lost, he reaches a tollgate under "a lamp shining bright as the moon":

> before I got through the man came out with a candle and eyed me narrowly but having no fear I stopt to ask him wether I was going northward and he said when you get through the gate you are; so I thanked him kindly and went through on the other side and gathered my old strength.

The narrative's overall structure also rewards careful study. Its most muddled section (from parting company with the gypsy in Buckden to arriving at Stilton) is written as a set of disconnected memories without a storyline. Rather than being the product of confused and impaired memory, however, its placement inside a repetition of the statement, like a pair of verbal brackets, that he can remember nothing between the two towns suggests that he has crafted it to convey a sense of suffering and exhaustion. Elsewhere he is concerned with creating an accurate narrative—for example adding a note to clarify that a town he thought "might be St Ives" was in fact St Neots. And he is careful to pin down the time frame of both the beginning and end of his account, because the distance he walked and the time it took him were crucial to the scale of his achievement.

The ending gives a clear indication of his ambitions for the *Journey*, with the final quotation from Byron's 'Prisoner of Chillon' drawing a deliberate comparison between his sufferings on his long escape from Essex and those of the prisoner Bonnivard. Clare clearly intends us to view his adventure as epic in scope, signalling its antecedents with echoes of Dante and Petrarch, and even suggesting a literary kinship with Homer by staging an ironic inversion of Odysseus' homecoming, in which he, the hero, returns to a wife he does not recognise.

BS

The Return

Love's Cold Returning

After John Clare

They bring him to the place they call his home,
but it's cold to his soul like the House on the Heath
where ruined walls and bloodstained floors
sheltered the wild cat and owl,
loud with the hissing cries of ghosts.

He knows this room, this is where Patty lives,
his second wife and children. But he cannot rest.
His heart is fraught with sweetest loss.
Mary's blue eyes and auburn hair
bright in memory, are not here.

She was his friend in the vestry school
at Glinton; in her father's house
meat and milk and fish were ever to hand,
but John had little beyond a barley loaf,
swedes and potatoes baked in the hearth.

Birds, whirring and chittering in the dovecote,
were the landlord's by law; and so were rabbits
and ducks and geese, pheasants and deer;
always the gamekeeper lurked with his gun,
a threat to the poet looking out for a wren.

That day in the woods, bundles of ripe hazel nuts
took their colour from her curls. He pulled them low
for her to reach and, at the touch of hands
and rush of sweetness, nuts dropped
with softest thuds into her pot.

As the sky set behind the disappearing sun,
the uncanny call of Whooper swans
marked Mary as his muse for ever.
Her smiles and the sweet stain of the sky
transformed him utterly.

Growing to womanhood, Mary's path was set:
domestic duties with her mother, finery
at the Assembly Rooms, dancing and merriment.
He saw her less and felt her ardour cooled
and, feckless, turned to pastures new.

Five spots on a cowslip, five eggs in a nest –
he discovered nature's laws, and found ways
of making time for rhyme: failing to please
as gardener, shoemaker, soldier,
perfecting poems and finding patronage.

Like Thomson, he ratified the seasons:
in summer speary barley and the startled frog
in rout; in autumn whispers of wind
in the leafless hedge; winter icicles
under the eaves, their tails afresht in the night.

Girls there were many when he was young and strong
and in his poet's frenzy he enjoyed
romantic song. It was no chance
that he would fall in love and marry –
though he called it accident – the bubble touched and gone.

Mary never married, alone on the day she died,
perhaps tripping on the fender,
her petticoat catching a new log's flame.
The fire scorched fiercely round the lintel
of the window: its dark fingers lie there to this day.

Did he know how she died? The newspaper
cutting was shown to him – and denied.
Mary's memory lived in the crucible
of his poetry, burning bright
in his creative insight – his poetical fancy.

Notes and Indexes

Abbreviations

Bate	Jonathan Bate, *John Clare, A Biography*, London: Picador, 2003.
By Himself	*John Clare, By Himself*, Eric Robinson and David Powell, eds., Manchester: Carcanet, 1996.
Champion	*John Clare, A Champion for the Poor, Political Verse and Prose*, P. M. S. Dawson, Eric Robinson and David Powell, eds., Manchester: Carcanet, 2000.
Critical Heritage	*John Clare, The Critical Heritage*, Mark Storey, ed., London: Routledge, 1995.
Early Poems	*The Early Poems of John Clare 1804-1822*, 2 vols, Eric Robinson, David Powell and Margaret Grainger, eds., Oxford: Clarendon Press, 1989.
Egerton	Egerton Collection of Manuscripts, British Library.
Harper	Charles G. Harper, *The Great North Road: The Old Mail Road to Scotland, Volume 1 – London to York*, Second Edition, London: Cecil Palmer, 1922.
In Context	*John Clare in Context*, Hugh Haughton, Adam Phillips and Geoffrey Summerfield eds., Cambridge University Press, 1994.
JCS	*The John Clare Society Journal.*
Later Poems	*The Later Poems of John Clare 1837-1864*, 2 vols, Eric Robinson, David Powell and Margaret Grainger, eds., Oxford: Clarendon Press, 1984.
Letters	*The Letters of John Clare, Mark Storey*, ed., Oxford: Clarendon Press, 1985.
Living Year	*John Clare, The Living Year 1841*, Tim Chilcott ed., Nottingham: Trent Editions, 1999.
Major Works	*John Clare, Major Works*, Eric Robinson and David Powell, eds., Oxford University Press, 1984.
Martin	Frederick W. Martin, *The Life of John Clare* (first published London: Macmillan & Co, 1865), Second edition, Eric Robinson and Geoffrey Summerfield, eds., London: Frank Cass, 1964.
Middle Period	*John Clare, Poems of the Middle Period*, 5 vols, Eric Robinson, David Powell and P. M. S. Dawson, eds., Oxford: Clarendon Press,1996-2003.
Midsummer Cushion	*John Clare, The Midsummer Cushion*, Kelsey Thornton and Anne Tibble, eds., Manchester: Carcanet, 1979.
Natural History	*The Natural History Writings of John Clare*, Margaret Grainger ed., Oxford: Clarendon Press, 1983.
New Essays	*New Essays on John Clare, Poetry, Culture and Community*, Simon Kövesi and Scott McEathron, eds., Cambridge University Press, 2015.

Poems and Prose	*Clare, Selected Poems and Prose*, Eric Robinson and Geoffrey Summerfield eds., Oxford University Press, 1966.
Sales	Roger Sales, *John Clare, A Literary Life*, Basingstoke: Palgrave, 2002.
Selected Letters	*John Clare, Selected Letters*, Mark Storey ed., Oxford University Press, 1990.
Selected Poems	*John Clare: Selected Poems*, Jonathan Bate ed., London: Faber and Faber, 2003.
Selected Poetry	*John Clare: Selected Poetry*, Geoffrey Summerfield ed., Harmondsworth: Penguin, 1990.
Shepherd's Calendar	*John Clare, The Shepherd's Calendar, Manuscript and Published Version*, Tim Chilcott, ed., Manchester: Carcanet, 2006.
SOED	Shorter Oxford English Dictionary.
Sonnets	*John Clare, Northborough Sonnets*, Eric Robinson, David Powell and P. M. S. Dawson, eds., Manchester: Carcanet, 1995.
Storey	Edward Storey, *A Right to Song, The Life of John Clare*, London: Methuen, 1982.
Tompkins	Herbert W. Tompkins, *Highways and Byways in Hertfordshire*, London: Macmillan, 1902.
Tibble	*John Clare, The Journals, Essays and the Journey from Essex*, Anne Tibble ed., Manchester: Carcanet, 1980.
Tibbles	J. W. and Anne Tibble, *John Clare, A Life*, London: Michael Joseph, 1972.
Wilson	June Wilson, *Green Shadows, The Life of John Clare*, London: Hodder & Stoughton, 1951.

Notes to Prose

The Journey—Essex
Pages 14–54

1. **Martin**, 279.
2. See Eric Robinson and Geoffrey Summerfield's introduction to **Martin** for an assessment of this biographer's methods.
3. **Wilson**, 229.
4. **Selected Letters**, 199.
5. **Bate**, 429.
6. Ibid, 429-30.
7. Clare taking on the guise of Byron was not necessarily a sign of madness. Will Ashton suggests he may have been trying to escape the disappointments of his past as a poet: "When Clare talked about 'being Byron' I wonder whether this was a similar vein to David Bowie being Ziggy Stardust. Reading Child Harold–along with Don Juan [...]–I couldn't help thinking of that old saw about Dylan going electric. A rebranding, an attempt to dig himself out of the hole he found himself in as John Clare–nature Poet." Will Ashton, *Strange Labyrinth*, London: Granta, 2017, 110-11.
8. **Major Works**, 309.
9. **Critical Heritage**, 247-56.
10. **Selected Letters**, 201.
11. **Major Works**, 308.
12. Ibid, 315.
13. **Living Year**, 141-2.
14. **Selected Letters**, 202.
15. **Major Works**, 322.
16. In one of the autobiographical fragments, Clare characterises his youthful feelings for Eliza Emmerson as foolish, conceited and one-sided (Pet. MS B3 82, reproduced **By Himself**, 137). While we can only speculate about the truth of this, she was without doubt his most intimate friend. She sent him Valentine's Day poems, wrote to him flirtatiously, was possessive of his time in London, and discussed with him by letter his extra-marital affairs; see inter alia **Bate**, 249, 283 and 285-6. She also gave him intelligent and compassionate advice when he most needed it. For a considered assessment of their relationship, see Emma Trehane's PhD thesis, 'The Epistolary Poetics of John Clare and Eliza Louisa Emmerson', Nottingham Trent University, 2011 (discussed this volume, 335-9).
17. Mrs Emmerson asked Clare to keep the portrait in his "own private drawer," as "Eliza [...] begs not to be exposed to public view, she would live with you in your happy cottage unknown to the curious or ill-natured." **Egerton** 2245, fol. 169, referenced **Bate**, 200; **Tibbles**, 143; **Wilson**, 92.

18 'Song' b, **Major Works**, 283.

19 Clare developed a reputation among the London Magazine circle for being a ladies' man (**Bate**, 262-3), and though he never refers directly to sexual adventures in London, they are hinted at heavily in Rippingille's letters to him. On August 1st 1824 Rip wrote, "When do you leave the atmosphere of smoke, smocks, smirks, smells and smutty doings...you are better I hope and you take care of yourself, no *pleughing* I trust, the Delia fever is abated I hope, or perhaps has given place to another..." Quoted in Peter Cox's paper '"A liking to use the pen": Edward Villiers Rippingille (c. 1790-1859) and John Clare', **JCS** 17 (1998), 17-33.

20 **Major Works**, 283.

21 All quotes from 'Don Juan' in this and following sections are taken from **Major Works**, 318-326.

22 **Selected Letters**, 199-200.

23 Ibid, 199.

24 Ibid, 200.

25 **Selected Poetry**, 213.

26 **Selected Letters**, 203.

27 Ibid, 202.

28 **Major Works**, 285

29 See **Bate**, 432.

30 Ibid, 424-5.

31 See Nicholas Haggar, *A View of Epping Forest*, Winchester: O-Books, 2012, 204-5.

32 Clare composed this poem in 1819 while lime-burning at Casterton. He wrote in his autobiography, "Crazy Nell was taken from a narrative in the Stamford Mercury in the same manner in which It was related   I was very pleased with it and thought it one of the best I had written and I think so still", **By Himself**, 110.

33 'The Crazy Maid', lines 31-48, **Early Poems**, II, 453.

34 'London Versus Epping Forest', **Later Poems**, I, 28.

35 William Morris, *News from Nowhere*, chapter III, as quoted by Clifford Bax in *Highways and Byways in Essex*, London: Macmillan & Co, 1939, 138-9.

36 Quoted in Peter Relph, *Four Forest Years*, Epping 2006, in the chapter '—and Places'. (Volume unpaginated.)

37 In 1984, octogenarian resident of High Beach L. S. H. Young recalled that when he was a boy "the small mounds of graves were visible" in the chapel yard. See his article in John Clare Society Newsletter no. 7, April 1984, also reproduced at John Clare Ephemera: http://bit.ly/lcrehb (retrieved February 1, 2019).

38 To defend his reputation Allen produced a pamphlet, *Allen versus Dutton*, which Taylor published. Other works followed—most notably the *Essay on the Classification of the Insane* (1837). Clare's admission to High Beach, resulting from their acquaintance, was therefore indirectly due to Dutton's legal proceedings.

39 As reported in **Bate**, 428.
40 **Sinclair**, 135.
41 'A Walk in the Forest', **Selected Poems**, 235.
42 **By Himself**, 84.
43 See James Canton, *Out of Essex, Re-Imagining a Literary Landscape*, Oxford: Signal Books, 2013, 39-40.
44 **Shepherd's Calendar**, 202. Both passages are taken from the first version of 'July', which was rejected outright by Taylor for being too descriptive.

The Journey—Middlesex
Pages 58–108

1 'Ponder's End Lock', LEA AND STORT: http://bit.ly/lcrpel (retrieved February 1, 2019).
2 Coordinates: 51°38'41.6"N 0°01'45"W; 51.644830, -0.028150.
   GOOGLE MAPS: http://bit.ly/lcrpln (retrieved February 1, 2019).
3 John Chambers, *A General History of the County of Norfolk*, London: John Stacy, 1829, III, 1159.
4 From papers lodged at Enfield Local Studies Archive, Record D1032, referenced in *The Charles Lamb Bulletin, The Journal of the Charles Lamb Society*, no 34, April 1981.
5 See 'Anglers vs the "Black Death"', THE GUARDIAN: http://bit.ly/lcrgcc (retrieved February 1, 2019).
6 'An Angler, A Hunter, and a Falconer', chapter 1, *The Compleat Angler* by Izaak Walton and Charles Cotton, first published 1653 (Walton) and 1676 (Cotton), reprinted Coachwhip Publications, 2005, 10.
7 **By Himself**, 233. The surveyors were working on behalf of the Northern Railway Company under the direction of George Stephenson, who had been hired to investigate two routes. The first was projected to run from London to Ware via the Lea Valley, then proceed through Cambridge, Peterborough, Oakham and Loughborough to join the proposed Derby Peak Railway bound for Stockport and Manchester. The second would also join the Derby Peak Railway, but take a more westerly approach via Northampton, Coventry and Birmingham. It was the former route the men were engaged in surveying when Clare came across them. See Victor A. Hatley, 'The Poet and the Railway Surveyors', *Northamptonshire Past and Present*, V, 101-5.
8 See 'Alma Estate tenants in Ponders End "desperate" for tower blocks to be demolished', THE ENFIELD INDEPENDENT: http://bit.ly/lcraea (retrieved February 1, 2019).
9 Letter from the Enfield Borough Librarian and Cultural Officer to a Cambridge scholar (name not on copy), 1982, lodged in the Enfield Local Studies Centre and Archive.
10 See **By Himself**, 338, Note 11.

11 **Selected Letters**, 203-4.

12 Neither the 1841 Census nor the 1851 Census has a record of a Mrs King living in Enfield Highway. However, as Clare lent her several books that we know he had obtained from Cyrus Redding following their meeting in May 1841, she almost certainly moved from High Beach to Enfield Highway sometime between the start of June and July 20th, and so would have missed the Census, which was taken in the spring and subsequently published on June 6th. By 1851 she may have moved again or passed away. She does not appear in the 1841 Census for High Beach.

13 In this context it is worth noting that Clare writes about coming across "a person" in Enfield Highway, not a "man" or "woman". This is the only place he does so. At every other point in the text he specifies the gender of those he meets—the "Man & boy coiled up asleep" on the road to Baldock, "the Man on horseback" who threw him a penny for a pint of beer, the "young country wench" and "young fellow" at Potton, and so on.

14 The name is unusual but not uncommon, and is likely to have appealed to Clare's sense of humour: pubs called the 'Labour in Vain' usually had a sign featuring a white woman scrubbing a black baby in a washtub. Over recent decades such images have been scrapped. The last known, at Yarnsfield in Staffordshire, was withdrawn in 1994.

15 Canton, *Out of Essex*, 44.

16 David Pam, *Enfield Town: Village Green to Shopping Precinct*, Edmonton Hundred Historical Society, 12.

17 Ibid, 5.

18 Though the school was demolished to make way for the railway station, its façade was preserved and is now housed in the Victoria and Albert Museum.

19 'Summer Images', **Major Works**, 124.

20   Þā wæs feohte nēh,
tīr æt getohte;   wæs sēo tid cumen
þæt þǽr fǽge men   feallan sceoldon.
Þǽr wearð hrēam āhafen,   hremmas wundon,
earn ǽses georn;   wæses on eorþan cyrm.

          Then was the fighting near,
glory in battle;   The time was come
that there fated men   must fall.
There a clamour rose up,   ravens circling,
eagles eager for carrion;   an uproar on earth.

The Battle of Maldon', lines 104-108, *Sweet's Anglo-Saxon Reader*, Oxford: Clarendon Press, 1967, 119.

21 'London versus Epping Forest', **Later Poems**, I, 28.

22 **Sales**, 36.

23 'Autobiographical Fragments', **By Himself**, 94.

24 Vic Gatrell, *The Hanging Tree: Execution and the English People 1770-1868*, Oxford University Press 1996, 617.

25 'January', lines 182-186, **Shepherd's Calendar**.

26 Gatrell, *The Hanging Tree*, 268.

27 Pam, *Enfield Town*, 6.

28 E. P. Thompson, *Whigs and Hunters, The Origin of the Black Act*, London: Allen Lane, 1975, 59.

29 See David Pam, T*he Story of Enfield Chase*, Enfield Preservation Society, 1984, ISBN 0 907318 03 7, 145-6.

30 Clare refers repeatedly to sitting on 'molehills', but from his descriptions it is clear these cannot be the small mounds of soil usually associated with the term. See Bob Heyes, 'Little Hills of Cushioned Thyme', **JCS** 12 (1993), 32-6.

31 'The Nightingale's Nest' is widely considered to be one of Clare's most important works. See inter alia Mina Gorji, *John Clare and the Place of Poetry*, Liverpool University Press, 2008, 1-4, and Hugh Haughton '"Progress and Rhyme": "The Nightingales Nest" and Romantic Poetry', *John Clare in Context*, Cambridge University Press, 1994, 51-86.

32 Charles Dickens, *Bleak House*, Harmondsworth: Penguin, 1971, 484-8.

33 *Short Guide 7, Scottish Traditional Brickwork*, Historic Environment Scotland, 2014, ISBN 978-1-84917-118-2.

34 A. C. Lynch, *The Turnpike Road to Hatfield*, Potters Bar and District Historical Society, 4.

35 H. J. Butcher, *Bygone Potters Bar*, Potters Bar and District Historical Society, 11.

36 'The Eternity of Nature', **Major Works**, 166-7.

37 Henderson almost certainly discussed with Clare the significance of the number five in nature. For two decades, from about 1820 to 1840, many British naturalists favoured William Sharpe Macleay's Quinarian taxonomy over Linnaeus's system of classification. Macleay and his followers believed that two sorts of relationship—*affinity* and *analogy*—existed among taxa, and that taxa existed in groups of five. Circular chains of affinity connected taxa within each group, and relationships of analogy existed among taxa occupying the same positions in different circles of affinity: see Robert J. O'Hara, 'Representations of the Natural System in the Nineteenth Century', *Biology and Philosophy*, April 1991, Vol 6, Issue 2, 255–274. Even if Henderson did not adhere to the Quinarian system, he would have drawn Clare's attention to it, and it may well have influenced Clare's idea of five being a significant number in the world of living things.

38 Pam, *The Story of Enfield Chase*, 156.

39 Ibid, 137.

40 **Harper**, 82.

41 Butcher, *Bygone Potters Bar*, 11.

42 The care home plans were rejected, and rejected again on appeal, as they involved demolition of part of the building. At the time of writing, the planners at Hertsmere Borough Council were considering an application to build homes at the rear of the site and convert the pub into a 'community hub'. See Welwyn Hatfield Times: http://bit.ly/lcrwht (retrieved February 1, 2019).

43 See **Bate**, 69.

The Journey—Hertfordshire
Pages 111–210

1. Lynch, *The Turnpike Road to Hatfield*, 4-10.
2. J. P. B. Clarke, *Inns at Bell Bar*, Potters Bar and District Historical Society, 16-21. Information on the inns at Bell Bar is taken from here unless otherwise indicated.
3. See 'The inns and alehouses of Bell Bar', NORTH MYMMS HISTORY PROJECT: http://bit.ly/lcraib (retrieved February 1, 2019).
4. Dorothy Colville, chapter 19, 'Bell Bar,' *North Mymms – Parish and People*, Letchworth, 1972, ISBN 9780900519239. Information about Bell Bar in the following paragraphs is taken from this source unless otherwise indicated.
5. Material on Greenwood's experiences on the road is taken from M. Tomkins, 'A Tramp through Hertfordshire', *Hertfordshire Countryside*, August 1977, 29.
6. Hon. John Byng, *The Torrington Diaries* Vol III, 189-90, C. Bruyn Andrews ed., London: Eyre & Spottiswoode, 1936.
7. See 'The end for The Swan in Bell Bar – a look at the inn's history', NORTH MYMMS HISTORY PROJECT: http://bit.ly/lcrslb (retrieved February 1, 2019).
8. **Harper**, 84.
9. Izaak Walton and Charles Cotton, *The Compleat Angler*, chapter XX, 'Of fish ponds and how to order them', first published 1653 (Walton) and 1676 (Cotton), Coachwhip Publications, 2005, 144-146.
10. 'The Journal', **By Himself**. 214
11. *Hatfield and its People, A Thousand Years of History*, Hatfield WEA, 1959, Book 5, 8.
12. Ibid, Book 1, 12.
13. Ibid, Book 3, 27.
14. **Harper**, 84.
15. Sadly, before this book went to press the Wrestlers' sign was replaced with a more anodyne version, in keeping with modern sensibilities.
16. *Hatfield and its People*, Book 1, 11.
17. Peter Rumley, 'The Great North Road', *Hertfordshire Countryside*, 50, issue 430, Feb. 1995, 16-17.
18. **Harper**, 88.
19. *Hatfield and its People*, Book 1, 11.
20. 'Don Juan', **Major Works**, 321, lines 96-104.
21. See Colin Brown, *Lady M: The Life and Loves of Elizabeth Lamb, Viscountess Melbourne 1751-1818*, Stroud: Amberley Publishing, 2018.
22. Nikolaus Pevsner, *The Buildings of England: Hertfordshire*, second edition revised by Bridget Cherry, Harmondsworth: Penguin, 1977, 112.

NOTES – PROSE

23 This and the following quote are taken from the 'Autobiographical Fragments', **By Himself**, 157-8.

24 CREDE BYRON: http://bit.ly/lcrcby (retrieved February 1, 2019).

25 Charles Thomas Samuel Birch Reynardson, *Down the Road: The Reminiscences of a Gentleman Coachman*, London: Longman Green & Co, 1873, 84.

26 **Harper**, 88.

27 Edward Young, *Night Thoughts*, lines 372-6, Edinburgh, James Nichol, 1853, 16. PDF available at ARCHIVE: http://bit.ly/lcrxnt (retrieved February 1, 2019).

28 Byron, 'Don Juan', Canto IX, stanza 1, *Lord Byron - The Major Works*, Oxford University Press, 2008, 678.

29 'Lines on Wellington', **Early Poems**, I, 54.

30 *Report on Welwyn*, English Heritage Extensive Urban Survey Programme, 12. PDF available at the ARCHAEOLOGY DATA SERVICE: http://bit.ly/lcrads (retrieved February 1, 2019).

31 'Welwyn Roman Baths', WELWYN HATFIELD COUNCIL: http://bit.ly/lcrwrr (retrieved February 1, 2019).

32 *The London Magazine*, John Scott and John Taylor, eds., April 1823, 380.

33 'Roman Antiquities' (unascribed) *Stamford Mercury*, Friday, 28 December, 1827, British Library Colindale Newspaper Archive. See also **Bate**, 236 and note.

34 For a discussion of Clare's interest in Roman artefacts, see Bob Heyes, '"Triumphs of Time": John Clare and the Uses of Antiquity', **JCS** 16 (1997), 5-17.

35 'Welwyn', BRITISH HISTORY ONLINE: http://bit.ly/lcrbhw (retrieved February 1, 2019).

36 Edmund Blunden, *Undertones of War*, 1928, reprinted Penguin Classics, 2010. See 23, 60 and 170.

37 'Welwyn', BRITISH HISTORY ONLINE.

38 'Strict and Particular Baptists', THE FAITH OF GOD'S ELECT: http://www.the-faith.org.uk/spb.html. Site written and maintained by John Cargill "as a personal contribution to the testimony of our Lord Jesus Christ." (retrieved May 28, 2018; page not found February 1, 2019.)

39 To James Hessey, after April 3rd 1824, **Selected Letters**, 85-6; see also **Bate**, 254-5.

40 'On Political Religion', **Champion**, 281, also quoted **Bate**, 351.

41 See A. C. Lynch, *The Stage-coach Through Potters Bar*, Potters Bar District and Historical Society, 18. (Lynch, referencing de Quincey, attributes the sudden decline in highway robbery in the 1790s to the introduction of banknotes.)

42 The complete line reads, "It was a dark and stormy night; the rain fell in torrents—except at occasional intervals, when it was checked by a violent gust of wind which swept up the streets (for it is in London that our scene lies), rattling along the housetops, and fiercely agitating the scanty flame of

the lamps that struggled against the darkness." Bulwer-Lytton's memory is now kept alive through San Jose State University's Bulwer-Lytton Fiction Contest, which invites annual submissions for the best worst opening line of an imaginary novel. For past winning entries see THE BULWER LYTTON FICTION CONTEST: http://bit.ly/lcrebl (retrieved February 1, 2019).

43   Peter Rumley, 'The Great North Road', *Hertfordshire Countryside* 50, issue 430, Feb. 1995, 3.
44   'The Hundred of Broadwater', BRITISH HISTORY ONLINE: http://bit.ly/lcrbhb (retrieved February 1, 2019).
45   'Langley Bush', **Major Works**, 30.
46   'Remembrances', ibid, 260.
47   Charles Dickens, 'Tom Tiddler's Ground', London: Chapman & Hall, 1861, 4-5. PDF available from THE HATHI TRUST: http://bit.ly/lcrttg (retrieved February 1, 2019).
48   Robert B. Black, 'The British New Towns – A Case Study of Stevenage', *Land Economics*, 27, 1, February 1951.
49   Quoted in Osborn and Whittick, *The New Towns. The Answer to Megalopolis*, London: Leonard Hill, 1969.
50   Information in this paragraph is taken from 'Stevenage New Town: "Building for the new way of life"', MUNICIPAL DREAMS: http://bit.ly/lcrdms (retrieved February 1, 2019).
51   Comment posted at 'Stevenage new town in 1962', YOUTUBE: http://bit.ly/lcrysn (retrieved February 1, 2019).
52   'First Visit to London', 'Autobiographical Fragments', **By Himself**, 134.
53   Ibid, 135.
54   Ibid.
55   **Harper**, 95.
56   **Tompkins**, 181.
57   **Martin**, 50.
58   Forster, John, *The Life of Charles Dickens*, London: Cecil Palmer, 1928, 820, quoted by Simon Kövesi and Scott McEathron, in the Introduction to **New Essays**.
59   *The Manchester Guardian*, 18 February 1862, available at THE GUARDIAN: http://bit.ly/lcrgsv (retrieved February 1, 2019).
60   **Tompkins**, 184.
61   *The New Annual Register, or General Repository of History, Politics and Literature for the Year 1807*, vol 50, London: John Stockdale, 1808, 173.
62   Pevsner, *The Buildings of England, Hertfordshire*, 347.
63   **Harper**, 102-3.
64   'There is a place scarce known that well may claim', **Sonnets**, 87.
65   **Harper**, 96.
66   **By Himself**, 338, Note 11.
67   See Chris Cooper, *The Great North Road Then and Now*, Harlow 2013, 50.

68 See Victoria Maddren, *Who was Jack O' Legs?*, Hertfordshire Library Service, 1992, for an examination of the story's folkloric context.

69 **Tompkins**, 234.

70 Doris Jones-Baker, *Tales of Old Hertfordshire*, Newbury: Countryside Books, 1987, 44.

71 Allan Whitaker, *Brewers in Hertfordshire, A Historical Gazetteer*, University of Hertfordshire Press, 2006, 140.

72 **Selected Letters**, 203; **By Himself**, 269.

73 The George is documented from 1797 onwards and known today as the George IV. See the *North Hertfordshire District Council Register of Buildings of Local Importance in Baldock*, 17th June 2003, 12. In 1841 the nearest pub to Baldock called 'The Plough' was at Wallington, about 2.5 miles east of the town.

74 See J. S. Rider, *Baldock History - Essays by J. S. Rider*, unpublished typescript, 1982, held at Baldock Local Studies Library.

75 **Tompkins**, 240.

76 See Alan Bates, *Directory of Stage Coach Services 1836*, Newton Abbot: David & Charles, 1969.

77 Referenced in Brendan King's 'The Coaching Inns of Baldock', Baldock Museum, 2006.

78 Daniel Defoe, *A tour thro' the whole island of Great Britain, divided into circuits or journeys*, London: J. M. Dent and Co, 1927, appendix to the Second Volume. See selection 26, available at A VISION OF BRITAIN THROUGH TIME: http://bit.ly/lcrvbd (retrieved February 1, 2019).

79 W. Albert, *The Turnpike Road System in England 1663-1840*, Cambridge University Press, 1972, 17.

80 Entry for Tuesday, August 6, 1661, *The Diary of Samuel Pepys 1660-1669*, O. F. Morshead, ed., London: G. Bell and Sons, 1935. Available at PEPYS DIARY: http://bit.ly/lcrspd (retrieved February 1, 2019).

81 *The Diary of Samuel Pepys 1660-1669*, entry for Monday, September 23, 1661.

82 *The Journal of George Fox*, Revised Edition, John L. Nickalls, ed., Cambridge University Press, 2010, 228, available at GOOGLE BOOKS: http://bit.ly/lcrgbp (retrieved February 1, 2019).

83 John Copeland, *Roads and their Traffic 1750-1840*, Newton Abbot: David & Charles, 1968, 80.

84 *North Hertfordshire District Council Register of Buildings of Local Importance*, 10.

85 John Gallas, *Mad John's Walk*, Nottingham: Five Leaves Publications, 2017, 9.

86 **Tompkins**, 241.

The Journey—Bedfordshire
Pages 214–280

1. **Harper**, 107.
2. Charles Thomas Samuel Birch Reynardson, *Down the Road: Reminiscences of a Gentleman Coachman*, London: Longmans, Green & Co, 1875, 61-2.
3. **Harper**, 107.
4. Pigot & Co., *National Commercial Directory*, 1839; Kelly, *The Post Office Directory*, 1847; *Slater's Directory*, 1850.
5. Clare's journal entry for Friday, June 3, 1825 records that he "got the tune of 'Highland Mary' from Wisdom Smith a gypsey", **By Himself**, 232-3. As the words were by Burns, the piece must have had a double significance for him. See George Deacon, *John Clare and the Folk Tradition*, London: Francis Boutle Publishers, 2002, 211n.
6. On June 29, 1820 Clare wrote to Hessey: "I mean to leave Taylor the trouble of writing my Life merely to stop the mouths of others – & for that purpose shall collect a great many facts which I shall send when death brings in his bill." **Letters**, 78-9. He subsequently produced 'Sketches in the Life of John Clare' (March 1821) and also the autobiography (1825), of which only fragments remain.
7. 'Central Bedfordshire', Topographic Map: http://bit.ly/lcrtmb (retrieved February 1, 2019).
8. There are no reliable records for the weather in Bedfordshire on the night in question, but the England and Wales Weather Precipitation Series (Hadley Centre, Met Office) records 1841 as having an unusually wet summer and autumn: "A wet sequence of months from July to November inclusive across England & Wales. Using the EWP series, the approximate anomaly for the period overall was 140-150%. No individual month was exceptionally wet by this series, but the consistency of high rainfall (May & June also had above-average values) led to local flooding later in the year. This was a period of feverish railway building in Britain, and work was often affected due to collapse of cuttings / embankments etc."
9. Moonset for Potton on July 21, 1841 was calculated at Greenwich Meantime: http://bit.ly/lcrgmt and verified using Predicalendar: http://bit.ly/lcrpdc (both retrieved February 1, 2019).
10. The map can be found on page 259 of **By Himself**, page 208 of **Poems and Prose**, and facing page 241 of **Martin**.
11. **Tibble**, 120.
12. See Matthew Beaumont, *Night Walking, A Nocturnal History of London, Chaucer to Dickens*, London: Verso, 2015, 227-8.
13. See inter alia 'The Welcome Stranger', **Early Poems**, I, 186, and 'Winter', **Major Works**, 96.
14. 'Autobiographical Fragments', **By Himself**, 91.
15. 'Sketches in the Life of John Clare', **By Himself**, 10.
16. 'Autobiographical Fragments', **By Himself**, 45.

17 Ibid, 155.
18 **Natural History**, 257; **By Himself,** 251;
19 See Jonathan Taylor, 'Lighting in the Victorian Home', reproduced from *The Building Conservation Directory*, Tisbury: Cathedral Communications Ltd, 2000, available at BUILDING CONSERVATION: http://bit.ly/lcrlvh (retrieved February 1, 2019).
20 'Autobiographical Fragments', **By Himself**, 150.
21 There were two establishments called 'The White Hart' in Tempsford: a coaching inn in Church Street—now a private residence called Gannock House—which ceased trading before 1822, and a beerhouse at Langford End that first appears in records in 1830. See Bedfordshire Archives and Records Service, Community Archives, Tempsford, WL800/5, available at BEDFORDSHIRE ARCHIVES: http://bit.ly/lcrbat (retrieved February 1, 2019).
22 See *Bedfordshire Magazine*, vol III, 273.
23 Unless otherwise indicated, information on the history of the Anchor Hotel is taken from 'The Anchor Hotel, Tempsford', BEDFORDSHIRE ARCHIVES: http://bit.ly/lcranh (retrieved February 1, 2019).
24 *Bedfordshire on Sunday*, April 10, 2011.
25 *The Torrington Diaries*, London: Eyre & Spottiswoode, 1954. Available at A VISION OF BRITAIN THROUGH TIME: http://bit.ly/lcrvbt (retrieved February 1, 2019).
26 **Harper**, 109.
27 Ibid, 110.
28 The information in the following paragraphs is taken from THE FENLAND LIGHTER PROJECT: http://bit.ly/lcrflp (retrieved May 30, 2018; page not found February 1, 2019).
29 Jim Brown of Gamlingay Historical Society, email to Ellis Hall, June 9, 2015.
30 'Forty Farmhouse Wyboston', BEDFORDSHIRE ARCHIVES: http://bit.ly/lcrbff (retrieved February 1, 2019).
31 'Autobiographical Fragments', **By Himself**, 74.
32 See **Bate**, 327; **Storey**, 203; **Tibbles**, 251; **Wilson**, 182.
33 The text has "it might be St Ives but I forget the name" but a note added after his return clarifies that the town was in fact St Neots (see **By Himself**, 338).
34 **By Himself**, 338.
35 Ibid.
36 'Sketches in the Life of John Clare', **By Himself**, 8.
37 Lines taken from Clare's sonnet '[Stone Pit]', **Major Works**, 270.
38 See Kristine Douaud, 'The tie that binds: Gypsies, John Clare and English folk culture', in *Romani Studies*, 5, 18, 1, 2008, 1-38.
39 'Autobiographical Fragments', **By Himself**, 134-5.

The Journey—Huntingdonshire
Pages 284–314

1. This passage is taken from Tim Chilcott's **Living Year** rather than **By Himself**. The latter has "the lumps lasshed in my face and wakened me from a doze" (339, note 14). In our view Chilcott's transcription makes better sense in the context of the passage, Clare having stated that the coach was in a hollow below him when it passed. Robinson and Summerfield's reading only makes sense if 'lumps' is taken to mean stone chippings, and on one occasion they depart from Clare's actual words when appearing to quote him verbatim, replacing "the lumps lasshed my face" with "the chips flew hard in my face": see **Poems and Prose** 214, footnote.
2. **Harper**, 124.
3. Ibid, 122.
4. Rev. Richard Barham, 'The Dead Drummer', *The Ingoldsby Legends*, London: J. M. Dent, 1840.
5. UK MYTHOLOGY: http://bit.ly/lcrmyt (retrieved February 1, 2019).
6. See John Goodridge and R. K. R. Thornton, *John Clare, The Trespasser*, Nottingham, Five Leaves Publications, 2016, 74. (First published as a chapter of **In Context**.)
7. Matthew Beaumont, *Night Walking, A Nocturnal History of London, Chaucer to Dickens*, London: Verso, 2016, 257.
8. Ivan Margary, *Roman Roads in Britain*, revised edition, Chatham, W & J Mackay, Kent, 1967, 18-22.
9. **Harper**, 124.
10. Ibid.
11. Ibid.
12. Margary, *Roman Roads*.
13. **Harper**, 125.
14. Defoe, *A tour thro'... Great Britain*.
15. Trevor Hickman, *The History of Stilton Cheese*, Stilton, Stilton Publishing, 1996, ISBN 9781445607634.
16. 'Autobiographical Fragments', **By Himself**, 153. See also Tom Bates, 'John Clare and "Boximania"', **JCS** 13 (1994), 5-17.
17. **Sales**, 238.
18. **Living Year**, 142.
19. Ibid, 143.
20. 'The Rise of Mendoza', *The Fort Wayne Sentinel*, Sat 26 February 1910, at BOXREC: http://bit.ly/lcrxbr (retrieved February 1, 2019).
21. Luke G. Williams, 'Fight of the Century Part 2 – Humphries vs Mendoza 2', BOXING MONTHLY: http://bit.ly/lcrbxm (retrieved February 1, 2019).
22. 'He eats a moments stoppage to his song', **Sonnets**, 69; **Middle Period**, V, 270.

NOTES – PROSE

23 Quotes from George Borrow in the following are taken from T*he Scholar and the Gypsy*, reproduced in ALL THINGS GEORGIAN: http://bit.ly/lcrncr (retrieved February 1, 2019).

24 'There is a place scarce known that well may claim', **Sonnets**, 87; **Middle Period**, V, 293.

25 'I cannot know what country owns thee now', **Sonnets**, 64; **Middle Period**, V, 263.

26 **Martin**, 281.

27 Ibid, 282.

28 Available online at JOHN CLARE EPHEMERA: http://bit.ly/lcrtnv (retrieved February 1, 2019).

29 Tobias Smollett, *Roderick Random*, Oxford University Press, 1979, 55.

The Journey—Northamptonshire
Pages 318–325

1 There is a 'Beehive' in Albert Street, Peterborough, close to the town bridge, but this cannot be where he was making for after passing through Walton.

2 To Matthew Allen, after 27 August 1841, **Selected Letters** 203.

3 To George Reid, November 17 1841, **Selected Letters**, 205.

4 **Selected Letters**, 204.

5 Clare was familiar with Homer's Odyssey: a translation by Alexander Pope is listed in the catalogue of his library. *The London Magazine*, 4, 1821, contains an article in 'Leisure Hours No III, "A Dialogue of the Living: on the Homeric Poematia"', which discusses the work of Bloomfield. Clare would certainly have read it as he received the *LM* regularly. There are also several mentions of Odysseus elsewhere in the same issue.

6 'Song b', **Major Works**, 283.

7 **SOED**, definition dated 1819.

8 See Oliver Sacks, *Hallucinations*, Basingstoke: Picador, 2012.

9 Byron, 'The Prisoner of Chillon', final lines of the introduction before the prisoner's monologue. Clare has inserted, "of my sad fate" in the first line, perhaps to refer more directly to his own journey of suffering. The final one and a half lines of Byron's sonnet read: 'May none these marks efface / For they appeal from tyranny to God.' (It's also possible Clare made a mistake as he was working from memory, having lent his copies of Byron to Mrs King and other women he met at The Owl before he left High Beach.)

The Man
Pages 329–365

1. Dr Nicola Blandford, psychotherapist, private correspondence to Bridget Somekh.
2. See Erving Goffman, *Asylums: Essays on the Condition of the Social Situation of Mental Patients and Other Inmates*, Harmondsworth: Penguin, 1961.
3. Ellis Hall and Martin Phillips, *The Great Spaghetti Scandal*, Cambridge: Trondheim Foundation Press, 1974.
4. **Sales**, 130-163.
5. 'The Literary Police Office, Bow Street', *The London Magazine* VII, January to June 1823, 158.
6. Richard Cronin notes that while contributors to the literary magazines of the time were for the most part anonymous, "a still more flamboyant magazine expression of the fluid identity that defined the metropolitan personality was the practice of pseudonymity." R. Cronin, 'John Clare and the London Magazine', **New Essays**, 215.
7. A particularly apposite phrase used by Clare in his letter to Matthew Allen on returning home: "where my poetical fancy is I cannot say for the people in the neighbourhood tells me that the one called 'Mary' has been dead these 8 years." **Selected Letters**, 203.
8. Sacks, *Hallucinations*, 56.
9. *John Clare in Context*, Hugh Haughton, Adam Phillips and Geoffrey Summerfield eds, Cambridge University Press, 1994, 272.
10. See Alan D. Vardy, *John Clare, Politics and Poetry*, Basingstoke: Palgrave Macmillan, 2003.
11. **Bate**, 429.
12. See page 18.
13. Emma Trehane, '"Emma and Johnny": The Friendship between Eliza Emmerson and John Clare.' **JCS** 24 (2005), 69-77.
14. Pet. MS B3 82, reproduced **By Himself**, 136-7.
15. **Bate**, 172.
16. Emma Trehane, 'The Epistolary Poetics of John Clare and Eliza Louisa Emmerson', PhD thesis, Nottingham Trent University, 2011.
17. **Egerton** 2245, fols 151r/v, 152r/v, quoted Trehane, 'Epistolary Poetics', 118.
18. **Egerton**. 2245, fols 183r/v, 184r/v, 185r/v, quoted Trehane, 'Epistolary Poetics', 126-7.
19. **Egerton** 2247, fol 2r/v, quoted Trehane, 'Epistolary Poetics', 223.
20. 'Don Juan', lines 153-82, **Major Works**, 322-3.
21. To James Augustus Hessey, 1 December 1820, **Selected Letters**, 33-4.
22. To John Taylor, 24 January 1831, **Selected Letters**, 168
23. 'Prose notes in Pet. MS A45', **Champion**, 293.

24 'Miscellaneous notes and fragments', **Champion**, 299-300.
25 To Marianne Marsh, late January 1832, **Letters**, 560.
26 'The Journal', **By Himself**, 219.
27 See E. P. Thompson, *Customs in Common*, Harmondsworth: Penguin, 1993, Chapter Two, 'Patricians and Plebs'.
28 Ibid.
29 'Letter to William Hone', **Major Works**, 486.
30 **Selected Poems**, 21.
31 See Sam Ward, '"This is radical slang": John Clare, Admiral Lord Radstock and the Queen Caroline affair', **New Essays**, 189-208.
32 Stanza 108, 'The Village Minstrel', **Champion**, 37; **Early Poems II**, 169.
33 'Miscellaneous notes and fragments', **Champion**, 298.
34 Ibid, 299.
35 To Taylor, 24 January 1831, **Letters**, 533; **Selected Letters**, 168. Clare's estimation was sound—Althorp was responsible for the 1833 Factory Act, which sought to improve working conditions for children.
36 'Miscellaneous notes and fragments', **Champion**, 298-9.
37 See page 150.
38 To Marianne Marsh, late January 1832; **Letters**, 560.
39 To Taylor, 18 August 1821, **Letters**, 208-9; **Selected Letters** 57. The last line, which Clare crossed out, is quoted in **Champion**, 312-3.
40 See inter alia John Lucas, 'Clare's Politics', **In Context**, 148-177.
41 To Eliza Emmerson, Dec 1830–Jan 1831, **Letters**, 527; **Champion**, 319.
42 Quoted W. E. Tate, *The English Village Community and the Enclosure Movements,* London: Gollancz, 1967, 188.
43 See John Barrell, *The Idea of Landscape and the Sense of Place 1730-1840*, Cambridge University Press, 1972, 102 and 107.
44 **Major Works**, 20.
45 Ibid, 150.
46 Ibid, 152.
47 Ibid, 260.
48 Ibid, 98.
49 Quotes from 'The Parish' in this section are taken from **Champion**, 52-7.
50 The Introduction to Poems *Descriptive of Rural Life and Scenery*, London: Taylor & Hessey, 1820, vii.
51 'A Visit to John Clare', *The London Magazine*, November 1821, IV, 540-8. Partially reprinted **Critical Heritage**, 157-65.
52 Clare owned a copy of William Render's 1807 translation of *The Sorrows of Werther*, and in response to reading it wrote the sonnet, 'Supposd to be Utterd by Werter at the Conclusion of his Last Interview with Charlotte' (**Early Poems**, I, 296).

53. 'Autobiographical Fragments', **By Himself**, 59.
54. To Charles Clare, Saturday 26 February 1848, **Letters**, 655-6
55. 'More Hints in the Life etc', **By Himself**, 32.
56. 'Autobiographical Fragments', **By Himself**, 59.
57. 'Sketches in the Life of John Clare', **By Himself**, 17.
58. 'Autobiographical Fragments', **By Himself**, 60.
59. Ibid, 62.
60. See Adam White, *John Clare's Romanticism*, London: Palgrave Macmillan, 2017 for a detailed examination of Clare's aesthetic in relation to that of the Romantic movement.
61. 'On Taste', **Major Works**, 45.
62. 'Essay on Taste', **Major Works**, 479-80.
63. 'Shadows of Taste', **Major Works**, 170-4.
64. See Goffman, *Asylums*.
65. **Major Works**, 414-5.
66. Eliza Emmerson retired from public life in 1837 and spent the next 17 years studying Dante in seclusion at her London house until her death in 1854. See Trehane, 'Epistolary Poetics', 255-7.
67. Ibid.
68. **Bate**, 267.
69. 'Apology for the Poor' appeared in Drakard's *Stamford Champion*—see **Bate**, 359. It evidently drew strong reactions from readers, as in several surviving drafts Clare mounted a robust counter-attack against his detractors: see **Champion**, 270.
70. In **By Himself,** the editors have moved the opening paragraph to the end of the text, presumably to present the narrative in date order. In MS8 Clare gives the date July 23rd but the following day changes it in MS6 to July 24th.
71. 'Autobiographical Fragments', **By Himself**, 134.

Notes to Verse

The Poet
Paradise Lost

Line 5   "a lively bonny wench": 'Sketches in the Life of John Clare', **By Himself**, 3.

10   "starnels darkened down the sky": 'Autumn Evening', **Major Works**, 241.

21   "his run-a-gate of a grandfather": 'Sketches in the Life of John Clare', **By Himself**, 2.

34   "shadow-shaping clouds": 'St Martin's Eve', **Major Works**, 174.

39   "the hedgehog's nest of grass and sedge": 'The Hedgehog', **Major Works**, 248.

40   "little trotty wagtails": **Major Works**, 'Little Trotty Wagtail', 401.

42   "the stillest and most good-natured child": 'Sketches in the Life of John Clare', **By Himself**, 29.

47   "to find the brink of the world and see earth's secrets below": 'Sketches in the Life of John Clare', **By Himself**, 40.

60   "wagtails trotting and tottering sideways": 'Little Trotty Wagtail', **Major Works**, 401.

The Journey
Musings I

M1, line 2   'What is it Allen's always telling me?': 'Self-Identity', **By Himself**, 271.

Musings II

M2, line 8   "Breakneck hills that headlong go, half the world below": 'A Walk in the Forest', **Selected Poems**, 235.

Musings III

M1, line 3   "in Allen's madhouse, caged and living": 'Don Juan: A Poem', **Major Works**, 325.

Musings IV

M1, line 4   "the bobbing heads and tumbler tails": '[The Fens]', **Major Works**, 239.

Musings V

M2, line 20   "starnels rush the sky": 'October', **Shepherd's Calendar**, 166.

           39   "trembling wings and feathers pricked on end": 'The Nightingale's Nest', **Major Works**, 214.

Musings VI

M2, line 14   "and his shadow struts by his side in pride": 'The Hue and Cry: A Tale of the Times': **Champion**, 176.

Musings VII

M1, line 9   "sandy places for fish to spawn": Chapter XX, 'Of Fish Ponds and How to Order Them' in Walton and Cotton, *The Compleat Angler*, Landisville, PA, Coachwhip Publications, 2005, 144-145.

Musings VIII

M2, line 3   "fearful people urged to the giddy brink": 'Summer', Thomson's 'The Seasons', 376.

           9   "an hour glass on the run": 'What is Life?', **Major Works**, 26.

           13   "Ten thousand tribes": 'Summer', Thomson's 'The Seasons', 249-50.

Musings IX

M1, line 14   "that sneering corporal": 'March to Oundle in the Local Militia', 'Autobiographical Fragments', **By Himself**, 95.

           20   "an angry dog ready to growl": Friday [11 May, 1835], 'The Journal', **By Himself**, 227

M2, line 6   "James Loudon McAdam improved the road": inscription on the plaque placed by Welwyn Archaeological Society on the restored 25th milestone at Welwyn. The name is incorrect as the work was carried out by James' son, John Loudon McAdam.

Musings X

M1, line 19   "some stranger soul had jumped into his skin": 'My First Visit to London', 'Autobiographical Fragments', **By Himself**, 134.

M4, line 3   "rich and poor are mulched in earth to nourish future multitudes": 'Elegy Hastily Composed and Written with a Pencil on the Spot in the Ruins of Pickworth, Rutland', **Major Works**, 12-14.

Musings XI

M4, line 1   "There's no trace today of the shed where he slept": 'Journey out of Essex', **By Himself**, 258.

Musings XII

M2, line 12   "his friend Rip's painting – 'The Stage Coach Breakfast' – ": Clare was introduced to the painter Edward Villiers Rippingille by Eliza Emmerson during his second visit to London in 1821. After two weeks together, they became firm friends. See Peter Cox, '"A liking to use the pen": Edward Villiers Rippingille (c. 1790-1859) and John Clare', **JCS**, 17, July 1998, 17-33.

Musings XIII

M1, line 1   "How great are my expectations": Letter to J. B. Henson, 1818, **Selected Letters**, 1.

         10   "a ribbon of lamps tapering into stars": 'My [Third] Visit to London', 'Autobiographical Fragments', **By Himself**, 150.

         15   "sweeing along the road": 'My [Third] Visit to London', 'Autobiographical Fragments', **By Himself**, 150.

         26   "stray cattle in the field": 'My [Third] Visit to London', 'Autobiographical Fragments', **By Himself**, 150.

Musings XIV

M3, line 1   "He wanted his pipe lighting and stood timid at the door": 'Journey out of Essex', **By Himself**, 260.

Musings XV

M1, line 5   "terribles with saucer eyes": 'for 3rd Visit to London', 'Autobiographical Fragments', **By Himself**, 155.

Musings XVI

M1, line 5   "a desent scraper": 'My first attempts at Poetry etc etc', 'Autobiographical Fragments', **By Himself**, 82.

         10   "John Barleycorn" was the personification of barley, and of beer, widely featured in British folk song during the eighteenth and nineteenth centuries.

         13   "that made a rare noise – and plenty" : Clare's letter to Taylor, Jan 7 1821, **Letters**, 138. Clare also says, "I get on 'like a house on fire' with my Cremoni & begin to be stil'd a first rate scraper among my rustic companions"; and adds "a professional at Stamford tells me she's a valuable instrument and her equal is not easy to be met with in our parts".

24   "Music might have saved him / as Farinelli's singing cured the mad king." The celebrated Italian castrato singer ended his stage career when Queen Elisabetta Farnese of Spain came to believe his singing could cure the madness of her husband, King Philip V. In 1737 he was appointed Chamber Musician and, for the remaining nine years of Philip's life, gave nightly private concerts to the royal couple.

Musings XVII

M1, line 10   "lengthy silver line": 'Autobiographical Fragments', **By Himself**, 91.

19   "sketches that breathe with living freshness": Letter to de Wint, Dec 19, 1829, **Selected Letters**, 151.

Musings XVIII

M1, line 10   Defoe's 'greatest meat market in the world': A.R.B Haldane, *The Drove Roads of Scotland*, Edinburgh: Birlinn Limited, 1997, ISBN 1-874744-76-9, 34.

Musings XIX

M1, line 14   "gone to roost": 'Journey Out of Essex', **By Himself**, 262.

Musings XX

M1, line 1   "I saw him soon as I came out the gate": 'Journey out of Essex', **By Himself**, 262.

Musings XXI

M1, line 3   "Fetching a hundred caterpillars in twenty minutes": entry for Thursday 26 May 1825 in 'The Journal', **By Himself**, 230.

7   "velvet moss and little scraps of grass": 'The Nightingale's Nest', **Major Works**, 215.

M2, line 14   "Now, he sees the road blurred and stupid": 'Journey out of Essex', **By Himself**, 263.

M3, line 4   "biographies of birds and flowers": Clare's preferred title for his book on natural history suggested by his publisher, Hessey.

10   "and thrushes in Royce wood, high in song": entry for Friday, May 4, 1825, 'The Journal', **By Himself**, 226.

Musings XXII

M1, line 10   "since the kingcups were shining like flame": 'Ballad', **Major Works**, 313.

Musings XXIII

M1, line 6   "Something like bread": 'Journey out of Essex', **By Himself**, 263.

M3, line 2   "his poetical fancy": Letter to Matthew Allen c. August 27 1841, **By Himself**, 269.

17   "my affection is unaltered": Letter to Patty Clare, Leppits Hill, March 1841. **Selected Letters**, 199.

4   "I'm determined to keep you both for ever": Letter to Mary Joyce [May? 1841], **Selected Letters**, 200.

Musings XXIV

M1, line 1   "We were up early to catch the cart home": 'Journey out of Essex', **By Himself**, 264.

Musings XXV

M1, line 2   "Charles": Clare's youngest son, Charles, born January 4, 1833 was eight years old when Clare returned from High Beach.

The Man

Father of the Queen of England

Line 9   "snuff box": "Prince Albert goes to Germany and must he / Leave the queens snuff box where all fools are strumming": 'Don Juan: a poem', **Major Works**, 320.

5   "a Cruikshank cartoon": See Vic Gatrell, *City of Laughter: sex and satire in eighteenth century London*, London: Atlantic Books, 2006, 10: "The prints of James Gillray, Thomas Rowlandson and George Cruikshank count among the great creative works of their era."

15   "a wry punster but not Byron – poh!": 'Don Juan: a poem', **Major Works**, 325.

Emma and Johnny

Line 4   "like the robin / in his poem singing of lost golden days": 'Helpstone', **Major Works**, 1-5.

7   "sympathy of thought": 'The Vow': **Early Poems**, II, 93.

17   "to leave the dinsome city": 'Song', **Early Poems**, II, 445.

Poet with an Oaken Bludgeon

Line 4   "Pope's regularities / of rhymes and John Donne's broken feet": 'Shadows of Taste', **Major Works**, 172.

12   "mob impulse of the moment": From Shakespeare's 'Henry VI', quoted by Clare in a letter to Marianne Marsh discussing riots in Peterborough. **Selected Letters**, 171.

25   "grand illuminations night": Letter to J. A. Hessey, 1 Dec. 1820, **Selected Letters**, 33.

Lament

Line 13   "curving darksome bawks": 'The Lamentations of Round-Oak Waters', **Major Works**, 21.

31   "willows grey-green boughs": 'Hares at Play', **Major Works**, 244.

34   "a senseless wretch": 'The Lamentations of Round-Oak Waters', **Major Works**, 21.

Laying out Plans for an Iron Railway

Line 2   "a pale rusty tinge with a root like pile wort": 'The Journal', **By Himself**, 231.

18   "laying out plans for an iron railway": 'The Journal', **By Himself**, 233.

The Education of a Man of Taste

Line 3   "sultry hours / and ever-fanning breezes": 'Summer', Thomson's 'The Seasons', 4-5. 'Summer' was the first part of 'The Seasons' that Clare read.

33   "You revelled in the picturesque": 'Within a pleasant lawn where pleasure strays', **Sonnets**, 13.

MS8 John Clare Collection, Northampton Library

Drafts of 'Child Harold', 'Jack Randall's Challenge', 'Don Juan' and the 'Journey out of Essex' are all in Northampton MS 8, the notebook that Clare carried with him on his escape from Allen's asylum.

Index of Persons

Allen, Matthew vii-xvi, 12, 14-7, 20, 22-7, 29, 31-2, 35, 38-41, 43-4, 76-7, 93, 120, 181, 196, 282, 320, 323, 325, 331
Althorp, Lord 344
Artis, Edmund Tyrell xi-xiii, 148-9, 163, 353, 355

Baines, Roy 296
Bate, Jonathan 32, 364
Beaumont, Matthew 292
Behnes, Harry xiii
Birch Reynardson, Charles 137, 214
Bird, Dennis 92
Birket Foster, Myles 162
Blake, William xiii
Bloomfield, Robert x, xii
Blunden, Edmund 149
Borrow, George 305-6
Boswell, 'King' Henry 3-4, 163-4, 271
Boulton, Matthew 65
Bowles, John 202
Brown, Jim 263
Browne, W. A. F. xv
Buckler, John Chessell 112
Burleigh, Lord 86
Butcher, J. H. 104
Brian, John 123
Bullimore, Mrs x
Bulwer-Lytton, Edward 153, 165, 167
Burgoyne, Roger, 6th Baronet 232-3
Byng, John 116, 251-2

Campbell, Thomas 20
Canton, James 46, 78, 80
Caroline, of Brunswick xi, 340-5
Carlyle, Thomas 23
Carrington, Anne 66, 78
Cary, Rev. Henry x, xi, xii, 363
Cecil, Robert, 1st Earl of Salisbury, 123
Chambers, John 65
Chatterton, Thomas 353
Cherry, John Law 162
Clare, Ann, *nee* Stimson xv, 3
Clare, Anna Maria xi
Clare, Charles xiv, 316, 320, 354
Clare, Eliza Louise xi, 19, 336

Clare, Frederick xii, 15, 21
Clare, John 'Jack' xiii, 358
Clare, Martha, *nee* Turner, xi, xv, 4, 16, 18-20, 22-3, 189, 239, 270, 273, 293, 303, 311-2, 314, 316-7, 320, 322-3, 325, 333, 335-6, 359, 361, 363, 369
Clare, Sophie xiv
Clare, Sophy x, xi
Clarke, Cowden 87
Cobbett, William xiv, 341
Cocks, Charles 111
Coleridge, Samuel Taylor x, xii, xv, 198, 221, 353
Colville, Dorothy 113
Corri, Haydn xi
Conyard, David 66-7, 78
Cowper, William 76, 280, 353
Cromwell, Oliver 93, 280
Crouch, Mr 214
Cruikshank, George 133, 330, 343
Cruikshank, Isaac 299

de Quincey, Thomas 221
de Wint, Peter xi, xvi, 245
Dante x, xii, 363, 365
Darling, Dr xii-xiii, xv, 364
Darwin, Charles xvi, 102
Defoe, Daniel 201, 259, 292, 296
Drury, Edward xiii
Dutton, Mr and Mrs 40

Emmerson, Eliza xi, xii, xiii, xv, xvi, ix, 19, 143, 329, 332, 335-9, 345, 363
Emmerson, Thomas xii, 335
Esterbee, Benjamin 139
Exeter, Marquess of 295, 335, 342
Fish, Miss 18, 42
Fitzwilliam, Earl xi, 335
Forster, E. M. 158
Fox, George 202, 204-5

Gallas, John 206
Gates, William 'Vulcan' 94
Gascoyne-Cecil, James, second Marquess of Salisbury 127
Gaussen, Robert 111, 113, 119, 126, 128
George IV 133, 341

Gilchrist, Octavius xii, 93, 143, 159, 161, 240, 280, 335
Goodridge, John 291
Goethe, Johann Wolfgang von 149, 353
Greenwood, James 114-5, 125-6
Grout, George and Joseph 65

Haggar, Nicholas 32
Hall, S. C. xii
Hamilton, Lady 19, 336
Harper, Charles 103, 107, 119, 125-6, 132, 142, 161, 163, 169, 186, 214-5, 252, 288, 290-2, 295
Harris, Jon viii-ix, 174, 178, 181, 184-6, 225-6, 238, 241, 244, 260-70, 272, 275, 277
Henderson, Joseph xi-xiii, 102, 353, 355-6
Henry VIII 123, 285
Hessey, James Augustus xi, xii, xiv, 93, 148-9, 283, 341, 364
Hill, Rowland xvi, 118, 120
Hilton, William xi, 198
Hobhouse, John 134
Hogg, James xii, xv
Hone, William 342
Hornbeam-Lane, Mr and Mrs 50, 80-1
How, Jeremiah xiv
Howard, Ebenezer 158
Hugh, Bishop of Lincoln 285
Humphries, Richard 298, 300

Jackson, 'Gentleman' John 299
James, Sid 250
Johnson, Samuel 149
Joyce, Mary xv-xvi, 4, 7, 15, 17-20, 22, 83, 124, 129, 143, 173, 187, 222, 273, 293, 303, 316-7, 322-4, 332-3, 347, 360-1, 363-4, 369-70
Joyce, James 347

Keane, Edmund 198
Keats, John x-xii, 87, 89, 353
King, Mrs 18, 42, 77
King, Brendan 207, 209-10
Lamb, Charles xi, xv, 89, 188, 353
Lamb, Lady Caroline 134
Lamb, Elizabeth 133
Lee, Lady Elizabeth 149
Lee, James 354
Linnaeus, Carl xii, 102, 354

McAdam, James 133, 135-9, 141-3, 153, 357
McAdam, John 153
Maitland, John Whitaker 35
Manners, John, Marquess of Granby 191
Margary, Ivan 294
Marsh, Herbert xi, xiii, xvi, 270
Marsh, Marianne xi, 318, 344
Martin, Frederick 15, 43, 76, 164, 166, 278, 312-4, 222
Marx, Karl 151
Matcham, Gervase 290-1
Melbourne, Elizabeth 134
Melbourne, Viscount 134-5
Mendoza, Dan 298, 300
Milton, Lady 342
Milton, Lord xv, 317, 335, 342, 344, 347, 350
Mobbs, James 164, 271
Moritz, Karl Philipp 233
Morley, David 96
Morris, William 35
Mossop, Rev. Charles 151

Nelson, Lord 19, 146, 336
Nicholls, Betsy 66, 78
Noronha, Mike 92

Olding, John 132

Paine, James 134
Paine, Thomas 342
Palmer, Samuel 58
Palmerston, Lady 139
Pawlett, Frances 296
Peel, Sir Robert xiv
Pepys, Samuel 201-2, 285
Pepper, General John 94
Perceval, Spencer x
Petrarch 363, 365
Pevsner, Nikolaus 134, 182
Phillips, Eliza ix, 18, 27, 336, 339
Phillips, Martin 331
Poe, Edgar Allan 153
Pole, William Wellesley 35
Pooley, John 120
Porter, Roy 333
Porter, Tom x
Pratt, Mrs 18
Prince Albert 20, 133, 330

Pryor, John Izzard 209
Pyne, J. B. 205

Queen Victoria xv, 20, 110, 133-5, 146, 270, 330, 332, 362

Radstock, Admiral Lord xi, xii, 335, 342
Randall, Jack xi, xvi, 12, 27, 141, 299, 300, 325, 331, 362
Redding, Cyrus 17
Reid, Geoff viii
Reid, George 320
Reynolds, J. H. 331
Rippingille, Edward Villiers xi-xii, 19, 270, 298, 338
Rolison, Kerry 30-2, 34, 36, 39
Rook, Tony 148
Rowe, Roger 336
Rumley, Peter 132
Russell, Rev. John Fuller 66, 77

Sacks, Oliver 325
Sales, Roger 93, 299, 331
Salisbury, Lady, Dowager 124
Salisbury, Lord 111, 115, 126-7, 342, 357
Salmon, Nathanael 193
Scott, Sir Walter xiv, 353, 364
Shelly, Mary v
Shelley, Percy Bysshe xi
Simpson, Frank xiii
Sinclair, Iain vii, 40
Silkin, Lewis 159-60
Smith, Wisdom 221
Smollett, Tobias 314
Stephenson, George xiv, 359

Taylor, John xi-xv, 193, 198, 296, 331, 335-6, 339, 341, 344, 353, 364
Telford, Thomas 136-7
Tennyson, Alfred Lord xiv, 31, 134
Thickpenny, Leonard 86
Thompson, E. P. 94, 342
Thomson, James 370
Thornhill, Cooper 295-6
Thornton, Kelsey 291
Thurgood, Robert 191
Tompkins, Herbert 163, 169, 193, 200, 210
Townshend, Charles, Viscount 94
Tradescant, John 195
Trehane, Emma 336, 338, 363

Trigg, Henry 182, 193
Turner, Martha see Clare, Martha
Turnill, John x
Turnill, Oscar 313-4, 318
Turpin, Dick 35, 119, 154

Van Gogh, Anna 152
Van Gogh, Vincent 152, 222
Vardy, Alan 335
Vestris, Madame xi, 198, 334-5

Walton, Izaak 53, 70, 120
Wagner, Richard 153
Wandesforde, Juan Buckingham 20
Ward, Sam 342
Watt, James 65
Wellington, Duke of xiii, 141, 143-4, 146, 361
White, Gilbert xii, 283, 364
Whitney, James 153
Wilkie, Sir David 85
Wilkieson, William 260, 262
Willingdale, Thomas 35
William IV xiv, 133
Williams, Luke 300
Wilson, June 15
Windsor, Barbara 250
Wolsey, Cardinal 193
Wordsworth, William x, 188, 352-3

Young, Edward 39, 143, 149, 151, 335, 338

Index of Places

16th milestone 111
18th milestone 115
25th milestone 149
32nd milestone 190-1
35th milestone 192
36th milestone 192, 196
51st milestone 256
53rd milestone 265, 294
70th milestone 292
73rd milestone 292
75th milestone 294

A1 road vii, 116, 138-9, 224, 227, 246-7, 252-3, 255-8, 264, 266-7, 272, 277-8, 284, 290, 295, 304
A1 Retail Park 224
A14 road 290
A1M road 132, 137, 139, 146, 148, 191-2, 289-90
A1000 road 128
A1010 road 76-7
Alconbury Hill 76, 287, 289-92, 294
Alconbury Weston 289, 291
Alma Estate (Ponders End) 58, 73-4
Anchor Inn (Tempsford) 248-9, 251
Anchor Hotel (Tempsford) 248-52
Angel Inn (Ayot Green) 135, 139; (Stilton) 295-7, 300
Ashmolean Museum 195
Ayot Green 133, 135-9

B197 road 133, 137-9
B1043 road 289
Back Street (Potton) 219
Baldock 196-7, 200-10
Baldock Museum 207
Baptist Church (Potters Bar) 102, 108
Barnet 90-1, 101-3, 113, 124, 177, 201
Barnet Museum 92
Bath 150, 215
Bedford Purlieus 149
Beehive public house (Peterborough) 320; (Werrington) 320
Bell public house (Bell Bar) 111, 117; (Stilton) 294-6, 300
Bell Lane (Bell Bar) 113-4, 116; (Stevenage) 181, 184

Bell Bar 111-7
Biggleswade 201-2, 209, 214-6, 224-6
Biggleswade Road (Potton) 219
Black Cat Roundabout 272
Bluebell public house (Helpston) x, 108, 237, 239, 317
Boat public house (Peterborough) 318-9
Boston, Lincs xiii, 200
Botany Bay (Enfield Chase) 92-3, 95, 262; (New South Wales) 262
Bowling Green (Stevenage) 159, 178-9, 181, 184-7
Broadwater 154-5
Brickwall Tollgate 133, 135, 138-9
brickworks (Potters Bar) 100, 103
Bridge Street (Peterborough) 318-9
Brocket Hall 133-5, 139
Brockman Park 111, 119
Broxbourne xvi, 74, 359
Buckden 274, 280, 284-7, 291-2, 364
Buckden Towers 285
Buckhurst Hill 81
Bull Inn public house (Bell Bar)

Cambridge 74, 94, 96, 146, 253, 290
Carpenter's Cottage (Bell Bar) 112, 114
Cask and Stillage public house (Potters Bar) 103-6
Caterpillar Island 132
Casterton xi, 239
Castor 353
Castor Hanglands Nature Reserve 96-8
Causeway (Potters Bar) 106, 108
causeway (Stilton) 294, 301
Chawston 265-6
Cheltenham 150, 215
Chingford 48, 51, 80-1
Chingford Reservoirs, see *King George's Reservoir* and *William Girling Reservoir*
Church End (Tempsford) 246, 255-8
Church House (Welwyn) 146-7
Church Lane (Stevenage) 178
Church Plain (High Beach) 36, 38
Church Road (High Beach) 23, 31, 34, 39-40

INDEX – PLACES 403

Church Street (Baldock) 201-2; (Enfield Town) 85, 90; (Tempsford) 255-8; (Welwyn) 144, 146-50, 152
Coach and Horses public house (Stevenage) 158, 174-5
Cock public house (Baldock) 197, 202
Compasses public house (Baldock) 210
Cold Arbour 235, 247
Coopers Lane (Potters Bar) 101
Crosshall 272-7
Crosshall Manor 273
Crossways (Chingford) 58, 80
Croydon 49
Crown public house (Biggleswade) 214-5
Crown and Woolpack Inn (A1) 292

Daws Hill 58, 73-4
Dew Drop Inn public house (Stevenage) 176
Dicket Mead (Welwyn) 148
Diddington 278-90
Digswell Hill 137, 146
Digswell Hill Viaduct 146
Ditchmore Lane (Stevenage) 168-71
Drapers Way (Stevenage) 176
Drewels Lane (Gamlingay Great Heath) 235, 244
Drove Road (Biggleswade) 226; (Gamlingay Great Heath) 228, 231-2
Duck Lane (Hatfield) 126

Eastwell Green 240
Eaton Oak public house (Crosshall) 273
Eaton Ford 272, 274
Eaton Socon 224, 265, 272
Ebenezer Strict Baptist Chapel (Welwyn) 150
Edmonton 43, 87, 89, 93-4
Eight Bells public house (Hatfield) 123, 125-6
Elmwood Park (Baldock) 196-7
Ely 253
Emmonsales Heath 83, 96, 164
Enfield Chase viii, 43, 90-5, 100-1, 103, 262
Enfield Highway 18, 42, 46, 66, 75-9, 86, 214
Enfield Market 82, 85-7, 89-90, 94
Enfield Town viii, 46, 75-6, 85-6, 90, 94, 214, 274, 288
Epping Forest vii, xv, 14-26, 29-43, 38, 42, 46-9, 57, 62, 78, 81, 119
Ermine Street 76, 201, 288-9, 294; see also *Old North Road*
Everton 232, 257

Everton Road (Potton) 219-20
Eynesbury 14, 234-5, 238, 244, 246

Falcon Inn (Baldock) 202, 206 (Ponders End) 72, 74
Fairlands Way (Stevenage) 167, 169
Fairmead Cottage (High Beach) 22, 31-2, 34, 39, 42
Fairmead House (High Beach) 15, 21-5, 30, 40
Fern Hill (High Beach) 28, 34, 36
Fletton 318
Fore Street (Hatfield) 110, 121, 123-6
Forty Farm (Chawston) 265-8, 272

Gamlingay 224, 233-4, 261
Gamlingay Cinques 233
Gamlingay Great Heath 216-22, 224, 227-31, 233-5, 238-41, 244, 259-60, 262-3, 265, 274, 280, 287
Gannock House (Tempsford) 256, 258
Gentlemans Row (Enfield Town) 89
George public house (Baldock) 201-2, 205-6; (White Hill) 196
George and Dragon public house (Graveley) 191, 193; (Stevenage) 174; (Potton) 218
Glinton x, xvi, 293, 316, 322-3, 346, 369
Granby public house (Stevenage) 190-1
Graveley 163, 188, 191-3, 195-6, 207
Great North Road 52, 90, 92, 95, 101, 106, 111-3, 115-6, 119, 121, 126-33, 135-6, 146, 153, 160-1, 163-6, 168, 170, 172, 187, 191-3, 201, 203-4, 207, 210, 214, 218, 224-6, 232, 241, 244, 246-8, 251-3, 255-7, 266, 272, 274, 277-8, 282, 284, 287-8, 292, 294-5, 304, 309
Great Ouse, River 227, 235, 238, 245, 248, 250-3, 258, 273, 284
Green Man public house (Potters Bar) 104, 106, 108
Green Street (Enfield Highway) 77
Greyhound Inn public house (Enfield Town) 87, 89-90
Grout & Baylis Crape Factory (Ponders End) 65-6, 75, 77-8
Guild of Literature and Art (Stevenage) 166, 168
Gwash, River 239

Hatfield 113, 119, 121-32, 136, 201, 257, 357
Hatfield House 111, 120-1, 123, 125-7, 127, 195, 357

Hatfield Park 110, 118-20, 136
Hatfield Road (Potters Bar) 106-8
Hatfield Viaduct 126-8, 357
Hawk Wood (Epping Forest) 49, 51
Helpston x-xiv, xvi, 19, 35, 52, 96, 149, 240, 275, 313-4, 317, 322, 335-6, 347, 353, 358-9, 364
Helpston Railway Station 359
Hertford Road (Hatfield) 128; (Ponders End) 76
High Beach vii, xv, xvi, 14-5, 20-4, 26, 30, 34-5, 40, 42-3, 46, 50, 77, 177, 318, 323, 325, 331, 335, 359, 363
High Street (Baldock) 197, 200-2, 206-7, 210; (Buckden) 284-5; (Ponders End) 76-7; (Potters Bar) 101-4; (Stevenage) 158, 171, 174-9, 181, 183-6; (Stilton) 295, 300; (Welwyn) 142-4, 146-50; (Werrington) 320
Hill Wood (High Beach) 34, 36-7
Hitchin Street (Baldock) 201-2
Holy Trinity Church (Stevenage) 174-5; (Weston) 193
Holyhead 137
Horslow Street (Potton) 219
Hounslow Heath 93
Hornbeam Lane (Sewardstonebury) 47-8, 50
Hucknall 124
Hull 200
Huntingdon 76, 241, 252, 278, 280, 289-90

Ickleford 164
Iron Church (Gamlingay Great Heath) 232, 235
Ivel, River 215, 252

Jack's Hill 191-2, 195
John O'Gaunt Golf Club 226, 233

Kimbolton Road (Crosshall) 272, 275
King's Arms public house (Enfield Highway) 77
King's Head public house (Enfield Town) 86-7, 89
King George's Reservoir 51, 54, 58, 62-3, 73
Knebworth House 153-5

Labour in Vain public house (Enfield Highway) 76-7, 80
Langford End (Tempsford) 246, 248
Langley Bush 45, 96, 155, 237, 271
Lea Navigation 51, 53-4, 58-9, 62-3, 65, 67, 70, 72, 85, 87, 209
Lea, River 51, 53-4, 57-8, 82, 85, 132-3, 337
Lea Valley 51-2, 58, 63, 82, 87

Lea Valley Road (Chingford) 51-2, 58
Lemsford 119, 133-9
Lemsford Bypass 133, 135-9
Lincoln 304
Lincoln Road (Werrington) 320
Lippitts Hill (High Beach) 21, 23-4, 39-41, 46, 196
Lippitts Hill Lodge (High Beach) 21, 23-7, 39-41, 43, 46, 53, 299, 333
Little Barford Power Station 235, 244, 246
Little Paxton 278
Little Heath 101, 111
Lockleys Drive (Welwyn) 148
Lolham 185
London vii, x-xvi, 19, 24, 26-7, 39, 43, 45, 49-51, 53-4, 57, 65-6, 73, 76-7, 80-3, 85, 87, 91, 93, 100-1, 111, 113, 123-4, 127, 129, 133, 135, 141, 143, 146-7, 149, 153-4, 156, 158-9, 161, 163, 165, 169, 173-4, 176-7, 188, 192, 195, 198-202, 204, 209, 214, 221, 225-6, 232-3, 239-40, 257, 270, 278, 287, 296, 299-300, 304, 310, 332, 334-6, 353, 359, 364
London Outer Orbital Path 49, 80
London Road (Enfield Town) 85
Loop Road (Tempsford) 241, 244, 252
Lopping Hall (Loughton) 36
Loughton 35-6, 42-3
Louth 304
Low Farm (Gamlingay Great Heath) 235
Ludgate Plain (Epping Forest) 46-7
Lytton Way (Stevenage) 160, 164-5, 171

Mar Dyke (South Marsh) 51
Mardley Hill 153
Market Place (Baldock) 200; (Biggleswade) 214-5; (Enfield) 85-8, 90; (Stevenage) 181-2, 184
Market Cross (Enfield Town) 87; (Helpston) 346
Marquess of Granby public house (Stevenage) 190-1
Marquis of Lorne public house (Stevenage) 174, 176
Matcham's Bridge 291
Matcham's Gibbet 291
Maxey 239, 346
Meridian Business Park (Ponders End) 59
Meridian Way (Ponders End) 70, 72
Methodist Church (Stevenage) 171, 174-5
Middle Row (Stevenage) 171, 176, 181, 183
Mill House (Welwyn) 150
Mill Lane (Welwyn) 150-2

Millennium Garden Sanctuary (Tempsford) 257
Mimram, River (Welwyn) 142-3, 146, 150-1, 153, 357
Monk's Wood 287, 291-2

Nag's Head Inn public house (A1, Chawston) 265; (Enfield Town) 85
Nag's Head Lane (Enfield) 84-5; (Ponders End) 46, 75-6
Navigation Restaurant (Ponders End) 63, 65
Nene, River 254, 311, 318
New River (Enfield Town) 82, 84-5
Norman Cross 76, 184, 254, 294, 304-6, 308-9, 312
Norman Cross Hotel 304, 309
Norman Cross Depot 305-6, 309-10
Norman Cross Memorial 308-9
Norwich 65
North Mymms Common 111
Northampton General Asylum xvi, 363
Northborough vii, xiv, 5, 19, 30, 52, 278, 312, 314, 320, 322, 325, 359, 361, 363

Oakmere House (Potters Bar) 104
obelisk (Alconbury Hill) 288-90
Old Anchor Inn public house (Tempsford) 248, 251
Old Bakery (Bell Bar) 114
Old Bushy Common (Gamlingay Great Heath) 235
Old Castle public house (Stevenage) 158, 182
Old North Road 76, 287; see also *Ermine Street*
Old Palace Gate (Hatfield) 121, 126-7
Old Plough public house (Eaton Socon) 272
Old Town Gyratory System (Stevenage) 170-1, 175, 185-6
Old White Horse public house (Baldock) 206
Our Mutual Friend public house (Stevenage) 165-6, 168
Owl public house (High Beach) 18, 39-40, 42, 46, 77
Oxey Wood 148

Park Farm (Gamlingay Great Heath) 231-4, 261
Park Street (Hatfield) 123, 126
Peterborough xi, xiii-xiv, 200, 295, 304, 308-10, 312, 318-20, 347
Pickworth xi, 157, 163, 189

Place House (Baldock) 197
Plough public house (Enfield Highway) 77; (White Hill, Baldock) 196
Ponders End 43, 46, 54, 57-9, 61, 64-9, 71-3, 75-7, 87, 104, 357, 359, 364
Ponders End Lock 54, 59, 61, 62, 64, 67
Ponders End Station 71-2
Potters Bar 76, 90, 99-104, 107, 113, 119, 174
Potton viii, 192, 197, 214-5, 217-9, 222, 224-6

Ram public house (Crosshall) 273; (Gamlingay Great Heath) 217-8, 221, 228-31, 260, 262-3
Red Lion public house (Ayot Green) 138-9; (Enfield Highway) 77-8; (Hatfield) 128; (Stevenage) 158, 176-8, 180
Ridgeway 82, 90-5, 100, 103
Rose and Crown public house (Baldock) 202, 205-7; (Enfield Highway) 77-8; (Peterborough) 318-9
Round Oak Waters 346, 348,
Royce Wood xii, 73, 283, 317, 356, 359
Royston 76, 162, 202

St Andrew's Church (Alconbury Hill) 292; (Enfield Town) 86-7, 90
St Benedict's Church (Glinton) 322
St Etheldreda's Church (Hatfield) 110, 120, 125, 127
St Ives 365
St James's Church (Enfield Highway) 66, 77-9; (Little Paxton) 278
St Lawrence's Church (Diddington) 278-9
St Mary's Church (Buckden) 285; (Welwyn) 143-4, 146-7, 149
St Mary Magdalene, Church of (Stilton) 298
St Neots 224, 234, 238, 241, 252, 272, 365
St Nicholas' Church (Stevenage) 182
St Paul's Chapel (High Beach) 32, 36, 38, 42

Salisbury Arms public house (Hatfield) 123-4, 128
Sawtry 14, 287, 292, 313
Sawtry Abbey 292
Sawtry St Andrew 287, 292
Sewardstone Green 48
Sewardstone Paddocks (Chingford) 54, 63, 80
Sewardstone Road (Chingford) 51, 80
Sewardstonebury 47-8
Shefford 278, 280

Shoulder of Lamb public house (Ayot Green) 139
Shrewsbury 137
Sish Lane (Stevenage) 171
Six Hills (Stevenage) 156, 160, 162-4, 173, 295
Six Hills Roundabout (Stevenage) 160
South Marsh 51-2, 54, 59, 61-2, 75, 78
South Corner (Wyboston) 266-7, 269-70
South End (Stevenage) 170-1, 174, 181, 185
South Street (Ponders End) 62, 68-9, 72, 74-5, 78
Southbury Road (Ponders End) 76-7, 85; see also *Nag's Head Lane*
Southgate Road (Potters Bar) 100, 102-3
Sporting Green public house (Enfield Highway) 77-8
Springfield (High Beach) 23-4, 29, 39-42
Stamford xiii, 100, 143, 156, 159, 200, 214, 270, 320, 335
Stanborough 131-3, 137
Stangate 292
Stangate Hole 290
Station Road (Baldock) 201; (Tempsford) 246, 255, 258
Stevenage viii, 14, 141, 146, 152, 156-171, 174-187, 191, 193, 195, 200-1, 209, 217, 295
Stevenage Arts and Leisure Centre 165-6
Stilton 76, 287, 291-2, 294-301, 305, 319, 364
Stilton Tunnels public house (Stilton) 296, 298
stone pit (Crosshall) 272, 275
Swingate (Stevenage) 165, 167
Suntrap Forest Educational Centre 30
Sutton Park, see *John O'Gaunt Golf Club*
Swan Inn (Bell Bar) 111, 114-7; (Stevenage) 158; (Welwyn), see *Wellington public house*
Swanley Bar 111, 119
Swordy Well 346, 348

Tempsford viii, 218, 226-8, 235, 238, 241, 244, 246-8, 252, 255-8, 265-7, 280
Tempsford Bridge 250, 252-4
Tempsford Hall 228, 246, 248, 255, 257
tollgate (Ayot Green), see *Brickwall Tollgate*; (Marquess of Granby) 191; (Tempsford) viii, 221, 235, 238, 240-1, 244, 246-7, 252, 265, 364; (Potters Bar) 101-2, 106; (Stevenage) 174-6, 181; (Waresley) 233-4
toll house (Ayot Green) 139; (Potters Bar) 99, 104, 106-7; (Stanborough) 132-3

town lockup (Stevenage) 174-5
Trinity Road (Stevenage) 171

Upminster 49
Upper Farm (Bell Bar) 112-3
Upwell 253
Uxbridge 49

Valley Golf Course (Chingford) 51
Vanilla Alternative (Tempsford) 250

Waggon and Horses public house (Graveley) 192-3
Waggoners public house (Ayot Green) 137-9
Walton 53, 70, 120, 320
Walthamstow 30
Wansford 149
Warden Hill 226, 228, 257
Ware 76, 85, 209
Waresley Turnpike 231, 233-5
watch house (Enfield Town), see *Enfield Town Watch House*
Waverley Woodgate (Gamlingay Great Heath) 235
Weaveley Clay Wood (Gamlingay Great Heath) 235
Wellington Inn public house (Welwyn) 141, 143-4, 146
Welwyn Old Town 132, 136-7 141, 153, 177, 201, 269, 295
Welwyn Garden City 147-8
Werrington 14, 314, 320
Weston 193
Wharf Road (Ponders End) 48-9, 67, 69, 72
Wheatsheaf Inn (Alconbury Hill) 288-91, 294
Wheatsheaf public house (Tempsford) 256
White Hart Inn (Bell Bar) 111, 113, 116; (Stevenage) 176-7; (Tempsford) 256, 258; (Welwyn) 142, 177
White Hill 196-7
White Horse Inn (Eaton Socon) 272; (Welwyn) 150-1
White Horse public house (Potters Bar), see *Cask and Stillage (Potters Bar)*
White Horse Tap public house (Baldock) 205-6
White Lion public house (Baldock) 197 199, 202-3; (Stevenage) 158, 173, 176, 178, 181-2, 184, 187

INDEX – PLACES

White Swan Inn (Bell Bar), see *Swan Inn (Bell Bar)*; (Biggleswade) 214-5
White Wood (Gamlingay Great Heath) 229
Whitehorse Street (Baldock) 201-2, 206, 210
Whitney's Pightle (Woolmer Green) 153
Wildhill Road (Woodside) 119
William Girling Reservoir 58
Windmill public house (Graveley) 192, 195
Windmill Hill (Enfield Town) 85, 90-1
Wisbech 254
Woodbury Manor (Gamlingay Great Heath) 262
Woodman's Glade (Epping Forest) 47
Woodside 118-9
Woolmer Green 153, 155
Wrestlers public house (Hatfield) 130-2
Wrestlers Bridge (Hatfield) 130
Wrestlers Hill (Hatfield) 130
Wyboston 235, 266, 269, 272
Yardley Hill 49, 51, 63, 80
Yardley Lane Estate 51
Yaxley 304-5, 310

About the Authors

Ellis studied Modern Languages at the University of Manchester before completing a Masters there in Comparative Literature. In 1983 he abandoned a PhD in English to work for a number of Cambridge software companies before joining the then nascent ARM Holdings in 1993. He left ARM nine years later, following its growth from a small firm to a publicly listed multinational, to set up a digital media consultancy. *Love's Cold Returning* is his second literary collaboration. In 2013 he contributed to, edited and produced *Hideous Cambridge: A City Mutilated* by David Jones, which was a *Spectator Magazine* Book of the Year.

Bridget grew up in Ireland and read English at Trinity College, Dublin, before working as an English teacher in Cambridge. Fascination with the process of learning led her into Educational Research and a professorship at Manchester Metropolitan University. Her poetry has been influenced by Irish writers' love of natural imagery, human idiosyncrasy and heritage. In recent years both her poetry and prose has been mostly about John Clare. She is passionate about poetry and theatregoing, and reads poetry and attends plays on almost a daily basis. Her one act drama *Aliens* was given a rehearsed reading in the Cambridge ADC bar.